Jan 2008

To Verne

Best wishes,

Kurt Holm

Coining Corruption

Coining Corruption

THE MAKING OF THE AMERICAN

CAMPAIGN FINANCE SYSTEM

KURT HOHENSTEIN

NORTHERN

ILLINOIS

UNIVERSITY

PRESS

DeKalb

© 2007 by Northern Illinois University Press

Published by the Northern Illinois University Press, DeKalb, Illinois 60115

Manufactured in the United States using 30% postconsumer-recycled, acid-free paper

All Rights Reserved

Design by Julia Fauci

Library of Congress Cataloging-in-Publication Data

Hohenstein, Kurt.

Coining corruption : the making of the American campaign finance system /
Kurt Hohenstein.

  p.   cm.

Includes bibliographical references and index.

ISBN-13: 978-0-87580-377-7 (clothbound : alk. paper)

ISBN-10: 0-87580-377-6 (clothbound : alk. paper)

1. Campaign funds—Corrupt practices—United States. 2. Political corruption—
United States. I. Title.

JK1991.H57 2008

324.7'80973—dc22

2007016730

To Mom and Dad

Contents

Acknowledgments

When I began to write this book while living in Charlottesville, Virginia, it was anything but a labor of love. It was hard work—but I had the good fortune of being surrounded by a great group of supportive colleagues. We often relaxed in the shadow of the Blue Ridge Mountains at Kate's place over good food, cold beer, and copious encouragement. I am thankful for the endless collegiality of all of my friends—Kate Pierce, Ethan Sribnick, Robert Parkinson, Andre Fleche, John Mooney, Chris Nehls, Peter Flora, Carl Bon Tempo, Kristin Cellelo, Carrie Janney, Eric Hamrin, Laurie Hochstetler, and Chris Loss—without whose support this project would have been dull duty indeed.

The staffs at the University of Virginia Alderman Library and at the National Archives, College Park, Maryland were unfailingly helpful in my search for answers. The Department of History at the University of Virginia offered me a chance to teach while I wrote, the only way I am effective at either, and the faculty and staff in that department made my journey through graduate school the trip of a lifetime. My students at the University of Virginia and Hampden-Sydney College constantly challenged me to understand American history from the inside out, and the results of that are reflected in this book. Other fast friends in Nebraska and Virginia and at my new home in Minnesota at Winona State University provided me with a challenging and comfortable place to work and finish this book. To all of them, I want to express my deepest gratitude.

My thanks also to those who supported me financially during my education. The University of Virginia College of Arts and Sciences provided generous scholarship support. The Supreme Court Historical Society allowed me to present my ideas on campaign finance at the Summer Seminar, arranged by Maeva Marcus and ably led by Chuck McCurdy and Harry Schieber. Thanks to Brian Balogh and Sidney Milkis, the Miller

Center of Public Affairs provided me with both regular employment and opportunities to present formative chapters of this book at seminars and a special colloquium. Special thanks also to Chuck McCurdy, Brian Balogh, Barry Cushman, Daniel Ortiz, Adam Winkler, Mark Wahlgren Summers, Robert Mutch, Paula Baker, and to two other, anonymous readers who provided immensely helpful comments on drafts of this book. Any errors in interpretation or emphasis remain mine alone. My editor at Northern Illinois University Press, Melody Herr, had the steadfast faith of a true believer in this book from the outset. The advice and encouragement that she offered, and the intellectual demands that she placed on this project, have been instrumental in the completion of this book.

Thanks to my family—Chad, Mandi, Shane, and my brothers and sisters—who patiently waited as I began this new life and who supported my renaissance. My grandson, Espen, was born during the writing of this book— and that has reaffirmed my belief in the magnificence of new opportunities. There is little doubt but that this project, and my life, would have foundered were it not for the sustaining love and encouragement of Cory Jaques. There may be better places with better people in the world than on the bench at the foot of the Lincoln Memorial, but I can't think of any.

This book is dedicated to my mom and dad. Dad passed away in the middle of my research, and Mom continues to live on the family farm in Nebraska. I am proud to return this piece of my life to Mom, in Dad's memory and as a token of the love she has always offered me. Small recompense indeed, but for now, it is the best I can do.

Coining **Corruption**

INTRODUCTION

Ignoring History and the Conundrum of Reform

T he two men stood barely ten feet apart on the Senate floor during the October 1999 debate over the bill that would become the Bipartisan Campaign Reform Act ("BCRA," called "Bic-Ra") of 2002. In a rare direct challenge to another senator, lanky Senator Robert Bennett (R-UT) had stormed to the floor at the egging of opposition leader Senator Mitch McConnell (R-KY). Bennett confronted Senator John McCain (R-AZ) about allegations posted on McCain's website "It'sYOURCountry.com," which implied that Bennett had corruptly used his office to benefit the 2002 Winter Olympic Games to be held in Salt Lake City by earmarking an appropriation of $2.2 million for sewer infrastructure associated with Games. McCain had labeled this corrupt pork barrel spending.

"I plead guilty," Bennett countered, admitting on the Senate floor that he was responsible for earmarking the appropriation in the bill to avoid committee testimony and debate. But Bennett, using the argument McConnell had pressed earlier in the debate, demanded proof of the connection between the earmarking and the corrupting influence of soft money. In a question reminiscent of the 1974 Watergate investigation, Bennett diverted the focus of the debate by asking McCain to make clear the corruption of which he was accused. "My question for the Senator from Arizona is who gave the soft money? How much was it? And where did it go? And where was the quid pro quo that I delivered on?"[1]

McConnell joined the fray, challenging McCain and supporters of the pending McCain-Feingold campaign finance legislation, which proponents argued would end the practice of using soft money from contributors seeking access to power. Soft money is unregulated by the legal restrictions of the campaign finance regimen because it is not given to candidates but to parties who ostensibly use it for legal purposes. McCain sought to expose those corrupt politicians who had lapped at the soft money trough in order to promote their piggish spending. "The Senator from Arizona," he contended, "has not named the Senators who were allegedly responsible for" the pork barrel spending, "which he suggests were inserted in the bill as a result of soft money contributions to political parties. My question remains," McConnell challenged McCain, "who were the Senators? How can it be corruption if no one is corrupt?"[2]

McCain steadfastly refused to name names beyond the connections he made on the website. To do so, he maintained, would defeat his purposes, because "this system makes good people do bad things." The system, more than the individual senators, was corrupt because the "influence of special interests has a pernicious effect on the legislative process." Exasperated at the attempt of members of his own party to delay and kill the bill, McCain defined the corruption targeted by BCRA by citing Webster's dictionary— corruption is the "impairment of integrity, virtue, and moral principle." For campaign finance reformers, he cited the even more authoritative definition announced in the 1976 Supreme Court decision of *Buckley v. Valeo,* which held that only direct "quid pro quo" corruption or the "appearance of corruption" were legitimate grounds for congressional regulation. For McCain and the supporters of BCRA, the plasticity of the language of corruption meant that you would "know it when you saw it." But for McConnell, Bennett, and other BCRA opponents, the imprecision of that definition proved the lack of direct connections between the use of soft money by political parties and political corruption in elections, which exposed the very senselessness of the reform effort.

The 1999 Senate debate over the meaning of corruption and congressional efforts to regulate federal elections left observers wondering about the rationale and legitimacy of yet another round of reforms. At the heart of that controversy was what campaign finance reformers called the *Buckley* problem—the resiliency of the 1976 Supreme Court definition of corruption that arose from the post-Watergate attempts to reform the electoral system enacted by Congress in the Federal Election Campaign Act (FECA) of 1971 and 1974. The *Buckley* court narrowly defined corruption as quid pro quo—that "get for giving" corruption where campaign contributors bought direct favor or indirect access to successful candidates. In its decision, the Court found that Congress's interest in regulating elections was necessarily balanced against the free speech rights of political participants. Money was the mother's milk of modern politics, essential to promote dissemination of political ideas in campaigns. Whereas the Court did not say that money equaled speech and thus possessed near absolute rights of First Amendment protection, it did find that regulation of campaign contributions and spending could only be justified to combat quid pro quo, or the appearance of quid pro quo corruption. It therefore held that campaign contributions that appeared to more closely resemble get-for-giving corruption damaged electoral integrity and thus were within the regulatory power of Congress.

Campaign spending, on the other hand, did not foster that same kind of corruption, and the Court struck down the limits on candidate and campaign spending. Free political speech interests might give way where direct or apparent quid pro quo corruption could seep into the campaign finance system. Spending limits, however, had no relation to that kind of corruption and therefore could not be imposed without violating free speech interests. After *Buckley,* policy makers and campaign finance reformers faced a circumscribed ability to enact broader reforms that regulated campaign expenditures as well as campaign contributions. The *Buckley* court left the campaign finance system as a Janus-faced remnant of what reformers had intended to create with FECA 1971 and 1974.[3]

The rise and regulation of political action committees provide an example of how *Buckley* cabined the congressional debate about campaign finance reform options. For nearly seven decades prior to the decision, campaign finance law had prohibited corporate contributions to federal campaigns. FECA 1974 and *Buckley* encouraged the creation of separate political action committees (PACs) whose organizational and operating expenses could be paid for by corporations. Contributions to the PACs came from individuals, parties, or other PACs, and this "hard money," regulated and disclosed, could then be contributed by the PACs to campaigns in strictly limited amounts. Individuals could contribute up to $5,000 to a PAC (up to an annual maximum of $25,000), and PACs in turn could contribute up to $5,000 annually to a candidate per election. The increased limits made PACs the preferred fund-raising vehicle, allowing candidates to maximize their time for larger contributions to pay for increasingly more expensive campaigns.

After *Buckley* gave its approval to the PAC provision in FECA 1974, the number of PACs grew from 1,600 in 1978 to over 4,000 six years later. Aggregate contributions from all PACs increased from $92.6 million in 1978 to around $220 million in the 1996–2000 annual election cycles. By permitting spending by PACs, *Buckley* muffled the hue and cry about ridding the campaign finance system of corporate donations, provided they came from special PACs and not from general fund treasuries of corporations and unions. But the mere increase of campaign money had not been the biggest concern of most critics. Many experts on both sides of the debate acknowledged that the costs of campaigns have increased dramatically, and the increased political spending by itself added little corrupting potential to the political marketplace. Yet what remained a concern to the most vocal proponents of campaign finance reform was not simply the aggregate increase of money in campaigns, but the origins of the money, how it was raised, the nature of the contributor, and the political access available to large contributors but denied to the average citizen.

In 1995, when President Bill Clinton and his political consultant Dick Morris devised the legal loophole of contributing to parties to fund electioneering on behalf of candidates, unregulated soft money poured into the cash box of campaign funding, as PAC funds had two decades earlier. The loophole permitted corporations and unions to contribute unlimited and unregulated amounts of money to parties, who were free to allocate the money in local and national races, provided that the parties did not coordinate the spending with a candidate. Soft money raised by Republicans in 1992 totaled nearly $50 million; by Democrats nearly $37 million. Four years later, the totals for each party rose to $141 and $122 million respectively.[4] Since *Buckley,* reformers, legal scholars, and historians have lamented those limitations, but few have considered how *Buckley* fit contextually into the long history of American campaign finance regulation. For most, *Buckley* originated in the political crimes of Watergate and was formed by the constitutional doctrine that preferred free speech rights over congressional attempts to regulate money in elections. After 1976, *Buckley* established the backstop to any reform of the system. All assumptions, all constitutional law, and all history stopped at 1976 in regard to any guidance about legitimate constitutional rationales for reforming the system.

Critics claimed this soft money loophole destroyed the post-Watergate reforms, which had limited contributions. BCRA proponents, in attempting to close that loophole, relied on the *Buckley* definition of quid pro quo corruption as the constitutional basis for their legislation. While restricting certain contributions, *Buckley* employed different rules for contributors and campaign spending that did not directly advocate for a candidate. The Supreme Court permitted Congress to regulate contributions by independent groups that specifically advocated for a particular candidate ("vote for Smith") because those contributions could actively corrupt a candidate under the *Buckley* rationale. It then upheld limits on the aggregate amount individuals and groups could contribute overall as well as to individual campaigns. While the *Buckley* court found spending limits unconstitutional, these two regulations meant that after 1976 individuals and political action committees, which under FECA 1974 were specifically permitted to contribute to campaigns, faced limits to the contributions they could make to individual candidates. Faced with the increasing costs of campaigning, candidates and political parties searched for a way around those limits. Soft money contributions evaded the *Buckley* hard dollar limitations. Political parties then used the money to organize party activities and voter registration efforts and to fund get-out-the-vote drives.[5]

Yet the renewed debate over the source and effect, and not merely the increased usage, of soft money contributions (contributions that were not regulated by federal law before BCRA because they came to the national or state political parties and not to campaigns) propelled the new round of BCRA reforms. Reform proponents opposed soft money not simply because of its aggregate size, but because it was funneled into elections as an end run around the contribution limits of *Buckley* from those very corporations and labor unions that for decades had been prohibited from contributing directly to federal election campaigns. If, reformers argued, campaign finance policy prohibited the direct financial contributions by corporations, labor unions, and wealthy individuals because those contributions created avenues for political access unavailable to the average citizen, why should those same groups be permitted to actively evade the prohibition merely because they gave the money to political parties who served as a conduit to fund party activities and election advertisements that were otherwise illegal?

But what if corporations, admittedly a large and influential segment of the American economy, found a way to contribute to the political marketplace? So what if labor unions, seeing their economic base decline, sought to gain the influence to stop that decline through the aggregation of membership contributions? So what if wealthy Americans, interested in financing political candidates that supported their views, contributed huge, unregulated amounts of money to political parties? How, people cut off by the *Buckley* backstop began to ask, did channeling of these contributions through political parties tend to directly or indirectly corrupt any candidate? Americans at the dawn of a new century, considering the goals and consequences of the BCRA reforms designed to address the problems of political corruption, engaged in a rousing debate over the reasons to limit campaign contributions because of their source and their presumed effect. That debate roiled across the airwaves and legislative chambers of America and finally settled, as do many of our most salient political questions, in the chambers of the United States Supreme Court.

The debate over the definition of political corruption has been central to the passage of and reaction to campaign finance legislation beginning with the Anti-Assessment Act of 1876. It reached a crescendo a century later in the 1976 *Buckley* decision. That issue has risen again in the new millennium in the controversial 2003 *McConnell v. FEC* decision and, most recently, in the 2006 decision of *Randall v. Sorrell*. But that controversy rested uneasily against the concept of corruption that the *Buckley* court had used to legitimize its decision because the *Buckley* backstop prevented reformers from questioning the very narrow "quid pro quo" definition of corruption that the Court adopted in that case as the only legitimate rationale for free speech regulation of campaign contributions. Yet beyond that backstop lies a rich and undiscovered history about how Americans defined and then sought to address concerns about political corruption in campaigns.

Coining Corruption retrieves the foul ball of corruption beyond that *Buckley* backstop and throws it squarely back into the rich historical game played out over the century-long making of the campaign finance system. Reformers defined corruption by addressing concerns about both the source of campaign money and the amount and effect of campaign spending. The *Buckley* court ignored that history when it focused on direct or indirect quid pro quo corruption. Yet by 1976, because this sort of corruption had mostly disappeared, questions remained about the cause and consequences of the *Buckley* court's narrow definition.

For a century before *Buckley,* conflicting conceptions of corruption created the need and then provided the legitimacy for campaign finance reform. Since the Anti-Assessment Act of 1876, the courts have defined the concept of corruption to justify the regulations. Assessments in 1876 were the "viggerish," so to speak—the 10 percent coerced by the party in power from the employee as a condition for gaining and retaining their employment. Assessments opponents defined corruption as the coercion that made public employees slaves to the party weal instead of the common good because the practice denied the independent exercise of voters' judgments. Public conceptions of corruption have changed over time, often to reflect emerging and evolving political realities. With each change, Congress and the courts redefined corruptive evil as they sought to purify the system. Each newly coined definition of corruption challenged the legitimacy of turning economic wealth into political power and the resulting damage to principles of deliberative democracy practiced in elections. The history of the way corruption in the *Buckley* decision was redefined to include only the rankest form of bribery is the story of legal and political institutions clashing and coinciding to make the campaign finance system.

But the making of the campaign finance system was always about more than process. Reformers sought to address genuine concerns about how money influenced public deliberation in political campaigns relevant to broader concepts of political corruption that affected deliberative democratic ideals. Reformers wanted to eliminate bribery, but they also were concerned about creating an electoral system that provided opportunities for political deliberation for a wide range of voices. The *Buckley* backstop has hindered legal scholars, election law experts, and historians from considering the history of the campaign finance system from its Gilded Age origins to the cumbersome, complicated system of today because it seemed to suggest that the history before *Buckley* was irrelevant to contemporary issues and concerns. By examining the evolving definition of corruption that was used as justification for a litany of campaign finance reforms, *Coining Corruption* exposes the untold, ironic story of that development. Recognizing that the most significant historical concerns that campaign finance reformers promoted were the principles of deliberative democracy and political equality, as they then understood them, allows us to more fully understand how campaign finance reform shaped and altered American politics in often unexpected and unintended ways and provides contemporary reasons for measured reform of the system.

Just as important, the creation of the campaign finance system involved real winners and losers far afield from the regular lineup of candidates and parties. The making of the campaign finance system has not been merely an esoteric collection of rules and regulations; it has not simply been a battle between free speech supporters and Mugwumpian political purists; it has not only been a story of ironic and unintended effects and legal misunderstandings. While it has been all of those, the campaign finance system has consistently done more than regulate money in elections. It has created opportunities and obstacles for political deliberation for public employees, political parties, corporations, newly enfranchised women, and labor unions. It has catalyzed emerging and declining political coalitions, minorities and interest groups, and vitalized and regulated electronic media technologies. And it has worked to differentiate political ideas while both opening and restricting democratic access and deliberative involvement for incumbents, challengers, and third parties.

Organized both chronologically and thematically, *Coining Corruption* examines the major legislation and court decisions from the American centennial to the most recent Supreme Court decisions. Chapter 1 discusses the first federal act and the Supreme Court case *Ex Parte Curtis*, which restricted the collection of assessments from federal employees, effectively cutting off the parties' main source of funding. The chapter describes the shift away from patronage assessments as the primary source of party campaign funds, and reassesses the impact of the Pendleton Act of 1883. Concepts of Gilded Age corruption as shaping coercive tactics, which denied voters the free expression of their electoral will, led reformers to limit the power of parties over public employees by ending the assessment connection. Consequently, parties began to seek alternative sources of money for increasingly expensive campaigns. Questions about how to purify party politics led ironically to the separation of spoils employees from direct involvement with parties, which led to an increased inability of parties to raise sufficient funds from those employees to support party practices and goals.

Parties, alarmed by their diminished ability to raise funds, increasingly relied on national corporations. Chapter 2 describes how, in the last three election cycles of the nineteenth century, corporate power increased as business leaders worked with political parties to fund campaigns. The potential for corporate wealth to overwhelm the electoral debate made the source of corporate funds in political campaigns a major concern. The vast corporate campaign spending that became evident after the 1896 presidential election led reformers to challenge the fairness of the system.

Reformers responded with the 1907 Tillman Act. Chapter 3 examines the passage of the first comprehensive state and national corrupt practices acts and the dual-federalist impediments that divided power between the national and the state governments that challenged their full implementation. Progressive ideas of corruption called for political campaigns that educated voters on the issues that led to congressional hearings for campaign finance reform, including disclosure and limits on campaign spending. The ineffectiveness of the Federal Corrupt Practices Acts ironically created opportunities for women in 1920 as they used their newly acquired political skills and franchise status to become professional campaign fund-raisers in state and national campaigns.

The rise of the free speech doctrine began to complicate the constitutional regulation of political speech. Detailing this development, Chapter 4 focuses on how the courts, while privileging individual free speech interests, nonetheless promoted communal concerns by regulating new communication technologies. During this period, corruption was defined as the lack of access or political opportunity to share ideas and opinions. Congress passed the Radio Act of 1934 to respond to emerging fears that the excessive power of this medium might deny access to candidates and ideas by drowning out deliberative debate. Congress, intent on promoting communal political speech interests by regulating excessive individual speech, adopted the public interest standard for mass media and imposed the fairness and equal time doctrines. The protection of communal political deliberation in the electronic media continued unabated until 1969, but was mostly ignored and forgotten by the court in *Buckley*.

The rise of class antipathy and concern over the manner in which lobbyists, government employees, and labor unions aggressively pursued their political interests led to a reaction against them as coercive and antidemocratic. Chapter 5 describes and analyzes the New Deal legislation that restricted the political activity of lobbyists and government employees, and that treated labor unions as analogous to ordinary corporations to justify the campaign finance regulations. The passage of the two Hatch Acts, the War Labor Disputes Act, and the Taft-Hartley Act, in reaction to a new kind of corruption that many felt had evolved from the New Deal reshaped the political speech and campaign opportunities of these groups, ostensibly to level the playing field. The subsequent rise of labor political action committees created new concerns about the aggregate power of those organizations to adversely influence deliberative discussion of political issues.

The 1950s signaled a wave of professionalization in politics. Chapter 6 describes how the use of consultants, pollsters, and advertising specialists, and the rise of television began to transform political speech and campaigning. Congressional reorganization and its reaction to lobbying abuses led to new reform efforts intended to promote the widest public deliberation over issues. Even as the Supreme Court became more involved in political questions, President Eisenhower established new procedures for nominating justices, with the result that the Supreme Court privileged particular values as it considered election law cases.

Chapter 7 reassesses the myths of the Watergate story, explaining how the legal reforms of FECA 1971 and 1974, which began as broad reforms of the entire political process, became more circumscribed, dealing only with the campaign finance system. By 1976 when the Supreme Court reviewed this legislation in the seminal case *Buckley v. Valeo,* it formalistically privileged individual free speech rights and defined corruption in a way that ignored political reality. The *Buckley* case continues to prove a constitutional impediment to regulation that promotes ideals of deliberative democracy, which the legal-political history of the campaign finance system had long recognized.

The divided Supreme Court opinions announced in *McConnell v. FEC* and *Randall v. Sorrell* dramatize the continuing misguided debate over corruption. Justices Kennedy, Thomas, and Scalia insisted that the BCRA reforms were an unconstitutional violation of free speech because they did nothing to stop quid pro quo corruption. Each hearkened back to the *Buckley* decision but no further, ignoring more than a century of campaign finance history as well as the continuing pragmatic political developments that make the "quid pro quo" definition most unhelpful to maintaining vital democratic institutions. The anachronistic debate about whether campaign contribution and spending measure political support, or buy political access, continues to focus on the most limited kind of quid pro quo corruption, and fails to deliver us from the evils that afflict the building of a more deliberative democratic system.

Understanding the history of the American campaign finance system remains a work-in-progress. But this book does not attempt to examine every reform effort, and its focus is not on the legislative process. *Coining Corruption* instead tells the story of how Americans grappled with evolving conceptions of corruption and deliberative democracy to make the modern campaign finance system and how, since 1976, that broad reformist vision has been obscured and obstructed by the backstop of *Buckley.* Rediscovering that vision is a vitally important project because it addresses our most basic democratic concerns, such as, How can we protect the marketplace of free political speech at a time when it is increasingly dominated by big money talkers? How can the campaign finance system promote deliberative campaigns that truly educate the public rather than those that appeal to our basest prejudices? How do we create an electoral system that challenges its players to earn and deserve the respect of an increasingly skeptical electorate? How can we ensure that all ideas have an opportunity to be heard so that Americans can deliberate and freely choose those ideas that best provide for the most citizens? These concerns and more are the box score reflecting the effectiveness of the reforms that made and remade the American campaign finance system.

My goal in *Coining Corruption* is to disclose the century-long pre-*Buckley* history to demonstrate how reformers built a campaign finance system intent on reviving the first principles of deliberative democracy. My hope is that this book will provide some historical answers to the campaign finance conundrum that has afflicted and continues to bewilder teams of reformers. Using history to examine the deliberative democratic foundations of the legal and political changes to the campaign finance system provides a reasoned path to debate and create campaign finance regulation true to the democratic ideals fundamental to our political history.[6]

Chapter One

THE BEGINNINGS OF THE
CAMPAIGN FINANCE SYSTEM

Reforming Spoils, the Anti-Assessment Act,

and *Ex Parte Curtis*

Civil War Union general Newton Martin Curtis faced a very different battle in January of 1882. Born in DePeyster, New York, on January 8, 1835, Curtis, a former teacher, postmaster, farmer, special treasury agent, and representative from St. Lawrence County in the New York legislature, had led troops as a major general in some of the war's bloodiest campaigns. At Cold Harbor in 1863, he commanded the 142nd New York Infantry. At Petersburg, he led the First Brigade, Second Division of X Corps. In the bloody assault on Fort Fisher, North Carolina, near the end of the four-year conflict, he won the Congressional Medal of Honor for his part in leading Terry's Corps of Ames Division in the attack, which cost him an eye while earning him the sobriquet "the hero of Fort Fisher." His was a distinguished military heritage.[1]

Yet as General Curtis awoke in his New York home on January 6, 1882, political charges leveled against him by the Civil Service Reform Association threatened to destroy his reputation. The Association alleged that, while acting as a special agent of the Treasury of the New York Customhouse, Curtis had violated an 1876 act of Congress prohibiting the solicitation or receipt of political assessments, not from corporations but from federal employees. Congress focused on the funding of elections because they were the core of representative democracy. By regulating the practice of coercively assessing public employees for party campaign funds, Congress defined and addressed what they considered to be the most prevalent form of corruption. What lay at the heart of these charges was a sea change in the manner in which political parties would raise and spend campaign funds. The obscure 1876 amendment to an appropriation bill cutting federal employee salaries lay unenforced for six years until the tides of reform grew strong enough, eventually washing over General Curtis and much of the previously unrepentant party machinery.[2]

Historians credit the Pendleton Act of 1883 with permanently separating the spoils of office from the hard currency of campaign finance. Most contend that it was the Pendleton Act that created a meritocratic system for hiring government employees and prohibited the levying of political assessments, signaling the end of the spoils era and the origins of the systematization of political neutrality in the distribution of political office. But prior to Pendleton, a series of events broke the symbolic, if not actual, symbiosis between patronage and party, and led to a fundamental reconfiguration of the campaign finance system in the last three presidential election cycles of the nineteenth century. These events ensnared General Curtis, involved the Supreme Court in the most important political question of the day, generated the foundations of policy that eventually led to widespread civil service reforms, and caused both political leaders and American businessmen to reexamine their role in national campaign finance issues.[3]

SPOILING FOR PARTY REFORM—
The Centennial Challenge to Democratic Ideals

The great exhibition hall of the 1876 Centennial Exhibition in Philadelphia represented a nation coming together and moving ahead. The exhibition at Fairmont Park, which would draw tens of thousands of visitors from across the country that summer, celebrated American ideals that the organizers hoped would prove lasting and worthy in the next century. In orations across the nation, speakers lauded the "breed and disposition of a people in regard of courage, public spirit and patriotism, the test of the working of their institutions, which the world most values, and upon which the public safety most depends." Recounting the last century, the greatest lesson of history had been the "preponderance of public over private, of social over selfish, tendencies and purposes in the whole body of the people, and the persistent fidelity to the genius and spirit of popular institutions."[4]

It is altogether fitting that the story about the making of the American campaign finance system should commence in 1876, characterized as the zenith of organizational party politics. The striking growth in the number of government employees from 51,000 in 1871 to 100,000 in 1881 paralleled a similar increase in state and local officeholders and employees. Accompanied by the decline of the active state, that growth commented ironically on the nature of American understandings about government and democracy. The adhesive character of party politics became the glue that bound parties to public employees.[5]

For many, however, the celebration of democracy remained a conflicted one. Many observers could not hide the despair they felt when assessing the state of American democratic institutions. Democratic ideals of independence and freedom, they feared, had become mired in the corruptive realities of the political party system. National party competition, which focused on developmental issues such as the tariff and the monetary system, often remained secondary to local political issues involving social norms, ethno-religious conflict, and voter identity. Yet while local issues remained important, national developmental issues nonetheless dominated state party declarations of principles. Similarly, party adherents realized that they harvested the fruits of their labors only in the fields of victory. Electoral victory became more than simply the means to acknowledge democratic choice—it determined how the spoils of political success were regularly awarded to loyal supporters of the successful party. As the patronage system grew at both the federal and state level, voter interest in campaigns became increasingly passionate and personal. What political historian Joel Silbey describes as the "common law of democracy," that articulating set of rules that formerly had imposed restraint on party behavior in the 1840s, had by 1876 been replaced by a spirit of partisanship where spoils sparred with principles, and where coalitions were held together "only by the cohesive power of public plunder."[6]

In that heady atmosphere, organizational revolution and growth reshaped the nature of the political process. Turning out votes became instrumental to the allocation of patronage employment. Moreover, turning out votes, then as now, came cheap to no one. The increasingly complex political system grew costlier with each election. Buying votes, organizing campaigns, promoting great parades, and exciting the mass of mostly disinterested voters cost money. Increasingly, although contractor kickbacks and contributions from individuals and companies still fueled the engine of the political machine, systematic assessments from an escalating number of government employees provided the main and steadiest source of campaign contributions. In 1878 the Republican Campaign Committee assessed all federal officeholders 1 percent of their salaries, fattening campaign coffers by $100,000. During the 1880 campaign, when General Curtis served as the Republican treasurer for the New York State committee, twelve separate assessment letters dunned New York's federal employees.[7]

Yet even as the breadth and extent of this assessment practice increased, substantial reformist voices chimed in a chorus of opposition. Drawing on idealized democratic conceptions of the public interest and the common good, Gilded Age reformers demanded civil service reform. Their larger quarry, however, became the system of organizational politics because they believed that it subverted a generalized sense of the public interest. Most reformers still believed in the principles of a common good, and the spoils system profited individuals whose claim to reward lay not in common good but in party loyalty. By enriching political parties, reformers contended, the spoils system sacrificed ideals of credible, efficient, and meritorious public service. Their efforts to pass the Pendleton Act in 1883 were intended to reform the civil service system and limit the corrupting effects and benefits of political assessments.[8]

While the 1876 act was the first act of Congress that specifically made solicitation or receipt of political assessments a criminal offense, officials had made previous efforts to curtail and limit the ties between parties and patronage. In 1841, President Benjamin Harrison, acting through Secretary of State Daniel Webster, issued an order preventing "the payment of any contribution or assessment on salaries or official compensation for party or election purposes" and making it cause for removal. In the corrupt aftermath of the Civil War, Congress passed the Naval Appropriation Act, which subjected an officer or employee of the government to dismissal if he required or requested any workingman in the Navy Yard to contribute or pay money for political purposes.

Later, President Rutherford B. Hayes issued a circular letter to department heads cautioning against the active engagement in elections or political organizations by federal officers. While specifically recognizing their right to vote, the letter stated "[n]o assessments for political purposes on officers or subordinates should be allowed." But enforcement had been weak at best, and when General Curtis was confronted by a *New York Times* reporter about the criminal allegations against him, he denied that he had been directly involved in the collection of customhouse employee assessments. He explained that the Republican State Committee, of which he was treasurer, customarily sent out invitations to all who were supposed to be friendly to the Republican Party and "as far as I know, all contributions that were made were voluntary." Curtis then added, almost naively, that he knew of no motivation for the charges. Soon General Curtis would find himself asking about these charges and more from inside a jail cell as he awaited a hearing on his habeas corpus petition before the federal courts of New York.[9]

Civil service reformers wanted to separate the spoils of office from the fruits of electoral victory in order to reorder government along efficient scientific principles. They first trained their sights on what they saw as the biggest and most egregious target. Competitive employment examinations based on merit, they argued, ought to replace partisan political appointments. Organized bureaucratic institutions should replace pell-mell operations of local and state departments often rife with corruption. Professional managers should supplant a system that wasted untold public bounty on kickbacks, bribes, and inflated contracts. Civil service reform would, they argued, promote revitalized democracy responsive to the common good and efficiently run by elitist professionals like themselves.[10]

Reformers recognized that the customhouse, with its nexus of political assessments and party loyalty, had become the most powerful political machine for controlling elections, and they called on Congress to end those same political abuses. As political assessments, levied since 1842 on a graduated scale according to the salary of each officer, had raised untold thousands for the party in control, reformers decried the coercive tie of public employees to political parties. The assessment practice thrived in the quid pro quo of political expectations inherent in the spoils system, of which the New York Customhouse remained the most glaring, though not singular, example.[11]

It was precisely that political nexus to the involuntary and coerced financing of campaigns that reformers described as corruptive. Customhouse employees, coerced to pay assessments on the direct or implied threat of dismissal, often made up for their personal loss by exacting from merchants unlawful gratuities, acting as employees of the party instead of as public servants of the people. While the loss of voter free will and independence and the attendant damage to the ideal of popular sovereignty was bad enough, what made the assessment arrangement intolerable for many reformers was that the customhouse operated as "a political machine," run not in the interest of the common good, but "exclusively and constantly in the interests of the party." The assessment practice was corrupt not merely because it was individually coercive, but because it led to institutional governmental corruption and inefficiency.[12]

Leading commentators, critical of the sickened condition of American politics, sought to regenerate those democratic ideals through political, institutional, and legal change. William Graham Sumner, in a series of articles for *Princeton Review,* argued that the art of government consisted in "adopting means to ends" and insisted that the "aim is the welfare of the community." The device of elections justified the idea of popular sovereignty. Mass elections of representative officials put into the hands of the people the power of patronage; elections were consequently struggles for power—war between the two parties—with the goal not conciliation but conquest. Since political parties were the "natural and direct outcome of the political dogmas which are accepted and believed," abuse of the spoils system was a symptom, not a cause, of vice and political disorder, and reform only of the party system not an adequate cure.[13]

Sumner argued that political parties actually stimulated voter interest through campaign techniques (party organs, tracts, processions, meetings, and clubs—in other words, the warp and woof of Gilded Age political campaigning), because most voters were otherwise disengaged from politics. Voters do not, Sumner contended, have their opinions made up ready to decide on Election Day, and party action was necessary to inform and encourage voter participation. Yet the act of voting remained an individual sovereign act, and "a voter cannot be a voter and let somebody else make up his mind for him." When the election process degenerated by whatever means into one where parties, spoils, and campaigns manipulated voter free will, it was not an election system fit to be called democratic. Only truly informed voters exercising free-will suffrage sufficed to sustain Sumner's democratic assumptions.[14]

Sumner believed that politics in the Gilded Age had already advanced beyond any rational conception of a common good, into an arena of competing interests best managed by improving opportunities for open, fair, and free deliberation. Sumner advocated that elections be reformed to provide for open deliberation among competing interests in order to arrive at the best political solution. No one questioned the propriety of an individual volunteering his time or treasure to the political party or candidate of his choice. But, when men retained, by virtue of the employment-assessment nexus, property over another, the wide sphere of public life was poisoned and "trailed politics to in the lowest depths of intolerance and corruption." It was not the active participation of employees in party politics that the reformers decried, but the partisan coercion of public servants into a form of political slavery. This assessment coercion against public employees by party officials created a violation of communal democratic freedom explicitly because of the coercive use of the public position to promote the party, ring, or office seeker.[15]

Envisioning a return to the democratic ideals in which an educated electorate deliberated over competing claims, reform groups contended that the parties improperly used campaign funds to influence or coerce voters to sustain their selfish political interests. Reliant on their belief in a common good, they viewed principles of deliberative democracy as essential to arriving at public consensus. These reformers believed that open deliberation over disputed issues was the best way to arrive at decisions for the common good, which they maintained was essential to a representative, popular democracy. In that climate, civil service reform became the essential national question because it would dry up the mother's milk of campaign financing at which the parties lapped for their authority, sustenance, and coercive power.[16]

THE ATTACK ON POLITICAL ASSESSMENTS—The 1876 Anti-Assessment Act and the Earliest Regulation of the System

The story of the Anti-Assessment Act that placed General Curtis's liberty in jeopardy demonstrates the earliest beginnings of a distinct body of democracy law connecting legal and political developments, and the nascent origins of a separate path of free speech law that promoted a communal legal doctrine over individual rights. The pattern of judicial-legislative interaction in campaign finance history involved shifting definitions of corruption that defined principles of equality and access, as well as individual voter free will. Even as Congress restricted assessments in 1876, an increasingly complicated story played out thereafter in the party meetings, corporate boardrooms, and courtrooms of America, which set the tone for the late nineteenth-century interpretations of free speech doctrine and acted as a catalyst for the development of the modern campaign finance system.

The attack on assessments was driven by three assumptions. The increasing need for money in campaigns due to their variety, scope, and increasing cost drove the reliance on political assessments. Assessments, in turn, localized the corruption, and provided a ready and legally accessible target for reform. Second, the uses of money for elaborate campaign artifice designed to obscure issues and influence less-educated voters, which lured attention away from the common good, epitomized the kind of corruption reformers most feared. Additionally, the potential grew for men of wealth with political ambition to buy a nomination or election. Finally, the illegitimate use of money to buy votes, the use of "floaters," and the actions of corrupt election officials continued to be a substantial problem. Only institutional reform, which cut to the heart of the problem and reshaped those corrupt historical symptoms of American political life, would remedy those ills.[17]

At every stage of debate, contested understanding of democracy demanded answers to political questions from legal institutions and actors. Questions of political boundaries, suffrage rights, federalism (especially in election matters), civil and social rights, and the nature of individual liberty roiled through the debates of the period. Even as northern politicians decried the electoral outrages being perpetrated against African-American voters in the redeemed states, other reformers questioned the viability of a democratic system driven by an uneducated electorate. The contested definition of corruption was central to all of those issues.[18]

In response to those concerns, the highest success of the Gilded Age moment for civil service reform culminated in the passage of the Pendleton Act in 1883. In the post–Civil War years leading up to Pendleton, the civil service system became the primary source of political patronage. Andrew Jackson's initiation of the spoils system, with rotation in and removal from office as the just reward for political supporters, had cemented the symbiotic relationship between party and patronage. Jackson considered federal jobs the plums of electoral success, and distributed them as a way to build party support and to end what he considered the professional politician's grip on power. Extended white male suffrage, the elimination of property qualifications for voting, and increased costs for increasingly national campaigns demanded that the successful politician recruit and reward supporters. Consequently, their political benefactors expected those supporters who were rewarded with jobs to contribute a portion of their salaries back to their party. The assessment system, which had developed as integral to the spoils system, became the most important financial source for campaign contributions.[19]

Spoils system employees paid an annual assessment to coffers to support party activities. The going rate for top New York customhouse officials, for example, was $25 annually. Inspectors and clerks paid assessments of $15 per year; night watchmen, at the lower end of the political hierarchy, paid $7.50. From the customhouse, the party annually collected over $6,000 from political assessments. In President James Garfield's victorious 1880 campaign, estimates of his campaign assessments averaging 5 percent on aggregate federal salaries yielded to the national Republican campaign fund a staggering $1,000,000. In the early years of the Gilded Age, officeholders, political candidates, and public employees provided the parties with their most significant and reliable source of campaign financing.[20]

While the payment of political assessments was technically mandatory, by 1876 the assessment collections had grown unreliable. The Republican National Congressional Committee, the first "extortion committee," dunned 100,000 employees, yet only 11,500 responded. That poor return, however, hardly diminished the vigor with which party officials prosecuted this coercive system of campaign finance. Besides national assessments, the party faithful also contributed to state, county, municipal, ward, and district campaigns. Often, bosses added emergency levies to the increasing burden. One Philadelphia postal employee in 1881–1882 paid his party's assessment of $16, a state assessment of $20, and a ward assessment of $5. His total political assessment tax was 5 percent of his $800 annual income. Commonly, assessments ranged from 2 percent to 6 percent annually. In New York, public payrolls often ran $14–15 million annually, generating a huge assessment base upon which the party bosses could draw.[21]

Although unregulated, onerous, coercive, and incessant, assessments remained the favored method of financing party operations and campaigns. Furthermore, while proponents called the assessments voluntary, employees and party officials alike recognized that dismissal from office was a real threat for recalcitrant officeholders. In fact, Republican Party officials, who between 1865 and 1871 had removed 1,600 employees for refusal to pay party taxes, now faced a far less amiable prospect. Reformers objected to a democratic system that obscured deliberative debate on principles and issues through the use of assessment to pay for parades and political entertainment, and that enslaved independent electoral action to party zeal. They called for reform of the assessment system. That concern clashed head-on with the reality of the political class that asserted partisan victory as essential to the promotion of the public good. Winning elections during the highly competitive and incomparably close party elections of the 1870–1890s required money, and the political class recognized those connections and the instrumental value of assessments to those ultimate goals. The assessment system thus became the political bogeyman for Gilded Age reformers because it was the singularly most pernicious tie between the parties—which they saw as democratically uninterested in the common good—and the financing of party campaigns. Assessments underwrote a system that they felt seriously undermined electoral independence and ensured a government run by men whose first allegiance was to party plunder instead of public interest.[22]

During the 44th Congress, debate on the general appropriation bill centered primarily on the cutting of salaries of federal employees in an effort designed to balance the budget. Over a period of several months during 1876, Congress debated various cuts in the salaries of clerks, postmasters, and other government officials. At times, the discussions over the salaries of customhouse commissioners, deputy commissioners, and clerks grew acrimonious. After all, the Democratic proposal would effect a broad reduction in the salaries of those same patronage employees that the parties controlled and on whose assessments their campaign finances largely depended.[23]

During the debate on April 27, 1876, Representative John Osborne Whitehouse (D-NY) offered to the general appropriation bill an amendment that prevented any public officer or employee of the government from soliciting, giving to, or receiving from another employee, any money, property, or other thing of value for political purposes. The penalty for a violation of the act included dismissal from office and conviction of a high misdemeanor, punishable by a fine of not less than $500 nor more than $3,000, and imprisonment for not more than one year. In case any member misunderstood the significance of the amendment, Representative Whitehouse explained that since salaries were being reduced by an average of 10 percent due to the national budget deficit, it was necessary to eliminate political party assessments to prevent any real salary reductions. "It is estimated," he proclaimed, "that the reduction in salaries will not make any material difference to the employee of the Government, as my amendment will relieve them from the assessments made for party purposes," and, he continued, will "enable each party to enter upon its political campaign or canvass on equal terms."[24]

Historians have wondered if this was a serious effort at legislative reform, or merely a partisan attempt by Democrats to starve the Republican assessment machinery. After all, since most officeholders were then beholden to Republicans, assessment benefits would accrue to the Republican Party. Evidence shows that Whitehouse's was a serious attempt to reform the assessment system of campaign contributions. First, Representative Whitehouse offered his proposal as a friendly amendment, acknowledging the support of the Committee on Appropriations. Second, despite strong resistance and failed attempts to limit assessments in the past Congresses, the House readily adopted the amendment on a voice vote. Finally, the amendment underwent revision in the Conference Committee, with Republican cooperation and involvement, and it became part of the statutory law. The New York Civil Service Reform Association began a campaign to enforce the law, and though delayed for several years, it eventually called into question General Curtis's activities, as well as those of many others who continued to assess and collect campaign funds from employees. Finally, the law was upheld by the United States Supreme Court in a then-celebrated, if now largely forgotten, case involving General Curtis, once the "hero of Fort Fisher," who became, by virtue of the Anti-Assessment Act, the first political casualty in the reform of the campaign finance system.[25]

In 1876, while the political landscape remained untilled for the emergence of civil service reform, piecemeal legislation like Whitehouse's amendment abolishing and criminalizing the collection of certain political assessments planted the first legislative seed in that growing movement. Representative Whitehouse surely realized that his measure could as easily harm his party if the spoils of office were to tip its way in the next election. The *New York Times'* skeptical response to the act was typical: the country would rid itself of the evil of spoils only with real reform. Real reform came first from the inquiry into the activities of General Curtis.

EX PARTE CURTIS—The 1876 Act and the Role of the Supreme Court in Reform of the Campaign Finance System

Calls for change resounded across the political landscape after the hotly contested presidential election of 1876. Many Americans wondered about the vitality of our democratic institutions, in light of the circumstances surrounding the corruption-ridden contest. In 1880 President Hayes, sensing his own political vulnerability, issued an executive order that prohibited the rankest form of patronage abuse that mostly went unenforced. Yet critics of these half measures remained. "Political assessments," opined one editor, "will always be levied and paid so long as employment under the Government is regarded as part of the spoils of victory." While President Hayes had issued an executive order prohibiting assessments, which in a limited way expanded the categories of included employees, they "are only one turn of the numerous evils which inhere in the system of patronage in the civil service, and it can only be done away with by a reform which does away with the system." The New York Civil Service Reform Association, less content to await that penultimate reform and demanding enforcement of the existing act, lodged a complaint charging General Curtis with a violation of the 1876 Anti-Assessment Act.[26]

Riding a strong wave of reformist impulse that had emerged out of the Hayes-Tilden election, General Curtis's indictment evoked strong support from the New York editors. Curtis, acting as New York State Republican Committee state treasurer, had unlawfully and knowingly received $5.00 from Peter Vogelsang and $100.00 from Charles Treichel for political purposes. All three were then employees of the United States government and therefore subject to the Anti-Assessment Act. Curtis's counsel filed a demurrer arguing the congressional regulation of a government employee raising campaign funds in his capacity as a private citizen was beyond the constitutional power of Congress. The government tried Curtis in the Circuit Court for the United States for the Southern District of New York. The jury returned a guilty verdict on two counts and fined him $500. Imprisoned by the court until his fine was paid, Curtis filed a motion for a new trial and a petition for a writ of habeas corpus with the United States Supreme Court. Chief Justice Morrison Waite issued a recognizance to allow General Curtis his release from custody on July 24, 1882, four days after his conviction and imprisonment.[27]

In December 1882, after submission of briefs and oral arguments, the Supreme Court issued its opinion in *Ex Parte Curtis* sustaining his conviction and upholding the constitutionality of the Anti-Assessment Act. In this case of first impression, the opinion of the Supreme Court, written by Chief Justice Waite, found that Congress's purpose in "promoting the efficiency and integrity in the discharge of public duties, and to maintain proper discipline in the public service" was a legitimate exercise of congressional authority. Echoing the sentiments of a litany of reformers, the Court recognized that employment independence under the law was "conducive to faithful public service, and nothing tends more to take away this feeling than a dread of dismissal" often attendant upon those employees who refused to pay their assessments. Since the act did not prohibit voluntary assessments, it was constitutional to prohibit only coerced political assessments.

Furthermore, the Court considered the potential, expressed by Congress in the rationale of the 1876 act, that salary increases would provide the means to pay the assessments. This would, the Court contended, indirectly require the public weal to furnish those extra funds to keep in power the political party that had control of the public patronage. Congress, the Court ruled, citing the Constitution's Article I, Section 8 "necessary and proper clause," clearly had the means to regulate compelled contributions. General Curtis, guilty of violation of the 1876 act, was remanded to the custody of the marshal for the Southern District of New York to pay his fine, or to sit in jail until he did.[28]

Justice Joseph Bradley dissented, evoking First Amendment principles that would, a century later in the case of *Buckley v. Valeo*, dominate campaign finance constitutional issues. General Curtis's attorneys had raised free speech issues in their brief to the Supreme Court. Curtis drew a distinction between the language and the effect of the Anti-Assessment Act, contending that, while Congress had the right to intervene when a federal employee's conduct adversely affected the public service, the act as drafted was overbroad because it restricted all forms of campaign fund solicitation. According to the Court ruling, a crime occurred even if the solicitation bore no relation to any official duty. Bradley argued that this regulation went beyond congressional authority to regulate elections because it was too attenuated from the wrong it sought to remedy.[29]

More importantly, Bradley held that association and contribution of money were among the necessary and proper means of promoting political speech. "To deny a man the privilege of associating and making joint contributions with such other citizens as he may choose," continued Bradley, "is an unjust restraint on his right to propagate and promote his views on public affairs." Bradley viewed the act of campaign contribution as a form of deliberative political speech. The overreaching interpretation of the act that limited all government employee solicitations, voluntary or otherwise, created First Amendment problems that Bradley felt insurmountable. "Neither men's mouths nor their purses can be constitutionally tied up in that way"—wrote Bradley, and, in a prescient statement that congressmen would later cite during their debates over the Pendleton Act reforms, he added that "We are not infrequently in danger of becoming purists, instead of wise reformers, in particular directions, and hastily pass inconsiderate laws which overreach. The mark aimed at, or conflict with the rights and privileges that a sober mind would regard as indisputable . . . the legislature may make laws ever so stringent to prevent the corrupt use of money in elections, or in political matters generally, or to prevent what are called political assessments on government employees, or any other exercise of undue influence over them by government officials and others. That would be all right. That would clearly be within the province of legislation."[30]

So there it was for all to see—for the reformers, for the party officials, for the government employees chafing under the weight of multiple, coerced assessments. There may have been a constitutional question about the scope of the 1876 Anti-Assessment Act, but after *Ex Parte Curtis,* no continuing legal dispute remained about the power of Congress to prohibit raising campaign funds by assessing federal employees. The legality of political assessments died in the opinion of *In Re Curtis.* The Pendleton Act merely performed the official and most solemn last rites.

The *New York Times* heralded General Curtis's original conviction, calling the decision "a decided change in one important feature of your political machinery," asserting "that the very bond between customhouse and the (political) committee is snapped." It printed in full the Supreme Court opinion the day after the Court announced it. Curtis, by then out of office, paid his fine and served no additional time in jail. He spent his remaining years on the outside of Republican Party politics, reliving his Civil War experiences, writing his memoirs, respected and honored for his service to country and party.[31]

THE PENDLETON ACT DEBATE ON *EX PARTE CURTIS*—Congress Interprets the Court's Interpretation of Congressional Action

The Anti-Assessment Act and the Supreme Court decision in *Ex Parte Curtis,* considered together, affirmed congressional authority to make illegal the assessment of political contributions from public employees and thus severed political parties from their most lucrative source of campaign funds. While voluntary contributions remained lawful under the 1876 act, President Hayes reaffirmed by executive order the civil service prohibition on compulsory assessments. Even as party officials continued deft efforts to solicit "voluntary" assessments, the best available evidence indicates that in the years between 1876 and 1883, the amount and regularity of voluntary political assessments from patronage employees to political party coffers declined precipitously.[32]

Even more significantly, an analysis of the congressional debates over the Pendleton Act, which occurred in the lame duck session after the 1882 elections, demonstrates the influence of the Anti-Assessment Act, and especially of *Ex Parte Curtis,* on the Pendleton debates. Considered historic because it was the first significant civil service reform initiative, the Pendleton Act initially affected only slightly more than 10 percent of the federal civil service, which in the 1880s averaged over 140,000 employees. This classified civil service included mainly clerical positions in Washington, D.C., and in the post offices and customhouses with fifty or more employees. The rest of the civil service remained unclassified, until brought under the system by later executive order or congressional action. Despite the reformers' rhetoric, even they realized that the Pendleton Act was but a first, small step in the civil service reform efforts.[33]

Making all political assessments illegal, however, would substantially and significantly alter the political campaign machinery and have an immediate impact on the connection between federal employees, political parties, and candidates engaged in campaigns. Debate surrounding the Pendleton Act's anti-assessment provisions, which occurred a month after the Supreme Court's December 1882 *Curtis* decision, show Congress recognized that the assessment restrictions and their connection to and impact on ideas of deliberative democracy, free speech rights and the campaign finance system were more important reforms than was civil service reform itself.[34]

Senator George Pendleton set the tone for the debate on December 12, 1882, as Congress reconvened after the fall elections. Republicans, facing popular reproach for years of spoils system partisanship, suffered electoral losses in New York, Pennsylvania, Indiana, Connecticut, New Jersey, and Massachusetts. New York voters elected Grover Cleveland governor by what was then the largest margin in history. Many Republicans, smarting from the losses and anxiously anticipating the 1884 elections, blamed the losses on the party's failure to take civil service reform seriously. When Pendleton introduced his legislation, he painted the goals with a broad, popular political brush. "I do say," Pendleton contended, "that the civil service is inefficient; that it is expensive; that it is extravagant; that it is in many cases and in some senses corrupt; that is has welded the whole body of its employees into a great political machine; that it has converted them into an army of officers and men, veterans in political warfare, disciplined and trained, whose salaries, whose time, whose exertions at least twice within a very short period of time in the history of your country have robbed the people of the fair results of Presidential elections."[35]

Yet while Senator Pendleton intended that civil service reform be the primary goal, both proponents and opponents observed that only Section 6 of the bill, the provision that prohibited assessments by and of federal employees, was, in any sense, real reform. Section 6 stated "no person in the public service is for that reason under any obligation to contribute to any political fund, or to render any political service, and that he will not be removed or otherwise prejudiced for refusing to do so." Pendleton admitted that the reform goals of the bill were "not perfect," and would not "immediately spring into life [a system] which will perfect and purify the civil service," but he added, that the bill remained "the commencement of an attempt to lay the foundation of a system . . . which will correct the abuses" of the spoils system.[36]

While Senator Joseph Brown (D-GA) questioned the necessity of expanding the civil service reforms to cover all federal employees, he supported the expansion of the assessment prohibition. Recognizing that the "practice of soliciting and virtually compelling donations of part of their salaries from subordinates in the different Departments" constituted a political evil, depriving men of their free will to decide how to spend their money, he nonetheless supported the remedy proposed in the bill. The people in the 1882 elections have spoken "in thunder tones of condemnation and denunciation, which can neither be ignored nor misunderstood," but he openly wondered, how civil service reform that affected only the very lowest grades of federal employees would solve the abuses that the Pendleton proponents promised.[37]

Opponents of the Pendleton bill recognized the limitations of the proposed civil service reforms and called into question the public demand for a bill that did little to remedy the abuses of the higher-grade employees. Senator Daniel Voorhees (D-IN) doubted the popular demand for the bill, stating that "[y]ou might as well claim that a man can be cured of the small-pox by homeopathic doses of rainwater as to say the public service of this country can be reformed by a bill providing for competitive examinations of the men, women, and children who strive to enter the lowest branches of Government employment." It was this false sense of reform, at least with respect to the modest goals of the Pendleton Act, that informed much of the debate on the competitive examinations and classification provisions of the act. Mocking Senator Pendleton's caution that the demoralization of the civil service permeated every office across the country, and if allowed to fester, would kill the republic, countless members asked, If that were true, how could the diminutive remedy proposed in the Pendleton Act actually solve the problem? "Do you propose to stop the frauds," questioned Senator Samuel Maxey (D-TX), "do you propose to stop all that fraud, all that peculation, all that corruption, by a competitive examination of men who have nothing whatever to do with that fraud, with that peculation, with that corruption?" "I ask," he continued, "is it possible to make a more lame and impotent conclusion from these grave and weighty premises?" For many of the opponents and proponents alike, spoils system corruption, where federal jobs became the quid pro quo for political support of parties and politicians, would not be truly reformed by the Pendleton Act because it would affect only the lowest 10 percent of lower-paid, entry level positions.[38]

The political assessment restrictions in the Pendleton Act, however, were a very different matter. They affected the nature of individual political rights, the democratic electoral ideal of voluntary free will voting, and the specter of political coercion that underscored the venality of the assessment practice. Congress thought it had ended the solicitation of political assessments in the 1876 act, which the Supreme Court approved in *Curtis,* but Section 6 of the Pendleton Act extended those restrictions to all solicitations and contributions of and by federal employees. Even more than the civil service provisions of the Pendleton Act, the anti-assessment restriction transformed political fund-raising and reconfigured democratic assumptions about the role of money in campaigns, and the ability and free will of individuals to engage in political expression.

Congressmen realized the implications of those new restrictions, even as they debated the meaning of *Curtis* in an attempt to clarify their own ideas about corruption, democracy, and individual political expression in the campaign finance system. The most discerning representatives made the connection, and as the Senate debate continued into late December 1882, the focus on the assessment provision grew. Senator John Sherman (R-OH) cut to the heart of the issue. Drawing on the *Curtis* decision, announced only weeks earlier, and from ideas of republican democracy and history, Sherman called into question the criminalizing of voluntary contributions by federal employees, something that the 1876 act had not done. "If any official of the Government chooses to give money to aid his political party," Sherman contended, he has a right to do it and he ought not to be interfered with in doing it. On the other hand, "he ought not to be compelled or coerced, or put in a position where he cannot refuse to do it . . . requests in the nature of an imperative demand to contribute for political purposes, were wrong and ought to be corrected. I would not allow any Senator or any member of Congress or any officer of the Government," Sherman concluded, "whoever he was, to ask for political contributions, nor would I deny to any officer, high or low, the right to give money in aid of his party for the legitimate expense of political warfare. I would not deny him that privilege." For Sherman, it was the coercion of political assessments that made them corruptive. In a society where individual free will remained the essence of democracy and popular sovereignty, a system that put an employee's job at risk for fear of noncompliance with party officials' assessment demands seemed the antithesis of republican values.[39]

For others, the nature of official duties and the position of public authority made their direct connection to partisan political affairs an abuse of power. "That the officer may exercise his mere personal influence for his faith or party like any other citizen," remarked *The Atlantic Monthly,* nevertheless did not imply a "right to use his official authority or influence, or to take the time required for the discharge of official duties, to propagate any opinions or to give strength to any sect or party," nor any right to make use of his office to electioneer, collect or coerce assessments, or act as the political agent of any party. To allow otherwise would convert the entire administration into a vast partisan propaganda machine where public duties became a secondary matter. While the reformers understood the necessity of assessment reform, something more than executive action such as that undertaken by the Hayes administration, which came apart in the 1880 election, was demanded. "The employees have been assessed, the office-holders have managed the campaign, the rules have been broken over," lamented one political commentator, "and we are back again at the beginning, only worse off than before, because the reform has become ridiculous." And, in a statement reminiscent of reforms before, and many campaign finance reforms to follow, he cautioned that, "[i]n politics, when a thing becomes ridiculous before it is widely or fairly understood, it suffers great harm."[40]

General Curtis fared only slightly better in congressional debate than he had in front of the Supreme Court. Congressional concern about the extent of their authority to limit assessments, especially voluntary assessments, drew them to the *Curtis* case and the 1876 law, and the Supreme Court's interpretation of both. Democratic congressmen, anxious to tie their Republican counterparts to the assessment evil, found in General Curtis a perfect foil. Democrats cited numerous instances of Republican efforts to collect assessments by General Curtis and a vast array of Republican officials for the party, as evidence of rhetorical hypocrisy on civil service. Many Republican supporters of civil service reform had not long before been its greatest opponents. Senator Francis Cockrell (D-MO), an early opponent of spoils system reform, reluctantly announced his support for the Pendleton Act. After affirming his ironic shift in position, Cockrell stated that only a change in the party in power would create real reform, ending the "greatest danger to our republican institutions . . . from the corruption of the source of political power," and from the "loss of political purity and the appearance of money as a determining factor in great political contests." "Corruption," he concluded, "kills honor, virtue, and patriotism, and saps the very foundations of society and brings down the structures of States and nations in ruins and disorder."[41]

Slowly, it became apparent to Congress that political assessments and their attendant evil were as important an objective of the Pendleton Act as was overall civil service reform. Then politicians from both parties, intent on positioning for the next election, attempted to outdo each other in reforming the assessment evil. Oregon's Senator James Slater (D) proposed an amendment to ban all contributions, voluntary or otherwise, to make clear that the Pendleton ban on solicitation would not be circumvented. But Senator Joseph Hawley (R-CT) objected, contending that the fatal flaw in Senator Slater's amendment prohibited any officer from giving any money or thing of value for political purposes. Drawing the distinction between voluntary contributions and the kind of coerced assessments the Supreme Court in *Curtis* had permitted Congress to regulate in 1876, Hawley argued that "to attempt to forbid any person in the United States, whether an officer, employee, or what not of the Government, or a citizen of any rank or degree, from giving his own money as he pleases, is something that this Senate and this House of Representatives can not do; it is utterly beyond their power." At stake was the right of citizens to participate in the electoral process, to use their own money for political speech, to voice their opinions through the fruits of their own labor. Slater contended that any such blanket restriction violated the powers of Congress, even with respect to federal employees.[42]

Others, however, disagreed. Senator Hawley, brandishing a copy of the recent Supreme Court decision in the well of the Senate, interpreted the *Curtis* decision as authorizing Congress, with respect to all federal employees, to "say to all officials and employees of the Government that they shall not solicit or take from each other anything for political purposes," because those employees were open to corruption from the process, and the possible coercion from each other. Furthermore, Congress could prohibit the use of government offices and rooms to solicit money for political purposes. The question then was, if the Supreme Court in *Curtis* permitted Congress to prohibit executive officers and employees from giving to other officers or employees of the government, why could it not prevent them from giving to anybody sent to them directly, or indirectly, by any political campaign committee to do the same thing?

For Hawley, congressional failure to prohibit voluntary assessments meant opening the door to assessments from government employees that appeared voluntary, yet carried with them the indirect threat of dismissal or reprisal. Senator Charles Van Wyck (R-NY) called the assessment provisions in the Pendleton Act "the most important feature in this bill" and noted the situation facing clerks from his own state. Cautioning political operatives that coerced assessments were illegal under the 1876 act, party operatives had ignored that act and sent out several notices to those clerks who had failed to respond to the political dun for contributions. Even after the election in the state of New York, described Senator Van Wyck, some of that same class of political patriots actually discovered "that the election had come and gone and that the clerks in the New York post-office, where they had civil-service regulations, had suffered an election to come and go, and after it had passed and all had been forgotten a certain political committee notified that class of men that they were surprised to find that they had suffered an election to pass and had not made a voluntary contribution." The chamber convulsed in laughter at the suggestion.[43]

Senator James George (R-MS) concurred, remarking that the assessment proposition was "one of the most material connected with civil-service reform," contending that the measure could be successful only if it included all contributions. Noting that the government had previously prohibited certain officers from investing in public securities and lands, George contended that the issue was a broader understanding of the corrupting effects of the assessment system. Limiting the prohibition to coerced assessments would fail, he contended, to "allow, and to provide for, the determination of elections by the people fairly, uninfluenced and uncontrolled by the use of money." This broader understanding of the object of the Anti-Assessment Act of 1876, of the *Curtis* decision, and of Pendleton Act prohibitions against assessments failed to win enough votes to prevent all contributions from all government employees, but it emphasized a new realization about the deleterious effects of the assessment-funded campaign finance system on ideas and institutions of American democracy. Even in 1882, the deliberative foundations of democratic participation shaped the debate and forged the skeletal structure of the emerging campaign finance system.[44]

In the end, those who sought the stronger rules against assessments, prohibiting both coerced and voluntary contributions, and enlarging civil service reform to prohibit all contributions and collections by federal employees, failed to convince their colleagues. While Congress generally recognized that its authority extended broadly to prohibiting the quid pro quo corruptive use of money such as vote buying or bribery during federal elections, it hesitated to adopt Senator George Hoar's (R-MA) vision that "we have the constitutional power to say to employees of the Government that they shall not pay for political purposes any money to any person whatsoever." Senator Benjamin Harrison (R-IN) understood the evil to be "not the collection of money for political uses" or the "corrupt and unlawful use of money in elections," but rather "to remove from all those in the official service of the United States any other influence or control in their giving than that which may operate upon a private individual." The emancipation from undue influence, the freedom to make independent choices, the right of the individual to contribute, to vote, and to voice his opinion free from the threat inherent in the assessment system was the goal of the legislation. Senator Harrison contended that Congress could prohibit the use of money for "illegal purposes, for purpose of fraud or corruption in elections," but not the use of a man's own money for any legitimate purpose.[45]

DELIBERATIVE DEMOCRACY AND THE "SUCCESS" OF REFORM

The Senate passed the Pendleton Act on December 27 and sent it to the House, where it would pass quickly in January 1883. The civil service reform provisions remained the weakest aspect of the bill; the anti-assessment provisions the strongest, providing the most significant changes to the political system. When it became law, the Pendleton Act prohibited the involuntary solicitation and collection of assessments from a limited group of lower-level employees to which the act applied, but, more importantly, along with the Supreme Court's decision in *Ex Parte Curtis*, it permanently established the end of the assessments as a foundation of civil service reform.

The effect of diminishing and unreliable party revenues, caused by the newly constricted assessment provisions, transformed political fund-raising even as new forms of campaigning dramatically increased the need for party revenues. Newspapers and "bought press" increased dramatically from 1870 to 1890. Campaigns at all levels became more expensive as advertising and pamphleteering blanketed a larger and more diverse electorate. Parties clamored to add or subtract voters, expanding and limiting the franchise, while struggling to justify the ideals of democracy that promised equality and voting rights. Special interest groups developed around issues such as the tariff, pensions, and budget and monetary policy, which increased the partisanship of elections and added to their costs.

The regulation of spoils diminished the assessments they provided, which forced parties to turn to individuals and businesses to finance their campaigns. As the cash cow of assessments eventually dried up, political organizations foraged elsewhere for those vast sums necessary to run campaigns. Business organizations, emerging then as national players in an increasingly national market, took their cue from the *Curtis* prosecution and sought out party officials in a distinctly new political effort. The parties, to court corporate interests, promoted legislation on their behalf, seeking to elect politicians sympathetic to the emerging ethic of economic individualism. "What power partisanship relinquished in setting the agenda, special interest would take up," creating a party system married to "business principles" and betrothed in the veil of laissez-faire.[46]

National corporations, welcomed by legal doctrine into an enlarged panoply of citizenship rights, sought the means to insert that nationalist vision into the political arena, intent on preserving their economic power against increasingly hostile threats from state legislatures. Businesses soon became involved in the campaign finance arena, first by reifying the conception that their national market interests equaled the public good, and then by backing that assertion with vast sums of campaign finance money directed to the election of like-minded officials. Between 1876 and 1896, national corporations and political parties redefined the conception of corruption and the nature of their mutual relationship, and forever altered the campaign finance system. It was to these corporate financial spigots that parties turned in the late 1880s, thus creating a new method for financing political campaigns that opened avenues of access for a wide array of nascent national interests. Emerging constitutional doctrine opposed to the redistribution of economic or political power reconfigured and reshaped those political institutions and processes. During the election cycles of 1888–1896, the legal system reconstructed end-of-the-century conceptions of corruption and democracy, catalyzed the emergent role of national corporations as campaign fund-raisers, and transformed the institutional development of the campaign finance system.[47]

The origins and ideology of Gilded Age campaign finance reform reaffirmed the belief in the free exercise of political deliberation. Reforms intended to end assessments demonstrate the central connections between democratic ideals and the campaign finance system. Increasingly, questions about our democracy would be resolved decisively by the Supreme Court, then emerging as part of the strongest branch of government capable of mediating political disputes over the connections between political speech, campaign financing, and a democracy with diminished opportunities for deliberation. In the late Gilded Age, political reformers clashed with political bosses and party adherents, and legislators clashed with each other as the judiciary assumed a greater role in the mediation of political disputes over tripartite rights, political machinery, election laws, apportionment, and corruption. This body of law addressed fundamental issues of democratic participation and deliberation, voting rights and privileges, and political free speech issues, and created the beginnings of the campaign finance system. In the tumult of the reform of the civil service and assessment system that sought to end political corruption then understood to involve the denial of free electoral will by the coercive connection between employment and party support, campaign finance reformers defined the corruption and then remedied to end it. These issues came to the judicial fore in the 1880s–1890s, as increasing social and political pressures to remedy the abuses of industrialization, immigration, and urbanization conflicted with a growing antiredistributive legalism on the Court.[48]

Chapter Two

FUNDING THE NATIONAL INTEREST

The Rise of National Corporations in the

Campaign Finance System, 1884–1896

On July 12, 1893, a thirty-two-year-old University of Wisconsin professor of history addressed an assembly of historians at the Chicago World's Fair. Frederick Jackson Turner's topic, "The Significance of the Frontier in American History," forever changed the interpretative retelling of American history. In calling the ever-retreating frontier the key to America's development, Turner sought to eradicate the germ theory of European infection and heritage from accounts of American expansion, relying instead on uniquely American factors, which he argued had shaped the "process of evolution" of expanded opportunities. In his view, American society was best understood as "a kind of biological organism evolving from frontier beginnings."[1]

Jackson's frontier thesis of free land, limitless opportunity, and advancing settlement promoted an emerging "frontier individualism" that, in turn, promoted democracy and forced "a composite nationality for the American people." It was, according to Turner, the nationalizing tendency of the westward expansion that transformed Jefferson's democracy into Madison and Jackson's national republic. Popular mobility meant the death of localism, the invigoration of individualism, antipathy to direct government control, and the extension of the franchise as a means to attract new settlers to the vast open lands of the West. But Turner's story was not all good and glory. He cautioned that the same forces that brought to the American intellect "coarseness and strength combined with acuteness and inquisitiveness" combined with "a masterful grasp of material things—a restless, nervous energy" also brought "a laxity in regard to governmental affairs which has rendered possible the spoils system and all the manifest evils that follow from the lack of a highly developed civic spirit." American ideals dug from the hardpan of the frontier influenced our economic and political history, for good or ill, toward a developmental ethos.[2]

Indeed, Turner's evolutionary analogy left him much concerned about the future of the United States democracy. Turner believed that the law allocated economic and political rights in an ethos anxious about the diminution of opportunity. He believed that the formerly abundant gift of free land—that essential frontier fuel—was gone, never again to provide a transformative medium for America's brand of democracy, and that the law had failed to militate against the consequences of that loss. He implored for an examination of the relationship between the end of the frontier and legal-political developments because he considered the legal-political connections that had gone ignored and unexplained to be essential to understanding American history. "What constitutional historian," asked Turner, aware of the impact that the law had on the changes he described, "has made any attempt to interpret political facts by the light of these social areas and changes?"[3]

Turner's argument coincided with a national redefinition of the concept of corruption from one focused on the coercion of individual voters by party spoils, into a conception that promoted national business interests as essential to the common good. As Americans came to terms with the limits on opportunities, national corporations began to promote their own economic interests as national goals. While associating national corporate economic goals with the common good permitted the continued expansion of the frontier of opportunity despite the limits of available free land, developing that ethos caused many Americans to view the expansion of economic and political rights as a zero sum game. In the last two decades of the nineteenth century, the law created and implemented an economic and political doctrine that encouraged the involvement of emerging national corporations in national politics and made them the leading financiers of the campaign finance system.

Reformers concerned with growing Gilded Age corruption were most concerned with the power of money in elections that "induced officials who ought to guard the purity of the ballot box to tamper with returns" and the use of campaign funds to supply "the funds for maintaining party organizations and defraying economic costs of electoral campaigns" in return for favors, clauses in bills, and grants for special interests. Only the criminal law, and the redeeming power of elections—of "inflicting condign chastisement not only on the men over whose virtue wealth has prevailed, but even over the party in state or nation, which they have compromised" remained viable tools to right a corrupted democracy. While many remained optimistic about the power of democratic elections, others cautioned against "the peculiar facilities of the great corporations, wielding enormous pecuniary resources."[4]

While elections offered a political solution to the corruption, the Supreme Court was more concerned about how state legislatures, addressing the inequality of economic power, passed laws that the Court considered assaults on property rights. In 1890 Supreme Court Justice Stephen Field addressed the New York State Bar Association on the centennial of the Supreme Court, expressing his understanding about the role of the Court in economic redistribution. A Californian, Field had seen firsthand the growth opportunities since the end of the Civil War. He, like Turner, contemplated the end of the frontier, realizing that booms did not last forever, and that while California offered "a realization of the wild and extravagant fiction of the East," his legal training involved resolving disputes tempered by a Jacksonian belief in limited government and faith in natural law. There could be no winner, economically speaking, without taking something from the loser. His understanding of class legislation made that equation crystal clear. Field believed in a difference between the inequality that existed naturally, which would secure, by a leveling process, liberty good and true, and artificial inequality foisted upon society by unnecessary government influence.[5]

To the New York Bar, Field argued that "[t]he Court, whilst cautiously abstaining from assuming powers granted by the Constitution to other departments of the government, must unhesitatingly and to the best of our ability enforce . . . not only all the limitations of the Constitution upon the federal and state governments, but also all the guarantees it contains of the private rights of the citizen, both of person and of property." Field asserted a broad constitutional power to protect property rights. The disappearance of free land and unlimited bounty caused by the end of the frontier led Field to forecast the inevitability of class conflict, which would become, by 1892, the Populists' protest and William Jennings Bryan's theme in the 1896 presidential campaign. The conflict caused by growing inequalities of wealth created a discontented population calling for government intervention in the affairs of business. Only the Court stood in the way of the inevitable attack on property, which Field felt formed the basis of American progress and prosperity.[6]

Field's construction implied two certainties. One, inequalities, especially those regarding aggregations of wealth and property, were natural and not to be disturbed by misguided democratic assumptions of legislative authority. Where the masses excited animus against that natural process, the Court must stand as a bulwark to preserve those rights of property that Field's conception of liberty deemed essential. Second, because of the end of the frontier, population pressures would most assuredly push up against the limits of American economic bounty. To grant to the "angry menaces" the authority to impose upon those great but natural aggregations of wealth necessarily implied a redistribution of that wealth. Under Field's constitutional theory, the public trust with which the judicial branch had been empowered permitted no "timidity, hesitation, and cowardice . . . whether moved by prejudice, or passion, or the clamor of the crowd," which assent would "constitute a robbery as infamous in morals and as deserving of punishment as that of the high-wayman or burglar." Courts, reflecting broad public concerns about diminishing economic opportunity, developed a doctrine that allocated economic and political rights among groups and individuals.[7]

Reformers focused their concerns on a conception of corruption that extended beyond the limited framework of quid pro quo electoral coercion and bribery. "If the average man," one commentator opined, "believes that his only concern with the government is to get through it all he can of mercenary profit," then bribery laws accomplished those ends more effectively. Abstractly, bribery purchased the power that the sovereign people for "the great security as the legitimate end of government" confided to a functionary. Bribery purchased absolutism and bought "the omnipotence that civilization had committed to the state." When limits to "a fair chance in the struggle for place" appeared in the public mind of the late 1890s, America's "excessive individualism gradually led the ordinary voter to regard the fruits of government as everybody's legitimate prey. The debased standard of citizenship," one commentator concluded, "is the radical public evil in America." Quid pro quo corruption, like that evident in the spoils system, may have been the most recognizable form, but Americans began to view the corruptive influences more broadly and considered them intrinsically damaging to American democratic idealism. The definition of corruption shifted from the individualistic coercion emphasized in the 1876 Anti-Assessment Act and the Pendleton civil service reforms, into a concept concerned with the effects of the rise and exertion of special interests fighting over an increasingly limited economic and political pie.[8]

Inherent in that definition was a peculiar kind of democratic theory. Although liberty was proclaimed as the self-evident *sine qua non* of American democracy, it became circumscribed with every political contest. Democratic theory and economic liberty became inextricably associated, and democratic thinkers, guided by the hard choices caused by the end of the frontier, failed to establish any hierarchies of value. There was no appreciation inherent in Justice Field's doctrine, for example, of a humane or moral freedom higher than freedom of property and contract. Yet it was not merely the rise of industrial capitalism, but the growing gloom about the extinguishing of what Turner called "the perennial rebirth, the fluidity of American life, this expansion westward with its new opportunities, its continuous touch with the simplicity of primitive society" that dampened the hopes and ignited the fears of many Americans. Hand in hand, the Supreme Court constructed that democratic faith into a legal doctrine, as the capitalist ethos converted the American dream from a theory of communal moral improvement into a singular doctrine of individual material progress. The right to labor and freedom of contract thus fulfilled this reconstituted founding ideal, any derogation of which corrupted America's promise and destiny as the land of the free.[9]

That new ideology infused business leadership, which was then embarking on national consolidation and expansion, with high politico-legal aspirations that supported their business plans. Coupled with the growing nationalization of economic and democratic thought, their survival seemed fated by a national market meant to sustain that national growth. This ideology promoted extensive corporate involvement in the campaign finance system. And when the most significant challenges to those assumptions arose, in 1892 from the Populists, and in 1896 from Democratic nominee William Jennings Bryan and the Populist fusion, the parties and corporations birthed a campaign finance system conceived in the principles of an emerging national market and swaddled in the garb of antiredistributive economic and political principles.

CONGRESSIONAL AND CORPORATE POWER IN THE ELECTORAL SYSTEM—
The Waite-Fuller Courts, 1874–1888

As Americans lamented the closing of the frontier, the reformist impulse of the Pendleton Act and the legal doctrine of the Waite-Fuller Supreme Court chugged alongside the twin track of an increasingly national market. Major corporations, most notably the railroads, oil, steel, and meat processing industries, combined and expanded their market reach across the nation. The story of that expansion, of the conquest of the western frontier, of consolidation of the market, and of the professionalization of their corporate management style, documents the connections between national corporations and federal and state politics. But that story has generally ignored, except anecdotally, how the rise of those national corporations, supported by this emerging legal doctrine, reshaped the campaign finance system and transformed American understandings of corruption and democracy.[10]

Before his appointment to the Supreme Court, Morrison Waite, like his fellow Supreme Court brethren Stephen Field and Melville Fuller, had engaged in political careers, albeit ultimately unsuccessful ones. In 1861 a split Republican Party in Ohio nominated Waite for Congress. Strongly supporting the Union war effort, he advocated a limited constitutionalism, fearful of the growing power and excesses of the Lincoln administration. His legal stand for the constitutionality of slavery and the necessity for a constitutional amendment to abolish it probably cost him the election to the radical Republican candidate. Exposed to the unforgiving calculus of American politics, Waite thereafter refused to submit himself to the equation of electoral politics, preferring to develop his private law practice and serve on appointed conventions. On May 7, 1873, Chief Justice Samuel Chase died at the age of sixty-three, and President U. S. Grant, having been turned down by Senator Roscoe Conkling of New York for the nomination, and after seeing his two subsequent nominees rejected by the Senate, nominated Waite.[11]

When Waite first took his seat as Chief Justice, he found associate justices Ward Hunt, Joseph P. Bradley, David Davis, William Strong, Noah H. Swayne, Nathan Clifford, Samuel F. Miller, and Field on the Court. In 1877 Justice Davis resigned and President Hayes appointed John Marshall Harlan of Kentucky. Three years later, Justice William B. Woods replaced Justice Strong. A general absence of overt political ambition of the members of the Court, due in large part to the political acumen and management of Chief Justice Waite, marked his tenure.[12]

Despite the lack of political activism, the Court did not avoid addressing political questions. In fact, it was to a great degree the apolitical tint of the Court, contrasted against the highly partisan nature of party politics off the bench, that accorded the Court its high public confidence. In 1876, despite Waite's best intentions, political issues intruded onto the Court's apolitical stage. *Ex Parte Curtis,* as we have seen, required the Court to consider the power of Congress to regulate elections and methods of campaign financing. The disputed presidential contest between Hayes and Tilden dragged on through early 1877. Congress appointed an electoral commission on which Justices Miller, Strong, Clifford, Field, and Bradley served. Chief Justice Waite, though acutely interested in the election's outcome and a friend of Hayes, refused to sit on the commission that eventually cast a series of decidedly partisan votes against his former classmate, Samuel B. Tilden. Similarly, in late 1876, *The Granger Cases,* which affected the power of states to regulate national business enterprises, were before the Court awaiting final decision. Waite would eventually author that opinion, which he considered "perhaps the most important series of cases in [the Court's] history." *The Granger Cases* signaled the Court's increasing involvement in national economic issues involving the dual-federalist conflicts over state regulation of national business that were becoming a major problem for many national businesses.[13]

Before Waite's tenure, the Supreme Court had decided several cases that poured the foundation for the conception of rights that the Waite court would cement. Catalyzed by the Fourteenth Amendment, the Court faced new issues about how to define equal protection, privileges and immunities, and due process within the constitutional confines of the federal system. The development of this doctrine of political, civil, and social rights entitled to varying degrees of constitutional protection, and the emerging ideas of an antiredistributive ethos, shaped the composition of the body politic, deliberative politics, and the campaign finance system. Although the Supreme Court decided relatively few cases directly affecting campaign finance between *Ex Parte Curtis* and the early years of the Progressive era, its election law decisions defined the power of Congress to regulate elections, and changed the nature of electoral politics and political speech afforded First Amendment protection. These decisions were the beginnings of a distinct body of law that contemporary legal scholars refer to as election law. In the 1890s, this body of law developed into a powerful doctrine that permitted congressional regulation of elections, specifically, the regulation of the use of money in elections, which created the modern campaign finance system.

Beginning with the Waite court and continuing through the tenure of Chief Justice Melville Fuller (1888–1910), the Supreme Court promoted individualistic ideas of work liberty, corporate authority, and property rights that outweighed conceptions of democratic deliberation and the communal value of a politically engaged citizenship. Although the Constitution recognized in Article I, Section 4 congressional power to regulate elections, the right to vote became a commodity of state privilege. By so defining and categorizing voting rights, the Court affected the ties between franchise reform efforts and federalism that espoused a formal articulation of state supremacy that was previously only implicit in the Constitution. Taking their cues from the Court, parties and national corporations then cooperatively transformed the campaign finance system from 1888 to 1896 into a system of massive contributions, raised mostly from the emerging national corporations. This transformation severed the connections between parties and individual voters, and ultimately redefined public conceptions of political corruption in the early twentieth century.[14]

This transformation helped produce a unanimous 1884 decision in *Ex Parte Yarbrough*. Commonly referred to as the "Ku Klux Klan cases," *Yarbrough* involved federal prosecution of coerced attempts at voter fraud. A court convicted defendant Jasper Yarbrough and multiple others of "going in disguise, and conspiring to prevent, by force, intimidation, or threat" Barry Sanders, a black citizen entitled to vote, from casting his ballot. The brothers Yarbrough, along with Lovel Streetment, Bold Emery, State Lemmons, Jake Hayes, and E. H. Green, worked their nefarious ways to prevent Sanders from voting in an election for his Georgia congressman. At issue was the federal power to supervise congressional elections against electoral corruption. While the Supreme Court had not clearly established the separate federal and state spheres in the electoral processes, it ruled in the Ku Klux Klan cases that with respect to elections, "[i]f this government is anything more than a mere aggregation of delegated agents of the states and governments, it must have the power to protect the elections on which its existence depends, from violence and corruption." "If it has not this power," the Court concluded, "it is left helpless before the two great national and historical enemies of all republics, open violence and insidious corruption."[15]

The special power of elections and their real and imagined value to democratic institutions complicated the political and legal tensions between federal and state governments. Congress's past hesitance to regulate elections out of deference for dual-federalist ideas did not diminish its right to do so when those elections faced threats to the "free, the pure and the safe exercise of the right of voting." Significantly, in *Yarbrough*, while the Court established the right of elections free from coercion for the individual voters, it also upheld "the necessity of the government itself that its service shall be free from the adverse influence of force and fraud practiced on its agents, and that the votes by which its members of congress and its president are elected shall be the free votes of the electors, and the officers thus chosen the free and uncorrupted choice of *those who have the right to take part in that choice.*"[16]

The Court maintained that once the state had allocated suffrage rights to its citizens, the federal government could then enforce legislation to protect the purity of that process. Voting rights had, by 1883, become the essential component of citizenship, and those public rights demanded public protection by the federal government in order to ensure against the corruption of elections that would coerce voters, undermining their free will to cast their ballots.[17]

Free choice guided the Court's decision in *Yarbrough* because the Court viewed coercion in the exercise of political and civil rights, similar to that discussed in *Ex Parte Curtis,* as corruptive to the democratic ideal. The right to choose one's own vocation and the right to exercise the franchise free from coercion were natural rights of man. Corruption meant the exercise of power to control elections and the electoral process through threats, or violence, or through less obvious means, because fundamental to democratic understandings of the electoral process was the belief that elected representatives, in order to be legitimate and accountable, must fully represent the free will of the electorate. The Court stated in the *Ku Klux Klan* cases that in a republican government where political power was reposed in representatives of the entire body of the people chosen by popular elections, "the temptations to control these elections by violence and by corruption is a constant source of danger. Such has been the history of all republics, and, though ours has been comparatively free from both these evils in the past, no lover of his country can shut his eyes to the fear of future danger from both sources. *If the recurrence of such acts as these prisoners stand convicted of are too common in one quarter of the country, and give omen of danger from lawless violence, the free use of money in elections, arising from the vast growth of recent wealth in other quarters, presents equal cause for anxiety.* If the government of the United States has within its constitutional domain no authority to provide against these evils—if the very sources of power may be poisoned by corruption or controlled by violence and outrage, without legal restraint—then, indeed, is the country in danger, and its best powers, its highest purposes, the hopes which it inspires, and the love which enshrines it, are at the mercy of the combinations of those who respect no right but brute force on the one hand, and unprincipled corruptionists on the other." Concern about maintaining democratic elections free from corruption originating from direct violence and the power of money remained a sustaining principle of election law in the late 1880s.[18]

In 1886 the Court extended the legal rights of the corporate entity in *Santa Clara County v. Southern Pacific Railroad*. With the country facing increasingly partisan political battles over the benefits of tariff legislation, budget policy, the futile Republican attempt in the form of the Lodge bill of 1890 to restore black political rights in the South, and inequities in wealth distribution and corporate power, the Supreme Court in *Santa Clara* created a constitutional doctrine none dreamed possible at the time of *Munn v. Illinois*. The case involved the equalization of tax assessments from Santa Clara County, California. The Southern Pacific Railroad brought suit to recover certain taxes it had paid pursuant to a state tax assessment that failed to give an offset from actual value for debt incurred by the railroad. California law permitted such a reduction from actual value for tax purposes, particularly for mortgage indebtedness, but specifically excluded railroad corporations from that benefit. The railroad claimed that such an assessment violated the equal protection clause of the Fourteenth Amendment, since the railroad corporation was a "person" entitled to equal treatment with all similarly situated persons. Justice Waite decided what should have been the most significant issue in the case, whether a corporation was a "person" under the Fourteenth Amendment, before argument, ruling that "the court does not wish to hear argument on the question whether the provision of the Fourteenth Amendment to the Constitution, which forbids a state to deny to any person within its jurisdiction, the equal protection of the laws, applied to these corporations," with Waite stating anticlimactically, "We believe that it does." Implicit in its decisions granting equal protection to corporations and locating the power to control corporate abuses in state law was not merely the spirit of laissez-faire, but concern about federal-state relations, the interpretation of the commerce clause, and an overwhelming judicial reluctance to alter the "natural arrangement" of political or economic power.[19]

The Court affirmed the citizenship status of national corporations, broadly reflecting both public and elite legal opinion. Convinced that money affected and corrupted elections by coercing voter free will, the Supreme Court reaffirmed the power of Congress to regulate the electoral processes to protect basic practices of deliberative democracy. At the same time, the Supreme Court evoked a powerful legal doctrine that promoted the political involvement of national corporations. The doctrine promoted national corporate interests in a complicated story of laissez-faire constitutionalism, which shaped the political economy and ultimately the political machinery, including the campaign finance system. The Court established a doctrinal milieu that promoted the national market for national corporations at exactly the same time corporations began to reexamine and then expand their own role in national politics. In conjunction with that changing role, national corporations turned to a more efficient instrument to effectuate that growing political influence, which helped create the system of corporate campaign finance that emerged full-blown in 1896.[20]

NATIONALIZING THE SPECIAL INTEREST—Redefining Corruption in the Tariff and Tax Debates of 1888–1894

When President Grover Cleveland in 1887 addressed the 50th Congress, his annual message offered cause for optimism. Facing the dilemma of a budget surplus caused primarily by tariff revenues that exceeded annual government expenditures by nearly $100 million, Cleveland took on the battle of tariff reform. Traditionally, the president's annual message was little more than a bland document of moderate legislative recommendations given little brook by Congress. Sensing an opportunity for reform, Cleveland seized the momentum of the civil service reform movement and delivered a pungent message—it ran only ten and a half pages—that took a strong position on tariff reform and set the tone for the upcoming session of Congress and for the 1888 election.[21]

Fresh from their victory over the corrupting effects of the spoils system, the civil service reformers of the Gilded Age looked with promise to the upcoming election. The Pendleton Act of 1883, combined with the decision in *Ex Parte Curtis* restricting political assessments, invigorated the reform movement and provided a growing impetus against the abuses of special interests in politics. Tariff opponents such as E. L. Godkin, Carl Schurz, R. R. Bowken, Melville W. Fuller, and James Russell White, all seasoned veterans of the civil service battles, were ecstatic. Their long fight against the corrupting effects of the spoils system girded them for this new contest against the protective tariff. Cleveland believed that the surplus damaged the economy by placing too much of the limited supply of money in government coffers, leaving but two realistic options: hoarding by the U.S. Treasury, or worse, allowing the budget surplus to be lavishly spent on special interests "with all the corrupting national demoralization which follows in its train." The very nature of tariff legislation, reformers argued, with its redistributive legal adjustment of schedules and free lists, created the perfect opportunity to practice political corruption because it permitted the political adjustment of the tariff to benefit a special class of manufacturers, often incompatible with the common public good.[22]

Deriving arguments from the discourse of corruption successfully used by civil service reformers, Cleveland contended that the crisis over the surplus involved the "most basic theory of your institutions," which protected individual freedom and promoted individual opportunity. Any tax, he declared, that took more from its citizens than required by "the careful and economical maintenance of Government amounted to an indefensible extortion and culpable betrayal of American fairness and justice." Cleveland's belief in a minimalist economic role for government was consistent with Jacksonian ideals of democracy. Any manipulation of trade through protective tariffs, which specially benefited certain business sectors, was antithetical to those beliefs, especially when it resulted in budget surpluses. Huge surpluses posed an even greater moral danger. Republican proposals to spend the surplus on an early redemption of Civil War bonded indebtedness and more liberal veterans' pensions simply magnified the corruption on the expenditure end, by benefiting the special interests at the expense of the public weal. Worse still, using the surplus for "unnecessary and extravagant appropriations" invited corruption and "an unnatural reliance in private business upon public funds."[23]

Yet what appeared to be an issue tailor-made for the apparel of reform turned out to be an ironic and ill-fitted disaster. Tariff reform, and its model of republican disinterestedness, failed to sway the practical application of the hard grind of political reality. Many historians focus on the tariff battles of 1887–1888 as the contested middle ground, the space into which reformers moved their struggle against political corruption in one long, lineal path toward Populist reform and Progressivism. The facts tell a far more nuanced story.[24]

Cleveland's message made tariff reform the preeminent issue facing Congress because the tariff controversy encompassed issues central to America's political, economic, and legal disputes. The tariff raised ancillary issues about industrialization and the role of business in the economy, about laborers' wages and farmers' prices, and about special-interest influence and corruption. During a time of increasing budget surpluses, it also raised fundamental questions about the appropriate role of government and about federal tax and spending policies that concerned Republicans and Democrats alike.[25]

During the 50th Congress, the House debate on the tariff galvanized public opinion across the country. Congress debated the House bill (HR 9051) referred to as the Mills bill after its chief sponsor, Roger Q. Mills (D-TX), the free trade chairman of the Ways and Means Committee, over fifty days consuming more than 240 hours of congressional time. The tariff issue was significant because it would become the singular issue in the upcoming elections, and tariff proponents and reformers presaged their election year rhetoric during the congressional debates.[26]

Mills opened the debate, given extended time to speak at the request of arch-protectionist, Pennsylvania representative William "Pig Iron" Kelley (R-PA). From the outset, the tariff opponents relied on a class-based argument that pitted wealthy Americans against the poorest masses. The Civil War income tax, by then repealed, had affected only the wealthiest Americans, but the tariff remained to raise federal revenues by taxing the most basic of consumer goods. Mills challenged the House to answer why it had repealed the "odious" income tax measure, which had at its height taxed only 460,170 people with income totaling $707,000,000, yet had left tariff taxes untouched. "Why," he asked, "had Congress lent a willing ear to the demands of wealthy corporations and individuals and took all the burden from them . . . and rolled all the taxes off the shoulders of the wealthy and lay them upon the shoulders of those who could only pay as they procured the means of their daily toil?" Mills framed the question to gain the support of the working classes, and to counter the traditional arguments of protectionists that high tariffs protected domestic jobs.[27]

The enormous taxes on the necessities of life, on products taxed under the tariff used by common folk, was the crowning abuse for the Democratic opponents. In addition, the corruptive effects of the surplus, which imposed "enormous taxation upon the necessities of life—taxation not only to support all the expenditures of Government, but taxation so contrived as to full the pockets of a privileged class," became the second leg of the rhetorical attack of the free-trade reformers. Taxes paid through the tariff effectively raised prices paid by the laboring classes for necessities, and the manufacturers benefited from this scheme by virtue of higher domestic prices for their products. Similarly, excessive taxation beyond the needs of the government bloated the federal surplus, corrupting politicians looking for electoral support who freely spent the money on impolitic and inequitable pension enhancements for longtime party supporters or on plans to subsidize special business interests.[28]

This class-based debate offered no concrete solutions for the economic and social ills Mills detailed. Many of the free-trade reformers had led the battles for civil service reform, and their solution was to create a scientifically based and rational system of tariffs that protected only industries that needed protection from unfair foreign competition, and then only to the extent of that foreign competition. Mills's first speech reiterated that traditional approach, and while reformers hailed it as wildly successful, it failed to investigate or challenge the underlying causes of economic disparity. Given the boundaries of acceptable discourse, however, Mills effectively stated the arguments against protectionism.

Representative Kelley's defense of protectionism admitted the indefensibility of the excessive budget surpluses, instead proposing alternative reductions in excise taxes on tobacco and some spirits to lower the burgeoning surplus. Kelley presented a parade of horribles that included the total abolition of tariff protection, paralysis of business, and national bankruptcy if the Mills bill passed. Similarly tied to the old arguments, Kelley then launched into a defense of protectionism that relied on the tired issues of sectionalism, prohibition, and fear. He too failed to promote the tariff in this opening salvo as a positive force for economic development in a growing national economy.[29]

Leading reformers defined the tariff and surplus issue in relation to their concept of corruption. Godkin wrote a constant barrage of articles about the tariff debates in 1888, relying on the familiar dialect of special interest used during the civil service reform efforts. At the same time, protectionists articulated a new language of emerging economic nationalism that redefined protection and muted the power of the Republican corruption discourse that had once been the reformers' most persuasive.

The Republican Party, in the tariff debates before 1888, had gradually abandoned its own doctrine of tariff for revenue only, and unashamedly adopted the belief in protection for protection's sake. This, wrote Godkin, revealed "the moral side of the tariff issue . . . to the apprehension of the dullest mind." He railed against government extravagance, against special pension bills that he viewed as corruptive efforts to promote special interests through the profligate spending of the surplus. In opposing the sugar bounty, a direct government contribution to sugar producers in return for placing sugar on the nonprotective or free list, Godkin complained that in our government of limited powers, bounties were unconstitutional. To make any business the recipient of taxes would be akin to subjecting the taxpayers to supporting a special interest that would give to business "the feudal privilege of legal robbery." The surplus was alarming because it "betokens an irresistible impulse toward extravagance and waste of the taxpayers' money" but not because it dramatically shifted the ideology of the function of government. In his argument, Godkin used a definition of corruption that ignored the class-based implications of the ongoing debates. One commentator contended that "everything that relates to protection means corruption," saying "the system of taxation on which it is based is a system of corruption," and "the surplus is a continual source of corruption." The tariff battle of 1888 was a "fight of law and justice against the anarchy of dishonesty" and a fight of the old patriot "who would sacrifice everything . . . to the welfare of the country, against the friend of the prostitute who would sell for money the most precious possessions of humanity," but he failed to connect that corruption to the altered dynamic between business in the emerging national market and party politics. For many reformers corruption remained the connection between unrepublican individual gain to the detriment of the public good, the limiting discourse of quid pro quo interestedness.[30]

Corruption, to be sure, was on the minds of the people, but Godkin naively painted the protectionists with too broad a brush. Idealistically, he contended that even as a Democratic defeat in 1888 might be disastrous, it would be "better both for the party and for the country that it should appeal to the intelligence of the country, even if it suffer a temporary defeat, than that it should win a temporary success by avoiding that appeal." For Godkin, the classical republican model of special interest versus the greater good remained the definition of corruption. When the Republican protectionists in Congress altered their argument, connecting protectionism to the growth of the national economy and protecting the wages of the laboring classes, Godkin and his reform accomplices failed to respond.[31]

With the boundaries of the debate established, reformers looked for broader ideas on which to build their coalitions. Tariff reformers attempted to create a system consistent with the classical political economists, relying, as did many reformers, on economics distanced from "purely political, ethical or social concerns." Protectionists, on the other hand, struggled to adapt old ideas to new economic realities. What they needed was an economic theory that altered the debate and that demonstrated the national value of protective tariffs. They needed to demonstrate how tariffs could promote the interests of the national market, and how localist special interests were part of the broadened national interest. Their ultimate success in reconfiguring their rhetoric during the tariff debate to adapt to the realities of the emerging national market led by business corporations and supported by judicial doctrine became a significant factor in their successful involvement in the electoral battles of 1888.[32]

What the tariff supporters did was ingenious. Recognizing that "Pig Iron" Kelley's opening sectional defense had proven inadequate, they offered during the debates an increasingly sophisticated defense of protectionism that emphasized the protection of property rights as a fundamental and constitutionally protected value. This effectively broadened the appeal of tariffs beyond the divisive and less defensible boundaries of private corporate weal. First, they disputed the venality of budget surpluses and argued that there were national needs, such as a strong navy, public education, internal improvements, and increased veterans' benefits that were legitimate outlets for increased federal spending. This deft blend of interest group appeal and nationalistic impulse, along with a tepid but popular promise to reduce excise taxes on alcohol and tobacco, was never effectively countered by Democratic appeals, and limited the effectiveness of Democratic assertions about the corruptive effects of large federal surpluses.[33]

Secondly, unlike in past debates, the protectionists threw off the emperor's clothes and openly paraded as protectionists, but not simply for protection's sake. By tying local interests that benefited from tariff provisions to broader national economic interests that had wide popular support, they created a new argument that appealed to nationalists and which undercut reformist arguments that tariffs were just a form of special interest quid pro quo corruption. Local interests, they contended, were simply coordinate facets of the general interest, and protectionist tariff policy that encouraged home industry, invigorated national markets, and protected the wages of the laboring class served the overriding national interest. Courts, they argued, had for that very reason protected entrepreneurship through judicial elimination of local obstructions to a national market. Congress, through the tariff, thus had a concomitant duty to encourage the capitalists by guaranteeing their investments and cushioning them from foreign competition. Protectionism brought government directly into the market as its chief booster. That new rhetorical tactic enabled free traders to overcome the old-fashioned split over the public and special interests, which was, after all, the epitome of specialized tariff legislation, and redefined local tariff protections as integral parts of a broader public interest promoting the emergent national economy.[34]

Two factors inclined many Gilded Age reformers to accept that argument. Many reformers came from business backgrounds and maintained a natural affinity toward capitalist enterprise. A good number of the reformers were self-made men who shared a profound faith "in the free play of competitive economic forces." They assumed the inevitability of natural economic growth, because from their vantage point, the frontier of opportunity still lay open or would remain open through the removal of artificial impediments to the operation of natural economic laws. Secondly, most reformers maintained only loose ties to political parties. Their commitment was to principle, not politics. Their distaste for nitty-gritty politics, though not uniformly held, was primarily a reaction to the class of people they found active in the political arena. They despaired most for the country where they found ignorant mass democracy, unprincipled government, and institutions without rules.[35]

Given that disposition, the reformers' most admired institution became the Supreme Court. Despite the fact that some vocal reformers decried the monopolies, the railroads, and the huge corporations which possessed unequaled power, many reformers believed in the preferential property doctrines the Court had developed in the preceding two decades. Labor organizations and farmers soon began a raucous chorus against specific business abuses in the early 1870s, demanding legislative action on behalf of the "industrial class . . . now suffering at the hands of arrogant capitalists and powerful corporations." Still, before the Populist movement in 1892, most reformers supported the political integrity and legal principles espoused by the Waite and Fuller courts. The formalism of the judiciary and its adherence to precedent satisfied the consistent, reasoned, and deliberative decision-making that those tariff and tax reformers considered the highest ideal of civic life. It was natural, then, that those reformers aligned with the judicial elimination of barriers to the national market consistent with those reasoned principles.[36]

When the Fuller Court in *Santa Clara County* put its judicial imprimatur on the corporate personality as a legitimate actor in the national market, reformers welcomed the Court's logic. During the tariff debates of 1888 and the election that followed, the result was not to silence critics of the most egregious monopoly power and abuse of public trust. Instead, the effect of that changed tactical strategy was subtly to alter the language of corruption. As national corporations gained acceptance as legitimate interests in the growing economy, their influence bled into other arteries of national life. Legal restrictions on strikes or work stoppages that sustained the processes of production allayed reformist fears about the chaos and unpredictability of labor unrest. Reflecting the conflicted and shifting notions of reform and the role of national corporations in the economy, and imbued with notions of reasoned order and policy making, Mugwump reformers cheered when courts struck down Granger statutes, which had been proposed by cash-poor farmers bonded to the financial extravagance of railroad speculators. These ideas mirrored renewed definitions of corruption as attempts to gain individual favor at the expense of the public good. During the election cycles of 1888–1896, the Republican Party and national corporations recognized and celebrated their mutual interests in that blessed union. However, the clarity of the ideal of a public good grew murky when business interests were married to the improvement of the national economy.

THE CAMPAIGN FINANCE SYSTEM TRANSFORMED IN THE ELECTION CYCLES OF 1888–1892

During no period, with the possible exception of the post-Watergate era in the mid-1970s, did the campaign finance system experience more dramatic changes than it did from 1888 to 1896. The post-Pendleton weaning of the parties from assessment-sourced funding, coupled with the growth and rising influence of national corporations within the political system, by 1896 reshaped the structure of campaign financing that would remain essentially unchanged until 1971. While these reform efforts were often dramatic, the basic rationale for using the campaign finance system to achieve their political goals was firmly established during the last three national election cycles of the Gilded Age.

Dramatic changes occurred in the period after 1896. Commonly held assumptions about corruption and democracy, the role of the government in regulating the power of wealth in politics, the judicial conception of status quo neutrality as a reactionary policy, and the development of individual and group civil rights, particularly speech and association privileges protected by emerging First Amendment doctrine, all fueled the transformation of politics. These legal, economic, and social changes influenced the evolution of the campaign finance system and ultimately affected Progressive efforts to regulate it in the twentieth century.

The tariff debates of 1888 demonstrated how the shifting discourse redefined the concept of corruption away from special self-interest and coercion. That shift encouraged political parties and national corporations to cooperate in financing national election campaigns. Government employees, relying on the anti-assessment statutes and *Ex Parte Curtis,* ignored party calls to pay a percentage of their salaries to the parties, and consequently party assessments grew increasingly less reliable as a means of raising party revenues. Business, concerned about the growing power of labor, assumed an aggressive role in political campaigns. Nationwide business organizations such as the National Association of Manufacturers began actively to represent business interests in local communities, political parties, and Congress. Business recognized that the courts were a propitious venue for the resolution of disputes that pitted localist regulation against the interest of the emerging national market. Where the Supreme Court addressed commercial matters that were "in their nature national," it attempted to create a category of regulation that promoted the national interest. As reformers supported the national economic goal of reducing barriers to the national market, parties sought out new sources of campaign finance revenue to replace the now-illegal assessments.[37]

President Cleveland had taken a calculated risk in making the tariff the key election issue in 1888. Congressional reaction to Cleveland's tariff message in 1887 led to an electoral conundrum—both Republicans and Democrats realized that the fall election results would salvage or doom Cleveland's proposed tariff reform. The Republican campaign, funded by the industries that had grown rich protected by the high tariffs, nominated Benjamin Harrison. Wealthy manufacturers, contributing mainly from their own purses (reflecting the relative close-corporate nature of their national businesses), financed a Herculean campaign machine that produced pamphlets and speakers extolling the public benefits of tariff protection, and warning that Cleveland's tariff proposal would lead to depression, low wages, unemployment, and starvation.[38]

Cleveland inexplicably selected two protectionist supporters, William H. Barhum of Connecticut and Calvin S. Brice of Ohio, as his campaign chairmen. Aware that a massive education effort aimed at winning labor support and overcoming the economic threats rolling out of the Republican electoral machine would be necessary, the campaign nonetheless started off slowly, intent on conserving its limited funds until late fall. On the other hand, Republican national chairman Senator Matthew S. Quay (R-PA) epitomized the alliance between national business and politics. Republican treasurer W. W. Dudley of Indiana, a Civil War veteran and former pension commissioner, allied with the veterans and their pension-dependent families in an attempt to seal the support of that key voting bloc. Quay appointed John Wanamaker to organize a national committee of businessmen focused on the critical states of New York and Indiana.[39]

The organizing work of several high-tariff associations, among them the American Iron and Steel Association led by James M. Swak of Pennsylvania, became important to the Republican campaign effort. "Its purse was almost bottomless," boasted the supporters, because the existing tariff schedules deposited hundreds of thousands of dollars of profit in the tills of the iron and steel industry. Within nine months of Cleveland's 1887 call for tariff rate reduction, the association had distributed 1,387,864 pamphlets advocating the benefits of high tariffs and the necessary defeat of Cleveland.[40]

In addition, the Protective Tariff League organized and funded by "One Thousand Defenders of American Industries," each pledging $100 annually, produced and distributed pamphlets across congressional districts countrywide. Alarmed by Cleveland's reform of their tariff bonanza, the League sent out 125,519 pamphlets, and in Minnesota they bought all available newspaper space and created special districts situated in industrial and urban communities where businessmen collected hundreds of thousands of dollars to fund the campaign. September 1888 opinion polls that showed Cleveland leading Harrison invigorated business contributions to the Republican campaign, and substantial money poured in from western businesses to support the established effort in the eastern industrial Northwest.[41]

By comparison, the Democrats adopted tactics that were particularly Mugwumpian. The American Free Trade League, headed by David A. Wells, distributed tariff reform documents, but reminiscent of the 1888 congressional debates they failed to connect tariff reform to the national interest. Most of the effective reform associations remained distinctly regional. Democrats successfully garnered the support of the best independent newspapers in the country such as the Springfield *Republican*, the New York *Evening Post*, New York *Herald*, *Nation*, and *Harper's Weekly*. Campaign chairman Brice reported a distribution of between eight and ten million documents by September 1888. However, the demand for educational pamphlets and Cleveland speeches seemed inexhaustible, and the supply grossly inadequate. As the election drew close, the states of New York and Indiana remained the key contested battleground. The purchase of "floaters," mobile voters whose votes could be had for a price and who were moved by party operatives into closely contested districts, rose from $2 to over $500 a head, and only the Harrison campaign had the ability to pay the market price. On the Saturday before the election, the Republican National Committee paid $150,000 for the votes of three New York "movements"; the Cougan movement estimated to carry 30,000 votes, the James O'Brien movement with 10,000, and the John T. O'Brien movement, with an uncertain quantity. It was only the failure of the votes to stay bought that brought the bribery to light. John Wanamaker raised an emergency fund of between $200,000 and $400,000 in the last days of the campaign. Indiana, not content to be out-Hoosiered by New York, reported thousands of floaters and bribed votes, many of them disfranchised blacks who were paid the handsome sum of $15 per voter for their civic engagement.[42]

The election returns gave the Republicans the narrowest of victories. Out of 401 electoral votes Harrison received 233, Cleveland 168. In Indiana, the Republican plurality was 2,348; in New York, 13,002. Cleveland had a popular plurality of 90,728, with total votes of 5,537,857 to Harrison's 5,447,129. A slight shift in the popular vote in the states where Republican business campaign money funded the education effort and obvious vote fraud would have swung the election. Cleveland accepted the defeat philosophically, acknowledging that his tariff message had cleared the ground for ideological battle. "It is better," Cleveland opined, "to be defeated for a moral principle, than to win by a cowardly subterfuge. We are defeated—it is true—but the principles of tariff reform will surely win in the end."[43]

Even Cleveland's supporters found vindication in defeat. Horace White wrote that it was "a perilous and paralyzing superstition to suppose that a party which should boldly attack the protective tariff would be necessarily overwhelmed in the first succeeding election." A young Nebraska attorney, William Jennings Bryan, wrote, "we would rather fall with you fighting on and for a principal (sic) than succeed with your party representing nothing but an organized appetite." Yet these observers missed the point. Comparing the returns from the high-tariff states to those in the election of 1884, when the differences in partisan positions were muted, Cleveland and the Democrats had actually gained ground. Cleveland carried New Jersey and cut the 1884 Republican plurality by nearly 50 percent in Rhode Island, Pennsylvania, Michigan, Ohio, and California. Clearly, on the issue of the tariff, Cleveland had won substantial support. What Cleveland and most of his supporters seemed to ignore, despite their recognition of outright fraud, was the evolving but instrumental role that new corporate sources of campaign contributions played in winning elections.[44]

In 1888 the Republican campaign committees tied their political interests to the emerging national corporations and the associations that represented them. The lack of reporting requirements and the multiplicity of national, state, and local committees, which independently raised and spent campaign funds, complicates any accurate estimates of the total campaign expenditures. The best evidence, gleaned from state committee expenditure and national committee reports, shows that Harrison outspent Cleveland's campaign, in direct, legitimate, and illegitimate expenses by several-fold. Whereas Harrison filled all the orders for literature and speakers, Cleveland's campaign went wanting. Cleveland's tariff reform platform opened the protectionist spigots and out poured an ample supply of money for the purchase of electoral expenses and Election Day floaters.[45]

Furthermore, the amount of money available to each campaign, and the power of that money to engage in deliberative debate about the tariff issue, never corresponded to popular opinion. Aggregate corporate wealth replaced the spoils system assessment practice largely because *Ex Parte Curtis* restricted assessments to amounts insufficient to organize and run a truly national campaign. Cleveland's tariff message sharply divided the parties and their support—but it can hardly be said that, given his popular vote plurality, the aggregate spending during the campaign was a true indication of the strength of the deliberative debate in the marketplace of ideas. The sources of money from the national corporations opposing tariff reform far outweighed the sources supporting and available to Cleveland. Democrats clung to the same moral lifeboat that had salvaged earlier reformers, ignoring the changes that the 1876 Anti-Assessment Act, the Supreme Court's *Ex Parte Curtis* decision, the Pendleton Act reforms, and the rise of national corporations all had made to the campaign finance system. By 1892 the Populists would make clear they understood those changes and their ramifications on the legal acceptance of status quo neutrality. Their fight would become the first significant political objection to the marriage of national corporate power to American politics, and it would seriously attempt to redefine American conceptions of corruption and democracy.

THE POPULIST MOMENT—Challenging the Status Quo and Defining Corporate Political Corruption

The goal here is not a full retelling of the Populist uprising in 1892 and its failed fusion during the Bryan-McKinley election of 1896. Rather, what is important is how the Populist challenge to the major parties—to entrenched political power—and to the growing power of aggregate wealth in politics and elections threatened the status quo. In 1892 Populist candidate James W. Weaver carried the banner of change into battle winning more popular and electoral votes (over one million, and 22, respectively) than any other third party since the Civil War. Although the Populists' success was geographically circumscribed, failing to break into the solid South, winning only limited victories in the Midwest, and making almost no impression in the Northeast and Northwest, the Populists did succeed in building the momentum of a third-party movement. Originally comprised of Farmer's Alliance members, most expressly apolitical, the party in 1890–1892 transformed itself into a political machine organized around an ideology bent on challenging the social-political-legal status quo.[46]

The challenge to existing privilege and the power of aggregate wealth formulated new conceptions about the relationship of law to politics and government to business. Populists called into question the argument about the prepolitical nature of existing social and economic conditions as a natural baseline for deciding contested issues. Judicial constructions of neutrality rejected any change from that government-promoted baseline as class legislation, finding it both partisan and improper. That assumption "played a critical role in the judicial assessment of the relevant practices": the world of segregation, the condition of labor, the political role of men and women, and the interrelationship between government and business. While some argue that the New Deal marked the beginning of the rejection of this concept of status quo neutrality, it was during the election cycle of 1892–1896 when the Populist mind creatively challenged those status quo assumptions that later formed the foundation of the liberal idea during the New Deal.[47]

The Populists never demanded the abolition of industrialism. Jacksonian themes of "equal rights for all, special privileges for none" resounded in their proclamations and proposals. Populists respected the labor theory of value and constitutionism; yet they contended that there was nothing sacred about the status quo. Stressing reform through law and order, they expressly recognized that "existing law was class law, intended to protect the rich at the expense of the poor." Law was a disguise constructed to maintain the status-quo privilege and inequality. Populists felt that the law, because it was intended to be reflective of democratic needs, ought to change to satisfy the emerging needs of a changing society. Populist leaders, national and local, assaulted the power of the status quo as unresponsive, inegalitarian, and undemocratic. "The machinery of government has been arrayed against us," proclaimed Kansas leader Lorenzo D. Lewelling. "[T]he Courts and Judges of this country have become mere tools and vassals and jumping jacks of the great corporations that pulls the strings while the judges dance."[48]

The causes of liberty and individual freedom were at stake. Populists felt threatened by the corporation, "this individual, the creation of law which has absorbed the liberties of the community and usurped the power" of the state that created it. "The corporation has absorbed the community" through its control of the money supply, and indebtedness, and by those means denied men the fruits of their labor. Soulless corporations, artificial and unnatural, cared little for the well-being of the masses. The challenge to corporate power evidenced a greater truth that affected present-day freedom, and "civil liberty is never in such deadly peril as when men deceive themselves as to its danger."[49]

Whereas Justice Field criticized government interference with the natural processes of the market, Populists contended that the "real root of the evil lay in the law." Aggregate wealth annulled the natural laws of supply and demand. Battles over these issues involved not only immediate electoral victory, but also larger principles. While Populists understood that "politics, stripped of its glittering generalities, simply means the manipulation of public affairs in such a manner so that those who make politics their profession can direct the channels of trade—the distribution of wealth—to their special benefit," they also knew political victory could only be achieved by winning elections. While it was true that law created the inequity that needed remedy, only with political victory could that remedy be attained. Populists overtly made the connection between political success and legal change because they saw the law much as later Realist theorists and New Deal pragmatists saw it—as a peculiarly human machine hitched to the creation and maintenance of the status quo.[50]

Yet early Populist politics remained fundamentally an educational practice. In 1892 Weaver harbored no hopes of winning the election. His goal was to "educate, agitate, and organize" against the permanent vesting of powerful, antidemocratic interests. He particularly despaired of the growing wealth of U.S. senators and their continued employment during their terms by corporate and other moneyed interests. "Such things," he declared, "are incompatible with the faithful discharge of public duty." Service of the public interest became corrupt, he contended, when the ties to private corporate power were so direct. Similarly, unified corporation and Supreme Court interests were seen as corruptive as the "corporation glacier is now sweeping over this country and lifting out of place the solid granite of our Judiciary." Aggregate wealth corrupted every institution of government it sullied with its tentacled reach.[51]

While institutional corruption ran rampant, the Populists preached a social gospel that questioned the assumptions of natural law and the status quo, and challenged the belief that the end of the frontier limited economic and political rights. Their ideology called for separate spheres for business and government and demanded structural change so that industrialization would become a positive force subject to governmental control. Individual sovereignty ensured an economy supportive of a culture of democratic capitalism. Populists steadfastly rejected socialism and communism, satisfied that their reforms could transform, without destroying, American values and institutions. Populists also patently rejected Social Darwinism, maintaining that government had a duty and the ability to be a life-sustaining force. State power ought not be used, they contended, to integrate the strongest economic groups and it must be used instead to protect the weakest in society.[52]

Populist Frank Doster, who became in 1896 the chief justice of the Kansas Supreme Court, argued that government must curb self-interestedness and must promote equality to "raise man above the barbarous antagonisms of the natural state into relationships of social unity and fraternity." Further, Doster proclaimed "that the equality of man means something more than equal privileges in getting money." Personal liberty, he added, "does not mean selling 'hell' in original packages to the heedless and the weak. I know that the millionaire must go like the feudal lord has done. I know that the wail of the orphan is heard louder in the courts of heaven than the chuckling glee of the money-changers. I know that humanity is above property, and that profit making on the bread of poverty is an abomination in the sight of the Lord." The new industrial regime the Populists called for emphasized individual liberty coextensive with sovereignty, with property at the service and not in command of humankind.[53]

By 1892 the People's Party abandoned the political-educational methods of the Farmer's Alliance and plunged headlong into the turmoil of electoral politics. Many longtime Alliance members deserted this course of action out of disgust. Somehow the Populists needed to evoke for those doubters the value of participation inside the political process without all its grimy involvement. Tom Watson placed his trust in public opinion, tilting the Alliance toward political-educational programs, and toward a pragmatic program of consciousness building and effective political action. Popular opinion would act as the adhesive between farmers and laborers of all kinds and economic status. By ascribing to public opinion the embodiment of society's cultural and institutional foundations, Watson believed that public opinion could act to liberate man from the vassalage of aggregate wealth toward social improvement. Deliberate discussion of principles and real issues would, according to Watson, reveal the ultimate truth. Watson faithfully maintained his faith that the democratic system could be righted only by efforts to equalize the prevailing inequities. "Keep the avenues of honor free," he declared. "Close no interest to the power of the weakest, the humblest. Say to ambition everywhere, 'the field is clear, the contest fair; come, and win your share if you can!'" In a fair contest, one where economic power was evenly distributed, the best ideas would prevail, preserving democratic opportunity through equal distribution in the capitalist system.[54]

Reformers seeking substantial reform soon realized that Cleveland's victory in 1892 only modestly challenged the status quo. The McKinley Tariff of 1890, passed under Representative William McKinley's guidance, was a complicated hodgepodge of regulation. The bill, which added thirty-seven articles to the free list, left rates on many other items as high as or higher than before. The final law deeply cut revenue and pushed the government close to bankruptcy just as the economy slumped in yet another of its periodic boom-bust cycles. The economic crisis that resulted drew its long knives across the throats of many American farmers and laborers. On July 5, 1890, a bloody strike broke out at the Carnegie Steel Works in Pittsburgh, and some 270 heavily armed Pinkerton guards, recruited and paid by Carnegie, battled the workers over the small everyday economic issues and over the larger contest of labor-capital supremacy. Ten men were slain and sixty more wounded before the strike was broken.[55]

The mood of the country, and business, turned away from the Republican nominee Harrison. Cleveland's conservative opposition to free silver did more than any other issue to shut the purses of the campaign financiers who had generously supported Harrison in 1888. Deprived of the vast campaign funds boodled to Harrison's coffers, Cleveland took his deliberative campaign on the issues to the people, winning 277 electoral votes to Harrison's 145. A shift of 750 votes in Ohio would have given Cleveland another 23. Godkin, who supported Cleveland's conservative approach to tariff reform, remarked after the election that "the era of discussion" had opened which consisted "largely to appeals to reason" and that Cleveland's election had demonstrated the value of "patient reliance on the power of deliberation and persuasion on the American people." He added, "Nothing is more important, in these days of boodle, of cheap, bellicose patriotism, than that this confidence in the might of common sense and sound doctrine and free speech be kept alive."[56]

The Populist threat reappeared in the form of Bryanism, and the Republican response of raising and spending millions to sway the public would, in 1896, challenge that civic confidence in political deliberation. Bryan's fusion with Populist ideas fundamentally challenged the sociolegal status quo and the political power of aggregate wealth. In the electoral battles ahead, Republicans and their corporate supporters, fearful that Populist successes would redistribute political power amassed unheard of sums of campaign money to overwhelm the speech of their opponents and drown the debate over policy they believed to be the very foundations of the capitalist economy.

THE ELECTION OF 1896—Ginning the Threat of "Bryanism" and Priming the Corporate Campaign Pump

The election of 1896 pitted William Jennings Bryan, the Democratic boy-orator from Nebraska, against the longtime politician and tariff proponent from industrial Ohio, Republican William McKinley. The election firmly established the components of the modern campaign finance system. Professionalized fund-raising from an elite group of interested parties, massive organized campaign dissemination of literature, and unlimited campaign fund-raising by the successful party became in 1896, and remained for nearly seventy-five years, the key features of every national election. The election of 1896 marked the effective end of party reliance on inefficient small contributions (though, of course, they were still solicited), and the shift to larger contributions from the most wealthy supporters. This new alliance between business and politics sparked a reaction in the aftermath of the 1896 election that led to the first systematic effort at campaign finance reform specifically intended to reinvigorate the deliberative foundations of democratic thought that had been polluted by corporate wealth. After 1896 observers connected the effects of huge campaign spending to effective limitations on political deliberation that many felt acted as a threat to republican government. In so doing, they greatly broadened public conceptions of corruption beyond the limiting "quid pro quo" definition. These reformist impulses and efforts, reacting to the increased role of businesses in the campaign finance system evidenced in the 1896 election, created a counterreaction to those reforms, which once again transformed the campaign finance system by empowering free speech rights as a component in the evolving campaign finance system.

Bryanism symbolized social, political, and economic change; some said revolution. William Jennings Bryan, the surprise nominee of the Democratic Party, had led the battle for tariff reform during his two terms in Congress, and had supplemented the loss of tariff revenues with a moderate income tax in 1894, the first passed since the end of the Civil War. In 1895, when President Cleveland spurned the Silverites, reversing policy and encouraging government purchase of gold as the standard monetary support, he split the Democrat Party into two sparring camps. Instinctively, Cleveland knew the danger of tying the party to silver at 16 to 1. "If we should be forced away from our traditional doctrine of sound and safe money," he warned, "our old antagonist will take the field on the platform which we abandon, and neither the votes of reckless Democrats nor reckless Republicans will avail to stay their easy march to power."[57]

Currency contraction and the lack of credit spread undeniable hardship across much of the country in the 1890s. The idea of expanding the currency from the current market ration of silver to gold, which stood at 32:1, to free coinage of silver at 16:1, would halve the value of the dollar. Debtors celebrated the prospect of paying back their debts, which many thought unfair, excessive and unjust, with cheaper dollars. However, over 21,000,000 Americans had money in savings banks, insurance companies, and building and loan associations. They feared that their investments would shrink to half of their value. Cleveland defended his gold policy as a national policy, and he decried all sectional and selfish interests in politics as he cast his wary eye on the mine-owner proponents in the silver states of the West.[58]

The silver story is an important one, but not so much because it typified Bryan's radicalism. His policies, after all, were not nearly as radical as were those of Populists who fused their ideas into his nomination and campaign. What was significant is how William McKinley's campaign manager Mark Hanna used the silver and tariff issues to terrorize the financial prospects of eastern bankers and corporations. Hanna's use of this aspect of Bryanism as a fearful foil permitted the campaign to raise enormous campaign funds for the Republicans and McKinley's campaign that drowned out Bryan's message in a disproportionate flood of purchased speech.

Before the Democratic convention held in Chicago in July 1896, the Democrats had moved toward supporting the idea of free silver. In the state conventions of Missouri, Mississippi, Nebraska, Pennsylvania, Rhode Island, Michigan, and Iowa, sharp divisions between gold and silver supporters remained. As the delegate count grew before the Chicago convention, Silverites held a solid, if still contentious, majority. Those who contend that Bryan's "Cross of Gold" platform speech at the convention propelled him into the nomination ignore the substantial support silver had before the convention. His rhetoric played into that support, music to the ears of those ready and willing to give the nomination to someone who had fought their battle for years while in Congress.[59]

Bryan's "Cross of Gold" speech was an eloquent version of the stump speech he had tested across the fields and dusty back roads of Nebraska during his two campaigns for Congress. It evoked themes of national citizenship, opposition to special interests, and a belief in reasoned deliberation. Bryan, in fact, relied on the earlier silver debates in the state conventions to support his position. "[O]ur silver Democrats went forth from victory upon victory," he declared, "until they are now assembled, not to discuss, not to debate, but to enter up the judgment already rendered by the plain people of this country . . . we have assembled here under as binding and solemn instructions as were ever imposed upon representatives of the people." Bryan believed in deliberation—it was essential to his concept of popular sovereignty—but at the convention, the prior selection of silver delegates by state conventions meant that the debate on monetary policy was over, and that the national delegates had been instructed in their course.

Bryanism, as Hanna described its excesses as seen in the frantic corporate boardrooms of Wall Street in the late summer of 1896, challenged the role of the law as a protector of organized wealth and political power. To be sure, Bryan called for "an Andrew Jackson to stand, as Jackson stood, against organized wealth," but more significantly, Bryan stood against the legal status quo. "[C]hanging conditions make new issues," he contended, and though "the principles upon which Democracy rests are everlasting as the hills, they must be applied to new conditions as they arise." Even before the Legal Realists, Bryan understood that the law was formed not by absolutes, but by the principles of men, subject to and altered by political pressures. Hanna used Bryan's ideas to depict him as a judicial radical, willing to strike at the very heart of conservative Supreme Court doctrine to overthrow every protection, derived from the principles of status quo neutrality, that business enjoyed.[60]

Bryanism rejected the principle of trickle-down economics. "There are two ideas of government," Bryan declared in his speech. "There are those who believe that, if you will only legislate to make the well-to-do prosperous, their prosperity will leak through on those below. The Democratic idea, however, has been that if you legislate to make the masses prosperous, their prosperity will find its way up through every class which rests on them." The crown of thorns, one must recall, pressed *down* upon the brow of labor. Bryan evoked much of the Populist rhetoric, but in a broader sense, he espoused a distinctive political ideology that challenged aggregate wealth and legal institutions as partners in oppression, conspirators in a political economy of special corporate interest that denied equal opportunity to the masses. Hanna, in a masterful employment of political spin, used Bryan's own words to indict him with charges that he would, if victorious, destroy the constitutional protection of the national market that the Waite-Fuller courts had constructed.[61]

During the campaign, Mark Hanna professionalized the methods of campaign fund-raising he had begun in 1892. A businessman by trade, Hanna's business life was inextricably entangled with his domestic and social life. Political involvement became a civic duty and Hanna's support for fellow Ohioan McKinley logically extended those affinities. After being selected chairman of the Republican National Committee in July, Bryan's nomination in July caught Hanna off guard. The "bump" in public support often gained by the nominee occurred in the late summer of 1896. But Bryan's support did not wear thin in the dog days of August and September, and private Republican opinion polling signaled to Hanna, and many others familiar with the situation, that if the election were held in late September, Bryan would win. Hanna took the seriousness of the unexpected challenge to heart, and as Bryan trailed his unending campaign train of corporate abuses cross-country, Hanna used the specter of Bryanism to coerce out of corporate and banking leaders such sums of money for the McKinley campaign as had never before been raised in American history. A "campaign of education" was needed to dissuade the confused mass of public opinion from the promise of Bryanism, and to convince the voters about the full meaning of the Democratic platform and "its palpable error."[62]

And what a campaign it was. Unable to count on certain states as safely Republican or Democratic as it had in 1884–1892, the Republican National Committee engaged in a national campaign that included nearly every part of the country. Since the time was short, the National Committee, instead of being a central agency to the state committees as had been prior practice, became in effect the general staff of the entire army of campaign, with Hanna as its commanding general. He systematized the recordkeeping and accounting systems. He established two headquarters, in New York and Chicago, in close proximity to the undecided states. To counteract Bryan's personal stumping (Bryan traveled mostly by train to campaign stops covering over 18,099 miles), Hanna organized trainloads of voters to travel to meet McKinley on the front porch of his Ohio home. Where that was impractical, Hanna hired and paid for the travel expenses of over 1,400 campaigners to spread the gospel of gold and specter of Bryanism to the hinterlands. The Chicago office shipped out over 100 million campaign documents; the New York office, 20 million. Most of the literature, available in 275 different formats printed in German, French, Spanish, Italian, Swedish, Norwegian, Danish, Dutch, Hebrew, and English, spelled out the effects of gold devaluation on the wages and employment of the working man and the more prosperous small businessmen and farmers. The committee distributed material directly to friendly newspapers, which reprinted the specially prepared releases each week. County journals with an aggregate circulation of 1,650,000 received three and one-half columns of campaign matter weekly; another list of local papers got ready prints to circulate to their additional one million readers.[63]

Hanna's organizational efficiency parlayed the campaign educational tactic favored by the elite Mugwump reformers into a national machine of purchased speech. Much of the literature was of debatable authenticity, and some of it intentionally mischaracterized Bryan's positions. Hanna's mission was not to engage in open and fair deliberation on the issues so that voters could make a rational choice between competing ideas, but to win the election. The cost of this kind of campaign was extraordinary. By 1896, assessing government employees to raise the enormous funds necessary to run a national campaign, as was needed against Bryan, proved wholly inadequate. Even the perennial assessment of businesses employed in 1892 looked quaintly deficient in light of the demands of the 1896 challenge. Instead, Hanna transformed the campaign finance system, organizing an army of solicitors who contacted banks and businesses, irrespective of party affiliation, to come to the aid of the national committee and beat down Bryan's challenge to the capitalist status quo that had made America, and them, so prosperous.[64]

The amount of money raised by Hanna's machine has long been the subject of dispute. Some historians suggest that the high estimates of $12 million are gross exaggerations. Indeed, they put the estimate more reasonably at $3.5 million. Estimates of the contributions to McKinley's national campaign from corporate interests, bankers, businessmen, life insurance companies, other employers of labor, and public employees totaled nearly $7 million, with total national, state, and local expenditures approaching $16 million. Whatever the actual amount, there is general agreement that Bryan's campaign, always short of money, raised between $300,000 and $600,000, or between 3 percent and 17 percent of McKinley's total. With that disparity in available campaign funds, Hanna employed a campaign not of "publicity and again publicity" as Republican campaign official Chauncey DePew called it, but of widespread corruption, direct fraud, intimidation, and coercion.[65]

Postelection accounts by Republican editors and politicians disclosed the outright purchase of votes; the miscounting of Bryan ballots by paid McKinley poll watchers and officials; a specific instance in a Philadelphia district numbering 30,000 people where 48,000 ballots were heavily cast for McKinley; and instances of jailed men released to vote, all with the acquiescence of McKinley partisans. Numerous reports of employees receiving in their preelection pay envelopes notices stating that, if Bryan were to win they need not report to work the next day, epitomized both the fears of the business community toward Bryan's policies, and the widespread coercion of voters away from the exercise of their free franchise.[66]

Bryan's campaign, always on the edge of running out of money, preached the rights of the poor, of a renewed equality, and of a redistribution of economic and political power that bespoke a revolution against supporters of the status quo. Hanna championed plutocracy, legalism, and the status quo marriage of business to political power, and successfully raised and employed copious amounts of hard, cold cash against Bryan's message. Drowned out by the Republican sea of speakers, campaign literature and financed corruption, Bryan's message failed to register in the marketplace of ideas. The campaign of 1896 demonstrated, and cemented for the next century, the advantage of professional fund-raising and campaigning. During the campaign, when Hanna stated that, if Bryan continued to speak so predominantly on the silver issue that he was beaten, he was not simply acknowledging Bryan's simplistic and ineffective idealism. Hanna predicted that Bryan's singlemindedness on the silver issue would, if successfully employed, manifest a fear among national businessmen that would drive the money changers to the temple and into the burgeoning coffers of the McKinley campaign.

Hanna knew the campaign contest was a campaign for the soul of America. The election of McKinley seemed to herald the marriage of business interests to conceptions of the national economic good in 1896. Populist ideas of democracy, of open frontiers where honest battles and elections over principles and ideas could be fairly fought out, were offset by the power of money to mute and drown out deliberative political principles of equal opportunity and free speech. The defeat of Bryan and the rejection of his democratic ideals meant the continuance of a Supreme Court–managed constitutional system safe for national business, one that preferred legal doctrines promoting the expansion of a national market. The election of 1896 fully promoted and revealed an open collaboration by business in national politics. In the two decades before the election, the Courts had used the law to revalue property rights and institute hierarchical conceptions of political, civil, and social rights. By the end of the century, these ideas reflected broad agreement in American culture and greatly advanced the rise of national corporations in a fully revamped campaign finance system.

In 1896, although the majority of Americans accepted this alliance between political parties and national businesses, there would soon be reformist reactions. In the states, and eventually in Congress in 1907, reformers would challenge the consequences for democracy of the aggregate power of corporate wealth in elections. In the first twenty years of the next century, Americans, alarmed at these changes, would struggle to reform the campaign finance system. Renewing traditional conceptions of corruption as coercion, and recalling Jacksonian arguments favoring the common good and against special interests, Progressive era reformers again turned to the law to challenge the ever-changing meaning of corruption intent on promoting the developing principles of deliberative democracy.[67]

Chapter Three

THE PROGRESSIVE PROMISE DERAILED

The Myth of the "Common Good"

and the Dual-Federalism Impediment to

Campaign Finance Reform, 1905–1928

In the final weeks of the 1904 presidential campaign, the whispered rumors about massive corporate contributions to President Theodore Roosevelt's campaign burst into the open. New York judge and Democratic nominee Alton Parker publicly accused Roosevelt of accepting massive amounts of corporate contributions, and tried to make the contributions themselves the preeminent campaign issue. The private, unreported character of party campaign finances made public exposure difficult. While Roosevelt vehemently denied the charge, the truth was that as national businessmen realized the inevitability of Roosevelt's victory, they lined up with money in hand to overfill Roosevelt's campaign coffers. Chauncey Depew, chairman of the New York Central Railroad, gave $100,000. Henry Clay Frick gave $50,000. George Parker gave $450,000 on behalf of himself, J. P. Morgan, and the New York Life Insurance Company. George Gould, railroad magnate of the Great Northern Railroad, gave $500,000. Although congressional investigations later disclosed that approximately 73 percent of all of Roosevelt's campaign contributions came from corporations, the lack of public disclosure along with Roosevelt's denial and a solid electoral majority drowned out Parker's sensational allegation.[1]

Political reformers, citing the influence of corporate-money election abuses, began to call for a revitalized politics free from the limited concept of quid pro quo corruption. The disclosure that businesses had contributed to the Republican candidate's defeat of Cleveland in 1888 the sum of between $1 million and $3 million expanded their view of corruption to include a less distinct but evermore pervasive conception of corruption, which reformers believed affected not only the candidate, but also the marrow of the body politic. But they began to argue that political manipulation of the uninformed voter was the main problem, and the secret ballot, "honest campaign literature and an intellectual campaign that provided the antidote to uninformed opinion" became their solution.[2]

Many critics of the Gilded Age election processes believed that traditional American campaigning that featured persuasive speechifying, political lectures, republication of articles and speeches, and reasoned appeals that avoided public passion or prejudice ought to be the model for elections. They proposed reforming the campaign finance system to encourage the spending of money on political education in order to promote an electoral consensus on the issues. For those Gilded Age reformers, corruption was very much interrelated to the concept of the common good that they fervently believed could only be arrived at by campaigns of education and by ending the coercion of political parties over individual voters.

But Progressive Era critics, such as Herbert Croly, Walter Lippman, and John Dewey challenged those solutions as too simple. They displayed a pervasive skepticism about the vitality of democratic electoral processes and institutions to arrive at the common good. Croly blamed the "practical immutability of the Constitution," which often prevented reflection of "a large body of public opinion." Croly disputed the logic of Gilded Age reform that restored "American democracy to a former condition of purity and excellence" because he believed that the "public interest has nothing to gain by its restoration." Croly argued that Gilded Age reformers where "moral protestants and purifiers" who were condemned to failure, because they disabused the principle of "noninterference" by the national government in their reforms. The formalism of the Supreme Court and the laws themselves were partly at fault for the failure of reform to rationalize democratic institutions to fit pragmatic political decision-making.[3]

This new coterie of Progressive reformers contended that an activist national government was essential to curb the power of national corporations in elections. For example, they called for legal recognition of trade unions, which they believed would, along with national corporations, play a vital role in the development of a great society. What they most feared was the fragmenting of the American national identity that they believed was leading to the rise of special individual interests, due in part to the unchecked, outmoded, agrarian Jeffersonian individualism. Only by creating a strong, efficient national government as an intellectual equipoise would the country fully develop its democratic potential.

Walter Lippman also addressed these concerns in the early Progressive era. In his brilliant works of democratic intellectual theory, *Drift and Mastery* (1914), *Public Opinion* (1922), and *The Phantom Public* (1925), Lippman forecast changes that would reshape American law and politics over the next three decades. Lippman battled the antiquated ideas of religion and promoted scientific thinking to implement public policy. He saw in

Populism and Bryanism an irrational and conspiratorial belief, unable to command and conquer the power of the new economic forces that were tearing the country asunder. Lippman believed that emotional political appeals were destructive, and that only the rational discipline of science gave "any assurance that from the same set of facts men will come approximately to the same conclusion."[4]

Furthermore, Lippman later came to deny the myth of a common public that developed from common cultural beliefs. He examined the speeches that defeated Wilson's League of Nations proposal, and found that they appealed not to a universal cultural understanding, but instead to men's emotions. Symbols replaced ideas, he argued, and men eventually voted not their consciences but their self-interest. There was no longer, Lippman concluded, "a self-contained community . . . a homogeneous code of morals," guiding American democracy. The old forms of government were fading away, and the new form, based on a "highly developed system of information, analysis, and self-consciousness" was replacing them. "The secret of the great state-builders," wrote Lippman, was that they knew "how to calculate the principles" of cooperation based on force and terror and those based on the patronage and privilege.[5]

John Dewey developed his theory of democracy during that same period, when the undemocratic drift of the Gilded Age gave way to calls for government involvement to improve American democratic institutions. At the heart of Dewey's philosophy was a commitment to government of the people, particularly citizen voters who expressed the common will of their government. The principle legacy of democracy, Dewey wrote, was that "government exists to serve its community, and that this purpose cannot be achieved unless the community itself shares in selecting its governors and determining its policies." The Gilded Age forces of industrialization, urbanization, and the emergence of the national economy had, however, made the old democratic institutions obsolete. Dewey described a new public, one that had unfortunately been unable to understand the forces swirling around it. The institutions of democracy designed to work in a decentralized, agrarian, and simple market society "were completely inadequate for the organization of this new public." Dewey felt the first task of the new society was to find a way to define and express its interests.[6]

The Progressive reform ideas, however, clashed against the stubborn Gilded Age idealism that dominated the thinking of the first generation of campaign finance reformers. While both groups feared the effects that modern changes had on American democracy, their reform solutions remained at odds because of their distinctly different conceptions of corruption. While formalist legal doctrine and the dual federalism of election law played a role in the failure of the Progressive campaign finance system reforms to eradicate corruption from the political system, that failure can equally be attributed to those two very different views of the effect of corruption on deliberative democracy that evolved during the Progressive era.

PROGRESSIVE MISCONCEPTIONS OF CORRUPTION AND THE
COMMON GOOD IN THE DUAL- FEDERALIST SYSTEM

The Progressive era theories did not diminish the fear that parties used excessive campaign contributions to coerce voters from their free will. Along with concerns about the effects of unrestricted immigration, the lazy expansion of suffrage, or the rise of corporate money in elections, early Progressive reformers expressed their anxiety that American democracy would founder when its voters could not be relied upon to vote in the interest of the common good. For some, immigration and race policy that permitted a nonhomogeneous electorate and highly disparate social classes to participate in elections posed a unique threat. The class of uneducated voters responded, so went the thinking, not to appeals to reason and the common good, but to "the rapidly increasing use of money for the undisguised purchase of votes." Restriction of the franchise to those educated enough to read, understand, and act in accord with the common good became a crucial first step. Calls to limit the suffrage to the educated, literate, Americanized, and noncriminal went hand in hand with the demands that the "use of money in elections be materially abridged." Political campaigns of education became, as they had in earlier times, the salvation of popular government.[7]

For many, the most feared corruption remained the direct purchase of votes. While astute observers of practical politics understood the need to raise and spend campaign finances to print speeches, hire campaign speakers, rent halls, and pay other necessary expenses, in close campaigns it was still widely recognized that "by far the largest part of funds goes for the direct and indirect purchase of voters." "Floaters," whose mobility permitted their movement into precincts and districts to cast the essential final ballots, were commonplace. They were often kept sequestered and liquored-up by their handlers days before the election, and the going rate for their civic services ranged between $4.00 and $40.00 each. They were not confined to urban districts; it was common in New York State "for a farmer to drive in to the polls with his sons and hired help, and unashamedly auction off the lot to the highest bidder."[8]

There were many reasons voters sold their votes. Some voters saw their votes as commodities, available to a candidate at the highest price. Others, cognizant of the increasing sums of campaign money being spent in elections, simply opted to get their fair share. Still others, finding little policy difference between the major parties and less consequence to either party's electoral success, found the compromise of conscience easier to lever. The issue of voter corruption bore deeper into the disintegration of democratic ideals than into any particular election.

But the direct purchase of votes was not the only form of corruption that Progressives railed against. The ideal of the common good, to be attained rationally and systematically through public policies by an informed electorate, began to change the concept of corruption. Reformers redefined the difference between corruption and what they considered the excessive use of money in elections to be a pragmatic distinction between corrupt and legitimate electioneering. Because the proper objective of legitimate electioneering was the education of the voters so that they could arrive uncoerced at a consensus, Progressive reformers contended that funds acquired and spent in excess of the needs for campaigns of education were corrupt and illegitimate expenditures. In the final days of campaigning, when quiet reflection on issues should have been the practice of the intelligent voter, reformers saw no need for the continued expenditure of money. "There were," wrote one critic, "no more documents to be distributed, no more halls and headquarters to be hired, few or no more parades to be organized or mass meetings to be held."[9] Reformers believed that the end of the educational campaign signaled the end of the legitimate need for campaign spending.

Many observers felt the corrupting influence of money that exceeded the necessities of practical politicking corroded not simply the electoral process, but the essence of American democracy. Democratic majoritarianism, argued the reformers, only worked well when the people were given a rational choice, executing their ballots after calm and due deliberation about which choice more closely allied with the common good. While realizing the inevitability that self-interest would arise and act, observers continued to believe that the Madisonian competition of multiple factions advocating their interests over the extended republic would counterbalance partisan competition to the general benefit of the majority.[10]

As progressive reformers addressed the conflict between popular will and the common good, they first turned to their own localities—to their cities and states—to implement change, because they considered those places "more tangible and amenable" to the experiment of reform. Reformers implemented numerous changes to the electoral system. Ballot reform, direct primaries, the regulation of lobbyists, suffrage limitations, and the use of the Australian ballot became the most common general reforms implemented. These methods, proponents argued, would purify the democratic system by systematically removing the incentive and opportunity for direct and indirect fraud.

Increasingly, individual states enacted corrupt practices legislation, called "publicity acts," modeled on the English Corrupt Practices Act of 1883, which regulated the use of money in elections. The English act forbade the undue use of money and influence in any way, fixed a maximum for all campaign expenditures, and required the publication of all campaign expenditures. The apparent simplicity and proven effectiveness of the English law appealed to American state legislatures anxious for a model of reform. At their core, the early publicity acts offered a regulatory scheme centered on the moral belief that the public disclosure and opprobrium of a candidate's close ties to large campaign donors would dissuade excessive contributions to a candidate, as well as an excessive reliance on those contributions by individual candidates. This belief was especially strong in states or localities where communities were smaller and less diffuse, and where reformers thought publicity about the sources of campaign funding would affect the amount and demand for campaign contributions.[11]

States became the laboratories of campaign finance innovation. Minnesota was the first state to propose a corrupt practices act. Modeled after the English act, it limited expenditures of all candidates for state and federal offices to $1,000 each and forbade the use of money for any purpose save the "legitimate expenses of election." Before the turn of the century, legislatures enacted reforms in Michigan, New York, and Rhode Island to limit the amount and use of money in campaigns. Massachusetts passed a law requiring committees and organizations of any kind assisting in the nomination, election, or defeat of any candidate for political office to have treasurers and to file detailed accounts of contributions received and expenses paid. Before 1890, most of the proposed state legislation did not specifically limit the amount of campaign expenditures, relying instead on disclosure and publicity to force illegitimate money out of the system. These restrictions, along with secret ballot reform, which was thought to eliminate vote buying as the chief form of excessive contributions, were intended to barricade the free and corrupt flow of excessive money, and close the avenues of direct and indirect corruption in the electoral process.[12]

The belief that increased public disclosure of campaign contributions and expenditures would solve the problem of excessive money in elections was never universal. But coupled with ballot reform laws and the secrecy of the Australian ballot that greatly diminished the opportunity for vote purchase, the disclosure of excessive campaign funds would, the reformers argued, act as a deterrent to their acquisition and expenditure, effectively ending direct and indirect voter bribery. "Political managers will do well to make a note of the fact," opined one editor, "that money is certain to play a less important, and reason a more important role in the campaign." Free and uncoerced exercise of the ballot essential to democratic deliberation seemed safeguarded by this legislative limitation of illegitimate money in campaigns.[13]

By the mid-1910s, nearly every state had enacted a corrupt practices law regulating the purposes for which campaign funds could be spent, requiring the reporting and accounting of those funds and mandating treasurers for political committees, prohibiting attempts to influence voters, and limiting the solicitation of funds from public employees or by corporations. These legislative efforts invoked long-held assumptions about the threat of political corruption to American democracy voiced earlier during the Anti-Assessment and Pendleton Act debates. In *Ex Parte Yarbrough* the Supreme Court had given states the power to enact election regulation intended to ensure "the free voice and joint will of the people" for the promotion of the general welfare. Despite the innovative nature of the reforms the states implemented, states followed legal and constitutional doctrines of dual federalism, which placed the primary responsibility for insuring the purity of elections on the states that took that responsibility seriously.[14]

The enactment of state corrupt practices acts provided the formative impulse of progressive election reform regulating the amount of money in elections. Before 1904, however, political parties and the regulation of their campaign financing systems faced a public-private distinction that largely restricted their comprehensive regulation. Widespread public disengagement from politics and the complexity of connecting campaign spending to corruption limited public support for the proposals. Most politicians, facing the disinterested public, found the reform efforts and publicity requirements a nuisance. Between 1900 and 1904, 17 states passed laws comprehensively regulating the use of money in elections; but from 1900 to 1904, six of those states took advantage of tepid public support to repeal them. During the first decade of the 1900s, campaign finance reform shrunk to become the work of a small group of reformers who strove to emphasize the deleterious corruptive effects on the ideals of deliberative democracy resulting from excessive campaign expenditures. Not until the sensational disclosures of campaign abuses during the presidential election of 1904 and the New York insurance scandal of 1905–06 was the public persuaded that the amount and sources of money in the campaign finance system created a new kind of corruption. This reinvigorated the corrupt practice act movement at both the state and national level.[15]

CATALYST FOR REFORM—Corporate Scandals Reshape the Campaign Finance System, 1904–1911

While the denials and eventual disclosure of the massive involvement of corporations in funding Theodore Roosevelt's campaign dismayed the nation, in New York, separate developments shocked the public and politicians alike to investigate the spending practices of several insurance companies. The New York State Legislature established a committee to investigate insurance company contributions to finance the election campaigns of 1896, 1900, and 1904. The Armstrong Committee disclosed huge contributions made from the treasuries of the mutual insurance companies, whose assets were owned by policy and stockholders. The public felt that the campaign contributions represented the corporate misuse of policyholder money. The political interests of the insurance companies, many argued, were not necessarily the same interests as those of the policyholders. The findings of the committee were so sensational precisely because it was understood that what the insurance companies had done was to subvert, in effect to coerce, political contributions out of unsuspecting policy and shareholders into the campaign coffers of candidates the policyholders did not support. In the first decade of the twentieth century, legislators sought to prevent the inappropriate use of "other people's money" by corporate managers to finance electoral contests.[16]

Widespread publicity surrounding the scandal investigated by the Armstrong Committee hastened a new onslaught of state laws barring corporate contributions to election campaigns. The federal government, still in the business of granting corporate charters, soon passed what political historians call the "first federal campaign finance law." While this reform was not the first law, this broad new ban on corporate contributions built on similar conceptions of corruption that had formed the foundation of the 1876 Assessment Act, and the judicial decisions of *Ex Parte Curtis* and *United States v. Yarbrough*. The scandals catalyzed the attitudes and ideas of that coterie of reformers who had been developing Progressive ideas to affirm and strengthen American democratic institutions. Reformers connected the threat to republican assumptions about the freedom from coercion in elections to the excessive use of corporate money in elections used to influence, and not educate, the voters. The Armstrong Committee's disclosure of the reality and extent of corporate money in politics, until then mostly guessed at, encouraged more aggressive action by reform organizations that advocated publicity reforms like those implemented in the corrupt practice acts. It was in that renewed climate of fear about the corporate ability to convert wealth to political power disconnected from the common good that those nineteenth-century concepts of corruption were recoined into a new definition that promoted ideas of equal access to both the voting booths and the deliberative political processes.[17]

THE TILLMAN ACT RESTRICTIONS ON CORPORATE CAMPAIGN CONTRIBUTIONS

By 1907 public demand to restrict the power of national corporate wealth and influence in electoral politics had grown irrepressible. "[M]any people, fearing the consequences of unrestrained corporate growth, wanted more public control over corporations." Much of the opposition to corporate involvement in political campaigns arose from their activity in the 1896, 1900, and 1904 presidential campaigns. Two ideas animated the demand for regulation of corporate electoral influence. First, the corporation was an artificial entity created and accorded rights by the state. The state could thus lawfully regulate corporate electoral activities. Second, corporate ability to aggregate capital in immense concentrations led to a profound fear that, if left unregulated, corporate power would dwarf individual voter agency in the political process. Since corporations themselves did not necessarily reflect the views of individual stockholders, their exertion of power in electoral politics undercut democratic and egalitarian ideas. Individuals, on the other hand, exercised their free will to decide, and corporate money that influenced and corrupted that exercise of individual free will became fair game for regulation and restriction.[18]

The 1896 election had demonstrated how the disparity between the corporate resources available to William McKinley and William Jennings

Bryan had affected the outcome of the election. Disclosures of corporate contributions to the Republican Party in 1900 and 1904 also added to the heated campaign issues. More importantly, the disparity demonstrated the power of aggregate wealth hitherto unavailable to political fund-raisers for political "education." Special characteristics that the law accorded the corporate entity were antithetical to the unequal influence corporations exerted in politics. Corporations claimed, argued the reformers, more than their fair share of the political pie. By the time the Armstrong Committee began its high-profile investigation of the insurance company troika of the New York, Mutual, and Equitable Life companies, disclosing their heavy-handed use of policyholder funds to support the Republican candidates in 1900 and 1904, public demand for action was at a fever pitch.[19]

What animated these new calls for campaign finance reform however, were not generalized objections to national corporate involvement in politics. Instead, reform-minded legislators called for a return to the past to purify politics with a heady dose of republicanism and egalitarianism by eliminating the coercion of individual voters through the power of aggregate wealth. In 1904 Senator William E. Chandler (R-NH) had introduced a bill to prohibit corporate political contributions. By 1905, with the Armstrong Committee disclosures proving an embarrassment to the president, Roosevelt announced his support of a publicity bill and called for legislation banning "all contributions by corporations to any political committee for any political purpose." While the Armstrong Committee focused on the rights of stockholders not to have their money coercively spent for politics they did not support, Chandler focused on the egalitarian ideas of reform. "The republic is supposed to be individual government," Chandler reasoned. It was individuals who voted and held office and it was individuals, he continued, that "may give money and spend money in conducting canvasses (not too much, here is another evil—enormous sums)." But he feared that when corporations used their corporate treasuries to carry elections "individual free will and individual responsibility" would disappear. "When the custom grows broad enough the whole character of our government is changed," he contended, "and corporations rule, not men."[20]

Chandler's backing of the bill won him the animosity of the Boston & Maine Railroad, which successfully worked for his defeat for reelection in 1900. Unable to find a sponsor in the Republican Party for the bill, the bill's supporters turned to an erstwhile Populist, Senator Benjamin R. "Pitchfork" Tillman (D-SC), to sponsor the legislation. On December 7, 1905, Tillman introduced a resolution to investigate corporate and national bank contributions to election campaigns since 1896, and in February 1906, Tillman introduced a bill to ban corporate contributions in elections. Referred to the Committee on Elections, the Senate reported the bill to the floor, asserting that the power of Congress to prohibit "any national bank or any corporation organized by authority of the laws of Congress to make a money contribution in connection with any election to any political office" was unquestioned. Tepidly, the report added that "Congress has the power to go much further than this bill in legislation against corruption" but the proposed bill "is in the right direction, can not possibly do harm, and may do much good."

President Roosevelt, who had suffered allegations of his own duplicity by accepting massive corporate contributions during his campaign while denying them, came out strongly for the measure. "Action has shown," Roosevelt declared at a dedication of Pennsylvania's new capitol building in Harrisburg, "that states are wholly powerless to deal with this subject [of corporate wealth] and any action that deprives the nation to deal with it, simply results in leaving the corporations without any effective supervision whatever, and such a course is fraught with untold danger to the future of our whole system of government, and, indeed, to our whole civilization."[21]

Congressional debate focused on two issues: the constitutional authority of Congress to regulate nonfederal elections and the fairness of singling out corporations for strident campaign finance regulation. Representative James Mann (R-IL) led the opposition. Because Article I, Section 4 gave Congress the authority over only the elections of senators and representatives, and the Tillman Act prohibited corporate contributions in all elections, Mann contended that Congress had constitutional authority only over federal elections, and the bill as drafted to include all elections was unconstitutionally over-inclusive. Representative Joseph Keifer (R-OH) challenged Mann, and he called on those southern Democrats supporting corporate restrictions to address not only corrupt corporate contributions, but at "the principle things that in some sections of this country prevent the great majority of voters, white and black, from voting at all." This debate typified the substance of both the Tillman Act and Progressive concerns about voter disfranchisement in the South. Purifying politics, for many congressional reformers, meant both the regulation of aggregate wealth that influenced or drowned out the voting power of individuals, and the elimination of racist voting restrictions that prevented otherwise qualified voters from exercising the franchise. The racial argument caught many Democratic proponents of the Tillman Act in its contradiction. While they advocated federal power to regulate corporate election contributions at federal and state levels, they also realized that their argument might empower the federal government to obliterate the distinct dual federalist boundaries over racist election practices, which permitted southern states to deny the vote to many African American citizens.[22]

Furthermore, Tillman Act opponents contended it was unfair to single out corporate wealth, yet leave personal wealth untouched in any scheme of regulation. While the tide of public opinion remained too strong to stop the bill's passage, opponents such as Ohio Representative Charles Grosvenor (R-OH) remained skeptical. "So now, Mr. Speaker," he stated during floor debate, "as we go ambling along, wobbling along, to the destruction of the independence of the states in the management of their own corporations, wobbling along in the direction of undertaking to purify the franchise of the country without striking a blow in the real direction where corruption comes from, we may as well stop slandering the men of the country." Grosvenor promised to vote for the bill merely "to help give the American people an opportunity to test the thing, which in my judgment, will be a total and significant failure."[23]

The Tillman Act exemplified Progressive fears about unequal corporate power in politics, which required a restriction on the use of any corporate money for two reasons. First, because corporations intent on exercising their growing national influence consistently contributed sums of money considered excessive in a campaign of education; and second, because corporate money was thought to unfairly influence voter choice by coercing voter free will, stifling real choice (as Populists had argued) by drowning out the deliberative arguments of the competition. Both concerns shaped the concept of corruption during the Gilded and early Progressive eras. Few espoused any concern about the free speech rights of those same corporations.[24]

Despite the objections, public concern over corporate contributions coupled with congressional cynicism that the bill would eventually prove ineffective or be declared unconstitutional ensured its passage. On January 26, 1907, President Roosevelt signed the Tillman Act of 1907 into law. By 1928 popular demand for reform coupled with widespread belief that corporate contributions remained singularly distinctive and corrupting to elections led thirty-six states to enact their own legislation barring corporate campaign contributions.[25]

The courts eventually examined the constitutionality of the Tillman Act, although it took nearly ten years for a legal challenge. In *United States v. U.S. Brewer's Association* the government obtained indictments against a number of Pennsylvania brewing companies and against the U.S. Brewer's Association, alleging violations of the Tillman Act. The defendants challenged the constitutionality of the act. They argued the act went beyond the power of Congress to regulate corporate contributions made within a state to election campaigns, and that the Tillman Act violated the First Amendment of the U.S. Constitution by restricting the freedom of political speech in the discussion of candidates in such elections.

The District Court, citing *Ex Parte Yarbrough,* held that the Constitution vested Congress with ample power to regulate congressional elections. If Congress could regulate the conduct of elections, the voting procedures, and the accuracy of the count, could it be doubted, the court reasoned, that Congress could regulate those "artificial bodies" which are "not citizens of the United States and so far as the franchise is concerned, must at all times be subservient and subordinate to the government and citizenship of which it is composed." The bar on corporate campaign contributions was "wise and beneficent legislation" that protected the principle that "an election is intended to be the free and untrammeled choice of the electors." The court added that "any interference with the right of the elector to make up his mind, how he will vote is as much an interference with his right to vote as if prevented from depositing his ballot; that the concerted use of money is one of the many dangerous agencies in corrupting the election and debauching the election; that any law, the purpose of which is to enable a free and intelligent choice, and an untrammeled expression of that choice in the ballot box, is a regulation in the manner of holding the election—the power of Congress to prohibit corporations of the states from making money contributions in connection with any such election appears to follow as a natural and necessary consequence."[26]

The Court gave short shrift to the free speech argument of the defendants in *Brewer's Association*. Unwilling to equate money and speech, it flatly rejected any claim that the "general restriction on political contributions" was an infringement on the freedom of speech. Not until labor unions became part of the Tillman prohibition on corporate campaign spending in 1943 did corporations again seriously challenge the constitutionality of the power of Congress to regulate corporate campaign spending.[27]

THE PUBLICITY AND EDUCATION MODEL OF STATE AND FEDERAL CORRUPT PRACTICES LEGISLATION

While Congress banned corporate contributions under the Tillman Act, reformers in the several states advocated for the passage of disclosure and publicity laws. These reformers felt that public exposure of an excessive reliance on corporate contributions would dissuade candidates from accepting contributions beyond those necessary for a campaign of education and deliberation. By 1905 a dozen states had enacted laws that required, to varying degrees, reporting and public disclosure of campaign contributions and expenditures. Soon after the Armstrong hearings, in 1907, Perry Belmont, younger brother of Democratic Party financier and banker August Belmont, organized the National Publicity Law Organization (NPLO). His goal was to require the public disclosure of campaign contributions, particularly those of corporations, to give stockholders information needed to bring lawsuits against abusive corporate managers. The NPLO failed to attract bipartisan support until the 1906 disclosures about the corporate contributions to Roosevelt's 1904 campaign reinvigorated the movement. Representative Samuel McCall (R-MA) introduced legislation in 1906 that required reporting of receipts and expenditures by any political committee active in federal elections "in two or more states." Dual federalism concerns about congressional authority to regulate single-state campaign committees created this limiting qualification. The bill made little progress over the next three years.[28]

Finally, in the 61st Congress, McCall reintroduced a bill, similar to his own, that had been sponsored by Senator George Norris (R-NE) and had made it out of the Committee on Elections, but had died in the Senate. The bill copied the earlier McCall measure, but was amended by Indiana Republican Edgar D. Crumpacker. Crumpacker's amendment, he explained, "enabled Congress to apportion representatives among the various states in accordance with the second section of the Fourteenth Amendment."[29] The Crumpacker amendments would have reinstituted the Reconstruction era federal voting rights laws in those areas where African Americans were being denied the franchise. His amendment led to bitter and acrimonious debate before the bill passed the House by a straight party line vote, 160–125.[30] As expected, that bill died in the Senate. McCall's reintroduced version omitted the voting rights provision, and the House approved and sent that bill to the Senate.

The Senate committee deleted the provision calling for preelection reporting of contributions and expenses. It argued that such publicity before the election would divert public attention from the qualifications of the candidate and the issues involved in the character of the contributor. Further, such disclosure would create an opportunity to question every person making such a contribution intended to prejudice voters against the candidate by claiming that he was supported by persons with some personal end to serve or private interest to promote, and was therefore, undeserving of public confidence and support. The bill would become the Publicity Act of 1910.[31]

THE PUBLICITY ACT OF 1910—The "Free Fight and Fair Deal" Origins of Modern Campaign Finance Regulation

While the Publicity Act of 1910 would become the foundation of the campaign finance system, few historians have considered the act in any detail. Amended in 1911 and again in 1925 to become the Federal Corrupt Practices Act, its provisions remained the core campaign finance legislation until 1971. The political wrangling over the bill involved an account of partisan one-upmanship, and contentious finger pointing over past campaign finance abuses and present practices of voter disfranchisement. More specifically, the debate over the first comprehensive regulation of campaign finances demonstrated a choice between principles in election law, and those choices that had a direct though often understated relationship to fundamental assumptions about the effects of corruption on American democracy.[32]

The Publicity Act of 1910 (which later became the Federal Corrupt Practices Act of 1911) did several things. It defined "political committees" subject to the provisions of the act as all national party and congressional campaign committees, and all "committees, associations, or organizations which shall *in two or more states* influence or attempt to influence a federal congressional election." It required that every political committee have a chairman and treasurer and keep a detailed account of all money or equivalent collected, and any disbursement exceeding $10 paid. The act required the public reporting of such receipts and expenditures not more than fifteen nor less than ten days before an election by filing reports with the Clerk of the House of Representatives. It provided an exception permitting any person connected with such elections to pay for personal expenses for traveling and for purposes incidental to traveling, for stationery and postage, and for telephone and telegraph services to communicate with staff and voters. Finally, it made any violation of the act punishable by a fine of not more than $1,000 and imprisonment of not more than a year, or both. Comprehensive and complete, the bill's major exception to the principle of full publicity involved single-state committees, which the drafters felt were beyond the constitutional power of Congress to regulate, and those personal expenses normally paid for by the candidate himself, which they felt essential to the prenomination phase of an election. Both areas Congress left unregulated.[33]

Senator George Norris (R-NE), whose own bill had died in 1906 in the Senate, argued that Congress should reassert its plenary power to regulate its own elections. "The power of Congress to regulate and control all elections at which representatives in congress are chosen," he declared, "is practically without limit." The bill acted to purify elections, especially by exposing the secret workings of the party machine. Publicity, Norris argued, would end the secrecy essential to the machine's influence, and to its control over the "freedom of individual action." Disclosure would limit the machine's ability to prevent the enactment of "wholesome legislation demanded by the public."[34]

Representative William Rucker (D-MO) acknowledged that public concern about the scandals had finally pushed the bill out of the dim corners of the committee process onto the House floor. The purity of the ballot, for Rucker, was the main reform of the act. "Each ballot should represent the untrammeled will and best judgment of a free American citizen." Threatened by the accumulation of vast fortunes of business associates and corporations, those beneficiaries of special privileges used that money to debauch the voter and pollute the ballot box. Rucker believed the bill sought to regulate the twin evils of the overt power of money directly or indirectly to buy votes and coerce a voter to act against his will. His conception of reform was connected to the Progressive ideas about corruption that emphasized the model of republican common good and opposed self-interestedness.[35]

Yet it was not solely the increased amount of money used in elections that prompted congressional fears. Representative John Conroy (R-NY) refined the distinction earlier made evident during the Tillman debates between honest, essential money necessary for a campaign of deliberation and reason, and the extravagant and excessive campaign funds contributed by "those favored interests that seek special privileges and legislation as a reward for their generosity in politics." It was that very extravagance, which "exceeded in quantity what is necessary, *and only what is necessary,* to meet the legitimate expenses of a campaign" that "degenerated into a moral, social, and a political evil."[36]

Importantly, Conroy saw the publicity bill as the best means to expose the "corrupt alliance between business and politics," a market in which "special privilege and class legislation can be bought or sold" whose existence and operation lay hidden and unexposed to the public. By publicizing campaign spending, the act disclosed the hidden operation of that market and reestablished a broader public purpose. Universal confidence in a republican government was essential to its healthy functioning. Because the source of all authority resided in the people, and because governmental policies must "directly and sensitively reflect the ideals and aspirations of the people," the excessive use of money in campaigns that coerced or influenced voters away from individual deliberative reason, or which distracted the government's representatives from the common aspirations of its people, was "political corruption . . . especially fatal to the republic." While promoting the educational benefits of the bill, Conroy was subtly expanding the concept of corruption by directly considering how excessive spending in campaigns undercut the ability of individuals to speak and be heard.[37]

Finally, the public benefit of attracting political candidates unable to independently support their own candidacies so as not to be beholden to large contributors remained an important rationale for the bill. Although the law did not act to limit large contributions, the common assumption was that no candidate could afford to accept them from corporations in a climate where the public felt they came attached to an implied promise of support. Representative Andrew Peters (D-MA) cautioned that the unlimited expenditure of money would eliminate that class of candidate unwilling to submit to his largest backer, or unwilling to spend his own funds to win an expensive campaign.[38]

Objections to the bill came primarily from two quarters; those who felt the bill did too little because it failed to regulate primary or nominating elections, and those who opposed the publication of contribution and expense information before elections. The Senate succeeded in striking the provisions requiring preelection disclosure, and ensured that the 1910 Publicity Act would not regulate primaries, often the only "election" that mattered in many one-party regions of the country. Flawed as it was, House and Senate conferees agreed in the end, and both houses approved the legislation. President Taft signed the Publicity Act of 1910 into law on June 25, 1910.[39]

Four months later, voters elected a Democratic majority to the House of Representatives for the first time in sixteen years. As they had promised to do during the 1910 debates, Democratic campaign publicity proponents pushed to amend the 1910 Act in the next session of the House and to add the preelection disclosure provision the Senate had deleted. The new provisions did not regulate single-district congressional committees that did business wholly within one state, nor did the amendment impose filing requirements on congressional candidates for money they spent in their own campaigns. The avoidance of certain sensitive issues, such as the racial implications of federal control over state election law, was intended to keep the fractious Democratic majority unified. But Republicans, smarting from their midterm defeat and unwilling to give the Democrats a victory on the reform issue, countered that primary regulation was essential to real reform.[40]

For much of the South and nearly half of the Democratic caucus, the primary elections were the only elections that mattered. First-term congressman Fred S. Jackson (R-KS) proposed an amendment that required candidates to disclose all contributions and expenditures in both primary and general elections. The move succeeded in splitting the Democrats, as most northern Democrats voted with Republicans in approving the amendment. Clearly, the campaign finance disclosure issue remained closely connected with concern over black voter disfranchisement. Election regulation had long been an issue of dual federalist division of power. The 1911 campaign finance debates, which focused attention on assumptions about democratic ideas and ballot purity, could not honestly ignore the system of one-party nomination in the South that effectively disfranchised most black voters. Faced with this reality, campaign finance disclosure for Southern Democrats became a side issue. The dangerous logic of the reform lay in acknowledging the power of Congress to regulate intrastate political matters, particularly party primaries, which until then were widely regarded as wholly private affairs. If the national government could regulate the disclosure of campaign finances in nomination campaigns, it was but a small constitutional step to accepting congressional regulation of ballots, franchise rights, and voter access. For southern congressmen, this amendment sounded ominously like the return of the hated and long since dead Force bill.[41]

After the approval of the amendment, Congressman Rucker moved immediately to recommit the bill to the Committee on Elections, intending to forestall implementing the provision on primaries. Furious Democratic maneuvering reconstituted the caucus, and the motion passed 157–149. As recommitted with the offending amendment removed, the House then passed the bill unanimously, including only the preelection disclosure provision, with 82 not voting. Debate then moved to the Senate.[42]

Expectedly, the issue there revolved, not around the preelection disclosure, which by that time had taken on a logic of its own, but around the constitutional propriety of primary election regulation. Interestingly, while the Senate considered the bill, both the House and Senate debated a resolution to amend the U.S. Constitution to elect U.S. senators directly. Proponents of direct elections contended that congressional regulation of primaries was permitted under Article 4, Section I of the Constitution, which authorized the states to regulate the "times, places, and manners of holding elections for Senators and Representatives," but permitting Congress any time "to by law make or alter such regulations, except as to the place of chusing [sic] Senators." Senator William Borah (D-ID) argued that Congress, because it had the power to "protect the purity of elections," could enact extensive legislation regulating campaigns and campaign financing. Senator Joseph Bailey (D-TX) accepted Borah's argument, announcing his belief in "the right, the power, and the duty of the Government to limit the expenditure of money in elections" and adding, "the States ought to limit it within their jurisdiction . . . and the Federal Government ought to limit it within its jurisdiction." "If," Bailey asserted, objecting to the apparent demolition of dual federalist boundaries Borah appeared to accept, "we have the power to require the publication of funds contributed to a primary election, . . . the power of the General Government over a primary is as plenary as it is over a general election—I cannot subscribe to that doctrine."[43]

Proponents countered that the Supreme Court had recognized congressional regulatory powers over election registration, including the time of holding the polls open and the form of the ballot. Were not the primary laws, they questioned, just as much a part of the final selection of members of Congress as those federally controlled regulations? Central to this dispute were the widely accepted assumptions about the baneful effect of money in elections, and the much disputed premise about the public-private distinctions of the party nomination process. Furthermore, the essence of the debate underscored the conflicted nature of the concept of the common good upon which reform proponents had founded their argument. Although money was a taint unmatched in its "evil effect" because it corrupted fundamental democratic ideas, that did not resolve the complicated dual federalist issues about the power and boundary of federal election regulation, especially given the emerging regional differences about race relations. Senator Bailey made clear the differences, supporting the regulation of money in elections, but leaving the regulation of primary election processes to the individual states. "I would make it so that a man's addresses to the judgment of conscience of the voter should control," he argued, "rather than the subtle and secret influences that addresses itself to the cupidity of the voter. I would make it impossible for any man's bank account to be a potential in either a primary or a general election." Yet he recognized the limits of the federal system, concluding that "our Government is so organized that the primary must be directed by the state, while the Federal Government has ample power to protect its elections for Federal officers against this baneful influence."[44]

Southern senators willingly admitted the powerful corrupting influence of excessive money in elections, but steadfastly refused to acknowledge the same corrupting influence of racial prejudice. In part, this was because of their long-held beliefs about the connections between voter capability and voter rights. While money could coercively influence even the most incorruptible voter, insuring the purity of the franchise demanded that black voters, having proven their unworthiness as electoral participants, incapable of reason and calm deliberation, be excluded from the electoral processes.

This belief, along with a second argument, strengthened the position of campaign reform opponents. Although they shaped public policy, most Americans considered party institutions and processes wholly private affairs. Political parties did not grant universal membership, and they constantly emphasized that active organization, not voting, was how one came to belong. Political parties, like clubs or churches, freely possessed the right to determine their own membership, nominate party candidates, choose their leaders, and frame party platforms. State regulation of party activity and election procedure previously handled by parties during the Gilded Age remained an uneven proposition in the first decade of the twentieth century. Many southern states reasonably expected to retain their practices concerning the private, club-like nature of their political parties and processes. Progressive reform at the state level signaled changing attitudes about political parties, but many senators, determined to maintain the all-white membership in their exclusive political clubs, had not yet felt the pressure of that persuasion.[45]

By July the Senate had reported a new bill out of committee that included language regulating primaries. The bill passed 50–7, with all seven southern Democrats opposing it, and with 33 Democrats not voting. Senator James A. Reed (D-MO) offered an amendment, hastily written in pencil during floor debate, that placed a $10,000 ceiling per election for each candidate. Intended to equalize candidate opportunity by regulating overall expenditures, Reed emphasized the coercive nature of a campaign that spent money beyond that necessary to educate voters on the issues. "There is no question about this fact," Reed stated, then he added that "money has been playing too great a part in every election in this country for many years" and there was no denying that it had come to be used so extensively "that we have almost begun to believe that it is legitimate." But Reed believed that outside any campaign money spent on legitimate candidate travel to visit voters or the hiring of a hall in which to meet them, or beyond those expenses necessary to the writing of letters and sending out of addresses, "not one penny can be legitimately expended in politics."[46]

For Reed, expenditures for direct methods of voter engagement and deliberation remained the only noncorrupting uses of campaign money. The close connections between ideals of deliberative democracy and legitimate methods of campaign spending animated every part of the Publicity Act debates. Ultimately, the Conference Report proposed a bill that regulated both nominations and elections, required preelection disclosure, and placed limits on nonpersonal candidate and committee expenses of $5,000 for representative elections and $10,000 for Senate elections, unless their respective state corrupt practices acts specified lower limits.[47]

Before the final vote, southern congressmen, still adamantly opposed to the consequences of this new federal involvement in state-regulated primaries, made one final attempt to defeat the bill. Representative William Adamson (D-GA) opposed the provision as "an overshadowing menace to our liberties to be fought at all points and resisted to the death." "A state," he chided, "which is not competent to regulate [its primary elections] ought to ask the Federal Government to relieve it of further responsibility, and divide its territory among the states that are able to do their duty. The elections in the South are honest, free, and fair, under adequate state laws—everybody votes who wants to, and his vote is counted." Defiantly, he concluded, "representatives do not purchase their elections there, but enjoy their positions . . . because they are elected by the free suffrage of the most enlightened, upright people in the world—the only true American and English constituency left solid in any State of the Union."[48]

In rebuttal, Congressman Jackson, the Kansas freshman still tinged by the Populist sentiment that had riven Kansas in the 1890s, drove home the real point of the legislation. Denying that the bill was another Force bill intended to punish southern racism, Jackson contended the gravity of the three great threats to the purity and integrity of elections, those of "race prejudice, the prejudice which grows out of conflicts between organized labor and capital, and most eminent of all, the danger of the use of money in elections," demanded a national solution. But among the three, Jackson contended, "the use of inordinate sums of money in campaigns is un-American and undemocratic. It puts a premium on greed and avarice and magnifies these qualities into political ideals of the nation."[49]

Jackson feared the power of money to disrupt the most fundamental right of the free election of free representatives. More broadly conceived than the limited evils of quid pro quo corruption, Jackson feared the power of political machines and bosses, which drew money from the "favored interests, pampered political pets, and jack-pot politicians." These corrupt political machines, he warned, "sometimes disturbed the judicial mind, and thus the scales of justice, by rude hints of the rights of property and vested interests when the rights of the public were on the other side in a lawsuit." Finally, Jackson concluded that the corruption reached the "public press, and therefore poisons the public mind itself." "I have not argued," he concluded, "nor do I intend to intimate, that public opinion has ever been overridden by the power of money in politics where the issue was clearly drawn and the public aroused, nor can it ever be. But the people of this country have the right to a free fight and a fair deal on every public question. The courts have given to the corporation and the property interests the rights of persons under the law, but they have never yet been given the right to vote or the power of the ballot." Jackson and other Publicity Act proponents expanded the definition of corruption in response to their fears of how aggregations of excessive money in elections undermined the foundations of deliberative democracy.[50]

The bill overwhelmingly passed by roll call vote, 282–27. The 1910 Publicity Act (later amended in 1911 and 1918 and referred to in 1924 as the Federal Corrupt Practices Act or FCPA) was, until 1971, the most significant national campaign finance legislation ever enacted. Although it relied on what would become largely antiquated ideas of the common good, it established the legal template for reform that stood for broad principles of political deliberation based on a communal understanding of the threat of electoral corruption.[51]

THE CONGRESSIONAL RESPONSE TO CAMPAIGN ELECTION SCANDALS

Over the next decade, Congress and the courts would struggle to implement the competing patchwork of state and federal campaign finance legislation. A series of high profile election scandals involving the FCPA occurred from 1914 to 1926, and led to lengthy congressional hearings that disclosed both the evolving nature of political fund-raising and the effective limitations of the Publicity Act. During that period, the Supreme Court also decided *Newberry v. United States,* and that decision sharply limited the power of Congress to act to remedy the emerging pattern of abuses. The congressional hearings, election disputes, and judicial intervention revealed stark differences between congressional and judicial assumptions about the nature of American democracy. Additionally, the hearings exposed the entrenched power of corporate wealth in the electoral process, the emerging role of women in political campaigns, the ambivalent and ironic legacy of progressive reforms such as the direct election of senators and campaign finance regulation, and the pervasive, often obstructive role of dual federalism in legal and political reform.[52]

While separate and sundry scandals created public concern, three major hearings on campaign finance abuses occurred over the next fifteen years, leading to legislation that defined the scope of the campaign reform legislation. Referred to as the Kenyon hearings, the Borah hearings, and the Reed hearings, they provided the first comprehensive record of campaign spending in the twentieth century, and established the argument for and against national regulation into the 1950s.[53]

The Kenyon hearings, chaired by William S. Kenyon (R-IA), with Senators Selden B. Spencer (R-MO), Walter E. Edge (R-NJ), James A. Reed (D-MO), and Atlee Pomerene (D-OH), were charged by the Senate Committee on Privileges and Elections to "investigate forthwith and report to the Senate as soon as possible the campaign expenditures of the various presidential candidates in both parties," including the names of all contributors, individual and corporate, and the expenditures of each committee. The committee conducted the investigation during the primary campaigns of seventeen different candidates in the Republican and Democratic parties, including unannounced but apparent candidates. The committee found the total funds expended for seventeen different candidates ranged from zero for Republican senator Joseph France and Democrat William McAdoo, to more modest sums for a number of favorite son candidates like Senator Hiram Johnson (R-CA) ($194,593) and Governor Calvin Coolidge ($68,375). At the high end was General Leonard Wood, running a national campaign with national resources, who spent $1,773,303. Neither the Socialist nor the Fair Labor party provided testimony on contributions.[54]

The committee also uncovered the activities of what they called "semipolitical" organizations, which were independent of candidates but raised money and exerted influence in the election. In the general election held on November 2, 1920, the party disbursements for the Republican National Committee totaled $5,319,729.32; the Democratic National Committee spent $1,318,274.02. The Republican Congressional Committee expended $375,969.00 while the Democratic Congressional Committee raised and spent a mere $24,498.05. On the Senate campaigns, the Republican Senatorial Committee spent $326,980.29 and the Bureau of Senatorial Election for Democratic Committee, again badly trailing the Republicans, spent $6,675.00. In addition, during the general election, state, county, and township party organizations, as well as independent semipolitical organizations, contributed and directly spent additional funds on behalf of the candidates. The committee developed evidence of the joint efforts of state organizations to collect and then remit contributions to the national party committees, who, in turn, returned a portion of those funds back to the states for local election expenses. Total estimates for the Republican presidential, congressional, and Senate campaigns were $8,100,739.21; the Democrats spent $2,237,770.71. The disclosure of the expenditures, far in excess of the amount permitted under the Corrupt Practices Act, posed a dilemma for the committee. Recognizing the constitutional impediments to national regulation that the *Newberry* decision (decided May 21, 1921, but not applicable to the expenses in the election of 1920) posed, the committee recommended consideration of a constitutional amendment that would permit broadened campaign finance regulation by Congress.[55]

The Borah hearings, chaired by William E. Borah, with Senators Wesley L. Jones (R-WA), Thaddeus H. Caraway (D-AK), Thomas F. Bayard, Jr. (D-DE), and Henrik Shipstead (Farmer-Labor-MN) as members, investigated the campaign expenditures of candidates for president and vice-president, and for the U.S. Senate, including the source and amount of all campaign contributions and expenditures in the election of 1924. It found that the national Republican organization collected for the presidential campaign $4,360,478.82 and spent $4,270,469.01, returning $573,599.20 to state organizations. The national Democratic organization collected during the same period for its presidential campaign $821,037.05 and spent $903,908.21, returning nothing to the state committees. The National Progressive Organization collected $224,837.21, spent $221,977.58, and likewise, sent nothing to its state committees. The report recommended changes to the Federal Corrupt Practices Act, specifically adjusting limits on expenditures in Senate contests to reflect wide variations in state population. Further, the committee recommended a restriction on the practice of collecting huge sums of money in one state, then sending it into other states for the purposes of carrying on party campaigns and controlling elections. It did not specifically recommend a solution to this practice, which it said "may well become the subject of abuse and lead to evil and corrupt practices and results."[56]

The Reed hearings, chaired by Missouri senator James A. Reed, had as its members Senators Charles McNary (R-OR), Guy Goff (R-WV), William King (D-UT), and Robert M. Lafollette, Jr. (R-WI). The Senate charged the committee with investigating senatorial primary and general expenses for the election held in 1926. Again, the committee investigated the various political campaigns while the campaign proceeded. The committee subpoenaed witnesses under a broad mandate to investigate all contributions of any kind for any Senate candidates, reported the amount and names of contributors, and documented all expenditures in the various campaigns. Relying on the Federal Corrupt Practice Act of 1924 (the Publicity Act of 1910, as amended in 1911 and 1918) and upon the relevant state corrupt practices acts of the several states where the investigation led them, the committee produced a massive amount of testimony on the campaign practices in Senate elections. Most of the testimony disclosed a consistent pattern of widespread disregard of the spending limits of FCPA 1925. The Committee also took testimony on the exclusion of Senators-elect Frank Smith and William Vare, both of whom had violated the FCPA spending limits during their elections, but who nonetheless had violated no constitutional spending limits as interpreted in the *Newberry* decision.[57]

Precipitated by sensational allegations of excessive campaign fundraising among the candidates, each of the hearings, often facing recalcitrant witnesses and a complexity of interlocking or independent fundraising, struggled to uncover the facts. Though discovering the facts about fund-raising was central to the hearings, the hearings also disclosed in detail the changing nature of campaign fund-raising, and the legislative complexities involved in its regulation. The Supreme Court decision in the 1921 case of *United States v. Newberry*, decided after the Kenyon but before the Borah and Reed hearings, added substantial complexity to any plan to regulate campaign spending because it prohibited congressional attempts to regulate campaign spending in primaries. The judicial doctrine of *Newberry* represented a sharp break from prior judicial doctrine on campaign financing and regulation, though it remained consistent with the Court's formalist pattern regarding the separation of state and federal political power.

The three separate investigations provide the best evidence for how Congress addressed the emerging conceptions of corruption in the campaign finance reform movement. The first of the three, the Kenyon hearings, detailed the nominating process in the 1920 presidential campaign. No fewer than seventeen declared candidates, many of them favorite son candidates, were in the field. Initially, the nominating process in most states required individual candidates to obtain sufficient signatures on nominating petitions to be placed on state ballots. Republican Warren G. Harding would eventually face Democrat James D. Cox in the general election.[58]

Testimony disclosed that Leonard Wood, a distinguished military leader, former "Rough Rider," major general, and Philippine governor, had attracted substantial support from prominent businessmen who had underwritten his campaign. The "Wood boom," as it was called, benefited from the fund-raising prowess of Dan R. Hanna, son of Mark Hanna; Edward J. Doheny, the president of Mexico Petroleum Company; Harry F. Sinclair, president of Sinclair Oil; W. B. Thompson, director of the Federal Reserve Bank; and several other national businessmen. Wood's campaign took the position that the Federal Corrupt Practices Act did not apply to the prenomination campaign, which was the exclusive province of state law. This position permitted the collection of vast sums of money used to pay for petition circulators, professional speakers, newspapermen, and as was widely alleged, the direct purchase of votes and the employ of floaters, all without regard to the limitations on campaign spending expressly provided for in the Federal Corrupt Practices Act. As the enormity of the Wood campaign fund-raising effort became known, the committee members focused on the rationale of the FCPA in limiting senatorial campaign expenditures to the lesser of $10,000 or the amount provided by the respective state's corrupt practice act, if one applied. At the core of that dilemma was the rationale that regarded as corrupting any campaign funds raised and spent in excess of that amount needed to educate the electorate. Among the many problems that the hearings disclosed were the increasing costs of political campaigns that made the $10,000 limit seem inadequate, especially for lesser-known candidates.[59]

THE SEVENTEENTH AMENDMENT AND THE RISING COSTS OF NATIONAL CAMPAIGNS

Witnesses also testified about the effects of two Progressive constitutional changes that had recalibrated electoral politics since passage of the 1911 Publicity Act and thus had made campaigns broadly more expensive. The Seventeenth Amendment, ratified in 1913, established the direct election of U.S. senators, removing their selection process from the various state legislatures. Second, the Nineteenth Amendment, ratified in 1920, granted women the right of franchise and substantially added to the complexity of fund-raising and campaigning. Both constitutional amendments worked to substantially transform electoral politics, but in ways not anticipated by most of their Progressive proponents.[60]

Before 1913, the strong and long-festering distrust of state legislatures often controlled by party bosses, along with a progressive urge toward democratization, led to repeated attempts to break the state legislative lock on senatorial selection. The eighty–six-year campaign for direct elections changed the nature of American federalism, shifting what the framers envisioned as a body "dependent on [state legislatures] for reelection, vigilant in supporting [state] rights against their infringement by the legislature or executive in the United States," to a more democratic, politically accountable body. The consequences of this change to the dual federalist system were little noted at the time, but grew more apparent as the Senate came to see itself as a body representing a more national constituency. The structural protection for state legislatures envisioned by the framers, abandoned in the progressive wave of Seventeenth Amendment democratization, redesigned the dual federalist structure and effectively undermined state legislature power. With ratification of the Seventeenth Amendment, the direct primary also became the most common means to nominate presidential electors to national conventions. The rationale of those progressive changes—to democratize participation and to purify politics by removing the taint of bossism and corrupt party politics from elections—created new problems for candidates and for the electoral system.[61]

During the Kenyon hearings, candidate after candidate testified as to the necessity and added expense of making a campaign in each state under the direct primary system. Appealing to the newly popular and increased electorate, candidates of limited means found it impossibly expensive to contend in states where they were unknown. I. T. Jones, manager of the presidential campaign of James Gerrard, testified that the campaign spent but $14,040, all in Gerrard's personal funds, focused solely on the state of South Dakota. Gerrard won the primary, but found the political ground harder to till elsewhere. Jones testified that the campaign limited itself to the single state where Gerrard had the most support. "We took a rather altruistic view of the thing," he commented, "and felt perhaps it would be the right thing to do just simply to submit the candidacy, sow or seed, and let the sunshine and the rain do the rest, but when we got to South Dakota and discovered there was something more than sunshine and rain required, we decided it would be best not to go into the other states."[62]

By contrast, the Leonard Wood campaign spent between $100,000 and $200,000 in South Dakota alone, and the realization that Gerrard would have to compete with Wood's vastly superior resources forced Jones to recommend that Gerrard not attempt to compete in any other state primaries. "Judge Gerrard did not feel he could go into that sort of campaign without besmirching himself and besmirching the dignity of the presidential office," said Jones, defending the decision to limit expenditures. "I think there certainly ought to be some better method of restricting the presidential candidates," recommended Jones. "In practice it is chaotic, and is, as I have said, the plaything of men and organizations having great resources, and it is prohibitive to men of greater ability but lesser financial strength."

Senator Reed suggested that Jones was arguing for getting back to the old fashioned idea of party organization as a much better scheme than the direct primary scheme reformers had implemented. The colloquy disclosed that the theory of the Seventeenth Amendment had had some unintended and negative consequences, pricing Judge Gerrard out of direct competition in more than one state because of the cost of campaigns, which defeated his ability to compete nationally. The theory seemed well intentioned, said Jones, but Senator Reed added, "Well, a theory is never correct that does not work in practice."[63]

The Wood campaign countered that the large amounts spent on his behalf were particularly necessary because Wood, as a relatively unknown political figure, had an acute public need to make his name and qualifications known. Questioned about expenditures in West Virginia, J. S. Darst, Wood's state campaign manager, acknowledged that while spending much less than rumored, a conservative amount essential for a campaign of education would be $55,000, or about $1,000 per West Virginia county. Lower advertising rates in West Virginia accounted for more limited expenditures there, but Darst emphasized his view that spending money was not only good in campaigns, but necessary. "Under the present system of electing men," Darst questioned, "how are you going to hope to get any support whatever if you do not get the facts to the people of your state? Is there anybody hurt, Mr. Chairman, if $100,000 is spent in West Virginia to get that campaign of education to the people of the state? Should not the people vote intelligently? If that money is used for educating the people, what is the harm?" The increased cost of campaigns created by the system of national direct primaries, the necessity for a broad campaign of education, and the added difficulties of making known an unknown candidate all justified the Wood campaign's enormous expenditures. Passage of the Seventeenth Amendment, intended to democratize the electoral process, had ironically increased the necessary campaign costs for candidates involved in that process.[64]

The Kenyon hearing disclosures of large donations and business underwriting of campaigns created other concerns about the kind of coercive practices that reformers believed limited real deliberation among voters. Some witnesses offered proposals to limit contribution amounts and to regulate the still unregulated interstate contributions. The committee continued to struggle with questions about the proper amount of money essential to, but not in excess of, a truly educational campaign meant to offer voters a deliberative choice.

If the problem of candidate expenditures was not enough, numerous interest groups, most notably the Anti-Saloon League and antiprohibitionists, as well as supportive and opposition forces contending over United States involvement in the League of Nations, raised substantial nonparty funds to influence the nomination. Testimony indicated that the Anti-Saloon League raised $27,000,000 over the election cycle at all levels to oppose "wet" candidates. The National Retail Liquor Dealers Association, a small organization, assessed its 4,000 members a minimum of $1.00 each to raise money for sympathetic candidates. Federal law regulated none of these groups, and the Kenyon committee found obtaining accurate information on the amount and methods of their fund-raising activities difficult. In the end, the Kenyon committee's most significant achievement was to uncover and disclose the complicated nature of presidential fund-raising, the interlocking and independent national and state committees ill-regulated by a hodgepodge combination of inconsistent state and federal laws that failed to fully account for emerging political realities about the costs and complications of campaigning. What became apparent was that only a national system of campaign finance regulation that addressed individual, party, and independent fund-raising, that demanded full and complete publicity of all contributions and expenditures, and that regulated the process from the primary to general election, would ensure the goal of limiting those coercive and corruptive expenditures that exceeded the needs of a fully deliberative campaign.[65]

THE NINETEENTH AMENDMENT AND THE EMERGENT ROLE
OF WOMEN CAMPAIGN FUND-RAISERS

Ironically, the constitutional enfranchisement of millions of women voters in 1920 also created both problems for suffrage reformers and opportunities for the newly enfranchised women. The hearings revealed a revolution in the practices of campaign fund-raising, which increased the responsibilities of women as high-profile members of the campaign staffs of many of the presidential candidates. Historians, oblivious to the important connectivity between the campaign finance denominator and the larger political equation, have mostly missed this point. While the Populist movement encouraged the active and direct participation of women in political campaigns, far beyond the symbolism of the 1840 Whig parades and pageantry, many historians have concluded that after ratification of the Nineteenth Amendment, those newly enfranchised women were politically worse off than before. Their argument that women lost power as they gained the vote focused on national political campaigns, where direct influence and agency have proven difficult to calculate. However, a new group of women's suffrage historians have shifted the focus back to local and state campaigns where women interested in issues such as child labor, public health, and mother's pensions and rights fought and won significant victories. In neither account, however, do the changes in the campaign finance system play any role. An examination of the congressional hearings uncovers a very different story. While the post-1900 disillusionment with parties and the political machine's inept handling of social, economic, labor, and social welfare issues colored much of women's political rhetoric, by 1920, during the first presidential campaign in American history that welcomed their participation, women ironically transformed their roles from the vocal opposition into integral components of that very party machinery against which they had so long contended. The campaign finance component offered women an immediate opportunity for direct involvement in party politics. Women who had led civic movements for social welfare and temperance reform, and who had raised millions in the war bond fund drives of World War I, were soon hired, becoming active and engaged participants in the political campaigns of the leading presidential candidates.[66]

The Kenyon debates illuminate that heretofore hidden involvement. In testimony before the committee, numerous women recounted their employment by the campaign committees and their view of their new roles. The greatly expanded franchise, candidates thought, called for a concerted attempt to engage women in their campaigns. Presidential candidates turned to experienced women, most of them former leaders of those same voluntary organizations that had battled the parties over social welfare policy, to lead that effort. Antoinette Funk, education director of the Democratic National Committee, testified that the Democratic Party specifically targeted women with a plan of "getting information to the women of the country on the principles of the party." Funk had suggested the plan in 1918 and implemented it under her own direction. She had made the same proposal to the Republican National Committee before ratification of the Nineteenth Amendment.

Funk, an experienced organizer, had been one of the women responsible for the National Liberty Loan Committee, organized to raise money for World War I obligations through the sale of bonds. She described as "natural" her move from one patriotic organization to another. "I have been interested," Funk testified, "in the Democratic Party since I supported Mr. Wilson in 1916, and I have done all I could for the party since then, all of the time." The committee questioned whether she had done party work while employed by the government selling five and a half billion dollars of Liberty bonds, but Funk maintained a scrupulous separation of her governmental from her political duties.[67]

While Mrs. Funk failed to convince the Republican Party to accept her plan for an educational campaign, by 1920 even the Republican National Committee recognized the role of women in the post–Nineteenth Amendment milieu. Mrs. John T. Pratt became vice chairman of the Republican National Committee Ways and Means Committee. The newly created franchise, Pratt argued in a circular entitled "Women's New Work," commanded women to participate fully in fund-raising for the campaign. "Usually women have been in a position of seeking the privilege in working with a political organization," she wrote. "This time the opportunity came to them unsought, and this time should be accepted by them in such a way as to prove their stability and earnestness of purpose." Thirty-four states chose women as vice chairmen of their state ways and means committees and the duty of raising the state quota of campaign funds became especially important to demonstrate their worthiness inside the parties. "It is especially important to push the work this year," she added, "when 12,000,000 women are at last looking forward to casting their first ballot for president, because it is bringing to their attention the necessity of *accepting party obligations and responsibilities* as well as party privileges." Women placed in important fund-raising positions urged other women to produce the campaign boodle in order to demonstrate their worthiness inside the parties that had so recently eschewed them. Mrs. May Giles, Tennessee vice chairman of her state Ways and Means committee, responded directly to the challenge, becoming the first woman in any southern state to contribute $1,000 to any state campaign fund.[68]

Illinois Ways and Means committee vice chairman Bertha D. Baur also testified before the committee that Illinois established a separate women's division with four employees. Her primary responsibility was to collect funds from women and women's organizations—and she successfully raised $35,367.57 during the first half of 1920. Her goal was to raise $100,000, or one-seventh of the Illinois state quota, from women. Chairman Kenyon inquired of Baur if she "had any sinister purpose in raising these funds" for the campaign. Baur, also a Liberty Loan veteran, recognizing her new role as political fund-raiser, and refusing to view her new cause as any less civic-minded, calmly replied, "No; the best purpose in the world."[69]

Individual campaigns also employed women in high positions. While some campaigns strove to adapt to this changing franchise dynamic, other campaigns seemed frozen by old attitudes. The Leonard Wood campaign allotted but $5,000 to women's clubs—specifically for teas and semi-social events, prompting Chairman Kenyon to wonder out loud if that was the way "women's campaigns are carried out? [laughter]." The witness responded by admitting he would rather "defer that to my wife." Even as increasing numbers of women moved into influential party positions, gendered attitudes about the social place of women in the political sphere continued to affect the seriousness with which men regarded their roles. Yet despite those constraining attitudes, the role of the Nineteenth Amendment, and its connection to the need to raise campaign funds to educate and influence the newly enfranchised voters, created an emerging opportunity for the involvement of women inside the campaigns of those same parties who for years had opposed their movement for suffrage rights. The evidence from the Kenyon hearings demonstrates that it was not merely the ratification of the Nineteenth Amendment that gave women increased power and visibility in the political system, but that opportunities to become active party workers as fund-raisers in the campaign finance system dramatically increased the personnel, purpose, and practice of women's involvement in the political process.[70]

THE SUPREME COURT DECISION IN *NEWBERRY V. UNITED STATES*—
Federalism and the Progressive Promise Derailed

Primary campaigns became the ground for weeding out candidates too local to attract a wide base of financial support, or those candidates unwilling or unable financially to contend in what was still widely regarded, though not in all circles, as excessive and corrupt fund-raising. The direct election of U.S. senators after 1913 and the enfranchisement of women made this political reality an increasingly expensive one. Because most reformers recognized that the real battles fought occurred in state nominating primaries, the 1911 and 1918 FCPA amendments imposed campaign spending limits in both primary and general congressional elections. The Kenyon committee exposed the increasing amounts of money raised and spent in primary campaigns due to their singular importance for election success, in direct violation of those limits.

The 1918 U.S. Senate campaign in Michigan led to a decision by the U.S. Supreme Court that compromised congressional attempts to regulate campaign fund-raising and spending, and for twenty years promoted the increasing exclusion of blacks in southern political society. The legal constraints imposed by the Supreme Court and the Constitution thus shaped politics through the campaign finance system. *Newberry v. United States,* like the 1882 Supreme Court decision in *Ex Parte Curtis,* illustrate how judicial decision-making over election law, particularly the campaign finance component of that broader system, shaped, defined, and delimited American conceptions of corruption and deliberative democracy.[71]

Part of the problem that developed before *Newberry,* evidenced by the Kenyon, Borah, and Reed hearings, was a congressional stalemate about how to deal with the problem of increasing campaign expenditures and widespread violations of the Federal Corrupt Practices Act. Ten years and several elections cycles after its enactment, FCPA maintained aggregate limits on senatorial expenses of $10,000 or less (if the state had a lower limit), which perplexed politicians running campaigns and regaling reform. In Michigan in 1918, the state corrupt practices act imposed a primary expenditure limitation on senatorial candidates of 25 percent of the senatorial salary, or a total of $1,875, defining the amount of legitimate campaign expenses essential to educate the electorate, as opposed to excessive campaign funds used to corrupt the electorate and the political process.[72]

The Supreme Court had two opportunities to consider the constitutionality of the FCPA before *Newberry.* In *United States v. Gradwell,* decided in 1917, at issue were the criminal convictions of numerous defendants charged with federal conspiracy to violate and defraud the United States and the states of Rhode Island and West Virginia by "corrupting and debauching by bribery of voters the general election of 1914 . . . preventing a fair and clean election." In the West Virginia case, the defendants were convicted of procuring a large number of nonresidents and enrolling them to vote in the primary election, depriving the United States, alleged the government, of "its governmental right to have the candidates of the choice and preference of said Republican and Democratic parties nominated for said offices." In effect, the defendants used "floaters," nonresidents of the state, to vote illegally in a primary election in violation of Section 37 of the United States criminal code detailing "Crimes Against the Elective Franchise and Civil Rights of Citizens."[73]

The Court examined the historical pattern of congressional regulation of elections and found that "the policy of Congress for so great a part of our constitutional life has been, and now is, to leave the conduct of the elections of its members to state laws, administered by state officers" and thus it would be a strained construction to apply the criminal law against government fraud in elections. Furthermore, the Court considered whether the criminal code, as used in this case against the procurement of fraudulent voters, applied to state nominating primaries. Sidestepping that federalism issue, the Court instead found that peculiar provisions of the West Virginia primary law (failed primary candidates could petition onto the general election ballot and only candidates belonging to a political party that polled at least 3 percent in the last general election could be candidates) made the primary legally distinct from a general election. Congress, the court held, "has yet shown no dispossession to assume control for such primaries."[74]

The year before *Newberry,* the Court faced a direct challenge to the constitutionality of FCPA's regulation of primary elections. Summoned before a grand jury in New York investigating alleged violations of the act in the 1918 Michigan senatorial primary, Owen M. Blair refused to testify and was found in contempt of court. Blair based his refusal on his belief that no grand jury acting under the grant of power of the FCPA could investigate primary elections of U.S. senators. Justice Pitney, citing *Gradwell,* refused to decide the question. The law of grand jury investigations permitted a refusal to testify to avoid self-incrimination, but nowhere could Justice Pitney find an exception based on incompetence or irrelevance arising from the alleged unconstitutionality of the FCPA. Accordingly, Blair was not entitled to set the limits of the grand jury investigation and had a duty to appear and fully answer the questions put to him unless protected by the Fifth Amendment.[75]

The Supreme Court could not avoid the issue in *Newberry.* The case arose out of the same facts as *Blair.* Truman Handy Newberry, businessman and secretary of the navy under Theodore Roosevelt, ran as the Republican candidate for the U.S. Senate in Michigan in 1918. Henry Ford, the auto magnate, ran in the primary against Newberry, but due to peculiarities of Michigan law, was a candidate for nomination on both the Democratic and Republican ballots. Newberry, at the time a naval officer, did not actively campaign in the primary or general election, preferring to let his campaign staff run the election from their Michigan headquarters. Michigan law limited U.S. Senate candidates to a spending limit of one-fourth of the annual salary for the office sought—in 1918, a total spending limit confined by the FCPA to $1,875. Newberry and his supporters raised and spent nearly $180,000 securing the Republican nomination, allegedly in violation of federal and Michigan law. After Newberry's successful election, the Ford campaign pushed for an investigation that led to Newberry's indictment under FCPA and his eventual conviction by a federal jury. The court sentenced Newberry, his campaign staff, and some of his financial supporters to two years in Leavenworth Federal Penitentiary and fined him $10,000. Appealing the conviction, Newberry hired Charles Evans Hughes to plead his case.[76]

Hughes's argument on behalf of Newberry left no further room for the Supreme Court to maneuver away from the central issue—did Congress have the constitutional power to regulate primary elections under the FCPA? The majority opinion of Justice McReynolds, following Hughes's reasoning, concluded that the source of all congressional power to regulate elections arose under Section 4, Article I of the Constitution, which provides that "the times, places and manner of holding elections for Senators, and Representatives, shall be prescribed in each state by the Legislature thereof; but the Congress may at any time by law make or alter such regulations, except as to the place of choosing senators."[77]

The specific constitutional authority was limited and did not create an unlimited grant of congressional power over elections beyond that which the Constitution specified. This textually formalist interpretation applied, because the majority reasoned, the only elections in existence at the time of the drafting of the Constitution were general elections. "Elections" thus could not mean primary elections, and congressional power to regulate the "manner of holding elections" was therefore not a broad grant of power to regulate them in all phases. The Court concluded that while there were many prerequisites to holding elections, "voters, education, means of transportation, health, public discussion, immigration, private animosities, even the face and figure of the candidate," the authority to regulate the manner of holding elections gave no right to control any of them. Relying on commerce clause analogies, the Court concluded that primary elections were "in no real sense a part of the manner of holding the election—and whether the candidate be offered through primary, or convention, or petition, or the request of a few, or as a right of his own unsupported ambition, does not directly affect the manner of holding the election."[78]

Justice McKenna concurred in part, but disagreed about McReynolds's opinion on the effect of the recent ratification of the Seventeenth Amendment providing for the direct election of senators. Justices Pitney, Brandeis, and Clarke would have reversed the criminal convictions on due process and vagueness grounds, but specifically wrote to sustain the FCPA and congressional control over primary elections. Chief Justice White would have reversed the criminal convictions on separate grounds, but dissented, separately sustaining the FCPA. The minority dissenters believed that the common sense reading was that primary elections had become, due to the direct election amendment, intimate to the general election such that "the influence of the former is largely determinate of the latter." Recognizing this practical reality made the regulation and control of the election of senators, a long-admitted congressional power, part of a broader and logical coextensive power of regulating nominating primaries held under state authority.[79]

Justice Pitney specifically considered the constitutionality of congressional power to pass the FCPA regulations. Opting for a broad construction of congressional power to regulate elections, Pitney found the authority to impose limits on campaign finance spending in the object and purpose of the Constitution to "deal in broad outline with matters of substance." For the majority to limit the meaning of "elections" to general elections, he contended, was to ignore the nature and adaptability of the Constitution to newfound evils from the corrupt use of money in primary and general elections. To suggest that Congress could exclude a member of its body for bribery in a primary, but could not regulate that same bribery or corruption, provided no "real check on corruption, or other irregularities in the primary elections."[80]

In the hands of the Supreme Court, the twin specters of dual federalism and strict formalism eviscerated the power of Congress to regulate primary elections after *Newberry*. States could regulate campaign expenses, but absent the federal power of disclosure and penalty found in the FCPA, most states instead chose to enact statutes that required reporting of contributions and expenditures, yet provided no criminal penalty. *Newberry* meant that Congress could regulate only general elections. This stifled attempts at reform in the one-party states of the South and the North, where the main campaign spending occurred in selecting the party nominees. Interestingly, the Supreme Court did not consider the constitutionality of FCPA campaign finance limits on First Amendment grounds, and they wholly ignored the congressional goal of eliminating corruption as a valid legal basis for exercising broad congressional authority. Dual federalist formalism provided a baseline of political power beyond which, no matter the goals or interests expressed, neither the legislative nor the judicial branch would trespass.[81]

The U.S. District Court, in its decision overruling Truman Newberry's demur to the indictment, had considered the broader public interest that the congressional reformers in 1910 and 1911 espoused when passing FCPA. The use of money to purchase the free will of voters, to coerce their votes, either directly or by the power of excessive spending, meant "our boasted freedom and equality have become mere mockery and delusion, and henceforth, the hopes and aspirations of every man for political preferment, whatever his learning, ability and talents, must be measured and bounded by the size of his pocketbook." For the District Court, campaign finance regulation was part of a broader system that demanded regulation by Congress to keep it pure from corruptive effects of aggregate wealth, in order to ensure free and open access to the machinery of its elections and equal and free debate on its most pressing issues. The Supreme Court preferred instead a formalist division of power and duty that smothered democratic ideals of political debate and deliberation, which the Court believed were best protected by state legislatures.[82]

THE CONSEQUENCES OF *NEWBERRY*—Using Congressional Member Exclusion to Regulate Campaign Finance Abuses

In the aftermath of *Newberry,* congressional supporters of campaign finance reform called for a constitutional amendment to permit federal regulation of primaries. Strong opposition to the proposal from southern senators intent on preserving state control over their elections and their limitations on suffrage prevented passage of any constitutional changes to overturn the decision. In 1924 and 1926, Congress, once again reacting to sensational allegations about excessive spending in U.S. Senate campaigns, held hearings detailing those abuses. The Borah committee, chaired by Senator William E. Borah, investigated national campaign expenditures of Republican, Democratic, and Progressive Party candidates. Spurred on by the Teapot Dome scandal, Borah's committee found increasing expenditures, and a multitude of local, state, and national committees acting in accord, and independent of one another, all beyond the regulatory parameter of the 1911 Act. Borah proposed changes to the FCPA, including the regulation of "all committees, local, state or national" and "all persons or parties" taking part in any House, Senate, or presidential election. Concurring with those recommendations, the Senate passed the Borah amendments unanimously. The House balked, substituting Representative John Cable's (R-Ohio) amendment for Borah's bill. The effect of Cable's amendment, which became the Federal Corrupt Practices Act of 1925, was to limit Borah's intended reform to committees operating in more than one state, to increase the amount of candidate expenditures permissible to $10,000 for Senate elections and $2,500 for representatives, or three cents per vote cast at the last election, all not to exceed $25,000 per senator or $5,000 per representative. The act restated the Tillman Act restrictions on corporate campaign spending, which became Section 313 of the new act. This bill remained the framework for all federal campaign finance regulation until the Federal Election Campaign Act of 1971.[83]

Increasingly, congressional campaign finance hearings shifted away from investigative proceedings intent on solving the *Newberry* dilemma into partisan wrangling over specific campaign expenditures as preludes to contests over congressional election credentials. Congressional reformers who had advocated the democratizing reform of direct elections and campaign finance regulation felt hamstrung by judicial doctrine and southern intransigence against federal involvement in state primaries. The regular congressional campaign finance hearing began to expose the antidemocratic and immoral, if not the technically illegal, violations of the spending limitations under FCPA 1925 as a justification for the exclusion of elected senators from Congress.[84]

The Borah hearings offered little fodder to substantiate the sensational allegations of excessive campaign spending, dispelling more often than proving the rumors of inflated campaign slush funds. The Reed Committee's voluminous hearings, on the other hand, disclosed a system of senatorial campaign spending rife with violations of the FCPA. Witness after witness, often combative and obstructionist, battled with Senator James A. Reed and his committee over charges and countercharges about huge campaign funds in Pennsylvania, Illinois, Arizona, Washington, Oregon, and Missouri. In each state, testimony demonstrated huge campaign expenditures spent to win the primary campaigns. Held during the 1926 election cycle, the committee's hearings uncovered facts showing that William Vare, the Republican nominee and successful U.S. Senate candidate from Pennsylvania, spent almost $700,000 to defeat his opponents, Gifford Pinchot and George Pepper, and win the seat. Pennsylvania, following a late 1920s trend of antireform backlash, had revoked its corrupt practices act and thus had no state campaign-spending limit. The only limits that applied to Vare's campaign were those found in the 1925 act, which established $25,000 or three cents a vote as the maximum legal expenditure. Accordingly, Vare was entitled to spend no more than $39,000 in his campaign.[85]

Vare's campaign committee hired newspapers, scores of speakers including women, and paid petition circulators to obtain the requisite number of names to place him on the primary ballot. On Election Day, Vare-hired poll watchers numbering more than 5,600 sat at polling places with pocketfuls of cash to supervise the election. Vare hotly denied allegations that his campaign had paid an opposing candidate $150,000 to withdraw from the race in order to make his campaign more appealing, but a stream of other witnesses confirmed the account. However, most of this nefarious activity had occurred during the primary campaign and Vare, citing *Newberry*, questioned the very power of the Reed committee to legally conduct the investigation, much less enact legislation to remedy any alleged abuses.

In Illinois, the committee found the campaign of Frank Smith similarly tainted. Smith, a Republican congressman, had been appointed to fill the vacancy opened by the death of William B. McKinley in 1926. Having successfully run for the seat in the 1926 election, Smith presented his credentials of appointment and election to the U.S. Senate. The Reed committee, while investigating the Smith campaign, uncovered campaign expenditures by Smith of more than $400,000, with $125,000 coming from Samuel Insull, a prominent opponent of the World Court. Numerous proponents and opponents of prohibition participated on both side of his candidacy, providing an additional $200,000 in support of Smith. Women's groups and the Ku Klux Klan, unregulated by the FCPA, which regulated only official campaign committees, provided money and organized support, and spent prodigious sums in the Illinois election. With Smith and Vare as senators-elect, the Reed committee introduced a resolution in the Senate similar to its actions in the Newberry case, challenging the credentials of senators-elect Smith and Vare on the basis that their elections had been obtained by fraud, and the corruptive and excessive expenditures of campaign moneys had been made.[86]

Recounting the congressional hearing testimony about corruptive and excessive campaign financing, the Senate resolution declared the credentials of Vare and Smith, due to their acceptance and use of contributions beyond the limits established by the FCPA, "contrary to said public policy, harmful to the dignity and honor of the Senate, dangerous to the perpetuity of free government and tainted with fraud and corruption," arguing that neither man was fit for membership in that august body.[87]

More problematic for Smith was the undisputed fact that, while serving as chairman of the Illinois Commerce Commission, he had accepted over $203,000 in donations from Samuel Insull and officers of Illinois public service corporations notwithstanding an Illinois statute prohibiting such a connected contribution. Yet all of Smith's campaign indecencies had occurred during the primary. He had violated, under the doctrine of *Newberry*, no federal law, and he contended the power of Congress to judge the qualifications of its members was limited by the Constitution. The challenge to Vare's and Smith's qualifications to serve as their respective states' senators became to some an infringement by meddling members of the Senate on the rights of state citizens to have their duly elected members sworn in. The right of the Senate to exclude an elected senator because of the acceptance of immoral even if technically legal campaign funds was a method of enforcing campaign finance standards many observers thought improper.[88]

Many senators, however, recalled their vote on the exclusion of Truman Newberry. Most of those who had voted to seat Newberry fared poorly in the next election. The sensational disclosure of excessive campaign spending in 1926, and the Supreme Court's restriction of alternative means to end excessive primary expenditures thought corruptive of the electorate, compelled the Senate to cast overwhelming votes of exclusion against both Senators-elect Vare and Smith. Senator George Norris summed up the collective frustrations and the last best hope of the Senate, stating, "We are going to establish a precedent one way or the other. Either we shall approve the resolution that was adopted in the Newberry case, and say to these powers, these trusts, these combinations, these multi-millionaires, 'You can get the courts, perhaps in some instances, you can get the executive department, you can stay the hand of justice in a criminal trial, but you can not buy the Senate of the United States. It, at least, stands in the road, in the way, of this kind of combination controlling the government of our country.'" Defeated by the unorthodox exclusion vote in the Senate, William Vare went back to his business and political activities in Pennsylvania. Undaunted, Frank Smith ran again for the office in the May primary and lost by 243,000 votes.[89]

Editorial writers celebrated the purification, announcing that the Smith case would "serve notice that no candidate can debauch public morals without incurring the grave risk of being thrown out when he attempts to pass through the Senate's door." Others, focused on the general state of affairs, on the Supreme Court rulings, and the inconclusive effects of two decades of reform, were not so sanguine. Some blamed the direct primary or the expanded electorate for the dramatic increases in campaign spending. Businessmen, increasingly involved in connections with an expanding federal machinery and administrative apparatus, questioned the denial of political access arising from the corporate restrictions in the Tillman Act. Black Americans chafed at the denial of their voting rights ingrained by the Supreme Court–sanctioned white primary. Women, now fully enfranchised, worked to carve out their own place in this confusing system, often becoming complicit in the very corruption they had for so many years contended against. And public opinion, recalcitrant and skeptical of reform, receded into the daily grind, wary of the next big disclosure.[90]

The Federal Corrupt Practices Act remained the backbone of campaign finance regulation until 1971, although in the next two decades, the advent of new means of mass communication and the rise of labor would require legislative revisitation of FCPA. The power of corporate wealth and dual federalism limited the Progressive-era election reforms that recalled a mythic democratic vision of the common good that began to seem more ghostly than genuine. Despite Progressive critics such as Croly and Lippman who challenged the reality of that vision, reformers continued to advocate reforms of the campaign finance system based on a conception of corruption that demanded regulation of corporate and other excessive money in elections to promote an equality of deliberation. Yet as they promoted those deliberative ideals, a different obstacle to campaign finance reform laid in wait. Ironically, the emerging doctrine of free speech would soon battle with the next great phalanx of reformers, once again challenging the definition of corruption and renewing debate about the principles of deliberative democracy.

Chapter Four

MANAGING THE MARKETPLACE OF IDEAS

Defining the Public Interest from the

Radio Act of 1934 to *Red Lion*

On Sunday evening, March 12, 1933, a troubled nation collectively gathered by its radio sets to listen to President Franklin D. Roosevelt. With nearly one-third of the nation's workforce unemployed, and every bank in America closed for eight days under the president's orders, the atmosphere was gloomy. But across those airwaves that night, and thirty more times throughout his twelve years in office, Roosevelt would use the medium to calmly, confidently, and with reasoned and measured rhetoric explain his administration's policies to the American people. Those radio broadcasts dramatically contrasted with those of another master of the medium across the Atlantic rousing the German people to racism, hatred, and war. President Roosevelt's appropriation of the radio medium for deliberation, reason, and straight talk was one of the great advances of American democracy.[1]

But the genesis of radio as an influential democratic tool came not from Roosevelt in the first years of his presidency, but instead years earlier from the work of his defeated opponent. In October 1924, as Commerce Secretary Herbert Hoover and his staff prepared their office for the Third Radio Conference, both the potential and the threat of the radio medium played heavily on their minds. During that summer, Americans across the nation had "attended" the Republican and Democratic presidential nominating conventions through radio hookups, and Hoover envisioned the advantages of the medium as a way to broaden democratic participation. While serving as Secretary of Commerce, Hoover came to understand and fear the unregulated power of big business. Hoover thought the best way to encourage business development while ameliorating its most serious excesses was through government stimulation of cooperative associations among business, labor organizations, and chambers of commerce. He believed in the economic advantages of scale, but cautioned against business becoming "so enlarged that they are able to dominate the community." Not content to rely on the unequal hand of laissez-faire, Hoover worked to create associational cooperation, and where that failed, he sought the use of government power to regulate business in the public interest.

In 1928, when he ran as the Republican presidential candidate, Hoover's political philosophy defined the primary problem of modern government as "maintaining the proper relation between the state and business." The fight "against economic and political domination," Hoover stumped, was ceaseless, and often the nation "lag[ged] behind in the correction of those forces that would override liberty, justice and equality of opportunity." While full economic regulation was not the answer, Hoover nevertheless recognized and sought to ameliorate the power of aggregated wealth where it threatened fundamental principles of American democracy and of American individualism as he understood it.[2]

Four formal Radio Conferences beginning in 1922, and occurring again in 1923, 1924, and 1925, were all chaired by Hoover. The voluntary cooperation promoted by Hoover created a "close-knit interrelationship between regulator and regulated." It was during those conferences, and in the Radio Acts that evolved from them, that the concepts of "public interest," freedom of expression, and equality of opportunity developed. Those public discussions over government regulation of the emerging radio media involved broad concerns about broadcasting, the public interest, and free speech rights.

By 1924, regulation of the radio industry became one of Hoover's most important Commerce Department projects. While he abhorred limits on expressive freedoms, he came to believe that excessive concentration in the industry ill-served the public interest. The conflict between free speech rights and the public interest required a balanced approach of exactly the type that Hoover had used in earlier business-government cooperative efforts. But free speech advocates, at this time emerging as the strongest legal proponents of civil rights protection, wanted an expansion, not a balancing, of those rights they felt necessary to protect individual liberties. The development of political speech over radio waves promoted by the development of the public interest standard created a branching of free speech rights that protected the access of the listener to a wide range of opinions. In that climate, free speech emerged as the new foundation for campaign finance reformers who once again redefined corruption to mean the lack of full and fair opportunities for political deliberation. Yet the cacophonous legal discourse about speech rights that emerged at about the same time as the Radio Act Conferences complicated the development of a popular and legal conception of the public interest in relation to the reform of the campaign finance system.

REMAKING THE METAPHOR—Holmes, Brandeis, and the "Free Marketplace of Ideas"

Conflicts between accepted understandings of libertarian and communal free speech rights and their implications for the ideals of democratic government arose in the early years of Progressive reform. The oft-told story of Justice Oliver Wendell Holmes's transformation from free-speech ambivalence to First Amendment champion due to the intellectual influence of Harvard Law professor Zechariah Chafee makes for great legal drama. Its usefulness as an explanation for the development of free speech doctrine and its relation to the public interest, however, remains unsatisfying because it failed for years to provide protection for any communal free speech values. Holmes, so the story goes, read Chafee's critique of the Supreme Court decision in *Schenck v. United States* in which the Supreme Court upheld the Espionage Act. He met with Chafee informally during the summer of 1919. The interaction between the two men led Holmes to reconsider his opinion.[3]

Schenck had mailed circulars to men about joining the army, claiming that World War I was a conspiracy of the capitalist class, and that the draft violated the rights of Americans. Federal authorities arrested and convicted him under a federal law prohibiting any actions detrimental to the prosecution of the war effort. Holmes wrote the *Schenck* decision, and opined that while an important right, free speech was not absolute and "the most stringent protection of free speech would not protect a man in falsely shouting fire in a theater." The question for those seeking to regulate that right was "whether the words used are used in such circumstances and are of such a nature as to create a clear and present danger that they will bring about the substantive evils that Congress has a right to prevent." Holmes's formulation of the "clear and present danger" test became the mantra for supporters of government regulation of speech liberties; at the same time, Chafee sought to convince Holmes that his creation would not provide adequate protection for those radicals seeking to exercise the full panoply of their First Amendment liberties.[4]

A few months later, aware of Chafee's critique, Holmes reconsidered the effect of his test. This time the defendants were Russian Jewish anarchists and aliens. Charged with violation of the federal Sedition Act, they had distributed leaflets in Yiddish and English protesting U.S. intervention in Russia, which had withdrawn from the war and made peace with Germany after the 1917 revolution. The government feared that the leaflets could incite readers to strike munitions plants and harm the war efforts. Fears of anarchist interference with war efforts led to a conviction of Abrams and his fellow defendants, and the trial court meted out twenty-year prison sentences. Holmes took this opportunity to dissent on the losing side (7–2) of the *United States v. Abrams* decision. In his eloquent dissent, he called the defendants "poor and puny anonymities," because the creed expressed in the leaflets was silly, finding that they posed no "clear and present danger" to the war effort. More significantly, Holmes clarified the understanding of his own test, finding that there needed to be a "present danger of immediate evil or an intent to bring it about" to warrant the state's restriction of speech rights. While the power of free speech, Holmes stated, made it politically logical for the state to seek to limit the expression of opinions, the theory of the Constitution, he countered, meant "that the ultimate good desired is better reached by free trade in ideas—that the best truth is the power of the thought to get itself accepted in the competition of the market." With Holmes, only Justice Louis Brandeis agreed.[5]

Despite all its legal drama, the enhanced protections of speech that Chafee and Holmes worked out that summer remained a losing argument for years. Even as the Court expanded the reach of the First Amendment and Fourteenth Amendment to cover the states in *Gitlow v. New York*, it held fast to Holmes's first version of the "clear and present danger" test elucidated in *Schenck*, not *Abrams*. Sustaining Gitlow's conviction for violation of New York's criminal anarchy statute, the court deferred to the legislature's determination that communist incitement to overthrow the government by industrial disturbances and revolutionary mass strikes constituted a clear and present danger to normative government functioning.[6]

Yet the seeds of change Holmes had planted in *Abrams* finally found fruition in a 1927 decision regarding the constitutionality of the California criminal syndicalism statute. A California court found Charlotte Ann Whitney, a niece of former justice Stephen Field, guilty of violating the law because of her membership and assistance with the state Communist Labor Party, which advocated the overthrow of the existing government. Although the Supreme Court again sustained the conviction, Justice Louis Brandeis, in a separate concurrence, reified the right of free speech as fundamental, using a distinctly deliberative rationale. Focusing on the degree of the danger the state must find to restrict speech, Brandeis reminded us that "the final end of the State was to make men free to develop their faculties; and that in its government the deliberative forces should prevail over the arbitrary." Those deliberative forces required that the "freedom to think as you will and to speak as you think are means indispensable to the discovery and spread of political truth; that with them, discussion affords ordinarily adequate protection against the dissemination of noxious doctrine; that the greatest menace to freedom is an inert people; that public discussion is a political duty; and that this should be a fundamental principle of American government." Given those ideas, Holmes's "clear and present danger" test, argued Brandeis, could only mean "immediate serious violence expected or advocated," because "confidence in the power of free and fearless reasoning applied through the processes of popular government" would act as a restraint on the effectiveness of any such incitement, unless the "evil apprehended is so imminent that it may befall *before there is opportunity for full discussion.*"[7]

Brandeis's belief in the power of rational democratic deliberation expanded Holmes's free market of ideas metaphor, adding to it a safeguarding filter for those ideas that may, at first glance, appear dangerous but which would through mature and rational debate be harmlessly discarded or ignored. The conception of free speech as an instrument of American democracy meant that Holmes's free market served both an allocative and educative function. Thus defined, the story of Holmes's transformation and Brandeis's contribution to free speech doctrine from *Schenck* to *Abrams* to *Whitney* becomes a Whiggish story about the development of the free speech doctrine from the Red Scare oppression against free thinkers and radicals challenging the status quo, which eventually set the stage for the expansion and constitutional sanctification of the First Amendment in the latter half of the twentieth century.[8]

That story, however, ignores two important currents of history that require a reassessment of the origins of the constitutional protection of free speech, and of the influence and scope of the Holmes-Brandeis market metaphor that so imbued liberal First Amendment theory after *Whitney*. The first current tends to place the Holmes-Brandeis debate at the midstream of doctrinal development, and thus less as an epiphany and more as part of a long procedural movement. The second calls into question the value of the market metaphor and its influence on the development of the doctrine, particularly regarding state regulation of certain kinds of speech, at the same time laissez-faire constitutionalism came under attack by Progressives like Brandeis. Free speech in the field of election and campaign finance law, and free speech doctrine as heavily influenced by the arguments that politicians and courts made over the power of government regulation of the radio industry, took a different turn. In the context of the making of the campaign finance system, First Amendment doctrine developed, promoted, and protected more communal democratic values than historians and legal scholars have described.[9]

Historians have detailed the pre–Red Scare history of free speech rights and described a radical libertarian tradition that challenges the perception that prior to Holmes's 1919 reassessment, individual rights were seen as a challenge to social reform. Under that view, Progressives like Brandeis began to defend free speech for its "contribution to democracy" rather than as a neutral right, stressing the social benefits to the polity of a free exchange of ideas. This movement had coalesced in the Progressive era, but its origins began earlier in the passage of the Comstock Act in 1876 prohibiting interstate mailing of obscene material. In that version, libertarian radicals formed the Free Speech League and the National Defense Association, then used those organizations to evoke a viewpoint that opposed government regulation of speech rights, especially for radicals like Emma Goldman and Margaret Sanger, who championed radical views like anarchism and birth control. Libertarians argued that free speech was an individual right of private judgment that no government could regulate. Lincoln Steffens, a member in good standing of the Free Speech League, opined that Americans "had freedom of expression in the sense that they were free to say what they thought," but it existed only in theory, since Americans, he maintained, "had not thought very freely." The lack of open discussion was due, according to the critics, to the repression of free speech principles, which were only valuable if applied to the views of the most radical thinkers of the day. Tying free speech liberty to larger ideals about how free speech protected community deliberation meant that free speech would become a right in which the public had "a genuine interest . . . quite distinct from the person or doctrine of those whom it seeks to help."[10]

Of the themes present before the Holmesian "creation" of liberal free speech doctrine, the regulation of public spaces, or "street speaking," was most significant for the history of the campaign finance system. The International Workers of the World (IWW) union speech fights over the right to speak on public street corners centered less on the rights of the speaker, than on the necessity for the opinions of the speaker to reach the workers. The street corner often was the most effective location to reach that audience. As local governments restricted IWW access to those public spaces, the union challenged those restrictions. When legal push came to shove, many courts considering the restrictions against Wobbly speech upheld the municipal restrictions. Often the distinction came from whether and how the speech incited illegal action, which nearly everyone thought could be prohibited. Opponents of freer speech rights argued that speech, especially speech that incited unrest or was "indecent," could be constitutionally regulated by the state. Many found incomprehensible the idea that minority viewpoints could be privileged in a forum if the majority rejected those views. While the rhetoric of democratic procedure for enacting the laws grew, few objected openly to the view that "democratic majorities could restrict the speech of minorities."[11]

Reconsideration of the prewar free speech cases challenges the accounts of the influence of Chafee's singular riposte to Holmes over tea and pleasant conversation in the summer of 1919. "Throughout the period from the Civil War to World War I, the overwhelming majority of decisions in all jurisdictions rejected free speech claims, often by ignoring their existence." In 1882 the Supreme Court ruling in *Ex Parte Curtis* was typical of the short shrift courts generally gave to free speech claims. Yet by 1930, in a growing minority of state and federal cases, courts saw the limitations of the "bad tendency test" and of the value of Blackstonian "prior restraint" as a doctrine that would promote a free press essential for functioning democratic institutions; as a result, they began to redefine the standards on which the court relied as they faced the twentieth-century sedition act cases.[12]

THE "FREE SPEECH TRADITION"—Balancing Individual Rights and State Democratic Interests

Judicial consideration of the constitutionality of the anti-assessment act and the Tillman Act occurred before *Schenck* and *Abrams;* consideration of the Federal Corrupt Practices Act shortly thereafter. In many ways, the

decisions involving the regulation of political campaigns became the catalyst for the emergence of more liberal free speech doctrine in the late nineteenth and early twentieth century. The principles of deliberation that imbued those decisions worked to invigorate the ideal of free speech as a
fundamental principle of democratic participation by establishing the
right of Congress to regulate speech to protect the institutions and practices of democratic participation. Implicit in that protection was a belief in
communitarian democratic values encouraging citizen participation in the
democratic processes. Individualist free speech rights were important, but
had to be weighed against the power of democratic institutions to involve
and engage a broad polity in public decision-making. In that sense, the
concept of corruption became transformed to include any impediment to
public participation in politics. When the courts evaluated the limitations
of free speech rights due to the regulation of the political system (the anti-
assessment act in *Ex Parte Curtis,* the Tillman Act in *United States v. United
States Brewers' Association,* and the Federal Corrupt Practices Act in *Burroughs v. United States)* they found no violation of free speech rights due to
the political regulation.[13]

On the other hand, the record of the states was not so clear-cut. Some
courts found violations of free speech in state attempts to regulate political speech. The Supreme Court of Virginia struck down a statute that prohibited public officials, including judges and teachers, from making political speeches and becoming involved in political campaigns. Based on a
state law modeled on the Pendleton Act, the court held that this state civil
service restriction violated state constitutional protections of free speech
"guaranteed to all the citizens of the state, not to any portion or any class
of citizens." The Supreme Court of Wisconsin invalidated state limits on
campaign spending by persons other than candidates (a model for the independent expenditure limits of FECA 1974, discussed in Chapter 7), finding a need for "agitation and discussion in the press, on the rostrum, and
in the open forum of personal contact" to guarantee the chance of substantial social and legal change. Absent that discussion, the Wisconsin
court felt that influential and wealthy parties could control the nature and
amount of debate, effectively stifling deliberation.[14]

In Idaho, the state supreme court upheld a law challenged on First
Amendment grounds that limited campaign expenditures to 15 percent of
the salary for the office sought. Though it was restrictive, the court found
no free speech violation since "the law did not attempt to prevent a candidate from freely speaking, writing, and publishing his views on all subjects."
This diversity of opinion over the constitutionality of state-created campaign regulations that often acted to limit political speech would continue
as the state and federal courts worked out their formula for the valuing and
protection of First Amendment rights. In both the federal and state arena,
government regulation of political rights worked to define and create the

doctrine that would become a distinctive part of free speech legal doctrine.[15]

Legislative regulation of the political system posed unique problems for lawyers and judges trained in classical liberalism, which decried the use of the government to regulate individual rights and liberties. A learned tradition of laissez-faire kept governmental power at bay, except when it was needed to loosen the barriers to free trade and open markets. While laissez-faire doctrine commonly permitted economic regulation of business, legal doctrine readily transposed the principles of government nonintervention to the regulation of the political processes and institutions. In conflict with the regulation of those political processes, a particularized doctrine of free speech that some have called the "Free Speech Tradition" emerged. It involves a shared understanding from both the core and the periphery about what free speech means. Yet despite that agreement, the tradition itself remains contested, as new facts build into new cases that challenge the historical assumptions and legal theory of the tradition, reconfiguring the meaning with each new generation.[16]

Two different principles remain stubbornly at odds within the tradition. The "individualist" understanding of the First Amendment privileges' self-fulfillment was a predominant and lasting value. Libertarian advocates affirmed that principle in *Schenck* and *Abrams,* and gave it full credence in *Gitlow v. New York.* In *Gitlow,* Holmes and Brandeis dissented in the losing 7–2 decision where the Supreme Court sustained the legislative prerogative of limiting speech rights that appeared to the majority to clearly and presently threaten the war effort. The individual had a right to speak, but that right must be balanced against the legislative decision about what imperiled the safety of the state. Free speech was an individual right, subject to a limited and moderate restriction by the government.[17]

What was significant about those decisions was that this branch of the political speech regulation often took on distinctive values and attributes not necessarily accorded to other kinds of speech. Long-accepted definitions of political corruption that denied individual voters free will and deliberative opportunities formed the foundation for these legal ideas. First Amendment definitions of and limits on political speech came to represent a subset of free speech doctrine as a whole, in which lawmakers and courts alike valued and took seriously the regulatory interests of the state in eradicating corruption. Increased regulation of the political process by Progressive reformers raised these issues at the same time that members of the Supreme Court struggled with the emerging controversies over free speech rights and political repression. Courts often treated free speech rights in disputes originating in electoral politics differently, regularly finding constitutional the legislative regulation of speech rights when those regulations directly related to the progressive goals of improving deliberative opportunities within political institutions or in the political process. Just as libel, obscenity, and "fighting words" came to be seen as distinct categories of speech deserving of lesser First Amendment protections, political speech limited by political reform developed into a distinct category of speech, protected by different constitutional tests and balances that supported different goals and values.[18]

Progressive challenges to traditional conceptions of individual rights would reorient the debate. Progressives, objecting to excessive individualism that they believed caused "destructive inequality and division" throughout American society, sought to shift the individualist protection of speech and other economic rights to one that permitted positive state action essential for needed social reform. Individuals demanding equal rights were often anathema to Progressives who thought self-interestedness destructive to the ideal of the common good. As a result, in the twentieth century, three rationales developed for the protection of free speech rights: the search for truth, self-governance, and finally self-fulfillment. These emerged at about the same time the Populists and then the Progressives advocated for the emergence of a democratic model of politics and a capitalist model of economics. The jurisprudence that developed slowly became more speech-protective, meant to improve the capacity of the democratic model of politics to expand influence to a broader range of citizens. In addition, the capitalist model of economics developed as the idealized model of laissez-faire economics in a free marketplace, characterized by limited government regulation, receded in importance. These two developments emerged as the "meaning and normative significance of democracy expanded," which distinguished the model of capitalism as an unregulated economic activity from democratic theory. "Freedom in the political sphere became embodied by democratic theory and practices, but freedom in the economic sphere was pictured as increasingly producing inequitable distributions of power and wealth. . . . The increasing influence of the democratic model of politics relative to the capitalist model of economics was reflected in a fundamental development in American constitutional jurisprudence. The emergence of free speech as constitutionally and culturally special was intimately tied to that development."[19]

Individualist free speech rationale embodied in the Holmes-Brandeis dissents of *Abrams* and *Gitlow* took a distinct and substantial step toward the communal, self-government rationale with Brandeis's concurring decision in *Whitney v. California*. Brandeis's democratic vision grew in his pre-Court career, as he fought against what he saw as the antidemocratic power of excessive wealth. Justice Brandeis did not shed his progressive habits and beliefs after President Woodrow Wilson appointed him to the Court in 1916. Conservatives, angered at Wilson by the appointment, fought his nomination with anti-Semitic comments, and many in his hometown of Boston charged that he was aloof, ill-tempered, and "not a fit person to be a member of the Supreme Court of the United States." His progressive legal career disturbed the conscience of the conservative bar, but eventually, the Senate confirmed him 47–22 on June 1, 1916. Despite this opposition, or perhaps because of it, Brandeis's progressivism endured while he served on the Supreme Court. His force of personality and his ideas would sanctify the budding marriage of free speech protection and deliberative democratic values. His work on this project on the Court, however, would not be a lonely tenure. As he prepared his affairs to start his new career in Washington, D.C., one of the many telegrams he received the evening after his confirmation was one that read, simply, "WELCOME," and was signed by Oliver Wendell Holmes.[20]

COMMODIFYING DELIBERATION AND MISREADING OF THE "MARKETPLACE" METAPHOR

That amiable beginning masked substantial distinctions between the free speech philosophies of Holmes and Brandeis. Often paired with him in common dissent supporting the protection of civil liberties, Brandeis did not merely mimic Holmes, but instead, through a creative misreading of the "marketplace" metaphor, extended Holmes's ideas espoused in *Schenck* and *Abrams* into broad, richly imaginative possibilities of free speech in democratic society. Where Holmes often judiciously enforced the law based on economic and social theories that he did not personally accept, Brandeis embraced the law as a means for social and economic change, and reconceptualized the First Amendment as the foundation of democratic society. Brandeis believed in progressive political ideas, and throughout his career on the Supreme Court, he expressed in his written opinions the rationale for those ideas.[21]

When in *Abrams* Holmes espoused his formula for protecting ideas that would reach the "ultimate good . . . by the free trade of ideas" and would, if powerful enough, "get accepted in the competition of the market," he was not as concerned with establishing democratic theory as he was with reformulating an intellectual boundary to his own "clear and present danger" test. Immediate danger, in both proximity and degree, became the standard—albeit for Abrams a Pyrrhic one—that Holmes intended to be a more substantial protection for speech. Yet the "free trade in ideas" market metaphor that Holmes created recalled a laissez-faire regulatory role for government over speech, one that relied on the invisible winning hand of absolute truth. Holmes, fearful of the raw power of government to suppress radical opinion, sought democratic popular acceptance as a mediating force, shifting the intellectual rationale for speech protection from a purely Lockean search for truth that provided a theoretical foundation for freedom. But Holmes remained committed to the impersonal market forces of reason and absolute truth to measure the argument and mediate the debate.[22]

Brandeis's contribution to the Free Speech Tradition, expanded in the *Whitney* concurrence, sought to ameliorate the impersonal power of the market and make speech a favored instrument of democratic reform. Whereas Holmes's metaphor implied the mediation of market forces,

Brandeis, long a critic of reliance on the market to ration political and economic deserts among a grossly unequal polity, recalibrated the "clear and present danger" test even further. Like Holmes's pursuit of "transcendent truth" to a "subjective individual freedom" and "intersubjective political deliberation," Brandeis's concurrence in *Whitney* sought to enliven the First Amendment with a power to affect and transform American democracy. The principles Brandeis established in *Whitney* formed the ideological font for the liberal free speech advocates in the 1930s and 1940s, and today provides the foundation for the resurgent movement of deliberative democracy theorists, a view that privileges a collective ethos that a "constitutional conception of democracy" does not reject the majoritarian premise but instead defines the highest aim of democracy as one where "collective decisions are made by political institutions whose structure, composition, and practices treat all members of the community, as individuals, with equal concern and respect." That recalibration demanded a hard and skeptical look at the rationale for Holmes's marketplace metaphor in the context of an emerging climate of political repression and rapid technological change.[23]

Brandeis began that reexamination in *Whitney v. California*. *Whitney* involved a conviction under California law for "assisting in organizing . . . the Communist Labor Party, [for] being a member of it, and [for] assembling with it." Whitney challenged her conviction under the California criminal syndicalism statute on the ground that the statute deprived her of her Fourteenth Amendment guarantees of liberty, due process, and equal protection. Her free speech claim was part of her Fourteenth Amendment claim, which the court had made binding on the states by incorporation in *Gitlow v. New York*. Brandeis agreed with the majority's finding that states could, if acting reasonably, suppress speech "in order to protect the State from destruction or from serious injury, political, economic or moral. That the necessity which is essential to a valid restriction does not exist unless speech would produce, or is intended to produce, a clear and imminent danger of some substantive evil which the State constitutionally may seek to prevent has been settled."[24]

Despite Brandeis's apparent agreement with the majority finding, he questioned the practicality of democratic limitations on the power of the state to regulate social, economic, and political doctrine imposed by the majoritarian consent of its citizens. Brandeis contended that "the final end of the state was to make men free to develop their faculties, and that in its government the deliberative forces should prevail over the arbitrary." Liberty served both as an ends and a means, and therefore, "freedom to think as you will and to speak as you think are means indispensable to the discovery and spread of political truth . . . that the greatest menace to freedom is an inert people, that public discussion is a political duty, and that this should be a fundamental principle of the American government. . . ." The founding fathers knew that order cannot be secured merely through fear of punishment for its infraction; that it is hazardous to discourage thought, hope, and imagination; that fear breeds repression; that repression breeds hate; that hate menaces stable government. The security of American democracy could best be protected by open thought and free discussion, and "the path of safety lies in the opportunity to discuss freely supposed grievances and proposed remedies; and that the fitting remedy for evil counsels is good ones." Believing in the power of reason as applied through public discussion, the founders "eschewed silence coerced by law—the argument of force in its worst form" and thus amended the Constitution so that free speech and assembly should be guaranteed.[25]

Brandeis's perceptive equating of the function of free speech in America's democracy with rational debate and full discussion meant that the clear and present danger test could be applied only where imminent danger was due to a failure of that reasoned, deliberative debate. In fact, for Brandeis, free speech was largely intended to encourage public debate and to promote that debate as the fundamental first principle of self-government requisite for the legitimacy of majority rule. Corruption meant a lack of public deliberation, leading to the failure of governmental legitimacy. For Brandeis, corruption of democratic institutions lay in the procedural inability of Holmes's marketplace to fairly encourage public debate, and to promote public opinion necessary to regulate political power. Unimpeded reason augmented by deliberative institutions and processes instead promoted a rich and valuable public debate sufficient to moderate the principles of personal autonomy and the self-interested right of expression and locate the collectivist principles of self-government.[26]

These legal-intellectual developments occurred contemporaneously with the emergence of radio technology. By the time of the *Whitney* decision in 1927, government officials, led by Commerce Secretary Hoover, were advancing a front of legal reasoning that co-opted Brandeis's collectivist ideas, but in a very different and ironic way. These disputes clashed and modified yet another process that began to look anew at the nature of voting rights, participation in political primaries, and, more central to a study of the campaign finance system, the power and authority of Congress to regulate those rights and that system. When those interests clashed, it was often due to the conflicting perspectives of the First Amendment and the pragmatic operational aspects of politics and the law.[27]

At the intersection of that dispute lay the contest over Holmes's marketplace metaphor as redefined by Brandeis. Laissez-faire conflicts about dual federalism, the political processes, and the state regulatory role to achieve egalitarian goals of deliberative democracy continued to surface in political question cases before and after 1927. The right of African Americans to participate in primary elections, the right of Congress to regulate federal election campaign spending and reporting, the right of a political party to set the nature of its own membership, the right of a state to exact a poll tax as a prerequisite for voting, the authority of the state to enact a "grandfather clause" or strict registration or literacy tests for voting, the state's right to set the time and manner of public financial solicitation, regulation of the rights of federal employees covered by the Civil Service Act to participate in political campaigns, control of the power of the media to publish attacks on elected officials, and the power of Congress to subpoena and hold in contempt any witnesses for refusal to cooperate with investigations of the Federal Corrupt Practices Act—despite the fact provisions of the act had been struck down in *Newberry v. United States*—all came before the courts during this period. At the same time the judiciary constructed a legal ethos regarding political rights, Congress considered the emerging role of radio in the American political process. Progressive thinkers merged their ideas with a Brandeisian skepticism of the market in a decade-long attempt to define and indoctrinate a "public interest" standard for nonprint media. In the late 1920s and early 1930s, they thought that "organized society must use its powers to establish the conditions under which the mass of individuals can possess actual as distinct from merely legal liberty," calling on government to regulate commercial and educational institutions to promote access to information and power essential for the protection of fundamental political liberties.[28]

THE RADIO ACT OF 1934—Promoting the "Public Interest" and Practicing Pragmatic Politics

The debate over the regulation of the radio industry exemplified the legal and political conflict over the role and power of the law to regulate political deliberation in the marketplace of ideas. Few observers denied the power of radio to influence the electorate; the real battles came over how to define the "public interest" and by what means state regulation could be constitutionally affirmed. Even libertarian free speech advocates, facing the unique nature of the broadcast medium, moderated their views about the role of government regulation in their idealized free speech marketplace. The development of public interest doctrine in the Radio Act of 1927 and the Federal Communication Act of 1934, which was later expanded by Congress and the Federal Communication Commission to include an explicit "fairness doctrine" and an "equal time provision" intended to protect that public interest, became a thematic unifier in the development of the campaign finance system. By 1969, the Supreme Court decision in *Red Lion v. FCC* appeared, not as an aberration to Free Speech Tradition, but as a familiar signpost along a distinct line of demarcation where the law accorded special respect to the ideal of preventing the corruption of public interest by regulating and rationing political speech access in order to achieve an equality of political opportunity and voice.[29]

In the early 1920s, when national newspaper circulation reached nearly 28 million readers and became the primary source of news and information, America saw the introduction of commercial broadcast radio. The easy accessibility of commercial broadcast radio offered the public a comprehensive and immediate means of receiving a wider variety of news, information, and entertainment sources. While radio competed with the entertainment industry, it soon embraced the technology. On November 2, 1920, radio station KDKA first reported the presidential results of the Harding-Cox race. This marked the first time that radio disseminated news before the public could read about it in the newspapers. By August 5, 1921, a major league baseball game was broadcast, and a year later, President Warren G. Harding became the first president to broadcast an address to the American public. As the public came to accept radio as a source of news and entertainment, business advertisers began to use radio to promote their products. By 1926, there were 526 licensed radio stations and 5.7 million radio sets, with a weekly audience of nearly 23 million listeners.[30]

Political leaders in the first half of the twentieth century, most notably Franklin D. Roosevelt, saw the political value of radio and used the medium to communicate directly with the people. His "fireside chats" provided public reassurance during the Depression, and increased the communal sense of authenticity and connectedness with the shaken political system in the nation's capital. Roosevelt's address on December 9, 1941, the day after Congress declared war against Japan, attained the largest single audience in radio history to date—an estimated 91 million listeners.[31]

The introduction of commercial television in 1941 slowly began the multimedia evolution of the industry. In 1945 there were fewer than 7,000 television sets in the United States, and they could receive programming from only nine stations. By 1947, however, momentum grew and the popular children's show *Howdy Doody* premiered on Sunday, along with the first television network series, *Meet the Press*. In the 1950s, television sets became cheaper, and television viewing skyrocketed. More than 108 stations broadcast programming to 15 million households with television sets in 1951. Advertisers flocked in droves to the new medium, and the competition between television and radio changed dramatically. The new medium that had started inauspiciously in the early 1920s emerged as the most important method by which most Americans obtained their daily news and information.[32]

In those early years, the Radio Conferences organized by Secretary of Commerce Hoover took a close look at the medium and found it disorganized, chaotic, and incapable of informing the public on the important issues of the day. Earlier attempts to regulate radio, such as the Radio Act of 1912, had made it illegal to operate a radio station without a license from the secretary of commerce but had failed to provide any discretionary standards for effective regulation of broadcasting. In two legal decisions, courts struck down the authority of the secretary of commerce to exercise discretion over broadcast programming. The Fourth National Radio Conference recommended to Congress that it pass a comprehensive regulatory act that would authorize under the commerce clause the licensing of all radio stations under one government agency. President Calvin Coolidge addressed the 69th Congress on December 7, 1926, decrying the present regulatory morass and calling for action. "The authority of the department under the law of 1912 has broken down," Coolidge stated, with many more stations then operating or under construction than could be accommodated within the limited number of wavelengths available. Unless the government developed a scheme to allocate and regulate the available spectrum wavelength among those emerging competitors, this important public function was likely to "drift into such chaos as seems likely, if not remedied, to destroy its great value."[33]

The Radio Act of 1927 resulted from that charge. Passed and signed into law by President Coolidge on February 23, 1927, the act created a five-member Federal Radio Commission, a temporary body that remained in power through annual reconstitution by Congress. Most significantly, the 1927 act established "public interest, convenience, and necessity," a phrase borrowed from earlier public utility legislation, as the discretionary standard. Regulation of the bandwidth dilemma was an important component of the legislation, with the Radio Commission allocating a spectrum in order to prevent overlapping signals, providing a solution to the problem of physical scarcity. The act gave the commission authority to prescribe licensing rules and regulations based on "the citizenship, character, and financial, technical, and other qualifications of the applicant to operate the station" only after a determination "that the public interest, convenience, or necessity would be served" by the granting of such license to such person. The statute regulated the physical scarcity of wavelength, but more importantly, it also established the right to hold a license based on a broad criteria regarding the citizenship and character of the applicant, and a requirement that the station be operated in the public interest.[34]

Additionally, the act provided for "equal opportunities" for political speech to ensure that the power of the media did not silence the very speech that had broadened radio's public appeal, which imbued the "public interest" standard by which all licensee qualifications would be measured. Section 18 of the act stated "[I]f any licensee shall permit any person who is a legally qualified candidate for any public office to use a broadcasting station, he shall afford *equal opportunities* to all other such candidates for that office," and the act authorized the Radio Commission to make rules and regulations to carry out those provisions.[35]

The "public interest" and "equal opportunity" provisions, first appearing in the 1927 act, became the ultimate criteria by which all later Federal Communication Commission regulations were measured. Yet the legislative history of both standards, first in the 1927 act, and later as reaffirmed in the 1934 act, provided scant guidance about what Congress intended by that scheme of regulation. The public interest standard was a constitutional standard originally applied to public utility common carrier regulation, dating back to Justice Waite's opinion in *Munn v. Illinois*. When Senator Clarence C. Dill (D-WA) referred to the standard during debate on the 1927 act, his casual usage of the "public convenience and necessity" standard was alternately phrased as "public convenience *or necessity*." The vagueness of the public interest standard apparently bothered few of the bills' congressional sponsors, since early efforts at legislative regulation often took a broad sweep, preferring to define administrative functions and allow the agencies to implement more specific regulations.[36]

The 1927 act and the Federal Communication Act of 1934, which generally ratified and reenacted the public interest and equal opportunity provisions, were backed by a broad public consensus supporting a comprehensive scheme for radio regulation. That the FCC would eventually act as the arbiter of the definition of "public interest, convenience, and necessity" was clear; what remained contested, and evolving, was exactly what that standard would come to mean in the context of the development of the collectivist free speech doctrine emerging in the constitutional quarters of the Supreme Court.[37]

During hearings on the 1934 Federal Communication Act, Senator Dill discussed a recent Nebraska Supreme Court case, *Sorenson v. Wood,* which created liability for each radio station that broadcast any libelous information. If broadly followed, the *Sorenson* standard would severely hamper the "equal opportunity" provisions of the act by making radio stations liable if a candidate who was offered such time to respond slandered or libeled another person. Dill's view was that the "equal opportunity" provisions, unless amended to prevent this vicarious liability, would severely hamper the ability of radio stations to broadcast political information. Under then-existing free speech doctrine, while they were not permitted to censor content, they could be held liable for libelous speech emanating from their studios over which they had an affirmative legal duty to permit. Senator Dill wanted to protect the stations, and stated that "there was no requirement in the law that a broadcasting station shall admit partisanship discussion on the station." Henry Bellows, chairman of the legislative committee of the National Association of Broadcasters replied, "[t]hat, it seems to me, amounts to less than nothing. The greatest value that radio can serve is to give the public, give the people a chance to speak and to speak freely. . . . If we are in the position where we have to say . . . we dare not let you go on because we do not know what the other fellow is going to say, then . . . I think one of the greatest values of radio will be lost." Even the real fear of potential libel liability did not dissuade the radio industry from advocating the advancement of the fundamental values of open and robust debate and deliberation for the industry. It was, after all, the industry itself which had called for the additional regulation after experiencing the ineffective efforts of the Commerce Department under the first Radio Act of 1912.[38]

After passage of the 1927 act, the Radio Commission began the daunting task of cleaning up the chaos of proliferation caused by the failure of the first regulatory scheme. When the Radio Commission organized, there were 732 operating radio stations competing for 90 frequencies. The commission divided broadcast time, allocated frequencies, categorized and created different classes of radio stations, and shut down some stations completely. The commission acted in all these instances under the auspices and interpretation of the "public interest" standard.[39]

From the outset, the scarcity rationale for federal regulation of the radio medium always meant more than simply the limited supply of the physical radio spectrum. To be sure, the 1920s problems with radio competition and overlapping spectrum broadcasting created a chaotic situation. Once the determination had been made that the airwaves were publicly owned, the 1928 division of broadcast rights into five geographic zones under the Davis Amendment required the FRC to delete several hundred competing stations whose service overlapped and conflicted with one another. This allocation of spectrum indeed was based on the technological limitation of available, usable radio spectrum. When the courts were asked to rule on the constitutionality of this power, facing a challenge to property rights jurisprudence of the station owners, they routinely found that the FRC acted in the public interest even though such allocation would, of necessity, take away the "property rights" of some station owners.[40]

Some observers conclude that the 1927 and 1934 acts demonstrate that the "public interest" and "equal opportunity" standard originated exclusively from the chaos of radio wavelength scarcity. The introduction of non-broadcast networks, such as cable television and other satellite dish networks, recorded media, digital compression and the Internet, claim the critics of the regulatory scheme of the FCC, have long since eliminated the physical scarcity on which the entire regulatory rationale was based since 1927. The number of media outlets has grown significantly since the 1960s. By 2000, there were more than 12,615 radio stations, 1,616 broadcast television stations, 68.5 million cable subscribers, 14.8 million direct broadcast satellite subscribers, and 1.2 million home satellite dish subscribers. There were 1,480 daily newspapers with a total circulation of over 55.8 million readers. There were also 281 nationally distributed nonbroadcast networks and 80 regional nonbroadcast networks. Approximately 42.5 million households subscribed to an Internet access provider by 2000. They argued that since it was the rationale of physical scarcity of available wavelengths that required the regulatory allocation, the advances in broadcast technology had ended that physical scarcity and therefore necessitated a new look at the "public interest" and "equal opportunity" standards.[41]

The development of the public interest/equal opportunity standard, however, was required by more than the concept of physical scarcity. For those early radio industry activists, and for the FCC in its early years of working out that dispute through regulations and court rulings, the public interest/equal opportunity standard was necessary for the promotion and regulation of an industry imbued with principles of the public trust. In that regard, deliberative democratic theory played an important though unrecognized role in the development of both the promotion of the new industry and on concurrent legal restrictions on speech meant to promote public political deliberation. The regulatory scheme finally implemented by government officials emphasized the role of a radio industry that served the public by providing egalitarian access for information, political debate, and collective deliberation on the most important public issues of the day. During the 1927–1934 radio regulation debates, scarcity of and access to diverse ideas was as significant a factor as the physical scarcity of radio spectrum.

THE PUBLIC INTEREST STANDARD BEFORE THE RADIO ACT OF 1934

A series of legal challenges to the FCC's interpretation of the public interest standard reconstituted the scarcity rationale for lawful regulation from one solely for the physical limits of radio technology to one that defined scarcity in terms of democratic access to information in the media marketplace. The legal challenges arose from instances where the commission reviewed the granting or relicensing of applicants, and denied their applications on public interest grounds. Interestingly, immediately after the passage of the 1927 act, the public interest section provoked so little interest that when Congress returned to enact the 1934 act, it did not change the public interest section at all. Section 19 (renumbered in the 1934 act as Section 317) was neither debated nor amended.[42]

In *Great Lakes Broadcasting Co. v. Federal Radio Commission* the Supreme Court considered the reallocation of frequencies by the Radio Commission for three existing radio stations serving the Chicago metropolitan area. WENR, WCBD, and WLS had their frequencies and times of operation changed on November 11, 1928, in accordance with the congressional mandate from the 1927 act. At issue was the determination of the operating time between the stations. The Radio Commission granted very limited frequency and time to WCBD, based on the "comparatively limited public service rendered by the station," and allocated WLS and WENR time at the ratio of 5/7 to 2/7ths. The Court altered the allocation, instead awarding equal operating time to both stations "upon consideration of the excellent service heretofore rendered to the public by WENR, and its capacity for increased service . . . its large expenditures for meritorious programs for public instruction and entertainment . . . and the popularity of the station." It was, the Court held, "contrary to justice, and against public convenience, interest, and necessity to apportion the operating time" to the disadvantage of the one station most clearly serving that public interest.[43]

Great Lakes provided some early clues as to the Supreme Court's understanding of the evolving "public interest" standard. A year later, in *KFKB Broadcasting Association, Inc. v. FRC,* the Radio Commission expanded that understanding in denying the renewal application of the putative owner of the station, Dr. J. B. Brinkley. Brinkley ran the Brinkley Hospital and

Brinkley Pharmaceutical Association, along with the station in the prairie town of Milford, Kansas. The station broadcast a regular program during three one-half hour periods daily that was referred to as the "medical question box," devoted to diagnosing and prescribing the treatment of patients from symptoms given in letters sent to Brinkley or the station. The good Dr. Brinkley never saw any of these listener-patients, yet advised them about their medical treatment, often prescribing the drugs his association then sold to listeners. In its ruling, the FRC biblically admonished ("by their fruits ye shall know them") the public sins of the applicant and denied the license renewal. Broadcasts of a distinctly private nature that were not only uninteresting but distasteful to the listening public, it reasoned, also provided a basis under the public interest standard for license denial. Congress, the Court held, clearly intended "that broadcasting should not be a mere adjunct of a particular business but should be of a public character." Having found that Brinkley's use of his license was primarily to promote his own business, in a way that likely endangered the public health of his listeners should they be fool enough to follow his advice, the Court agreed with the Radio Commission's denial of the renewal application.[44]

This public interest standard required the commission to determine if the content of the shows broadcast over the airwaves served the public generally, but the broad, ambiguous "public interest, convenience, or necessity" standard appeared to grant great leeway to any determination. Yet the early courts appeared comfortable with the free speech concerns about prior restraint. It was common in the 1924–1926 election cycle for broadcasters to prohibit certain kinds of political advertisements, primarily to keep what broadcasters felt was distasteful material from their listeners. The equal opportunity provisions of the 1927 Radio Act substantially remedied overt censorship, so primarily the litigated issues revolved around the general public interest standard based on the past practices of the radio station. In that sense, physical scarcity, which most commentators contend was the rationale for the standard in the first place, took on a new and different meaning. To be sure, many of the legal battles were between competing stations over spectrum space and allocation, but the court decisions in *Great Lakes* and *KFKB Broadcasting Association, Inc.,* and then finally, in *Trinity Methodist Church, South v. FRC,* established guidelines for the public interest standard even before the passage of the 1934 act that remained consistent, if not always crystal clear, until the mid-1980s.[45]

The Reverend Doctor Robert Schuler of Los Angeles, California, was the lessee and operator of a radio station, KGEF. It operated for 23 1/4 hours a week, broadcasting reports alleging the sinister and ulterior motives of trial courts and judges. Schuler charged some judges with immoral acts, never providing proof or justification. He further alleged the labor temple in Los Angeles was a bootlegging and gambling joint. On one occasion, he announced that he had damaging information about an unnamed person, which he would publicly reveal unless a contribution to the church for

$100 was forthcoming. (He received several contributions from guilt-ridden and gullible parties.) He disparaged both Jews and Catholics, alleging that their institutional influence in all areas of government made them threats to American democracy. Faced with this litany of derision and abuse, members of the public filed several objections when the license of the radio station came up for renewal.[46]

The commission denied the license under the public interest standard, and the Court of Appeals upheld the denial against a charge that the power of the Commission amounted to censorship and a violation of the First Amendment rights of the station. In the most salient early announcement of the parameters of the public interest standard, the Supreme Court held that possession of a permit to broadcast in interstate commerce limited the use of broadcast facilities because they, in covering the entire country, could obstruct the administration of justice, offend the religious susceptibilities of thousands, inspire political distrust and civic discord, or offend youth and innocence by the free use of words suggestive of sexual immorality. If the broadcast station was answerable for slander only at the instance of the one offended, the Court held, "then this great science, instead of a boon, will become a scourge." This was neither censorship nor previous restraint, nor any whittling away of the rights guaranteed by the First Amendment, nor an impairment of their free exercise because the broadcaster could continue to challenge the characters of men in public office, freely criticize religious practices of which he did not approve, or even indulge private malice or personal slander. But no broadcasters, the Court reasoned, "demand, of right, the continued use of an instrumentality of commerce for such purposes, or any other, except in subordination to all reasonable rules and regulations Congress, acting through the commission, may prescribe."[47]

While physical scarcity of spectrum motivated the initial regulation of the radio industry, as the Radio Conferences and debate over the 1927 act demonstrate, the public interest standard adopted by Congress as rationale for allocation of that scarce spectrum invoked a concept of public trust that by its very nature extended beyond mere physical limits. Scarcity of both physical access *and* broadcast opportunity, coupled with the central public purpose of radio communication as a popular educational instrument, belied the limited rationale of physical scarcity that commentators and opponents of the equal access and fairness doctrine would later offer for ending the rule. The free speech principles implicit in the Radio Act regulations meant that "when self-governing men demand freedom of speech they are not saying that every individual has an unalienable right to speak whenever, wherever, however he chooses" because "the common sense of any reasonable society would deny the existence of that unqualified right." It was therefore essential to protect "not the words of the speakers, but the minds of the hearers. The voters, therefore, must be made as wise as possible. They must know what they are voting about. . . .

What is essential is not that everyone shall speak, but that everything worth saying shall be said." Enhancing the rights of listeners to a broad and varied range of public discussion was central to the public interest regulation of the early Radio Act enforcement.[48]

THE RADIO ACT OF 1934 (THE FEDERAL COMMUNICATION ACT)—
The Public Interest Ascendant

Remarkably little discussion about the public interest standard occurred when Congress reviewed the act in 1934. For the most part, the changes Congress sought to implement centered on the creation of the Federal Communication Commission and several minor regulatory changes relating to the appeals process. However, the judicial interpretation of the public interest standard had established a benchmark of congressional intent, and the debate that would later occur ratified and clarified that judicial standard.

The cultural belief that radio had immense power to shape attitudes, mold minds, and distribute and influence the ideas of the American people led to acceptance of a broader conception of scarcity as the rationale for regulation. The National Association of Broadcasters, cognizant of the intimate invitation into their homes that Americans had issued to radio, instituted an industry code of ethics at its January 26, 1928, meeting. The FRC, consistent with the 1927 Radio Act's Section 9 imprimatur against censorship, allowed broadcasters to regulate their own industry. Where elsewhere, like in Britain with its British Broadcasting System, the industry had been founded on a tradition of public service, broadcasting in the United States developed commercially without direct state subsidy or involvement. The industry code of ethics and the public interest standard administered by the FRC were the main components of instilling the American ideals of public service. In the early years, however, the debate over the proper role of radio, of the use of advertising to fund commercial operations, and of the effects of a medium whose message could not only assert the "unifying power of simultaneous experience but . . . [could] communicate meanings about the nature of that unifying experience" exposed itself fully in the Radio Act legislation.[49]

The Commerce Department *Study of Communications by an Interdepartmental Committee* issued in January 1934, discussed the issues of economic efficiency, the allocation of physical resources, and the fear of unrestricted competition in the industry. In hearings on the 1934 Federal Communication Act that followed, Congress considered the scarcity of radio outlets in the less-populated western states that had been limited under the Davis amendment. They also attempted to deal with the concerns of broadcasters about libel liability under the rationale of the *Wood* case from Nebraska. The legal right and appeal procedures from FCC determinations were formalized and streamlined. The hearings, however, did not address the public interest standard, then the most recognized and accepted rationale for the effective development of the radio industry.[50]

Some groups called for an allocation of 25 percent of all available frequencies, wavelengths, power, and time assignments for educational, religious, agricultural, labor, cooperative, and similar nonprofit associations, with the remaining 75 percent being assigned to commercial undertakings. For men like Rev. Father John B. Harney of the New York Missionary Society of St. Paul the Apostle, the public interest standard had too often favored "the viewpoint of popularity . . . instead of the real interests of educational information." The National Association of Broadcasters, on the other hand, strongly opposed this mathematical principle of allocation. "[T]he sole test of fitness for a broadcasting license," the organization testified, "is service to the public as a whole, as distinguished from service to any particular class, group, or denomination." This dispute exemplified the continuing cultural conflict between commercial radio development and the American system of public ownership of the airwaves, and the concurrent duty to use the airwaves to educate and inform the public. The issuance of radio licenses, subject to the affirmative duty to serve that public interest, remained the guiding principle of the Federal Communication Act of 1934 when it passed Congress on June 19, 1934.[51]

Despite the contest over specifically defined allocations, the 1934 Act provided that the newly created Federal Communication Commission make those decisions based on the same standard of "public interest, convenience, and necessity" that it borrowed from the Radio Act of 1927. But the concept of physical scarcity related to both the problem of allocation (which Congress addressed by providing at Section 307 that "the people of all the zones established by this title are entitled to equality of radio broadcasting service," accomplished as near as possible by the commission's "equal allocation of radio licenses"), and to concerns about access to a wide and robust diversity of political opinion. In that regard, the "public convenience, interest, or necessity" standard became more than mere physical scarcity. The democratizing influence and potential of the radio medium was a public trust that Congress nurtured and encouraged through the power of the FCC. Not insignificantly, many congressmen familiar with the role that radio had played in recent political campaigns considered it the most important emerging instrument of democratic education in the United States. The fear, expressed by congressmen during floor debate on the measure, was that wealthy owners could monopolize the physical radio system and thus deny access and opportunity to the vast and diverse expression of political opinion essential for the effective operation of the deliberative election process. For that reason, Congress enacted Section 315 of the act providing that if any licensee shall permit any person who is a legally qualified candidate for any public office to use a broadcasting station, he shall afford equal opportunities to all such other candidates for that office in the use of such broadcasting station, and the commission shall make rules and regulations to carry this provision into effect.[52]

This provision had a very limited connection to the concept of physical scarcity, since the understanding was that it would apply only where two or more candidates had physical access to broadcast media. Section 315 addressed the concept of scarcity as it related to democratic beliefs in equal opportunity and access to the means of expression, ensuring that the listener would have full and fair opportunity to hear all sides of a debate. The public interest standard solved both the physical scarcity concerns, and concerns about democratic access to diverse opinions in an unequal marketplace of ideas.[53]

By providing equal access and opportunity for all candidates, Congress addressed the threat most fundamental to the misuse and abuse of the nascent industry. Gross W. Alexander, Executive Manager of Pacific-Western Broadcasting Federation of Los Angeles, California, acknowledged during his testimony to the House on the 1934 act the concerns of many Americans. "Democracy," he stated, "is not doing well." Informed that there were dictatorships and despots in forty foreign countries that had "profaned, abrogated, and annulled" the highest achievement of the human race there, Alexander predicted "if democracy fails in America . . . it will be because of the nonuse, the misuse, the abuse of the instruments of communication—of the media of mass communication." "Not only is man in interaction with material existence," he continued, "but he lives and moves in an environment of ideas and personalities. It is by means of these social contacts, and the resulting exchange of concepts, sentiments, emotions, that cumulative racial experience is developed into a body of knowledge."[54]

The development of new means of communication that catalyzed such human interaction made possible unlimited panoramas of social organization and rational economic, social, and political reconstruction. For Alexander, the threat to this great possibility lay in "the rapidly accelerating concentration of economic control of machines of production and distribution." He called on Congress to preserve and protect the civic, social, and educational process in keeping with the old American tradition, which was the promotion and maintenance of educational and social services by the state. Many in Congress who had witnessed, in the last election cycles, the power of radio to sway the public and had themselves experienced the increasing costs of the medium to the political candidates, recognized that Section 315 was not meant to allocate scarce radio spectrum. Instead, the equal opportunity provisions of the act (which would later become through FCC rule-making the "equal opportunity" and "fairness doctrines" that helped regulate media influence in political campaigns) were intended to promote equal access to the airwaves as a means to ensure fundamental principles of political equality and practices of deliberative democracy.[55]

AFFORDING FREE SPEECH—The Equal Time and Fairness Doctrines and
Red Lion Broadcasting

Not long after its passage, the FCC began to address the practical application of the public interest standard and the equal time provision of the Communication Act. The commission, using only the "public convenience, interest or necessity" standard, formulated rules and enforcement procedures to implement the law. In 1943 the Supreme Court considered the constitutionality of the Communication Act, and specifically of Congress's delegation of rule-making and regulatory authority to the FCC. The case involved the Chain Broadcasting Regulations that permitted the FCC to fix and alter existing contracts between radio stations and the larger networks. The networks alleged the regulations rewrote existing contract law and violated the "takings clause" of the Constitution. In an opinion authored by Justice Felix Frankfurter, the court upheld in *NBC, Inc. v. United States* the provisions granting the FCC authority to determine and allocate radio frequency and spectrum, and found the public interest standard not so vague and indeterminate as to create First or Fifth amendment problems.[56]

The case considered the power of the FCC to regulate the increasing concentration of radio stations under the network umbrella. At the time, stations affiliated with the national networks of NBC and CBS used more than 97 percent of all nighttime broadcast power, and the three national networks controlled almost half of all the broadcast business in the country. Frankfurter, writing for the 7–2 majority, found that the historical background of radio regulation and the public interest standard were necessary due to the limited facilities of radio, and the "fixed natural limitation upon the number of stations that can operate without interfering with one another." The initial authority of Congress to regulate spectrum was extended to the scarcity rationale beyond spectrum limitations when the Court considered the validity of the public interest standard as the operational dogma for the regulations. The Court found that, while limited by natural factors, "the public interest demands that those who are entrusted with the available channels shall make the fullest and most effective use of them" in order to encourage the "larger and more effective use of radio." The significance of this decision was that it reaffirmed the scarcity dichotomy fundamental to the Communication Act: although the physical spectrum scarcity provided the public trust rationale for congressional regulation of an ostensibly private industry, it remained the scarcity of full and equal access for a diversity of ideas that permitted the development of the public interest standard, and the concurrent doctrines of equal time and the fairness doctrine, which created free speech restrictions founded on the principles of equality of access and opportunity.[57]

The fairness doctrine that the Supreme Court eventually considered in *Red Lion Broadcasting Co. Inc. v. Federal Communication Commission* developed from an FCC study commissioned in 1949. The commission defined "the fairness doctrine" to require that "when a broadcast station presents one side of a controversial issue of public importance reasonable opportunity must be afforded for the presentation of contrasting views." This principle was distinct from the "equal time provision" specifically set out for candidates in Section 315 of the act. That provision, which came from language borrowed directly from the 1927 act, required broadcasters to afford "equal opportunities" to all other candidates for office when the station permitted any legally qualified candidate to use the broadcast facilities. However, the fairness doctrine did not have a similarly defined section in the act, and arose primarily from the regulatory position of the FCC that its statutory mandate of "public interest, convenience or necessity" made it a necessary corollary to that standard.[58]

In 1949 the FCC addressed the concerns of broadcasters and the public. The "Mayflower Doctrine" used since 1941 disapproved of the licensee's one-sided presentation of political issues. In *Mayflower,* the FCC found that a radio station was, under the fairness doctrine, required to present both sides of any controversial issue because the public had an overriding right to the full and fair deliberation on those issues of public interest. The FCC expressly sanctioned any station that used its facilities to win public support for a political position by nonobjective or one-sided programming, stating that this type of activity demonstrated "a serious misconception of its duties and functions under the law." Again, the dual conception of scarcity determined the position of the agency when it held that because of the limitations in frequencies inherent in the nature of radio, "the public interest can never be served by a dedication of any broadcast facility to the support of [the licensee's] own partisan ends. Radio can serve as an instrument of democracy only when devoted to the communication of information and the exchange of ideas fairly and objectively presented." A truly free radio, the Court found, "cannot be used to advocate the causes of his licensee, support the candidacies of his friends," nor can it be devoted to the support of principles he happens to regard most favorably. In brief, the broadcaster cannot be an advocate.[59]

In the years ahead, the commission faced a dizzying array of scenarios that demanded more specific direction to broadcasters. In response, the FCC issued its *Report on Editorializing by Licensees.* This report presented the definitive statement on the fairness doctrine. It rescinded the 1949 *Mayflower* ban on editorializing so long as the station maintained an overall balance in its broadcasting "by affording opportunities for the presentation of conflicting points of view." The commission denied that its policy constituted an effective ban on the free speech of the broadcaster since "[t]he freedom of speech . . . does not extend any privilege to government licensees of means of public communication to exclude the expression of opinions and ideas with which they are in disagreement. . . . We believe . . . that a requirement that broadcast licensees utilize their franchises in a manner in which the listening public may be assured of hearing varying opinions on the paramount issues facing the American people is within both the spirit and letter of the First Amendment." In 1952 Congress amended Section 315 to prevent licensees from charging more for political time than was charged for other types of programming, this in response to increased broadcasting costs paid by candidates. No specific legislation formalized the fairness doctrine until 1959, which by then was regularly imposed by the FCC.[60]

In 1959 Congress finally formalized the fairness doctrine, amending Section 315 of the Radio Act of 1934 that exempted appearances by candidates on news programs from being considered a "use" of the broadcast facilities and adding the second sentence to Section 315 (a) which specifically stated that the regulation should not be construed as relieving broadcasters, in connection with the presentation of newscasts, news interviews, news documentaries, and on-the-spot coverage of news events, "from the obligation imposed upon them under this Act to operate in the public interest and to afford reasonable opportunity for the discussion of conflicting views on issues of public importance." This amendment did not settle the dispute over the fairness doctrine. The FCC, having failed to promulgate rules or regulations until 1967, continued to decide those questions on an *ad hoc* basis. Even the 1967 rules dealt only with personal attacks and political editorials, considered remnant subdivisions and not the whole cloth of the fairness doctrine.[61]

Broadcasters, attempting to comply with the FCC decisions, complained that the fairness doctrine compromised their ability to maintain the business viability of their broadcast operations. The crux of their complaints was an appealing argument: broadcasters, fearful of triggering application of the doctrine (which could result in the requirement of supplying free reply time, or worse yet, facing FCC licensee sanctions), determined instead to opt for a course antithetical to the democratic purposes of the public interest standard, and restrict their broadcasts to the "bland, the insipid, and the uncontroversial." Opponents contended that the fairness doctrine as implemented, prevented, rather than encouraged, the deliberative democratic opportunities central to the early Radio Act.[62]

The debate over fairness doctrine regulation and equal time access for political candidates merged in 1967–1969 in a set of cases involving the some of the most vocal and long-standing opponents of the doctrine. A case arising in the Seventh Circuit Court of Appeals involved the Radio Television News Directors Association, CBS, and NBC (referred to as RTNDA). These organizations sued the FCC, alleging the unconstitutionality of the 1967 rules on personal attack and political editorializing broadcasting, and directly challenged on First Amendment grounds the underlying foundation and legality of the fairness doctrine. A second case, *Red Lion Broadcasting Co., Inc., v. FCC,* arose in the United States Court of Appeals for the District of Columbia. In that case, Red Lion Broadcasting, Inc., acting as the licensee for radio station WGCB-TV, of Red Lion, Pennsylvania, sued the FCC, challenging a ruling that required it, under the fairness doctrine, to provide equal time to Fred J. Cook, who had been attacked during a

November 1964 broadcast. During that broadcast, Reverend Billy James Hargis, speaking on a program called *The Christian Crusade,* discussed the 1964 presidential campaign involving Lyndon B. Johnson and Barry Goldwater. He alleged that a book authored by Cook, called *Goldwater—Extremist on the Right,* was biased. During the radio discussion, Hargis further alleged that Cook had made false statements that led to his firing from the *New York World-Telegram,* that Cook, while writing for "the left wing publication, *The Nation,* had written an article absolving Alger Hiss of any wrongdoing," that he had attacked the FBI and J. Edgar Hoover, and "wrote the book to smear and destroy Barry Goldwater." The FCC ruled that the station had used their medium to attack Cook on an issue of public importance, and was required to provide Cook with equal time, at the station's cost if Cook could not afford the time, to respond.[63]

Both cases were ultimately appealed and were consolidated by the Supreme Court in *Red Lion Broadcasting Co., Inc., v. FCC.* Many observers who had examined the regulation in light of existing free speech doctrine expected the Court to strike down the fairness doctrine as an unconstitutional exercise of power beyond the statutory mandate of the Federal Communication Act. However, the development of a strong and substantive right of free speech during the Civil Rights era masked, for those observers, the equally strong free speech tradition that permitted state regulation of political speech to protect against electoral corruption. The briefs of the appellant RTNDA challenged the underlying rationale of the act. "The press (all mass media) is not a stagecoach obligated to carry all ideas ready to travel." The only legitimate rationale for the fairness doctrine was that "the success and viability of our democratic institutions are seriously and immediately threatened because the electorate is exposed in high degree to one-sided communications on political and social issues, and its judgments, therefore, will fall short of the intelligence that is demanded if our democratic institutions are to be secure."[64]

The short, 38-page brief of Red Lion Broadcasting Company argued simply that the electronic mass media in 1969 were no longer physically scarce, and thus, the 1934 rationale for regulation was no longer valid. Red Lion contended that the lack of scarcity made any regulation suspect, and the fairness doctrine, absent a clear and direct threat to American democratic institutions as a result of the lack of diverse news and public interest programming, was unconstitutionally onerous to the free speech rights of the station. This argument, gleaned from a selective reading of congressional documents from the 1934 act debates, focused only on the physical half of the scarcity rationale, ignoring the democratic purposes of the "public interest" standard and the free speech interest of the listener, which were the root of the public policy of radio regulation.[65]

The amicus brief filed on behalf of the United Churches of Christ, the National Council of Churches, the National Catholic Conference for Interracial Justice, the AFL-CIO, and the Young Women's Christian Association, took a different approach. These parties, interested in the educational and democratic values of broadcasting, claimed that there was, in practice, little real diversity in news programming. The increased number of network outlets over the past forty years had lessened the physical scarcity of radio. The number of on-air commercial stations since 1949 had increased from 69 to 626; educational television stations from 0 to 127; commercial AM stations from 2,006 to 4,135; commercial FM stations from 737 to 1,706, and educational FM stations from 34 to 318. That increase, however, did not equate to an increase in diversity of programming, and left almost 2000 communities in the United States with only one station. Furthermore, the consolidation of the industry meant for the stations that affiliated with one of the big chains a new level of standardized broadcast programming. The increase in the number of stations had been accompanied by a "trend toward increased network control over the production of programming." The monopoly and standardized programming created a new concern for viewers demanding broad access to the medium for controversial matters of public interest.[66]

Furthermore, the churches criticized what they called the "Fourth Network," the broad group of stations in small communities against which the vast majority of fairness doctrine complaints were lodged. Out of 800 complaints, only 173 involved personal attacks, and none of those complaints was lodged against one of the big three networks. All fairness doctrine complaints studied in 1967 had been lodged against local companies, with none involving a major market. These local stations often carried syndicated programming sponsored by "nonprofit" organizations established by an affluent person seeking to advocate his personal views. These programs came from "the Radical Right" that "spewed out a minimum of 6,600 broadcasts a week, carried by more than 1,300 radio and television stations—nearly one out of five in the nation. . . . A survey recently completed . . . indicates that 'call-in' radio programs are also widely used by right-wing sponsors and commentators . . . to promote extremist views and oppose liberal legislators." For these religious and civic groups, the increasing number of media outlets exacerbated, instead of eradicated, the need for regulation in the public interest since the "Fourth Network," owned by wealthy conservatives, tended to exploit broadcasting as an instrument for free expression. The free speech rights of the "Fourth Network" mattered less to those groups because they saw the programming as "one-sided abuse, which unanswered had very little social utility." They believed that the real free speech rights belonged to the listening public, and these groups called on the Supreme Court to affirm and strengthen the public interest purposes of the fairness doctrine.[67]

Thus understood, Congress expected that the public interest standard of the Federal Communication Acts might restrict free speech rights in order to promote democratic principles of deliberation, creating an informed public that deliberated over issues in order to arrive at the most rational choice. The economic costs of radio and television broadcasting, caused by both its spectral scarcity and by the substantial capital costs of plant and facilities, effectively put the business out of reach of most Americans. This gave Congress a legitimate commerce interest in regulating the industry. In 1969, few disagreed with that viewpoint. The second issue, however, remained hotly disputed. The growth of the media marketplace as the principal purveyor of political and social ideas demanded that Congress, once it determined upon regulation, do so in the public interest by providing full and free access to exactly the range and diversity of opinions that deliberative body required to make pragmatic decisions.[68]

The Supreme Court decided *Red Lion* on June 9, 1969. Chief Justice Warren, in one of his final cases on the Court, wrote a unanimous (7–0) decision that ruled in favor of the FCC and fully sustained the fairness doctrine as a proper constitutional delegation of congressional authority to regulate the media marketplace in the public interest. The Court considered the legislative history of the regulation of the broadcasting industry, recognizing that the scarcity rationale impelled the early decisions to regulate the industry. The assertion that "the right of the public to service is superior to the right of the individual" provided the original rationale for the regulation of the industry. Service of the public interest, the suppression of selfishness, supported the standard of regulation that Congress adopted when it required as a condition of licensing that the station would serve the public interest, convenience, and necessity. "Thirty years of consistent administrative construction left undisturbed by Congress until 1959," wrote Chief Justice Warren, "when that construction was expressly ratified, reinforce the natural conclusion that the public interest language of the act authorized the commission to require licensees to use their stations for discussion of public issues, and that the FCC is free to implement this requirement by reasonable rules and regulations which fall short of abridgment of the freedom of speech and press, and of the censorship proscribed by Section 326 of the act." The Court affirmed that the authority of Congress to regulate the industry and to delegate that authority to the Radio Commission through the FCC was a lawful exercise of its commerce power.[69]

Yet the significant First Amendment question remained: how would the rights of the broadcasters to be free from any law that prevents the station owner from saying or publishing what he thinks, or from refusing in his speech or other utterances to give equal weight to the views of his opponents, be protected? Interestingly, the Court used the characteristics of the modern media to justify the regulation. "The ability of new technology," it stated, "to make sounds more raucous than those of the human voice justifies restrictions." Furthermore, the problems raised by the new technology, "which supplants atomized, relatively informal communication with mass media as a prime source of national cohesion and news," compelled government regulation to eliminate the potential drowning out of "civilized private speech." This kind of communication was not face to face, and the reach of radio signals was "incomparably greater than the range of the human voice and the problem of interference is a massive reality." While spectrum interference clearly mattered to the issue of regulation, the purpose of regulating that interference was to prohibit the monopoly of a licensee because, the Court reasoned, "the free speech of a broadcaster does not embrace the right to snuff out the free speech of others." The Court embraced communal rights of free speech, of the public's "collective right to have the medium function consistently with the ends and purposes of the First Amendment," which was the right of the public to receive "suitable access to social, political, esthetic, moral, and other ideas and experiences" and was a right in the collective polity that could not be abridged by either Congress or the FCC. The Court, evoking free speech values, recognized that in a democracy, principles of equal access and deliberation were substantial constitutional principles that permitted the restriction, on the publicly owned airwaves, of the rights of broadcasters to unrestrained control of the medium.[70]

Resources and equipment likewise mattered, and the Court recognized that only a very few would ever be able to financially and technologically access the airwaves. The Court discussed the issue of scarcity of resources in economic terms, but refused to base the decision on those grounds. It also refused to directly consider the argument that Congress did not violate the First Amendment by "indirectly multiplying the voices presented on public issues through time sharing, fairness doctrines, or other devices which limit or dissipate the power of those who sit astride the channels of communication with the general public." Confronted with the historical reality that Holmes's marketplace metaphor turned ideas into commodities, the Warren court nonetheless found that in the pragmatic world of politics, ideas were not bought and sold like consumer goods. Appellants argued that the fairness and equal time doctrines cost broadcasters revenues, since they were often forced to provide broadcast time free of charge to air the opposing viewpoints. If this forced broadcasters to self-censor on the coverage of controversial public issues such that such coverage "would be eliminated or rendered wholly ineffective," the Court concluded, "[s]uch a result would indeed be a serious matter." But that remained speculative, and what was not speculative to the *Red Lion* majority was the congressional demand that licensees be "proxies for the entire community, obligated to give suitable time and attention to matters of great public concern," and the right of the FCC to condition the granting or renewal of licenses on a willingness "to present representative community views on controversial issues . . . consistent with the ends and purposes of those constitutional provisions forbidding abridgment of freedom of speech and freedom of the press."[71]

The *Red Lion* decision stunned many observers because the Court adopted the communal argument about First Amendment protections, elevating the public interest over those of individual broadcasters. Critics decried what appeared to be a setback for free speech advocacy. But for scholars of congressional regulation of the institutions of democracy, *Red Lion* ought to be seen instead as an extension of the line of cases involving elections and campaigns for federal office dating back to *Ex Parte Curtis*, sanctioning the power of Congress to regulate democratic institutions and processes. In that light, *Red Lion* becomes merely a modern bookend to long-held free speech doctrine wherein the Supreme Court decided that Congress had the power to regulate the democratic processes, and then sanctioned the regulations imposed by Congress on the campaign system when it furthered the democratic theory of those institutions and processes. The examples of legislation affirmed as constitutional in *Ex Parte Curtis* and *Red Lion* show that Congress defined corruption as a threat to open and full political deliberation and enacted remedial regulations to address those concerns. And in nearly every case involving congressional attempts to regulate that kind of corruption, the Supreme Court held that those regulations were both constitutional and legitimate political powers of Congress.[72]

The marketplace metaphor of Holmes and Brandeis had, in *Red Lion*, been reified though not replaced, by an approach to First Amendment political speech rights that preferred and protected the interests of the listening public. Inspired by the technological breakthrough of the mass media and by the scarcity of spectrum, by 1969 the scarcity rationale had been transformed into an anthem to the ideal of deliberative decision-making in a democratic society. By ensuring publicly supported access to speak out on controversial issues to those who could not afford access on their own, lawmakers hoped that political debate would promote campaigns settled, not by the size of a person's pocketbook, but by the significance of their ideas. Ironically, even as the Warren court grounded *Red Lion* in the Radio Act rationale of scarcity, actual physical scarcity of spectrum had by 1969 mostly disappeared. Although the issue of scarcity and access to a diverse range of ideas remained fundamental to the preservation of the fairness doctrine, in 1987 the FCC, responding to the kind of complaints presented in the appellants' briefs in *Red Lion*, formally abolished the doctrine.

Red Lion stands for the proposition that aggregate power could monopolize mass media leading to the scarcity of diverse opinions, which first compelled the Radio Act Congress to regulation. Equalizing the opportunity for voices to deliberate in the marketplace of ideas required that some voices, more powerful, more authoritative, and wealthier than others, could be regulated to speak less so as to ensure that all voices might be heard by a public fundamentally entitled to that debate. From the first days of radio regulation, implicit in the public interest standard was the belief that the value of democratic deliberation carried with it a duty and responsibility to ensure that equality of access to the means of dissent remained a public commodity. For the drafters of the radio legislation and for the FCC rule makers, and finally for the courts, the regulation of the marketplace of ideas demanded full and fair access to both the spectrum and the specie of mass communication.[73]

From 1912 to 1969 mass media served as the technological catalyst for changes in the campaign finance system. Questions about candidate access, equal time, and the corruption of the public interest catalyzed the evolution of free speech doctrine on a separate and distinct though not wholly dichotomous track from early Progressive ideas about the First Amendment. The courts, in promoting a theory of deliberative democracy, carved out a free speech exception that permitted, even required that some voices be silenced so that the deliberative function of political debate could be heard. At the same time, Congress began to address concerns over the growing power of lobbyists, labor organizations, and the civil service, which it felt threatened to corrupt democratic institutions and processes in similar yet distinctly different ways. The political power of those groups in the 1930s caused a reaction from conservative reformers seeking to limit their political influence, which, in turn, reconfigured the debate over deliberative democracy in American elections and set the parameters of the campaign finance system for the last half of the twentieth century.[74]

Chapter Five

CAMPAIGN FINANCE "REFORM" IN THE NEW DEAL

Silencing the Emergent Coalition

The House committee investigating campaign expenditures in August 1944 thought they had CIO union leader Sidney Hillman dead to rights. A year earlier, in reaction to increased congressional legislation restricting the ability of unions to contribute directly to political campaigns, Hillman had organized the first political action committee. Investigated twice by the FBI and once by the Senate counterpart to the House committee, Hillman's political footwork had thus far danced around the edges of illegality. Hillman welcomed the opportunity to scotch the "fantastic stories" about a labor political slush fund as he was sworn in, dapper in his neat, double-breasted suit, relaxed and looking amiable. The "National Citizens-PAC" had, he told the committee, spent so far a mere $408,070 supporting the Democratic ticket. What's more, he argued, every step he had taken organizing this new fund-raising machine had hewed strictly to the very laws that Congress had passed prohibiting union spending in political elections. Try as it might, the committee failed to uncover any legal misstep that would allow them to crack down on the political action committee. Hillman and the union lawyers had responded to congressional regulation in the Hatch and War Labor Disputes acts by creating and then implementing an innovative campaign finance scheme that permitted union members to support candidates despite the best efforts of Congress to prohibit those contributions.[1]

During the New Deal and the early postwar years, the campaign finance system underwent significant change, severely limiting the political and speech rights of average Americans. Through passage of a series of acts intended to limit the political power of corporations, political organizations, and the rising influence of government employees and labor unions, Congress restricted the ability of those organizations to contribute to campaigns and influence congressional policy. In enacting this legislation, the proponents of reform returned to a rhetoric of corruption reminiscent of the Gilded Age debates that sought to regulate aggregate economic power by reifying democratic conceptions of the public interest. Between 1935 and 1947 Congress debated and passed legislation that promoted the connection between free labor and free political will, including laws that prohibited public holding companies from contributing to campaigns; that registered and regulated agent-lobbyists of foreign countries; that prohibited political contributions and limited political engagement by the growing class of federal and state civil servants; regulated the actions of domestic lobbyists, and that made illegal the direct contributions by labor unions to federal political campaigns. Coming amidst the World War II debates over the value and survival of democracy, these campaign finance measures ironically limited political participation by millions of Americans in civil society, and helped begin the dismemberment of the New Deal coalition that had developed during Franklin Roosevelt's four terms in office.

Many historians contend that the New Deal coalition of labor, small farmers, and African Americans eventually succumbed to internal conflict and conservatism over the economic reordering that its most radical supporters proposed. "A broad suspicion of centralized bureaucratic power—rooted in traditions of republicanism and populism," writes one historian, "remained a staple of popular discourse and a constant impediment to many liberal aims." When World War II brought Americans out of the Depression, the middle class, fearful that the growing federal bureaucracy would limit their "freedom and autonomy," reaffirmed the powerful chorus of antistatism that Jefferson, Jackson, and the Populists had earlier sung. Liberals reacted cautiously to those fears, but recognized that an over-powerful state, examples of which had wrought unparalleled destruction in Germany and Japan, provided a warning exemplar about centralized state power involving economic and social regulation. Just as progressives like Brandeis had warned about the excessive power of aggregate corporate wealth and bigness, the Leviathan state posed for some New Deal liberals an equivalent fear. "A generation which has watched the extreme of police-state organization in Soviet Russia and its equally frightening off-shoot, the Nazi and Fascist organizations in Germany and Italy," said Adolf Berle at a University of Pennsylvania lecture, "is not likely to underestimate the possibility that an overmastering state likewise can become a tyrant."[2]

Others contend that the demise of the New Deal coalition is overstated, or misplaced in time. Some suggest that the "Democratic order" was, in fact, maintained for years after the New Deal in the face of serious and continual challenges. For example, even the conservative assault on the labor rights secured under the Wagner Act, accepted, in the end, the main elements of the principles of unionism. These historians contend that the disintegrating forces of declining Democratic Party capacities, excessively reliant on the state "as a means of organizing and mobilizing Democratic adherents," is the explanation. This "demobilization," defined as "the declining ability to turn political support into actions that immediately benefit the political order, including voting," resulted from decreasing political activism due to a statist Democratic order that accentuated the national over local political parties. The old political and economic machines, which had successfully mobilized voters in the 1930s and early 1940s, gave way to clumsy efforts to engage from afar an increasingly diverse electorate with the new media resources. This view disputes the account of a conservative thematic shift that crippled the New Deal coalition, suggesting that there was "no end of reform," since the regime committed to "sustaining recent reforms and undertaking new ones was still in place." What had changed was the increasing complexity and difficulty in retaining support from the traditional constituencies of the Democratic order while engaging and appealing to new groups committed to revitalizing the social and economic reforms of the New Deal.[3]

The ongoing debate over the demise or reconfiguration of the New Deal coalition and its most provocative social policies then remits itself to one of two central explanations: political ideas evolved to more conservative grounds due to World War II fears (and the Cold War corollary) of the power of the leviathan state, or institutional shifts in the Democratic Party away from local and state party-building and toward national policies left the coalition disinterested, discouraged, and disaffected from continued New Deal policies and goals. Neither story, however, accounts for the dramatic shift in political power due to the reconfiguration of the American campaign finance system from 1935 to 1947. During those twelve important years, changes in the system severed the relationship between millions of civil servants and union workers with political parties. Political action committees emerged as surrogates for their policy involvement in a deliberative democratic process. The significance of that divorce would resound in the kinds of thematic detachment and political demobilization where the language of politics came to be spoken not by the grass-roots engagement of individuals and groups seeking broad national change, but instead by the increasing amount of money raised and contributed through attenuated political action committees with particular objectives. During those years, corruption was once again defined to mean the economic coercion of voters away from their electoral free will and became the sustaining argument for advocates of reform.

THE PUBLIC UTILITY HOLDING COMPANY ACT—Regulating Wealth and Power and the "Ginned-Up" Lobby

Even before the stock market crash of 1929 sent shockwaves through the economy, politicians and economists challenged the growing aggregation of public utility companies. The holding company, a corporate form of business whose sole purpose was to acquire and operate other corporations, became a favorite device of accumulating investors in the public utility business. The holding company, a late 1920s development, was an outgrowth of attempts to accumulate businesses under the umbrella of a single entity able to raise and wield the necessary capital to buy up entire businesses. While not a pure monopoly, public utilities had long been subject to federal regulation where they affected aspects of interstate commerce. Where they remained principally state-chartered businesses, however, federal regulation conflicted with the federalist understanding of the limits of regulating interstate commerce.[4]

In 1928 Congress directed the Federal Trade Commission to undertake an investigation of electric and gas utilities. Holding companies, due to their labyrinthine structures, invested none of their own money in the utilities themselves. Because of the lack of direct at-risk investment in the utilities, opponents felt that the holding company device led to artificial profiteering, unfair and excessive consumer pricing, opaque financial disclosure, and the default of and loss of investors' savings in holding-company organizations. The FTC recommended regulation of the holding companies including the eventual breakup of the massive aggregations of finances. By 1935 the 74th Congress instructed the House and Senate Committees on Interstate and Foreign Commerce to investigate their formation and operation.[5]

Disclosures from the committee investigations shocked even the most ardent New Dealers. Thirteen holding companies held three-quarters of all privately owned utility companies in the industry. United Corporation, Electric Bond and Share, and Insull, the three largest companies, controlled nearly 40 percent by themselves. Within the companies, there appeared a hodgepodge of organizational unity, with companies holding private utilities without regard to geography, use, or consumer delivery. In addition, the committee added, the holding companies profited from the arrangement, selling the individual utilities management, engineering, and construction services, often at greatly inflated prices unrelated to their fair economic value. The effect of these arrangements, reported the congressional committees, was a substantially inflated price structure for domestic electricity, detrimental to the public at large, but extraordinarily profitable to the holding companies. Since the holding companies "manufactured nothing," they avoided state regulation and federal regulation, which in 1935 remained a dim prospect.[6]

The House committee, chaired by Representative Sam Rayburn (D-TX), called Federal Trade Commission (FTC) officials and experts from the industry to account for the nature and rationale for the holding company structure. The legislation that resulted from the hearings was the Public Utility Company Act included Title I, the Public Utility Holding Company Act of 1935 (PUHCA). The act declared holding companies "affected with a national public interest" due to their national marketing of securities by mail and multistate marketing arrangements, regulated the formation of holding companies in the electric and gas industry, and provided for licensing, reporting, and security regulation. Defenders of the holding company form, such as Wendell Wilkie, then president of the New York holding company, Commonwealth and Southern Corporation, reminded the committee that "about the biggest misconception in all that has been said here about a utility business is, that there is no business in the world that requires money, such as the utility business." Wilkie stubbornly defended the holding company form as the most utilitarian form in an industry where huge amounts of capital were required to construct the expensive infrastructure of the massive generating and distribution systems of consumable electricity. The most drastic provision of the act provided that the newly formed Securities and Exchange Commission would, after January 1, 1940, have the power to compel the dissolution of every holding company that could not establish an independent economic reason for its existence.[7]

While the death-sentence provision caused the most concern, the bill still maintained profoundly conservative principles. Witnesses testified against the bigness of holding companies, calling it the antithesis of individualistic entrepreneurship. Rayburn called the holding device a pyramid scheme designed to "give a few small but powerful groups control of the billions of the public's money invested in the utility industry." Many believed the holding companies stifled the growth of individual business enterprise, since the accumulation and consolidation of the utility industry shut off individual creativity and stewardship at a time when the industry most needed those entrepreneurial features.[8]

Although the holding company was a relatively new form of business, regulatory enthusiasm used older republican ideals of individual entrepreneurship and competition to advocate for broad regulations. The statutory regulation of the holding companies also extended to the regulation of their political contributions and, interestingly, due in large part to a clumsy, politically coercive attempt to sway congressional opinion about the bill, to the duty and responsibility of the industry's privately employed lobbyists. Title I, Section 12 (h) of the PUHCA proposed making illegal the use of the mails or any means of interstate commerce, directly or indirectly, to make any contribution whatsoever in connection with the candidacy, nomination, election, or appointment of any person for or to any office or position in the government of the United States, a state, or any political subdivision of a state, or any agency, authority, or instrumentality of any one or more of the foregoing, or to make any contribution to or in support of any political party or committee or agency thereof.[9]

In several ways, this language mirrored the anticorporate contribution language of the Tillman Act of 1907. Recognizing that the holding company was a complex form of corporate entity, it made sense to extend the Tillman Act restrictions prohibiting political contributions to this new form of corporate entity. Yet this new provision extended the Tillman Act rationale and restriction far beyond the intentions of the Progressive era reform. Congress was not content to rely on the Tillman Act rationale to regulate corporate contributions in national elections; in fact, Congress extended the PUHCA campaign finance restriction beyond merely regulating contributions to federal candidate and candidate political committees. By using the mail and interstate commerce rationale, Congress established solid constitutional grounds for regulating political contributions.

PUHCA presciently recognized that the regulatory scheme being established would affect not merely elected officials, but appointed federal and state officers enlisted to supervise and regulate the utility industry. Furthermore, while the Supreme Court had struck down congressional attempts to regulate primary contributions in *Newberry v. United States,* PUHCA explicitly regulated contributions to nominees and appointees, neither of which was permitted under the corruption rationale of the *Newberry* decision. This language, though never the subject of a Supreme Court interpretation, would later be validated in light of the Supreme Court decision in *Classic v. United States* and of the expansive interstate commerce rationale adopted in *NLRB v. Jones & Laughlin Steel Corp.*[10]

The expansion of the corporate campaign finance restriction to holding companies was a logical extension of the Tillman Act rationale in light of the public testimony about holding-company abuses. Investors in utility companies organized under the economic umbrella of holding companies feared their power, through their control of voting stock, to arbitrarily set prices and management contracts that ignored fair contractual bargaining. In a message to Congress, President Franklin Roosevelt called for the regulation of holding companies specifically because they failed to protect the investor. "We seek to establish the sound principle," Roosevelt wrote, "that the holding company, so long as it is permitted to continue, should not profit from dealings with subsidiaries and affiliates where there is no semblance of actual bargaining to get the best value and the best price." Roosevelt made it clear that the danger of the holding company form was the confusion "of the function of control and management with that of investment" and that he considered holding companies an unwelcome aberration of the corporate form. "It is," he maintained, "a corporate invention which can give a few corporate insiders unwarranted and intolerable powers over other people's money" and destroy local control, concentrating "tyrannical power and exclusive opportunity to a favored few." The protection of independent stockholders and investors and the fear of aggregate corporate power and wealth unresponsive to the interests of investors and dangerous to the democratic system (the principal rationale for the corporate campaign prohibition of the Tillman Act) remained the main arguments supporting the regulation and restriction of campaign contributions by holding companies.[11]

Significantly for the creation of the modern campaign finance system, the PUHCA congressional debates spurred an effort by the holding company industry to lobby Congress that backfired on supporters of the act.

As the industry witnessed growing support for the bill, it engaged in a dishonest lobbying scheme designed to persuade Congress of the radical, un-American nature of the legislation. John W. Davis, speaking before the American Bar Association, told the assembled crowd that "the holding company bill was the gravest threat to the liberties of the American citizen that has emanated from the halls of Congress in my time." During the 1935 hearings, congressmen began to receive thousands of telegrams from their constituents decrying the regulation of the holding companies. By early February 1935 letters and telegrams flooded into the Capitol Hill congressional offices from nearly every congressional district in the country. Individual representatives received visits from utility company officials claiming the bill would destroy their state utilities. Senator Harry S. Truman (D-MO), refusing to knuckle under to industry pressure, burned thirty thousand telegrams and messages sent to his office. Members were accustomed to, though not pleased with, the pressure from the utility lobby in Washington, D.C. The death penalty provision in the Wheeler-Rayburn bill, which would require the break-up of holding companies, however, ended any ambivalence from the utilities, and they fought the bill with all the tools at their disposal.[12]

Newspaper accounts indicated the public utility lobby employed more lobbyists (660) during the legislative fight than there were members of Congress (527). Intense outside pressure and face to face meetings with congressional opponents of the act left many fence-sitters exasperated. Congressmen received over 800,000 messages opposing the bill if it included the death penalty provision. Representative Denis J. Driscoll (D-PA), for example, received 816 messages from a single borough in his Twentieth District. When the death sentence amendment came to a vote in the House, it was defeated, 216–146. The weakened bill, without the death penalty provision, passed by a vote of 323–81 and went to conference committee with the Senate-passed version. Ironically, it was that same flood of messages from individual home districts in the early summer weeks of 1935 that turned the tide in favor of the bill and the death penalty provision those in the industry most despised. As the proponents settled into gloomy despair over the defeat of the death penalty provision, new revelations about the utility industry lobbying campaign roiled Congress.[13]

Late one evening, Driscoll noticed that the names on the messages did not ring his elective bell—he had not heard of many of these "constituents." When a new batch of telegrams came to him from yet another borough in his district, he personally checked with the local Western Union office only to discover that the return addresses were fake. The realization that holding companies had ginned up the "opposition" brought renewed vigor to the bill's supporters. As the debate continued amid unremitting pressure, many congressmen, now aware that their own constituents did not oppose the bill, resisted the bitter lobbying pressure.[14]

Other revelations created persistent concerns about the lobbying campaign. Representative Ralph Brewster (D-ME) alleged that Tommy Corcoran, in the employ of the lobby, had threatened to stop construction of a dam in his district should Brewster support the death penalty provision. While the charges were never proved, and may have been misunderstood by Brewster, they did lead to an announcement by the House and Senate of an investigation into the lobbying techniques of the utility lobby. The Senate appointed Senator Hugo Black (D-AL) to lead the investigation, and Black took immediate action. The Committee surprised chief lobbyist Philip Gadsden of the committee on Public Utility Education, serving him with a hastily prepared subpoena, then physically brought him before the Special Committee for questioning, without preparation, attorneys, or handlers. While the House investigated the Brewster-Corcoran dispute, Black began a skillful, trial-lawyer–like examination of Gadsden and Associated Gas and Electric executive Howard Hopson, that revived the holding company bill and demonstrated the undemocratic nature of the lobbying techniques employed in the fight to defeat it.[15]

In the first day of questioning from Black, Gadsden testified that the lobby had spent $301,865 to defeat the death penalty provision of the bill. Asked whether the lobby spent money on telegrams to members of Congress urging defeat of the bill, Gadsden replied, "Only on our own telegrams." It became apparent, however, that the lobby had indeed paid for mailing services and public relations firms, and solicited telegrams from a variety of sources, and when that failed to produce the public opinion onslaught intended to convince Congress of widespread opposition to the bill, the lobby simply manufactured the telegrams and sent them through their hired agents to "generate the storm of apparently spontaneous protest."[16]

Black's committee uncovered proof of hundreds of thousands of manufactured telegrams paid for by public utilities at a cost of more than $700,000. Senator Lewis Schwellenbach (D-WA) asked why the lobby of the Associated Gas and Electric System, which had not paid a dividend since 1928, could justify payment of those expenses out of profits properly due its shareholders. Although industry witnesses admitted burning some of the records of the lobbying campaign, there was proof enough to compel Ursil E. Beach, head of the securities department at A.G. & E., to admit that he had ordered both the destruction of the records and the payment for the massive telegram campaign with cash in order to hide the origin of the payments.[17]

Due to the revelations, the conference committee on the public utility holding company bill settled on a compromise worked out by SEC administrator Felix Frankfurter that revived a different version of the death penalty provision. Public utility holding companies would remain legal, but the Securities and Exchange Commission would have the power to regulate interstate arrangements, including the control of more than one integrated public utility system if additional systems could not economically stand alone or were so dispersed as to prevent efficient management, operation, or regulation. Roosevelt, acceding to the compromise, signed the bill on August 26.[18]

While opponents of the holding company corporate form were disappointed with the eventual compromise, the fight over the bill and the tactics of the utility lobby made the restrictive campaign finance provisions of the bill an easy call. With no significant opposition, the final bill included restrictions on campaign contributions to candidates, appointees, political parties, political committees, or agents. The restrictions applied to candidacies, nominations, and elections and extended to cover any federal government, state, state political subdivision, or any "agency, authority, or instrumentality of any one or more of the foregoing." Furthermore, the act made it illegal for any person employed or retained by a holding company, or any subsidiary of a holding company, "to present, advocate, or oppose any matter" before Congress, any member or committee of Congress, or any Commission or member of any commission unless they had filed a statement or retainer that disclosed the nature of the arrangement and compensation received and expenses incurred in the lobbying arrangement.[19]

These restrictions on campaign contributions and lobbying activities of public holding companies that arose out of PUHCA greatly expanded the reach of the campaign finance system, and diminished the free speech and association rights of corporate enterprises and their hired lobbyists. The utility company campaign to intentionally manufacture public opinion through telegrams from nonexistent constituents reaffirmed the New Dealers' zeal to remake a political society where the people spoke and were accounted for, even if it meant that the civil and political liberties of some segments of the polity were regulated and restricted. The actions of the utility lobby during the congressional fight over PUHCA reaffirmed the long-held belief that corporate economic resources could be misused to generate unequal and undemocratic political power, and that representative government had a legitimate right to regulate the use of that economic power in the electoral system. Only when the debate forum promoted a fair distribution of political access would deliberation on public policy represent the democratic ideal. For New Deal proponents, as for the Gilded Age and Progressive reformers before them, regulating campaign finances and disclosing lobbying expenses and connections were a rational means of expanding the opportunity for representative and open debate on public issues.

THE 1936 ELECTION—Business Fat Cats and the Emergent Purring of Labor

The first four years of the New Deal created the nascent beginnings of a coalition of groups seeking to expand the regulatory role of the federal government over economic and social affairs. Whether the New Deal was a radical innovation or a continuation of earlier themes in American politics, whether it was a "watershed in American history or a deepening and widening stream that had its sources in earlier periods," for New Deal supporters advocating for more fundamental political change, the election of 1936 became the first real political test of the American public's acceptance of New Deal policies.[20]

The growth in the size and scope of the federal government was the most visible ramification of the early New Deal. Washington, D.C. during the Depression grew from a population of 63,000 in March 1933 to 166,000 by 1940. The shift from a payroll of major industries to one that predominated with government workers demonstrated the growth of federal employees as a measure of the newly created responsibilities of the administrative government. The growth of the federal workforce outside Washington dwarfed the capital city growth by several-fold. Under the administration of Harry Hopkins, the direct relief of the Federal Emergency Relief Administration granted $500 million to states on a direct and matching grant program. Hopkins spent $5 million within two hours of taking office and by 1935 had spent over $3 billion employing hundred of thousands of previously unemployed workers. The Civil Works Administration spent $400 million of federal funds for relief work, and by November 1933, was paying out wages to 814,511 workers. By Christmas that year, the CWA employed nearly 3.5 million. A month later, that number had climbed to 4.2 million.

The Works Progress Administration (WPA) would prove to be the New Deal's most lasting and significant employment agency. Fearful that the "dole" would destroy a man's spirit, Hopkins convinced Roosevelt to ask Congress for $4.8 billion to launch the work program that envisioned labor-intensive public projects that paid a real day's wages for a real day's work. By December 1935 the WPA planned to employ at steady work 3.5 million of the nation's unemployed. The benefits of the program to national economic recovery remain disputed, but the WPA and other New Deal jobs programs created and emboldened a labor force that realized that in FDR, they had no better friend in the White House. The growing size and gratitude of the federally funded workforce led to concerted attempts by New Deal supporters and by local party bosses to employ that ready labor force, and its massive economic largess, on behalf of the candidacy of Roosevelt and others in the 1936 election. That effort ran counter to early civil service reformist concerns about the independence of the governmental labor force, and about the coercive effect of connecting government employment with political loyalty through campaign contributions and electioneering.[21]

Almost from its inception, the 1936 campaign proved a battle in which the legions of government workers were employed, or drafted rather, to finance and man the political ramparts. The Winnebago County, Illinois Democratic Jackson Day dinner called on 175 WPA staffers to pay $3 per plate, of which $2 would go to fund the 1936 national campaign war chest. Jackson Day fund-raisers became the initial assault to replenish the campaign coffers of the Democratic Party across the country. The party used the fund-raising dinners to pay off a $378,615 deficit left over from the 1932 election. Postmaster General James Farley, who also served during the campaign as Democratic

National Chairman, denied any wrongdoing in the dinners, although the political assessment of public employees remained illegal.[22]

Yet it was not merely the dinners that caused alarm from opponents and civic groups fearful of a political takeover of the civil service. The political assessment of federal officers and employees, disdained and illegal since 1876, once again rose throughout the country, especially among the postmasters that Postmaster Farley directly controlled. Speaking before a Republican group, Natalie F. Couch of Nynack, New York, charged that Farley had instructed all officeholders to "give one month's salary to the Rockland County campaign fund for use in the upcoming election" and thus, one employee had written his mother that he would be unable to buy an overcoat due to the assessment. As reports of coerced assessments began to roll in from across the country, Washington politicians, smelling a scandal, demanded an investigation.[23]

Senator Arthur Vandenburg (R-MI), asserting that "a small scandal now was better than a big stench later," called for a nationwide investigation of reports that politicians "were collecting campaign funds from relief workers." WPA administrator Harry Hopkins, while admitting sporadic incidents might have occurred, denied responsibility for what he called "the acts of dumb politicians" doing the soliciting. But Hopkins's denial did little to stop the growing concern in 1936 that public employees, the renewed focus of the reformist zeal, were in danger of having their free electoral will, and right of voluntary contribution to political campaigns, coerced and corrupted by the threat of job losses or postelection retribution. In nearly every region of the country, reports about the solicitation of campaign contributions from WPA employees appeared to confirm the worst fears about the Roosevelt campaign. The allegations became so intense that in September, Senator Augustine Lonergan (D-CT) announced that the Senate Campaign Expenditures Committee would hold hearings on some of the most egregious allegations of assessment coercion arising in the WPA field offices in Pennsylvania, Michigan, and Texas.[24]

Republicans also alleged Democratic Party corruption over a scheme to send out letters to all postmasters over Postmaster General Farley's signature, calling on them to contribute to Democratic campaign funds. Farley denied he ever signed such a letter, but the letter calling for each postmaster to sell a set of "nominator tickets" at $1.00 each, with those funds going to the campaign fund, did exist. Representative Charles A. Halleck (R-IN), who would later support the attempt to enact the "Clean Politics Act" (known as the Hatch Act), doubted the plausibility of Farley's "rubber stamp signature explanation."[25]

There were also allegations of administration coercion of businesses in two separate fund-raising schemes. One involved the withholding or canceling of government contracts to businesses antipathetic to the New Deal, and the second involved the infamous Democratic Convention Book of 1936. Rumors that the administration punished unsupportive businesses arose during the campaign. Republicans on the Lonergan Committee raised these concerns in retaliation for the investigation the committee conducted into charges that businesses had threatened their own workers with dismissal and layoffs should they vote for Roosevelt. Lonergan himself became subject to charges when, in response to allegations that Oil Country Specialties Manufacturing Company of Coffeyville, Kansas had "asked its employees to vote for" Republican candidate governor Alf M. Landon, he sent a letter threatening the company with "vigorous investigation." Reports alleged that the Jones & Laughlin Steel Company charged that administration officials threatened a loss of government contracts that seemed to be supported by Secretary of Commerce Harold L. Ickes's cancellation of a $40,000 steel contract the government had previously awarded. Company officials denied any coercion, however, maintaining that they had a good relationship with the government.[26]

The facts surrounding the Democratic Convention Book of 1936, however, are not disputed. Campaign books were not new ideas. Earlier campaigns published accounts of the campaigns or biographies of the candidates in order to raise funds. In 1936 the 300-page volume consisted of a history of the Democratic Party, the duties and history of Cabinet officers, and a recounting of the achievements of the first term of the Roosevelt administration. The Democratic National Committee sold the paperback edition for $2.50, the hardback for $5.00, and the deluxe leather edition signed by Roosevelt for between $100 and $250 each. Advertisements for the book, many purchased by national corporations prohibited from directly contributing to the campaign, cost $2,500 per ten-by-thirteen-inch page. Although the book directly violated no law, and raised only $250,000 for the Democratic campaign finance fund, it appeared to be a surreptitious attempt to evade the corporate campaign restrictions of the Tillman and Federal Corrupt Practices Acts by creating an opportunity for businessmen to "buy" advertising and souvenir books, and thereby contribute illegally excessive individual or corporate funds to the Roosevelt campaign. In 1937 the Lonergan Committee investigated whether the sales of advertising and the book violated the Federal Corrupt Practices Act of 1925, and it, along with the Justice Department, failed to find any significant violations of the act. The controversy, however, did much to expose the limitations of the existing campaign finance law. Since the purchase of either advertising or the books themselves acted to put funds into the Roosevelt campaign coffers, either by individuals or corporations subject to a contribution limit or prohibition, the failure of the FCPA to regulate such activity constituted a gaping loophole.[27]

Democratic allegations of widespread campaign finance abuses by businesses, reminiscent of those that occurred during the 1896 McKinley-Bryan campaign, also roiled the election waters during the campaign. The American Liberty League, a business-supported group organized to oppose many of the New Deal policies, paid salaries of $10,000 annually to several of its top executives. Its required reports filed with the House under the Federal Corrupt Practices Act also disclosed that the Republican National Committee was paying its research chief, J. Bennett Gordon, a salary of $13,400 (an amount equivalent to $177,000 in current dollars). The salary paid to political campaign professionals by the RNC shocked many observers since the salaries were often several times larger than the amount an entire state committee could lawfully raise and spend in a statewide election. The Committee heard witnesses describe a campaign by businesses to coerce their own employees, through threats, intimidation, and payroll check notices, to vote against Roosevelt or lose their income security. Democratic senator Charles Guffey (D-PA) called on the Lonergan Committee to investigate charges that Carnegie-Illinois Steel and Jones & Laughlin Steel companies of Pennsylvania had "coerced their employees by various means to do their political bidding." Throughout the industrial sections of Illinois, Indiana, Michigan, Ohio, and Pennsylvania, employers printed notices on employees pay envelopes alerting them to the likelihood of a 4 percent payroll deduction effective on January 1, 1937, due to the Social Security Act. These notices blurred the line between direct campaigning and advocacy by the corporations. Republicans countered and demanded that the committee investigate labor leader John L. Lewis, said to be "forcing members of the United Mine Workers to vote the Democratic ticket."[28]

The complaints, Democratic and Republican alike, were not simply that huge contributions would corrupt the politicians and lead to poor policy based on favors and fraternization. Instead, the main complaint that resonated in the 1936 election was that voters, denied their free will by the coercive threat of retaliatory dismissal (government and business alike), and by the corruptive tactics employed by government agencies or businesses, would lose their ability to cast a ballot based on a rational assessment of the candidates and their stands on the issues. The corruption was a coercion of the deliberative processes, compelling voters to cast their ballot inimical to the public interest. In response in March 1936, Congress proposed a bill that would have made illegal an attempt by any person or corporation to influence the voting of its employees "through fear or intimidation." The Senate passed the bill by unanimous consent on February 4, but the bill languished in the House. One member of the administration gleefully suggested the bill would "tie the American Liberty League into knots."[29]

By August reports surfaced that the Democratic campaign fund had reached $3,500,000. Republicans calculated that franking privileges by New Deal executive departments increased from 1931–1932 public expenditures by $45,000,000. Republicans appealing to supporters for their own campaign funds included the cost of public works projects as part of the Democratic "fund" available to win the election. After the campaign, the Lonergan Committee report disclosed that in 1936, the Democratic National Committee, which led to Roosevelt's stunning landslide, spent $3,400,000 and the Republican National Committee spent $7,400,000, both amounts far in excess of the legal limits imposed by the FCPA. The committee recommended closing the contribution language loopholes and simplifying the reporting requirements of the Federal Corrupt Practices Act, including limiting each major political party to total expenditures of $1,000,000 for all presidential, senatorial and congressional candidates.[30]

One of the most striking discoveries of the Lonergan Committee was the massive increase in independent labor union spending in the 1936 campaign. Union campaign spending during the 1936 campaign demonstrated that many unions began to reshape their role in the political system away from being outside activists and into becoming integral players in the nomination and election process. Not content to educate their own membership through union newspapers and local bulletins, unions organized to raise campaign funds in order to have a say in the nomination and election of candidates supportive of pro-labor policies. More importantly, as International Typographical Union president Charles P. Howard stated, unions must become active in the campaign finance system to counter the power of "industry where the great corporations have been successful in defeating trade union organizations in the past."[31]

Some unions still faced the dysfunction and division between the craft and trade membership, beset by race, class and organizational differences of opinion. Yet despite the differences, unions eager to support Roosevelt as a reward for the Democratic Party's passage of the National Labor Relations Act of 1935 (referred to as the "Wagner Act" after its principal sponsor, Senator Robert Wagner, Democrat of New York) connected the rhetoric of "unity and centralized control" with adequate financing that they intended to use to educate their workers on behalf of their political supporters. In the heated political and legislative battles of the first term of the New Deal, labor supporters (who witnessed the passage of the Agricultural Adjustment Act of 1933, the National Industrial Recovery Act of 1933, the Securities Exchange Act of 1934, the Banking Act of 1935, the Social Security Act of 1935, and the Wagner Act) came to understand that "unionization . . . requires a compelling set of ideas and institutions, both self-made and governmental, to give labor's cause power and legitimacy," and the decision to raise and spend campaign finances in the 1936 election recognized that unionization was "a political project" that could eventually transcend the ethnic and class differences that had limited labor's ultimate success.[32]

The results impressed even the most skeptical observer. Overall, unions invested over $750,000 in Roosevelt's campaign. John L. Lewis's United Mine Workers gave $469,000 and two other CIO affiliates gave $141,000 more. The United Mine Worker expenditure alone was fivefold greater than the total American Federation of Labor's total contributions raised for political purposes in the preceding thirty years. One-third of the campaign funds were direct contributions to the Democratic National Committee, with one-half going to Labor's Non-Partisan League and to the American Labor Party. Along with the indirect expenditures by national unions and local affiliates, union spending, which was regulated only by the relatively porous provisions of the Federal Corrupt Practices Act of 1925, exploded on behalf of their New Deal friends, and contributed to the massive outpouring of labor support in behalf of Roosevelt's victory.[33]

During the 1936 election, Democrats and Republicans drew partisan battle lines over sharp and bitter administration rhetoric about class differences, which created an emboldened political class willing to don the necessary armaments to win the war. Roosevelt fiercely attacked what he called the "economic royalists," selfish and self-interested businessmen who had counterattacked against New Deal policies intended to help the poorest in society. His willingness to use the power of the federal government to support widespread economic improvement, and his opposition to the judiciary's conservative belief in limited government and the protection of property, "divided the country on issues unlike [it] had been since the election contest of 1896." At the same time, the rising cost of campaigns, increasingly reliant on more expensive electronic media outlets and techniques, increased the demand for campaign finances.[34]

The 1936 campaign reinvigorated political life, at least for the short term. Unions especially witnessed the "great political game" being played out, and opted to join the fray in full force. While many observers dismayed over the "propaganda machines" of the Republican and Democratic parties, fearful that the use of patronage and job benefits, of public assistance or business contracts, were being used to coerce the voters away from their duty to vote their consciences, labor groups realized that campaign financing on behalf of their favored candidates or against their fervent foes was an essential part of that political game. But the addition of labor and the expanded federal workforce coincidentally increased concerns that labor would itself become a political power, or worse yet, a political party, that labor would coerce its union members, and that the administration would coerce the mass of new federal employees to exercise their free electoral will, not out of a communal sense of the common good, but out of fear of retribution and reprisal. These fears, coupled with a recognition of how integral campaign financing had become to the caliper of political power, created a conservative movement that adopted reformist rhetoric about coercive corruption, and then began in 1939 through the passage of the "Clean Politics Act" and continuing until the passage of the Taft-Hartley Act of 1947 to neuter and depoliticize an entire class of working Americans.[35]

THE CLEAN POLITICS ACT (HATCH I AND HATCH II)—Saving Democracy by Silencing Government Employees

The political involvement of federal employees during the 1936 and 1938 elections created a mood for reform in Congress. From the early origins of the campaign finance system, winning parties had used the political spoils of office to reward supporters and punish their foes. The 1876 Anti-

Assessment Act had led to the passage of the civil service reforms in the Pendleton Act of 1883, and the Supreme Court had sustained in *Ex Parte Curtis* the campaign finance regulation of civil service employees. The massive New Deal expansion of federal and state payrolls, financed in large degree by federal relief funds flowing into the states, created a renewed concern that unless some regulation occurred, public employees would again be coerced into becoming a political arm of the party in power.[36]

This use of government employees in the 1936 campaign led Senator Carl A. Hatch (D-NM) to introduce legislation to clean up the civil service. Hatch's bill was the outgrowth of abuses uncovered by the Senate Campaign Expenditures Committee chaired by Senator Morris Sheppard (D-TX). The hearings and report disclosed substantial political activity, much of it opposed by local farmers and relief workers who felt harassed and coerced by the implied threats from the activity, in all parts of the country. Senator Hatch described the bill, officially titled the "Clean Politics Act of 1939," as necessary for "the removal of politics from relief" with a goal to "place all non–policy-making officials and employees of the federal government under the same rules as the civil service." The bill made it unlawful "for any person to intimidate, threaten, or coerce, or to attempt to intimidate, threaten, or coerce, any other person for the purpose of interfering with the right of such other person to vote or vote as he may choose, or of causing such other person to vote for, or not to vote for, any candidate for the office of President, Vice President, Presidential elector, Member of the Senate, or Member of the House of Representatives" at any election. The act applied to any person employed by the United States or any "department, independent agency, or other agency (including any corporation controlled by the United States or any agency thereof)," but did not extend to state departments or agencies that may have federal government connections. Senate Bill 1871, coauthored by Senators Morris Sheppard (D-TX) and Warren Austin (R-VT), passed the Senate on April 13, 1939, but languished in the House.[37]

To address the threatened loss of employment, the law banned any promise, "direct or indirect, for employment, position, work, compensation, or any benefit" as consideration, favor, or reward for the support of or opposition to any candidate or political party in any election. The law reenacted the anti-assessment provisions of the 1876 Act, making unlawful any solicitation or receipt of any assessment, subscription, or contribution for any political purpose whatever from any person known to be employed by any employer who received funds from any act of Congress. Furthermore, the law banned the disclosure or receipt of the names of public employees to any political candidate, committee, or campaign manager for political purposes. For any of those violations, the bill set the penalty at a fine of $1,000 and a year in jail.[38]

Proponents contended that the law protected public employees from the coercive effects of political pressure exerted by the government or its political officers. Addressing the concerns of the reformers who saw the abuses in 1936 and 1938, Senator Hatch's bill effectively prevented all attempts, direct or implied, to put pressure on federal employees to vote against their conscience out of fear or coercion. However, Senate Bill 1871 was more expansive. Section 9 of the bill, its most controversial provision, accomplished two objectives. First, it prohibited any federal employee from using "his official authority or influence for the purpose of interfering with an election or affecting the result thereof." This provision seemed a reasonable regulation based on practical considerations about the potential for influence from superiors. The second half provision of Section 9 severely restricted the political rights of those employees themselves by providing that "No officer or employee in the executive branch of the Federal Government, or any agency or department thereof, shall take any active part in political management or in political campaigns. All such employees retain the right to vote as they may choose and to express their opinions on all political subjects." The penalty for violation of that provision was removal from office. That new restriction on the political rights of federally funded employees sparked major opposition, precisely because it extended the corruption rationale beyond the fear that employees would be coerced away from the free exercise of their votes, into a new assumption that all direct political activity by a distinct class of the polity was presumptively corruptive.[39]

Hatch explained the necessity for the provision by recounting the role of federal employees at political party conventions. "If there has ever been an abuse of patronage in the history of the country," he explained with hyperbolic understatement, "it has been in the packing of political conventions by employees." He decried the power of the party elite, supplemented by the use of the political employee class, to control the nominations. "It is a well-recognized fact that nominations by national conventions are the exclusive work of politicians," he claimed, "which the electorate of the whole U.S. is permitted only to witness in gaping expectancy and to ratify at the polls in the succeeding November." His fear, expressed perhaps by the lack of party representation at the convention from western state senators, was that the delegations were unrepresentative due to the increase of those federal employees, and that the national party could "usurp control of party conventions in the states."[40]

The opposition to the Clean Politics Act (Hatch I) in the House arose from a very different understanding of the role of parties and patronage in the political process. In debate on July 20, 1939, Congressman Claude Parsons (D-IL) rose to make a point of order before H.R. 251 was called up for debate. "Since this House is about to witness the demise of the political parties in this country," he warned, "I think a quorum should be present at this embalming." At issue was a key provision of the House bill, added to the Senate version that provided "[n]othing shall be deemed to affect or deny any person to state his preference with reference to any candidate, *or to participate in the activities of any political party.*" Opponents of Hatch I considered the parties not merely helpful, but fundamental to American democracy and the operation of its institutions. Many House members worried that the exclusion of the federal workforce from party politics would severely hurt the effectiveness and influence of the party system.[41]

Representative Emmanuel Celler (D-NY) put his objections in more blatantly political terms. "The Republicans," he argued, "seen to assume a 'holier than thou' attitude. I remind them that they perhaps have clearly in mind that they have easier sources of campaign funds than we Democrats. Any deficit they have can easily be made up by a mere plea to a Morgan, a Rockefeller, a Grundy, and others whom Theodore Roosevelt used to call malefactors of great wealth." So while supporters of the bill claimed a healthy need to disinfect the political system from the "political ghouls and vampires" and "venal political scavengers" who exploited those needy employees on relief by assessing their meager wages for political purposes, others viewed this forcing of a shift in campaign finances resources as nothing more than a crassly political adjustment of the medicine of reform. In August 1939, after over thirteen hours of debate, Congress passed Hatch I by a vote of 241–134. President Roosevelt, sanguine about the effects of the bill, noting that it failed to regulate the political activities of state and local employees, nonetheless signed the bill on August 2, 1939. He hoped, he said in his message to Congress, "that the bill would be administered so that the right to free speech will remain."[42]

Almost as soon as the bill passed, Senator Hatch began work on amending the bill to include those state and local employees the bill had excluded. Working feverishly to get the bill approved before the 1940 elections, Hatch introduced amendments to the 1939 bill (referred to as "Hatch I") that expanded the "act to prevent pernicious political activities" to include "officers or employees of any State or local agency whose principal employment is in connection with any activity which is financed in whole or in part by loans or grants made by the United States or by any Federal agency." Roosevelt had requested the change, and Hatch thought there would be little opposition to the amendment. Hatch I had, after all, passed the Senate comfortably and the House by a margin of nearly 2 to 1.[43]

The National Civil Service Reform League, a longtime proponent of depoliticizing the public employee sector, lauded the amendments, stating that "confidence in impartial, nonpartisan administration of government is greatly enhanced if public employees are kept out of partisan politics." But Hatch II ran into immediate opposition when senators learned that the amendments to cover state employees likewise would extend to federal employees in the District of Columbia, directly affecting many of their own congressional staff employees. Senator Sherman Minton (D-IN), a staunch New Deal supporter, promised to lead the attack on the floor. Minton, the majority whip, may have agreed about the value of depoliticizing public employees, but he focused on the primary dispute made during the Hatch I debate. He proposed an amendment that removed the restrictions on political activities of public employees, modifying Hatch II to provide only protection for those employees from coercive assessment pressure.[44]

The debate soon turned to a consideration of the conflict between the proper role and power of government to support and regulate partisan political activities, and the rights of citizens to exercise their inalienable American rights of free speech, franchise, and political engagement. "The curse of democracy," declared Senator Minton, "is that you cannot get citizens interested enough in politics to get out to the polls and vote—and here, we are outlawing all vigorous political activity." Hatch II opponents envisioned a system that promoted engaged political activity, but prohibited any activity that tended to coerce or threaten the free will of any voter. They argued that citizen involvement in party political activity was invigorating, not corrupting to the democratic process, and essential to open deliberation in political affairs.[45]

Opponents unsuccessfully tried to characterize Minton's authorizing of political activity as a fight between the elite and the grunts of the political processes. Hatch II contained an exemption for policy-making officials that meant that the Hatch II restrictions applied only to state, local, and non–policy-making federal employees. Senator John Miller (D-AR), an opponent of the regulation argued that this meant that high officials of the government would control the political policy and party platforms, while "the man who pushes the wheelbarrow, the clerk, and the other small employees can only vote." Some members of Congress who had voted for Hatch I now worried about the effect that Hatch II would have on legitimate party activity.[46]

Senate Majority Leader Alben Barkley (D-KY) shifted the tide in favor of Hatch II when he spoke in favor of the bill. Barkley, who had been instrumental in killing a 1938 attempt to enact the public employee regulations, bluntly told the Senate that some members of his party had asked him not to speak his convictions. "When the time comes," he intoned, "that I must stifle my convictions, I will call a conference of the Democratic members and tender my resignation as majority leader." The threat became reality when days later, Senator Fred Brown (D-NH) offered an amendment that barred from political activities and political contributions every corporate officer, stockholder, or corporate employee benefiting from federal grants, loans, tariffs, or contracts. Brown meant to expose the inequity of treating one group of citizens who benefited from federal employment differently from others who benefited less directly from that same government largess. Faced with an insurrection from inside his own party, Barkley offered to resign if the Democratic members determined to caucus over the stalemate.[47]

Brown's amendment dramatically shifted the focus of the debate from that of protecting workers from politically motivated coercion and toward the role of big money in elections. "Money is the thing that corrupts politics in this country," Senator Minton declared, and the Senate ought to fight hard to rid the system of the big contributors. What Minton had in mind were the kinds of contributions that the Senate Campaign Committee's investigation had disclosed in 1936, including campaign contributions made by the Pew family of Pennsylvania exceeding $310,000, John D. Rockefeller's $150,000 contribution, the Du Pont family aggregate contributions exceeding $600,000, and J.P. Morgan and George F. Baker's contributions from the Morgan banking empire, of $55,000 and $61,000 respectively.[48]

As the Democratic filibuster continued, other Senate business sat idle. Farm state senators, anxious to see appropriations in the farm bill passed to aid their ailing constituents, questioned the priority of the Hatch bill. A few days later, Senator John Bankhead (D-AL) offered an amendment unpalatable to Democrats and Republicans alike that he thought would kill the bill. The amendment, addressing the big money concerns, established a limit of $5,000 for any amounts "expended, contributed, furnished, or advanced by one person or corporation directly or indirectly" for political purposes. The amendment made violation of the contribution limit a felony punishable by up to five years. In a mixture of frustration to move the bill and an honest belief that the incessant violations of the Federal Corrupt Practices Act, which had not been criminally prosecuted since the Vare and Smith cases in 1924, required an enforceable remedy, a coalition of Democratic and Republican senators voted to adopt the amendment. Surprisingly, proponents failed when they tried to recommit the bill to remove the spending limits. Hatch II, which prohibited federal and state employee involvement in federal campaigns, and included the campaign contribution-solicitation provision, passed the Senate, 58–28 on March 18, 1940. Democrats represented 27 of the 28 votes opposing the bill.[49]

In the House, the judiciary subcommittee unanimously approved an amendment that further limited campaign contributions. Hatch II, which had begun as a modest extension of Hatch I to state and local employees paid out of federal funds, evolved into a major piece of campaign finance legislation. The subcommittee amendment limited party national committee expenditures to $3,000,000 annually, substantially below the $8,065,524 and the $5,030,848 that had been spent by Republican and Democratic national committees, respectively, in the 1936 elections. Senator Bankhead's poison-pill amendment, intended to kill the bill, had instead reconfigured the debate from one about the fairness of federal regulation and the role of the federal government in regulating the actions of state employees who were subject to the same kind of coercion Hatch I protected federal employees from, into a debate about congressional regulation of large contributions and party expenditures that could corrupt and coerce voters in elections.[50]

From the White House, Roosevelt, contemplating but demure about a bid for a third term, called on Congress to pass Hatch II. After House Judiciary Committee Chairman William H. Sumners (D-TX) pigeonholed the bill in committee, members of his own party moved to bring it before the full House for consideration. Roosevelt's call for passage encouraged House proponents to proceed, and under pressure from the president and the rebel Democratic House members, the judiciary committee sent Hatch II to the full House on May 7, 1940. Sumners bitterly denounced the action, calling the bill "a mess," and declaring "the Republic is being destroyed by the same sort of processes as those carried out in this bill." Sumners decried the power of the Civil Service Commission to define "pernicious political activity," a move he worried would create too much power in the "temporary God almighty up here in Washington." He called the members who had petitioned for discharge of the bill from his committee "fools," and declared that Hatch II, by making the Civil Service Commission the arbiter of state political activity, "slandered" the state citizens since it meant they could not govern themselves "and preserve the purity of elections in their own respective district—Talk about American citizenry! Talk to me about decency in American citizens believing in American government! Why don't you turn it over to Hitler and be done with it. That is where you are heading for."[51]

The debate on Hatch II carried into the summer of 1940. The House passed the bill with the new campaign finance amendments, and the Senate voted to agree to the House version. As finally approved, Hatch II also defined labor unions as organizations that could not contribute or loan more than $5,000 in any year to a political party. Hatch II also incorporated the criminal penalties of the Federal Corrupt Practices Act of 1925. President Roosevelt signed the bill on July 19, 1940.

FOREIGN AND DOMESTIC THREATS TO DEMOCRACY

Most experts have ignored the passage of Hatch I and II in their discussions of the making of the American campaign finance system. Seen as a continuation of earlier civil service reform, the Hatch Act debates and controversy seem strangely detached from the Corrupt Practices Act debates of the early 1900s. In a larger context, however, the passage of Hatch I and II demonstrated the compelling connections and contradictions between the rhetoric of corruption, economic and political power, and the democratic ideal. Even as the debates about the effect of coercing federally funded employees raged in Congress, the antidemocratic menaces of Nazism, fascism, and communism spread incessant fear about securing the safety and security of democracy and democratic ideals. Moreover, despite a general agreement on those ideals, there remained a much disputed route to getting there.

The specter of totalitarianism hung like a thick night fog during the debates on Hatch I and II. Nazi Germany had begun its march throughout Europe, crushing its opponents in Germany, occupying the Rhineland and Sudetenland, and in March of 1939, invading and taking Czechoslovakia. By August Hitler's armies looked invincible in Europe, and the Nazi-Soviet peace pact left Poland defenseless. By September Europe broiled in the deadly heat of war. Democratic nations fell under the coercive power and military might of Nazism and fascism, and communism. At home, Americans increasingly viewed the world events as a challenge, not merely to their comfort and security, but to democracy itself. World events engendered the fear that the American democratic experiment, already shaken by a decade of economic upheaval, might play out in the darkness of a flickering and then extinguished flame. On December 29, 1940, despite reluctance and recalcitrance from members of both parties, Roosevelt would tell the American people in a fireside chat that the obligations imposed on the nation by circumstances beyond its control required a steady purpose to become "the great arsenal of democracy."[52]

In 1939, Columbia University historian David S. Muzzey, writing in the *New York Times,* called the world situation a particularly cogent crisis because democracy was "derided by its foes and doubted by many of its friends. . . . [I]nstead of a world made safe for democracy," he wrote, we have "democracy desperately seeking to make itself safe in the world." The economic trauma of the Great Depression to the national conscience notwithstanding, Muzzey called on America to renew its faith in its democratic ideals, "the best form of government . . . and the only one that holds the promise of the free development of human personality." People, despite what the propagandists from Germany, Italy, and the Soviet Union declared, were not "tired of liberty." Americans must not, he cautioned, give ground to fatalism and despair; instead, ideals must "move in the upper air of theory—and we must devise policies to meet the complex situation of the moment."[53]

At a gathering of four hundred members of the Brown University Club, Jan Masaryk, former Czecho-Slovak envoy to Britain, appealed for American leadership in the fight for democracy and liberty. "Europe is now flirting with the devil; Munich has brought world peace no nearer and today democracy in Europe is fighting for its life." Educators and political leaders renewed calls to teach democratic principles in public schools. At hundreds of birthday celebrations honoring George Washington, speakers called on Americans to "adhere to the fond democratic tradition." At a ceremony held at the base of Washington's statue on Wall Street, a group of boy scouts, including Chinese-American Troop 150, marched through the Bowery and then stood attentively along with 3,000 others from over sixty patriotic groups and heard Mark Eisner, former chairman of the New York City Board of Education, address the crowd. "Those who really cherish the memory of Washington," he stated, "must patriotically adhere to our fond democratic tradition. They cannot subscribe to any system of government which reduces their fellow-men to a state of vassalage to any individual or nation," and they are, he continued, "duty bound when honoring the memory of Washington to endeavor to emulate him in his high moral purposes and to follow him in his abounding faith and his uncompromising respect for his fellow man." Five members of the board of the National Lawyers Guild split over ideological differences and issued a statement that "we stand unreservedly behind American democracy [and] we oppose all ideologies, political philosophies or isms, whether from the Right or from the Left, which challenge our democratic institutions."[54]

Political choice and deliberation free from direct and indirect coercion, as well as the freedom to cast a ballot without threat or repercussion from political forces, distinguished American democratic ideals and institutions from those in the Old World. The Hatch Act debates, which defined corruption as voter coercion made possible by the power of economic power to unfairly influence the electorate, were imbued with an understanding that elections were the most fundamental political act in the democratic play. Congressmen recognized and adopted those views while creating arguments in support of, or opposition to, the restrictions on political engagement and campaign finances. The sordid disclosures of WPA employee coercion against some voters in the 1936 election threatened the fundamental right of citizenship. Representative Hamilton Fish (R-NY) felt the main purpose of Hatch I was the preservation of a free ballot. "Our free institutions today by a free people under a free ballot are being attacked more than ever. We are told from abroad that popular government and democracy have failed—unless we pass legislation of this kind," he continued, "upholding a free ballot and our free institutions and thereby our representative form of government, it is the beginning of the end of free institutions and you will soon have some form of dictatorial government in this country." Representative Raymond Springer (R-IN) agreed, adding that "the right to vote and to vote as a free man, without intimidation, coercion, threats or restraint—and to vote as the dictates of his or her conscience may direct—is an American right . . . coupled with the right of citizenship."[55]

Similarly, opponents of Hatch I and II used the threat to democratic ideals to support their position that parties and party activity were the best antidote to totalitarian repression. Citing the undemocratic example of Hitler's totalitarian system, Representative Frank Hook (D-MI) claimed that the United States was born in politics and had advanced to the highest state of civilization through politics. Hook considered the role that parties played essential to the democratic functioning of government, and felt that the Hatch acts would severely hamper the parties in that role. "Might I be so bold as to say," he cautioned, "to you who are about to destroy our democracy that as long as you have Republicans and as long as you have Democrats, you will have neither Communism or fascism—but when you eliminate politics from government you will eliminate parties." For party believers, party politics and democracy worked hand in hand to make the electoral system work. Representative Charles Faddis (D-PA) called it "un-American" to establish a doctrine that denied any group of citizens the right to engage in political activity and the "beginning of an invasion of the civil liberties of the American people." The Hatch restrictions on political activities of federal employees, on which parties had relied for their labor and lucre, they contended, would result in democratic destruction.[56]

Almost before the ink had dried on Hatch II, questions arose over several of its provisions. Attorney General Robert H. Jackson issued an opinion that a federal employee may pray for his party without violating the clean politics act. A federal officeholder could open the Iowa State Democratic convention with a prayer asking the "divine blessings upon the Democratic Party, its principles, policies, platform and candidates." Harry B. Mitchell, president of the U.S. Civil Service Commission, soon announced that government workers and state employees "can still talk politics and contribute to the campaign chests of political committees—so long as the talking was done in private and the cash contributions . . . made voluntarily." The issue of how closely a state or local employee need be connected with federal funds before the act applied remained an open question, one of many issues to be enforced by the Civil Service Commission, which estimated it would need 200 additional lawyers, investigators, and administrators to enforce it. Additional claims that both parties and numerous campaigns continued to violate the contribution and spending limits of the act through the use of multiple committees, the device of campaign books, and the use of uncoordinated committees that spent independently of the campaigns, among other methods, led Congress to authorize another investigation into 1940 campaign expenses. The Senate special campaign investigating committee, headed by Senator Guy M. Gillette (D-IA), began investigating the campaigns of various presidential, vice presidential, and U.S. Senate candidates. Its stated purpose was to determine the expenditure of all sums and all facts in relation to those elections, which would be in the public interest in enacting legislation or in deciding any contest for the right to a seat in the United States Senate. The report of the committee disclosed numerous violations of Hatch II and the Federal Corrupt Practices Act of 1925. The rise of independent Wilkie-for-President Clubs and the independent Democratic organizations argued that each organization could spend up to $3,000,000 for the campaign, so long as they did not coordinate their contributions. But both national organizations spent under the $3,000,000 limit, if measured from the time of passage of the act. On the other hand, nonparty organizations pushed the Republican receipts to $6,618,158 and expenditures to $5,983,408, and Democratic expenditures to $5,855,082. If the independent state Wilkie-for-President organizations are added to the Republican numbers, the total expenditures climb to $14,941,142. The Hatch II limit of $3,000,000 never acted as an aggregate limit for either campaign.[57]

In 1947 the Supreme Court ruled on the validity of Hatch II in two cases, *United Public Workers of America (CIO) v. Mitchell*, and a companion case, *Oklahoma v. United States Civil Service Commission*. Involving both federal and state workers, the Supreme Court sustained the political restriction provisions of the act. Citing *Ex Parte Curtis*, Justice Reed, writing for the majority, deferred to Congress, finding that "the power of Congress, within reasonable limits, to regulate, so far as it might deem necessary, the political conduct of its employees" including the right to limit political solicitation and contribution of campaign funds, was necessary and lawful to promote the efficiency and integrity in the discharge of official duties. Political neutrality, it held, was a "sound element for efficiency." Dissenting, Justices Hugo Black and William O. Douglas found the political restrictions in Hatch II overbroad, the enforcement of which by the Civil Service Commission was sure to be uneven and uncertain. The right to express political opinion prohibited legislation "not only because it injured the individuals muzzled, but also because of its harmful effect on the body politic in depriving it of the political participation and interest of such a large segment of our citizens." Interestingly, neither the majority nor those dissenting spoke of the threat of corruption of the employee's free will, the fears on which the supporters of Hatch I and II most strongly relied.[58]

While both sides claimed democratic ideals as their mantle of reform, even more than the Federal Corrupt Practices Act of 1925, Hatch I and II established the connective language between the corruption of coercion and deliberative democracy. The corruption that the Hatch reforms regulated involved coercive forces that enslaved the voter—to his job, to the political parties, and to a fear of economic ruin—such that he became unable to exercise an independent deliberative vote. Congress adopted the spending and contribution limits in Hatch II not only because it feared the corrupting effects of big money on the politicians. Instead, those limits were adopted because the big contributions would decrease political opportunity by making it more likely that the democratic process would be financed, not by the masses of ordinary citizens, but by limited groups of wealthy insiders who could seek and gain inordinate and excessive power unrelated to the civic legitimacy of their ideas. Taking their cue from the history of the rise of Nazism, a solid congressional majority accepted the logic in limiting both individual contributions from a variety of sources and total expenditures for campaigns. Congress passed and Roosevelt signed the Hatch acts not because they limited the corruption of the politicians or parties, but because they ensured the free will and promoted the rough equality of the electorate.

LABOR RESURGENCE AND REACTION—The War Labor Disputes Act, Taft-Hartley, and the CIO Political Action Committee

The 1936 elections, during which President Roosevelt had "welcomed the hatred" of the economic royalists, and had cemented the emerging New Deal coalition grounded in the labor movement, signaled a new phase in the development of economic democracy. Under the protection of the Wagner Act (1935), reckoned as "perhaps the most radical piece of legislation in twentieth-century history," the labor movement thrived, grew, and became a powerful counterbalancing force to the aggregate power of national corporations. The Wagner Act leveled the economic playing field for American labor, promoting collective bargaining, recognizing unions as bargaining agents, and authorizing a litany of labor tactics that would substantially alter the scales of power between labor and corporate business from 1935 to 1947.[59] The harsh economic realities of the Depression caused many to believe that government economic policies needed a substantial readjustment away from disapproval and repression and toward open toleration of unionism and collective bargaining, and protected rights to organize under principles of freedom and democracy.[60]

The Wagner Act has a contentious history. Whether the act successfully promoted that original vision of economic democracy, or whether it shifted the resources of the federal government in favor of a union movement that denied by its heavy-handed actions the rights of the workers it pretended to protect, remain a disputed matter of perspective. What is unquestioned, however, is that the Wagner Act afforded labor new powers over bargaining rights and representation. This new power reshaped public support for unions, which were soon challenged in the tumultuous upheaval of world war.[61]

As the war came, wartime exigencies dramatically changed the focus of the argument over workers' rights and benefits. For the time being, at least, material production of the machinery of war took precedence. Yet on the political front, fought at home during the elections of 1936–1942, contention over the increasing power of national unions, over Labor's Nonpartisan League as a union campaign organization, and over the Congress of International Organizations' (CIO) increasingly effective involvement in direct electoral politics, created an opportunity for the opponents of the Wagner Act, who sought an antidote to the rise of labor political power. Congress fought the first campaign in that political war in 1943 over the passage of the War Labor Disputes Act (WLDA), commonly known as the Smith-Connally Act.[62]

The WLDA was offered as a war necessity intended to authorize the power of the president to protect the capabilities of the war industry to produce the necessary material for the war effort. Section 3 authorized the president to "take immediate possession of any plant" that held a contract for war material production with the United States, if the president found and proclaimed that there is "an interruption of the operation of such plant, mine, or facility as a result of a strike or other labor disturbance, and that the war effort would be unduly impeded or delayed by such interruption." In the event of such a seizure, the War Labor Board would be empowered to operate the facility, and resolve any disputes over wages, hours, or labor conditions. Furthermore, the act made it unlawful for any person to "coerce, instigate, induce, conspire with, or encourage any person to interfere, by lock-out, strike, or slowdown, or other interruption interfering with the operation of such plant, mine, or facility by giving direction or guidance in the conduct of such interruption, or by providing funds for the conduct or direction thereof, or for the payment of strike, unemployment, or other benefits to those participating therein." The act empowered the president to prevent labor disputes or to resolve them outside the framework of the National Labor Relations Act and the procedures and law established under that act during the duration of the war. It expired of its own accord six months following the termination of all hostilities as proclaimed by the president or by concurrent congressional resolution to end the act's provisions.[63]

WLDA also included a contentious, seemingly misplaced provision that restricted the power of labor organizations to contribute to political campaigns. Section 9 of the act amended Section 313 of the Federal Corrupt Practices Act of 1925 to make it unlawful for any national bank, or any corporation organized by authority of federal law *"or any labor organization* as defined under the National Labor Relations Act," to make a contribution in connection with any election to any political officer, or "for any corporation whatever, to make a contribution in connection with any federal election or for any candidate, political committee, or other person to accept or receive any contribution prohibited by this section." The penalty for violation of the act was a fine of not more than $5,000, and included possible imprisonment of up to a year for any corporate officer or director of labor officer who violated the act.[64]

At first glance, the inclusion of a campaign finance provision in a labor regulation bill seems incongruent. The context of the Hatch Act reforms of 1939–1940, driven by the rhetoric of freeing labor from the influences of coercive party partisans, however, allowed supporters of this new labor restriction latitude to argue that the provision really was a campaign finance reform, and not a restriction of labor power. They unpacked the rhetorical tools to paint labor organizations with the same broad brush of excessive corporation power used in earlier debates over the Tillman Act, FCPA, and the Hatch acts. They argued that labor organizations and corporations were similarly organized and equally powerful to coerce voting through campaign spending, and therefore ought to be regulated in the same manner. These strategies reflected wartime public opinion over the fear of union political power and successfully reshaped both the concept and institutional strength of labor political activity.[65]

New Deal and labor opponents, bruised and beaten by the political muscle of labor political contributions and activities in 1936 and 1938, were anxious to limit the strength of those practices. Adding the campaign contribution provision to the WLDA allowed labor opponents to support the war effort by limiting strikes in war industries, yet elude the charge that the campaign finance restriction was nothing more than a direct attempt to eliminate labor political money in campaigns. Supporters of the WLDA chose two rhetorical strategies, both with long historical antecedents from earlier campaign finance debates over corruption, to stake out their positions.[66]

The first strategy, borrowed from the earlier Tillman Act rhetoric about "other people's money," alleged that the undemocratic power of unions over their own members involuntarily collected workers dues and spent the workers' money without, or in some cases, adverse to their interests. Reports from around the country about the abusive power of national unions to subvert local elections using the Wagner Act prompted Representative Forrest Harness (R-IN) to offer an amendment during floor debate on the WLDA that largely rewrote the bill. Harness stated that he "would like to see secret and honest elections of union officers—I want the workers to have the same right I have to give free expression to my opinion without intimidation." Workers, Harness explained, often lost their right to free expression because the unions failed to provide full and free elections for union leadership. That same leadership then made choices about campaign contributions to political parties and candidates. Harness's amendment included language prohibiting union organization political contributions.[67]

The very fact that Congress was considering limits on labor activities during wartime seemed to suggest that labor might not have the public interest at heart. If the unions could reject the free electoral will of their local and national members, prohibiting their campaign contributions seemed a natural response to protecting the workers from the coerced exaction of their hard-earned money for contributions to campaigns they may not support. Proponents of the WLDA cautioned that many unions had become coercive and undemocratic, and used this rhetoric of corruption to call for their exclusion during the war from the most democratic of processes.

Although Hatch II had extended the $5,000 contribution limit by defining "persons" as "an individual, partnership, committee, association, corporation, and any other organization or group of persons," that contribution provision had failed to effectively restrict labor union expenditures. Because the Senate Judiciary Committee had amended that provision to permit $5,000 contributions to any number of different candidates and political committees, and then provided that any political committee could spend up to $3,000,000 directly, the Hatch II limits had no substantive effect on spending by the Labor Nonpartisan League or any other labor organization. Harness called this incongruity into question with the use of a second rhetorical strategy.[68]

Since 1907 the Tillman Act had prohibited corporate campaign contributions in federal elections. The provision, explained Harness, "merely included labor unions with national banks and corporations which are now prohibited by the Corrupt Practices Act from making contributions in connection with Federal elections." Arguing there was no difference between the corporate form and the labor unions that organized to fund political candidates, Harness challenged the House to distinguish labor unions from other corporations, which had been prohibited from making direct contributions to federal campaigns since 1907.[69]

Several members, surprised at Harness's amendment, tried to explain the difference between corporations and labor unions. Representative Matthew Merritt (D-NY) wondered why other "unincorporated associations" were not included in the Harness amendment and why the provisions should not instead be proposed in an amendment to the Hatch Act. Senator Guffey, considering the conference report that included the labor union restriction, questioned why Congress should enact a law that "picked on labor organizations, in view of the fact, as I think every Member of the Senate knows, that the Hatch Act and other corrupt-practices acts are being violated in every election." Senator Homer Bone (D-WA) lamented the attempt to regulate campaign finances at all. "We think we are going to accomplish something directly but we do not accomplish it either directly or indirectly. A man would have to be extremely dumb," he added, "if he were a banking corporation—if he could not find a way to get some of the bank's 'dough' into a political campaign." Bone wondered aloud if the House conferees had not "put one over on our friends in the labor unions."[70]

Those arguments only challenged the propriety of including the campaign finance regulation in the WLDA, or the evenhandedness of the new labor restriction. Fundamentally though, the issue was whether corporate and labor union campaign finance restrictions were really of the same ilk. Only Congressman Celler questioned that basic assumption. In a colloquy with Congressman Merritt (D-NY), Celler asked if "[i]t was not quite true that a man like Eugene Grace or John Pierpont Morgan could give $5,000 or more, for a dollar for every member of the CIO, or similarly, any other man, and there is no law to retard them whatever?" Celler's unartful query went to the heart of the question. Were labor unions, composed of memberships of workers, essentially like corporations, in terms of their power, influence, and ability, to spend the dues of their members for political purposes?[71]

By 1943, for a public in the midst of war and weary of the threat of strikes and perceived labor excesses, and for a majority in Congress, the answer was a resounding yes. During the House hearings on the WLDA, committee members heard testimony about the abusive practices of labor officials in denying individual workers their rights. Representative G. W. Landis (R-IN) proposed a bill to require reporting of all campaign finances and expenditures, but labor opposition to any alteration of the campaign finance system created an impression about "the huge war chests being maintained by labor unions, of enormous fees and dues being extorted from war workers." American trade unionism, Landis argued, having become "an established American institution has implicitly accepted certain definite social responsibilities" that demanded its policies be based on not merely the welfare of its members, but on "the welfare of all the people." The way to do this, argued Landis, was simply to require of unions that had become campaign financiers the same reporting and restrictions over campaign contributions and expenditures that corporations had been facing for nearly forty years.[72]

Labor leaders representing several unions testified against the bill. W. D. Johnson, Vice President of the Order of Railway Conductors, questioned the motives behind the bill. Landis argued the bill was to root out the "labor racketeers" who charged members high initiation fees and yearly union dues, then used the money to build up their political funds. Johnson challenged Landis's contention. "[I]f there are as many racketeers in the United States at the present time, or at any other time, as the press and other means of spreading poisonous propaganda would make us believe . . . and if there are state laws to take care of them, I am wondering why that has not been done." A long train of union representatives denied the charge of racketeering, offering instead a picture of labor responsibility and union-management harmony. Unions, they testified, instead of being corrupt institutions led by corrupt men, had trained the employees who entered the armed forces, and who were during the immediate war, "constructing every kind of material or piece of armament that is being used with such success by the armed forces of our country and its allies."[73]

Union leaders attempted to draw democratic distinctions between corporations and unions. American unionism, testified the supporters, represented men and women who voluntarily organized together as American citizens, joined in the efforts of their neighbors who may be members of a union, "to assist their choice of candidates . . . contribute their efforts . . . and make monetary contributions toward advertising to assist in that choice." They either favored or opposed the candidate on principle, and it would be repugnant to American democracy "that their efforts shall be made unlawful and that they shall be made subject to fines as provided in this bill."[74]

The argument that their unions were functionally unlike corporations because they were organized around the unified social goals of their members was an important distinction because they believed that their unions served the common good. John T. Corbett, Assistant Grand Chief Engineer of the Brotherhood of Locomotive Engineers, for example, declared the unions were like fraternal organizations—the Odd Fellows, the Masons, the Knights of Pythias—and thus intrinsically different from large national corporations that could affect the economy and thus the public interest. Locomotive engineers like Corbett, he declared to Landis, "could not take off his overalls on Saturday night and come in and discuss legal questions with you on Monday morning," unlike corporation and national bank officials. The Brotherhood of Locomotive Engineers, though organized and empowered, still held no sway in the halls of Congress because their power emanated from individuals joined for a common purpose; corporations and national banks, on the other hand, lost nothing from the Tillman Act restriction because their officers and directors retained direct political access to Congress. Furthermore, corporate officers and directors could individually give substantial funds to candidates from their personal fortunes, while the only means unions had to match that political cache was through collective action.[75]

In the end, distinctions between corporations and union organizations that played a political campaign finance role were muddled and unclear. The War Labor Disputes Act passed Congress on June 12, 1943, by wide margins in both houses. Roosevelt vetoed the bill, citing objections to the propriety of the political contribution restrictions. "This provision has no relevancy to a bill prohibiting strikes during the war in plants operated by the Government—If there is merit in the prohibition," he added, "it should not be confined to wartime and careful consideration should be given to the appropriateness of extending the prohibition to other non-profit organizations."[76] On June 25, 1943, with little debate, the House (244–108) and the Senate (56–25) overrode Roosevelt's veto and the bill became law.[77]

The WLDA prohibited direct labor organization contributions to campaigns until the end of the war, when Congress permanently established the campaign restrictions against labor unions in the Labor Management Relations Act of 1947. But labor leaders, unwilling to accept the political segregation envisioned by the WLDA, soon devised a plan that would revolutionize the institutional structures of campaign financing, they began to separate and differentiate the engaged activism of special interest membership groups that relied on social cohesion and unity of interest, from the political money changers of single-interest special interest groups focused on the power of money to buy access for their political views.[78]

THE CIO POLITICAL ACTION COMMITTEE OF 1944—Corporatizing the Communal Interest

Passage of the WLDA sent shockwaves through the labor movement. Labor leaders, like Sidney Hillman, head of the Amalgamated Clothing Workers Union, lamented the political retrenchment evidenced in the congressional hearings and elections from 1938 to 1942. Drifting away from the "social democratic vistas of the mid-1930s" alarmed Hillman. Labor's economic power had been enhanced by the political power it could marshal in elections, and Hillman worried that WLDA could cripple the labor–New Deal alliance that had successfully elected loyal supporters and ousted labor's most vocal opposition. In July 1943 the CIO executive board established created a Political Action Committee separately formed and operated from the CIO itself in order to avoid the prohibitory provisions of WLDA. Its first chairman would be Sidney Hillman.[79]

The CIO Political Action Committee (CIO PAC) established primary political goals that included mobilizing the full force of the CIO for local and statewide elections in 1944, securing united political action through united political committees, and "working toward the formation of a national united labor league . . . which will . . . weld labor into the mighty political force which its numbers, strength, organizing ability, and program entitle it to play in the life of our nation." Initial seed money to the

CIO PAC came from several union treasuries after the general executive board of each union had approved the transfer. Each of the four international unions of the CIO contributed $100,000 to the PAC. The CIO financial statement filed May 31, 1944, showed total receipts of $669,764.11 and disbursements of $189,112.12.[80]

Almost immediately after Hillman's announcement, opponents sharply denounced the principles and operation of the PAC. Harrison E. Spangler, chairman of the Republican National Committee, challenged United States Attorney Francis Biddle to investigate and prosecute the CIO for what he called "a flagrant and bold violation of the Corrupt Practices and Hatch Acts." Spangler's objections were twofold: first, he argued that the Corrupt Practices Act, with the WLSA amendments, made illegal any corporate or labor union expenditures for federal political campaigns, whether directly from unions or from PACs formed by unions. Second, he contended that the Hatch Act prohibited any one person, association, corporation, or other organization from making any direct or indirect contribution more than $5,000 to any federal campaign. The $100,000 labor union contributions to the fund would, argued Spangler, violate that law. But Hillman and CIO President Philip Murray countered that industrialists like A. W. Robinson of Westinghouse Company, "the Weirs and the du Ponts and Mellons can't understand why labor is interested in politics, in education work." "These interests," he reminded the critics, "have had their political action committees as far back as I can remember."[81]

The Senate and House soon called yet another set of campaign finance hearings over the controversy, expanding it to include the presidential and senatorial elections of 1944. In testimony before the House committee, Hillman claimed that the PAC violated no laws in soliciting the union seed money, or in the CIO PAC receipts from individual union members that amounted to $34,569.06. Hillman denied any violation, since none of the funds, he claimed, had been contributed to any campaign. Only direct money contributions were illegal under Hatch II and the WLDA, and the CIO PAC educational campaign would neither contribute to nor "directly spend [those funds] by such labor organization and not by agreement or prearrangement with the candidate or their political parties or their political committees." In addition to the CIO, Congress investigated other PACs, including the Peoples Committee to Defend Life Insurance and Savings, the State Republican League and Republican Citizen's Committee of New Jersey, G. L. Smith's America First Party, Frank Gannett's Committee for Constitutional Government, Inc., the National Economic Council, United Mothers of America, Anglo-Saxon Federation, the National Association of Manufacturers, and the National Industrial Information Committee. In no case did Congress find a clear violation of the campaign finance acts then in effect. The committee instead awaited the ruling of a test case on the act. Senators Ball and Ferguson wrote a minority report that recommended extending FCPA and Hatch to include expenditures as well as contributions, but the committee as a whole resisted that, fearful "the extension of the prohibition to include expenditures would tend to limit the rights of freedom of speech, freedom of the press, and freedom of assembly as guaranteed by the Federal Constitution." The line of demarcation between educational and purely political, the report found, "is difficult, if not impossible to draw, since it depends to a considerable extent on human motives."[82]

The Senate Special Committee to Investigate Presidential, Vice Presidential and Senatorial Campaign Expenditures in 1944 unanimously concluded "that prohibitions and sanctions [of the Federal Corrupt Practice Act] had failed to prevent pernicious political activity in Federal campaigns." The committee refused to find that the expenditure of funds by PACs by itself constituted pernicious political activity. Instead, it focused on specific examples of campaign finance abuse: incidents of published campaign literature not attributed to any candidate or political committee, the practice by political committees clearly working for the election of a candidate of calling themselves "educational" and thus seeking exclusion from regulations, the failure of the regulatory scheme to provide publicly accessible information about contributions and expenditures, and the failure to expressly extend the laws to cover primaries. The committee also found the $3,000,000 spending limit for presidential and vice presidential campaigns "utterly unrealistic," and called the limitation the catalyst for the propagation of the political action committees, which obscured the transparency of the reporting requirements. The committee called for raising of the expenditure amount to more accurately reflect the practical costs of campaigning, and for "intelligent and continuous publicity" about campaign contributions and expenditures that "will focus public attention upon the size of campaign funds and thus public opinion itself may regulate where prohibition without publicity has failed." Congress later addressed the problem of publishing or distributing any political statement relating to any federal candidate in the "Powers Act." The Powers Act required that any published political pamphlet, circular, card, dodger, poster, advertisement, or any other statement must contain the name or names of the persons, broadly defined, who were responsible for the statement or publication. Failure to include the name(s) constituted a crime carrying a $1,000 fine and up to a year in jail.[83]

The Senate Committee report discussed several important constitutional distinctions. The committee accepted the contribution-expenditure dichotomy permitting greater regulation of contributions because they found that contribution limits only weakly afflicted First Amendment rights. The committee recommendations, especially the limits on expenditures, affected free speech, association, and press rights, but not equally across the groups affected. The committee believed labor unions were different from corporations and banks, not being "legal persons," instead calling them "an aggregation of individuals like a church, or a fraternal organization, or a social club." This distinction, labor supporters argued, fundamentally distinguished labor unions from corporations, thus permitting a different class of regulation.

This distinction, however, would soon become indistinguishable because after the passage of WLDA, PACs would, unlike aggregations of individuals, or churches, or social clubs, become the most important campaign funding instrumentality of the labor movement. As PACs grew in political influence and power, the character of the original union PACs became indistinguishable from that of newly created corporate PACs formed by national corporations. The fraternal nature of union fund-raising, where each union member would pay for lobbying and political activity with a voluntary contribution from his weekly wages, and then rely on that political activity to provide him with political access along with thousands of other like-minded members, became attenuated when the unions organized specialized political action committees whose sole purpose was to raise and contribute campaign funds. The rising power of Sidney Hillman's PAC innovation made it increasingly difficult for union supporters in Congress, who in 1944 compared labor unions to social or fraternal organizations, to argue that labor PACs, organized as corporate campaign subsidiaries of the unions themselves, were significantly different from the PACs of business and industry.[84]

The House also held hearings into labor union activity during the 1944 elections. The report of the House Special Committee to Investigate Campaign Expenditures found even the distinctions between "educational and political activities" nearly impossible to maintain. "[T]here are still newspapers, magazines, and radio programs which are quite what they purport to be. But it is also true," the report concluded, "that major power and pressure groups show a growing tendency to participate in political campaigns indirectly through these traditionally nonpolitical forms rather than directly through political parties, party committees, and outright contributions to candidates." According to the committee, the problem involved drafting and monitoring a regulatory scheme that included "political" organizations and "opinion-molding, educational, or similar types of organizations," that engaged in political activity for "both reputable and subversive ends."[85]

The Committee cautioned that there needed to be a "broad base of agreement . . . with respect to practices deemed to be disreputable and intolerable, those to be treated as crimes." The committee did not define those activities, which it classified as subversive to the polity. It was clear, however, that they felt certain election offenses undercut the heart of the electoral process, having to do with not merely "the corruption of campaigns and elections but with the quite distinct problem of subversive activity and sedition." The House called for an assessment of the indirect patterns of political participation raised by the new PACs, and called on Congress to undertake a study to determine whether organizations like PACs were "detrimental to the general welfare."[86]

By 1947 the rise of labor PAC power and the conservative reaction to the vision of economic democracy represented in the Wagner Act reached full fury. The Labor Management Relations Act, called "Taft-Hartley" after its Senate and House sponsors, recalibrated labor-management relations in dramatic fashion. The campaign finance restrictions in WLDA expired six months after the end of World War II hostilities, and Taft-Hartley made permanent those restrictions that had affected direct labor involvement in the campaign finance system since 1943. These restrictions have played an important role in the ways in which labor gained, and exercised political power over the last sixty years.[87]

Labor historians offer three reasons for the decline of the trade union idea: "the declining reputation of the unions, the decay of industrial pluralism, the rise of a new discourse of individual rights," which they say impacted both the legal status and meaning of trade unionism. Labor unions, in accepting the National Labor Relations Act procedural machinery for adjudicating workplace rights, soon were overshadowed by civil rights claims advocated by African Americans, women, and cultural minorities. Those powerful notions, arising not out of procedure, but from emerging liberal notions of equality and substantive justice, overpowered the mechanical operations and underpinnings of the New Deal labor consensus. These historians also claim that judicial decisions began to "devalue union solidarity and privilege(d) a more individualistic conception of worker rights" that led to a distinction "between economic and political rights" of workers made more attractive with the demise of the group pluralist idea.[88]

The impact of Supreme Court rulings sustaining the legality of the Hatch II and WLDA/Labor Management Relations Act restrictions on campaign contributions played an important though unrecognized role in reshaping labor power. Those decisions about the proper role of labor money in the campaign finance system, much like decisions about the Tillman Act for corporations and the Hatch Act for public employees, divorced the economic and political power of unions by constitutionalizing the campaign finance restrictions in the Taft-Hartley Act. That divorce significantly undercut the ability of unions to gain and retain political power in the post–New Deal era. In *United States v. CIO,* the Supreme Court considered an indictment of the CIO and its president Philip Murray for violation of Section 313 of the Federal Corrupt Practices Act made applicable to labor unions under Hatch II and WLDA/LMRA. The indictment charged the union with publishing *The CIO News,* a weekly union newspaper that advocated support for federal political candidates. Prosecutors alleged that publication of the newspaper constituted an "expenditure" under the FCPA, and the union thus violated the contribution and expenditure provisions of the act. The Court, asked to rule on the constitutionality of limiting labor union political contributions and expenditures, instead found the indictment insufficient to reach these types of publications.[89]

Justice Reed's unanimous opinion thus cautioned Congress against restricting internal educational efforts directed at union membership or stockholders, but did not decide the constitutionality of restricting the campaign finance activity of labor unions like corporations. A decision treating labor unions and corporations alike in the campaign finance system would not come until 1957 in *United States v. UAW.* By then, union PACs operationally resembled corporate aggregations of wealth that the Tillman Act regulated. The campaign finance legislation of the 1930s–1940s disassociated unions from traditional forms of member political participation including the raising and giving of money, which led to the creation of the CIO PAC, an organization with less direct ties to local labor membership. As union PACs evolved into corporate fund-raising machines, those civic threads that union leaders, Congress, and the Supreme Court had demanded as a precondition for nonregulation had unraveled. As the PAC component of union political participation separated unions from traditional functions, labor unions and corporations involved in political fund-raising came to resemble one another—posing no problem for campaign finance regulators to cover both with the blanket of reform.[90]

The rise of political action committees as civic adjuncts to the campaign finance system posed a bigger problem for reformers. These new political actors were expressly political, and soon developed into money machines with different dimensions and understandings of participatory membership. All it took to "belong" was a contribution, and the kinds of political participation that local union membership and other civic organizations had engaged in during the heady days of the New Deal seemed lost in the distant past. Unions, whose members had long been used as campaign organizers, morphed into organizations generating PAC funds from their memberships. That development created a regulatory opportunity because the unions' PACs, in losing their fraternal-political character, became much like corporate forms of campaign organizations, which had been fully regulated since 1907.[91]

New Deal changes in labor-management relations exposed several interconnections between public policy and the hard pragmatism of electoral politics. Campaign finance reformers maintained a running discourse against the kind of corruption that denigrated the free will of individual voters through coercive tactics. This discourse resonated in the debates to limit union political activity, when reformers could point to other labor excesses that appeared to diminish the free will of workers in local elections, bargaining units, or industry-wide work stoppages. But it was the reaction of the CIO in organizing the first PAC, as a necessary though unintended reaction to those limitations, that eventually split individual workers off from the activism of local political participation. For many members, contributions, not local activism, became the coin of their civic engagement. By the time the Supreme Court ruled on campaign finance system regulation of union contributions, individual workers' political contributions were less voluntary precisely because they had become disconnected from local political activism, and as an ironic result, were thought less deserving of constitutional protection. Political action committees would, in the next two decades, become commonplace means of raising campaign finances. They would, however, be regarded as less deserving of constitutional protection because their origins were understood to be a surrogate form of citizen political participation. Yet even as politics became increasingly professionalized and surrogated during the 1950s–1960s, a movement of extraordinary civic activism would turn the legal-political landscape upside down and create vast new opportunities for both reform and corruption unseen since the politically engaged days of the Gilded Age.

Chapter Six

PROFESSIONALIZING POLITICS
AND THE "DE-POLITICAL" COURT

The Language of Reform from the
Political Thicket, 1946–1969

In the latter years of President Dwight Eisenhower's presidency, he remarked that his biggest mistake was "the appointment of that S.O.B. Earl Warren."[1] But Eisenhower's dissatisfaction with Warren arose, not simply because of the Warren court's decisions, but because Eisenhower felt that Warren had hoodwinked him by appearing to be a more moderate justice than he eventually turned out to be. Warren's unpredictability surprised Eisenhower, who had expected a justice more inclined to follow rather than make precedent. Future presidents, in attempting to avoid a similar Eisenhower "mistake," would seek to appoint judges with clear and consistent judicial records upon which they could rely, rather than politicians who had no track record of judicial decision-making. Judicial appointees with previous political and particularly electoral experience became the aberration instead of the norm. That changed the way courts looked at the connections between political free speech and political corruption. That the Warren court led a revolution in civil rights and free speech jurisprudence has been well documented; but what is less well known is that Eisenhower's reaction to the Court's activism led to a new procedure for evaluating and appointing judges that would transform the Warren court's free speech jurisprudence from a central means of protecting communitarian democratic equality into a formalistic impediment to the reform of the campaign finance system.

During the 1950–1960s, by addressing the grievances of the Civil Rights movement, the courts created opportunities for new voters to access the political system, and in so doing, increased the demands on Congress to more fairly regulate and administer that system. Changes in the electoral system created opportunities for the free-agent politicians and the growing coterie of political professionals to engage in a pattern of expensive advocacy, marketing, consulting, and election management that reconfigured American elections. The increasing costs of American elections led to the need for, and increasing influence of, campaign contributors to finance elections, and this in turn led to the rise of a newly reenergized coalition of reformers who saw the system emerging yet again, from the late 1950s through the 1960s, into a pattern corruptive of the basic principles of deliberative democracy.[2]

Despite broad reforms of the political system, those efforts failed to instill widely accepted democratic confidence in the political process. Some critics focus on the failures of the reform coalition to account for the power of the media, and on the declining importance of political parties, as important elements contributing to the failure of reform goals. Historians argue that by 1974, when Congress passed the Federal Election Campaign Act, the reform coalition had made "debilitating compromises such as accepting political action committees (PACs) and limiting public financing of campaigns" that eventually led to their failure to build and maintain grassroots support for fundamental campaign finance reform.[3]

But the story of that "Happy Days" interregnum of reform and of the rising tide of political dissent and voter enfranchisement in the turbulent 1960s cannot be fully or fairly told without incorporating the influence of the law, and particularly the role of the Supreme Court in those changes. Baked into that story is the development of a new type of Supreme Court reflecting a more traditional judicial philosophy reacting to the pattern of increasing political professionalization of and expertise in campaigns. As the Court began to address the most political of questions in the 1950s–1960s, it did so with a membership increasingly composed of elite law school graduates, law clerks, and judges, nearly devoid of the kind of practical political acumen that past Courts had long experienced.

The political campaign process became more professionalized and the membership of the Supreme Court, reflecting broader legal-community attitudes about judicial competence and the proper role of the Court in deciding issues entangled in complicated political questions, became increasingly separated from the kind of pragmatic, hands-on political experience that had epitomized its membership since its formation. As the Court became less experienced politically, its members being imbued instead with the formalist understanding of free speech taught in American law schools and preferred by judges, it ignored the pragmatic definition of corruption coined in the political trenches that had long promoted fundamental democratic ideas of equality and access. Even as reformers raised legal and political questions about the democratic principles of electioneering, voting, apportionment, media access, and campaign finance in the 1950s–1960s, the selection process for the Court was undergoing a depoliticization that refocused its vision on a narrowly defined conception of preferred rights that, ironically, began to sunder the long-standing connections between free speech and deliberative democracy. Increasingly less experienced in electoral politics, the depoliticized Court privileged a distinctly formalist theory of free speech to protect First Amendment freedoms in modern America.

By 1976 its decisions conflated the meaning of corruption with bribery because it failed to understand the complicated political relationship between the campaign finance system and deliberative democracy that had, since 1876, formed the backbone of the system. Responding to the civil rights demands of many Americans, the Court preserved and elevated individualist principles of free speech as the paramount method to protect American democratic institutions, and thereby transformed the meaning of political corruption to the severely limited conception of quid pro quo bribery that bore little relationship to either the history of the campaign finance system, or to the pragmatic necessity of American politics.

CONGRESSIONAL REORGANIZATION AND THE FEDERAL REGULATION OF LOBBYING ACT OF 1946

The necessity of congressional reform, made evident by the trial and tumult of the war years, became the first contest over the restriction of free speech as a means of eradicating political corruption. Congressional concern about the usurpation of its power by the administrative state and its ability to balance its power with that of President Roosevelt motivated Congress to pursue a program of self-evaluation and self-improvement. Congressional recognition that reform was essential to maintain its capabilities as a functioning deliberative body was a small but telling part of the changes to the campaign finance system. As Congress reorganized its committee structure and information-gathering and analysis capabilities, legal changes in the role of parties in primary elections further divorced parties from their candidates. Those legal changes were accompanied by the rise of the electronic media, expanding their reach toward the electorate with a focused message produced and paid for by candidates financing their own campaigns with their own funds and acting increasingly as free agents outside the party structure. New direct marketing campaigns financed through PAC donations began to burgeon after 1948. These trends contributed greatly to the reform of the Federal Corrupt Practices Act and to the development of a different set of values designed to rid corruption from the campaign finance system.

Senator Francis T. Maloney's (D-CT) 1942 resolution created a Joint Committee on War Problems to address the growing gap between the competencies of the executive and legislative branches. The goal was to ensure that Congress was better informed, thus addressing the principal complaint about the capability of the legislative branch to deal with multitudinous and increasingly complex issues. In addition, Congressman Everett M. Dirksen (R-IL) proposed that a select committee be organized to study congressional reorganization, and to "investigate and study the structure, functions, and procedures of the legislative branch to determine how they may be modified, revised or augmented." These efforts led to the development of committees committed to "riding herd" on the executive branch to ensure that congressional intent was fairly implemented by the growing administrative state created by the New Deal and the exigencies of war. After the armistice, Congress acted to fundamentally reorganize and reform its own institution.[4]

The Reorganization of Congress Act of 1946 stands at the midpoint of a complicated story about the increased professionalization of American politics, beginning in the mid-1930s and continuing through the full flowering of the electronic media age. The 79th Congress's plan of reorganization had several basic objectives. Congress intended to streamline and simplify committee structures, clarify committee duties and reduce jurisdictional disputes, improve congressional staff aids, reduce the congressional workload, strengthen legislative oversight of the executive branch, reinforce the power of congressional budgeting, and regulate lobbying. Congressional workloads created by the burgeoning size and responsibility of the national government had inundated senators and representatives with more information than they could responsibly manage.

In an address to the Southern Political Science Association, Senator Estes Kefauver (D-TN) described the problem as a "dangerous gap" between the executive and legislative branches arising from a "lack of teamwork . . . essential to our welfare and security." Reorganizing those responsibilities and providing new professional staff for each congressman, and for Congress itself, would, proponents hoped, alleviate the burden on Congress from the massive increase of information. Kefauver stated that the problem arose from "a lack of facts on particular issues" and the inability of congressmen to get the full facts, often relying on "fragmentary information from a constituent" that ends up "with an endless succession of requests for investigation" by Congress that "betrays the fundamental lack of information that plagues our Senators and Congressmen." Kefauver lamented the impossibility to keep "*currently* informed" because of the "human impossibility for any member to read" all of the annual departmental reports or attend all the committee hearings to which he was assigned. Proponents intended that the Congressional Reorganization Act of 1946 would decrease the number of standing congressional committees, eliminate overlapping responsibilities, and help solve the ad hoc approach to accessing and disseminating policy information to members of Congress.[5]

The central recommendations for reform were a result of concern over the emergence of interest groups, lobbying organizations, and political action committees that advocated for specific legislation, and which operated for narrow special interests that tended to "divert legislative emphasis from broad questions of public interest." Earlier state regulations during the Gilded Age commonly imposed substantive criminal prohibitions on lobbying activities. The Alabama Constitution in 1873, for example, criminalized the solicitation of legislators, or any public officials, and made illegal the practice of solicitation to influence their action.

By 1877 Georgia had made all lobbying a crime. In 1879 California passed a constitutional provision that said "[a]ny person who seeks to influence the vote of a member of the legislature by bribery, promise of reward, or any other dishonest means, shall be guilty of lobbying," and made the act a felony. These outright prohibitions later gave way to a more moderate distinction between corruptive and educational lobbying, as most state legislatures that enacted lobbying restrictions between 1900 and 1932 substituted comprehensive disclosure requirements for the outright prohibition of lobbying activities. After 1932 thirteen state legislatures enacted lobby regulation statutes, nearly identical to the disclosure regimen of the early Gilded Age.[6]

The impetus to regulate federal lobbying activities came primarily from inside Congress. The end of World War II released pent-up demands for domestic policies and programs such as veterans' housing, price controls, public power projects, and labor-management relations. These programs garnered support or faced opposition from a growing body of interest groups organized specifically to advocate for the individual interests of their members. Big battles over the shape of the postwar American economy created a huge demand for active lobbying organizations, and the lobbyists descended on Congress in droves. When Congress began to regulate lobbying activities, state experiences shaped much of the federal legislation. Political scientist Dr. George B. Galloway, who headed the Joint Congressional Committee, made recommendations to Congress as it conducted hearings.[7]

While many legislators decried the incessant contact with lobbyists, Congress's main concern was the power of lobbyists to sway public policy and the lack of information about the origins of lobby money and efforts. This lack of information about the sources of the influence and the potential for abuse by a hidden organization that manufactured public opinion came to the fore during the congressional battle over the Public Utility Holding Company Act in 1935. Many congressmen decried the holding companies' campaign to manufacture opposition to the bill as deceptive, undemocratic, and corruptive of the public interest. When Congress set out to reorganize its own house, the regulation of lobby activities seemed a natural extension of the process necessary to ensure that the entire public interest, and not simply the vocal voices of the narrow interest, would be heard. One of the fundamental requirements of the Reorganization Act was that "all groups, representatives of which appear before congressional committees, should register and make full disclosure of their membership, finances, etc.," so that members of Congress would receive and be able to assess the value and bias of the information from those lobbyists. The act promoted full disclosure and free exchange of information, with a goal of increased and informed deliberation on the issues. Passed in 1946, the Federal Regulation of Lobbying Act ("Lobbying Act") became Title III of the overall reorganization effort of Congress. President Harry S. Truman signed the act on August 2, 1946.[8]

Although Congress had investigated early abuses of lobbying activities, the Lobbying Act was the first statutory regulation of federal lobbying activities and lobbyists in U.S. history. The act created a schema of registration and reporting that mimicked earlier disclosure laws by requiring the registration of every person "who engage[d] himself to pay or any consideration for the purpose of attempting to influence the passage or defeat of any legislation by the Congress of the United States." The act also required detailed accounting of any person who "shall in any manner solicit or receive a contribution (in excess of $500) or any expenditure (in excess of $10) to any organization or fund" for anyone who "directly or indirectly, solicits, collects, or receives money or any other thing of value to be used principally to aid, or the *principal purpose* of which is to aid, in the . . . passage or defeat of any legislation" or to "influence, directly or indirectly, the passage or defeat of any legislation by the Congress of the United States." The Lobbying Act required those people to register with the Secretary of the Senate or Clerk of the House, detailing their lobbying arrangements, compensation, and expenses, and the information was to be compiled and published in the Congressional Record as soon as practicable at the close of each calendar quarter.[9]

The Lobbying Act was designed to avoid the manufacture of evidence of public support for proposals that did not actually have that expressed public support. The report of the Joint Committee stressed the undemocratic potential of lobbying pressure, cautioning that "[m]ass means of communication and the art of public relations have so increased the pressures upon Congress as to distort and confuse the normal expressions of public opinion The committee, recognizing the growing influence of special-interest groups, feared that without "full information regarding the membership, source of contributions, and expenditure of organized groups," Congress would be unable to weigh and measure the public support for the proposals those groups supported. During floor debate, while some members disagreed on the source of the potential corruption, they were in broad agreement that the modest registration and publicity provisions were needed to moderate the amplified voices of lobbyists in the arena of Congress.[10]

Representative Adolph Sabath (D-IL), recounting with considerable disgust the lobbying effort directed against the Public Utility Holding Company Act, argued that the Lobbying Act would prevent the lobbies from "acting under false pretenses or controlling votes." The organized effort to inundate members with the manufactured opinion of the few masquerading as the public interest, Sabath contended, was "insulting to Members of Congress" and "distracts us from our proper duties, prevents our accomplishing our proper work and wears us out." There were few open defenders of the lobbyists and the bill had strong support. Representative Chester H. Gross (R-PA), however, called attention to another growing lobby he claimed was more pernicious than the special-interest groups. "The worst and most pernicious lobbying," he argued, "comes from the various bureaus within the government to perpetuate themselves." His prescient view would not until later increase the legal attempts to limit the rights of interagency lobbyists to influence legislation as the administrative state grew larger and more pervasive.[11]

After passage, the Lobbying Act faced several immediate problems. Imprecisely drafted, it could not prevent many groups who felt that their group's lobbying activities were incidental to evade registration. Organizations that had regularly contacted congressmen to advocate their membership's or company's interests disputed whether they were covered by the statute. By 1950, of the 1807 organizations maintaining offices in Washington, D.C., less than half had registered as lobbyists. Despite these ambiguities, official reports filed with the Senate and House clerks demonstrated the pervasiveness of lobbying activities. By the end of 1949, a total of 2,878 persons and groups had registered, and their reports showed those groups had collected $55,000,000 since 1946, and had spent over $27,000,000 on lobbying activities in the three years since the act became effective.[12]

The Supreme Court considered the legality of the Lobbying Act in two cases in the early 1950s. In *United States v. Rumely*, the House of Representative sought to punish Rumely, secretary of a lobbying organization known as the Committee for Constitutional Government. Called before the House Select Committee on Lobbying Activities, Rumely refused to disclose the names of people who had made bulk purchases of books published by the Committee, which the Court described as being of "a particular political tendentiousness." The question before the Court involved the power of Congress to compel testimony about lobbying activities, and about the conflict between lobby disclosure and free speech and association rights. In *Rumely*, the Supreme Court held that since the mandate of Congress to the investigating committee was limited to investigating all "lobbying activities intended to influence, encourage, promote, or retard legislation," and since the sale of the political books did not fall under the statutory definition of "lobbying activities" in the act, the contempt conviction could not stand. Having ruled that Congress exceeded its authority in finding Rumely in contempt, the Court avoided ruling on the constitutionality of the Lobbying Act.[13]

However, just two years later, the Supreme Court squarely faced the issue of the power of Congress to require registration and reporting of lobbying expenses and payments. The National Farm Committee, a Texas corporation, and two of its officers, Moore and Harriss, were indicted under

Section 305 of the Lobbying Act and charged with failure to report the solicitation and receipt of contributions to influence the passage of legislation to raise commodity prices. The expenditures involved the payment of compensation to communicate face-to-face with members of Congress at public functions and committee hearings, and the costs of a campaign encouraging groups and individuals to communicate by letter with Congress concerning the legislation. The District Court declared the act unconstitutional, citing free speech and association rights, and the appeal proceeded to the Supreme Court.[14]

The Supreme Court, in *United States v. Harriss*, reversed the lower court and held the Lobbying Act constitutional. Writing for the majority, Chief Justice Earl Warren held that the main issue was whether the act was so indefinite that it failed to give an ordinary person notice that his criminal conduct was forbidden by the statute. The Court construed the language in light of the legislative history, which it discussed extensively in the opinion, and found the gist of the antilobbying provision (Section 307) constitutionally prohibited any direct or indirect solicitation, collection or receipt of money or other thing of value "to be used principally to aid, or the principal purpose of which person is to aid" in the passage or defeat or influence directly or indirectly the passage or defeat of congressional legislation. The act lawfully required that the registration and disclosure requirements of the statute be complied with. The Court held that the language of Section 307 of the act that defined illegal conduct was not indefinite, and that it provided legal notice. The substantive registration and disclosure provisions of the act thus stated a criminal violation.[15]

Despite strong objections that the Lobbying Act impinged on free speech and association rights, by upholding the Lobbying Act the Court deferred to congressional concerns about the corruptive potential of lobbying activities expressed by passing the act, according great weight to the deliberative rationale behind the legislation. Balancing the national regulation of lobbying activities with the potential limits on free speech, the majority found that the congressional rationale for the act did not violate "the freedoms guaranteed by the First Amendment—freedom to speak, publish, and to petition the Government." Explaining their deference to legislative motives, Warren, who himself had faced lobby pressure as governor of California, found that "[p]resent-day legislative complexities are such that individual members of Congress cannot be expected to explore the myriad pressures to which they are regularly subjected." Yet a "full realization of the American ideal of government by elected representatives," Warren cautioned, "depends to no small extent on their ability to properly evaluate such pressures . . . otherwise, the voice of the people may all too easily be drowned out by the voice of special interest groups seeking favored treatment while masquerading as proponents of the public weal." That, according to Warren, was the kind of corruption that the Lobbying Act was designed to help prevent.[16]

Furthermore, the Court realized the practical need for a congressional requirement that lobbyists "provide a modicum of information from those who attempt to influence legislation or who collect or spend funds for that purpose." To deny Congress the power of disclosure would be "to deny Congress in large measure the power of self-protection." Finally, when confronted with claims that the act would deter the exercise of First Amendment rights, the classic "chilling argument" that had become an accepted part of First Amendment theory, the majority dismissed that likelihood, calling the hazard of such restraint "too remote to require striking down a statute which on its face is otherwise plainly within the area of congressional power and is designed to safeguard a vital national interest."[17]

The lesson implicit in the judicial approval of congressional regulation of lobbying activities was that the Court would sustain the regulatory power when Congress addressed corruptive activities that it felt hampered the deliberative mechanisms of congressional lawmaking. The need for Congress to keep informed about the positions of persons and groups remained integral to a full deliberation of those issues, but that only worked with full disclosure about the real proponents of those positions. In *Harriss* the Court recognized the special political competency of the legislature to regulate those activities that directly affected its fundamental lawmaking function, and looked to the practical legislative considerations given during passage of the act, to sustain the modest political regulation over the theoretical legal claims of First Amendment imposition made by the dissenters. Because lobbying activities, absent disclosure of the sources of money and power that paid for those activities, prevented Congress from accurately measuring the real public support for those proposals, the Court found the restrictions on association and free speech rights from the law were outweighed by the congressional demands for a full and open process of legislative deliberation. In this battle between political regulation and free speech rights, the Warren court sustained the principles of free speech equality of the public voice over fears that the regulation may go too far in limiting the First Amendment rights of special interest advocacy.[18]

THE UNHAPPY DAYS OF CAMPAIGN FINANCE CORRUPTION—
Professionalizing Politics and the "De-political" Court

Congress continued its biannual congressional ritual of investigating the campaign finance system during the 1950s, investigating the presidential and congressional campaigns of 1948, 1954, and 1956 in a continuing but fruitless effort to produce a campaign finance system that was both transparent and accountable. Just as in the earlier years, the congressional investigations of the 1950s attempted to discover, then disclose the source, amount, nature, and effect that campaign contributions and spending had on federal elections. The 1954 Special Committee to Investigate Campaign Expenditures, composed of Representatives C. W. "Runt" Bishop (D-IL),

Kenneth B. Keating (R-NY), Howard H. Baker (R-TN), Hale Boggs (D-LA), and Frank M. Karsten (D-MO) compiled a final report detailing all the provisions of federal law that regulated national elections, including the Federal Corrupt Practices Act, the Tillman Act, the Hatch Act, the prohibitions on the solicitation and collection of assessments from federal employees, and limits on individual and aggregate party campaign contributions and expenditures.

The committee published an extended compendium of federal statutes regulating elections that offered Congress a complete view of the nature of federal election regulation, and demonstrated that the changes to the campaign financing of federal elections ought to address the problem of reform in a broad and coordinated way. In addition, Congress specifically sought to regulate the franking or U.S. Post Office privileges of members of Congress and drafted new regulations that provided equal time for all legally qualified candidates for any public office in the use of radio broadcast stations, prohibited the censorship by any broadcast licensee of political content, and required that the charges made for the use of any broadcasting station for political advertising not exceed the charges for comparable advertising at such station. Years of reform effort had created a campaign system that regulated contributions and expenditures, and established a system of measures designed to limit coercive practices on voters that would remove their free electoral will, but these new measures were intended to promote a full opportunity for fair democratic deliberation on the most pressing issues of the day through equal access and full debate.[19]

Yet substantive problems remained unaddressed in federal election law. Congress proposed to correct those deficiencies in the Federal Elections Act of 1955. Despite the Supreme Court's 1941 decision, *United States v. Classic,* which overruled *Newberry* and permitted the federal regulation of primary elections, Congress still had not amended the Federal Corrupt Practices Act to make it applicable to primary elections or state caucuses. This loophole, coupled with the equally obvious limitation of FCPA that exempted single-state political committees, effectively allowing the establishment of fifty state committees that operated outside the contribution and spending limitations, made FCPA impotent to regulate and force disclosure of campaign finance expenditures. Yet those problems had been evident since the 1920s; what compelled Congress to act in 1955 were the miserly contribution and spending limits on congressional candidates who faced an increasingly expensive marketplace for political campaigning.[20]

Proposed as an answer to those concerns, the Federal Elections Act of 1955 raised the spending limits for senatorial candidates to either a maximum of $50,000, or an alternative equal to 10 cents times the total number of votes cast in the last prior election for the office sought. House candidates would see their spending limit rise to $12,500 or higher, using the same formula. Proponents called the old spending limits "outdated" and "ridiculous" in view of "the new techniques in political campaigns." Opponents, led by Senators William E. Jenner (R-IN), Frank A. Barnett (R-WY), Joe McCarthy (R-WI), and Carl T. Curtis (R-NE), objected to the changes proposed in the bill. They particularly opposed three provisions that banned political contributions from any committee unless specifically authorized by the candidate, the bills' extension to cover primaries, and its failure to prohibit the use of union PAC contributions spent without specific authorization for those expenditures from union members. The bill, which would have enacted the most substantive reforms of FCPA since 1924, failed to win approval during the 1955 session, and was eventually defeated in 1956. But its main provisions, the closing of the single committee loophole and the raising of campaign spending limits to reflect the changing political campaign practices, along with the consolidation and streamlining of disclosure provisions, remained the main avenue of reform efforts until 1971.[21]

Congressional reform efforts in 1954–55 reflected a growing appreciation of the consequences and costs of the emerging professionalization of political campaigning. Astute political commentators foresaw the potentialities and problems of media advertising on political campaigns. The 1952 presidential campaign of Dwight Eisenhower was the first major campaign that featured television advertising. That year, both major parties ran television, radio, and print ads that played heavily on World War II memories. Techniques of mass persuasion, perfected by advertising executives, became the most common form of advertising in political campaigns. Many critics concluded that, given a reasonable receptivity among audience members, "radio and television (could) sell social objectives as they sell soap." With the increased use of broadcast advertising came other professional operatives—the public opinion pollster, the political consultant, the public relations advisor—all of which became integral to the modern political campaign. When Dwight Eisenhower announced his candidacy for reelection in 1956, Republican National Chairman Leonard Hall announced that "we are going to run a mass communication campaign."[22]

At the same time, a loose coalition of academics and reformers concerned about the democratic health of the campaign finance system began to study and critique the operation of that system. This group employed new social science methods to gather evidence to critique the use of mass communication technology in political campaigns. Different from earlier campaign finance reformers, this group was "neither a grassroots movement nor a group of elites" but instead "political actors operating at the margins of power who believed that representative government could be improved." Their concerns related to the representative boundaries of the polity, to ensuring that the principles of democratic deliberation were not warped by the methods of mass communication. This coalition studied the campaign system, particularly the inadequacies of the campaign finance component, and began to assert in published studies and congressional testimony that competent, targeted reform was needed to promote democratic ideals and "end the cynicism that now scars our politics."[23]

But the slow, accretive change in election law during the 1950s and 1960s motivated by the reform coalition outside of Congress, and a few concerned representatives inside it, was also affected by two other major factors. First, the role and influence of the judicial branch and its increasing willingness to tackle "political questions" during the 1950–1960s provided the modus operandi for the resolution of contentious issues that were often irresolvable inside the legislative branch. And second, the preappointment political background of the members of the Supreme Court, and the Court membership's growing institutional detachment from hard-core politics and electoral political experience, created and favored a formalistic model for the resolution of those "political questions." This led, ultimately, to a preferment of First Amendment rights over long-recognized legislative interests that had privileged communal democratic ideals thought necessary to protect electoral integrity. Those factors increased the likelihood that legislation affecting campaign finance would be examined using a judicial lens that considered the election reforms as justiciable questions, thus obscuring the very political questions from the practical aspects of politics they sought to regulate.

The 1956 Senate hearings on the campaign finance system reveal the growing divergence between practical politics and the constitutional impediments to electoral reform. The hearings before the Subcommittee on Privileges and Elections were chaired by Albert Gore (D-TN) and included Senators Mike Mansfield (D-MT) and Carl T. Curtis (R-NE). The primary objectives of the hearings, like nearly every biannual hearing on campaigns since the Progressive era, were first, to collect the fullest record of actual spending in the 1956 campaign, and second, to propose legislation to remedy defects in the campaign financing laws to be submitted to the next Congress. Though that purpose mimicked earlier hearings, the 1956 hearings, coinciding with the wave of electoral professionalization and concern about the way that the campaign finance system affected opportunities for democratic deliberation, took a very different approach. The 1956 hearings mark the beginning of serious congressional efforts to reform the FCPA, showing its irrelevance after thirty years of ineffectual service.

The committee worried that the multiplicity of campaign committees, taking advantage of the one-state loophole of FCPA, and the ingenuity of corporate and labor union contributors, permitted the widespread evasion of the law. Sensational revelations in 1956 that an oil company had offered cash to Senator Francis Case (R-SD) to support legislation favorable to the company added to that concern. Although Case rejected the bribe, President Eisenhower eventually vetoed the oil company bill to avoid any appearance of impropriety. The disclosure, coming as it did at the start of the investigation, spotlighted the issue of campaign finance reform. Public involvement in the financing of campaigns in 1956 included nearly $75 million in ready contributions to the campaign chests of the two major political parties, five times the amount reported spent in the election of the 84th Congress.[24]

The hearings provide evidence for this shift in approach and intent. Unlike earlier congressional hearings that focused on the disclosure of the amount of campaign funding and expenditures, the 1956 hearings drew conclusions about how the financing of political campaigns limited the opportunity for public debate. The professionalization of political campaigns and the effects of an increasing reliance on expensive electronic media outlets to express the message focused the hearings more than ever before on how money corrupted the electoral system by drowning out the potential for alternative messages.

At the outset, it was clear that this investigation would be different, reflecting the major changes in tactics and methods of political campaigning itself. Before the committee commenced taking testimony, it hired special counsel and a staff composed of attorneys, investigators, accountants, and statisticians, including E. Wayles Browne, Jr., an statistician and economist. The committee hired Alexander Heard, an expert who had compiled numerous studies of past campaign finance practices. His studies included direct testimony and responses accumulated from questionnaires directed to several hundred independent political committees and all candidates, all 21 national political committees, and more than 300 additional political committees active at the city and county level. The information, more voluminous than any previously accumulated, had to be reduced to an IBM punch-card system at the Library of Congress to sort and analyze.[25]

Heard testified that he had examined some 3,500 campaign finance reports for 1952. Over a third of all directors of the hundred largest corporations, Heard said, had made campaign gifts in 1952 of $500 or more, and a great many of those directors had contributed to both candidates in an election. Heard identified four problems with the American campaign finance system: the inequality of campaign finances between candidates, the assumption of large contributors that they could demand favoritism due to their campaign contributions, the fearsome amount of election regulation that often could not be enforced, and finally, the resulting attitude of apathy, distrust, and cynicism in politics and the situation that gave rise to it. Heard, under questioning by conservative Senator Carl Curtis (R-NE), admitted that the problem was rampant among corporations and labor unions, as well as Republicans and Democrats. The problem, he said, resulted from a failure to recognize that our electoral system demands that money be spent to inform the electorate about candidates, and second, from the fact that there was little accountability from political committees to record and report all contributions. Heard advocated tax-deductible donations to encourage public giving to political campaigns, guaranteed minimum electronic media access to radio and television at greatly reduced costs to candidates and political parties, and strong enforcement of violations of a streamlined and efficient reporting system. But Heard cautioned that the reform goals were unusually expansive. "Americans," he said, "must realize that they have been inordinately ambitious in their efforts to regulate money in elections. . . . Our failure is a failure to reach goals others do not attempt."[26]

Testimony from party officials complained about the rising costs of campaigns. Democratic National Committee Chairman Paul Butler testified that a thirty-minute advertisement on the three national networks would cost between $200,000 and $220,000. In the first three months of 1956, Democrats raised $269,000 as compared to the Republican total of $2,634,000. The concern of those involved with the conduct of political campaigns was how to "avoid a one-sided presentation of the issues" that necessarily resulted from the purchase of time and space in the electronic media. For Democrats, the only way to do this was to encourage "large numbers of small contributions from citizens."[27]

Yet the single greatest source of campaign funding for the Democratic Party came not from individual citizens, but as bundled contributions from labor unions. Senator Curtis questioned the union officials on the extent of coercion involved in accumulating the union contributions. These arguments recalled those made during the earlier debates over the War Labor Disputes and Taft-Hartley Acts when union officials had charged that corporations commonly evaded legal requirements by making off-the-book contributions to Republican candidates from officers or by coercing employees to contribute to particular candidates under an implied threat of dismissal. Curtis, turning the tables on the unions, questioned the union practice of using the educational component of the Committee on Political Education (COPE) fund for political purposes, thus subverting the contribution and reporting requirements of FCPA. Steadfastly maintaining the practice was legal, Jack Kroll, codirector of the recently merged AFL-CIO and its newly formed COPE, agreed that the law as written required separate funds, and that the "education" COPE conducted with the funds "talked about no candidate . . . we talk about issues as those issues affect our people." The distinction, for Curtis, was without a difference.[28]

The final committee report documented the ineffectiveness and inadequacy of the current campaign finance laws. Republicans and Democrats spent over $33 million in 1956 federal general election expenses, with television and radio advertising accounting for $9,504,000 of the total. The law limited the maximum aggregate expenditure by each candidate or party to $3 million, saying that "unrealistically low" limits "lead to the creation of numerous other political committees for purposes of a campaign" and "demoralize the political climate and breed contempt for the law" so easily and routinely ignored. The miracles of IBM technology permitted the committee to geographically analyze the source of the major contributions over $500, and they found that contributions to the State of

New York Republican Party ($2,382,047) nearly equaled the totals contributed to the Democrats in all states. More importantly, by segregating the larger contributions from individuals, the committee was able to sort through the inadequately reported contributions, and find, for example, that Lansdell K. Christie of New York, whose filings showed he had contributed only $23,000 to eight Democratic committees, in fact had given $78,164, including $26,000 to fourteen political committees of which the subcommittee had no prior knowledge.[29]

The committee ultimately recommended more stringent reporting requirements, a broadening of the base of the electorate, and equalization of "opportunities of candidates and parties to present themselves to the electorate." It also called for interstate limitations on the raising and spending of money. "We feel that it is the prerogative of the citizens of a given State," the report concluded, "to elect senators and representatives of their own choosing without undue interference from without." This prerogative is "in accord with sound principles of representative government" and is "endangered by the ever increasing cost of elections and the degree to which people and interests of other States seek to interfere with cash."[30]

The bill would have raised spending limits to "realistic levels," required strict reporting requirements and specific authorization from a candidate before any committee could spend money in his name, ensured free radio and television air time for major candidates, raised and made tax-deductible the contribution limits to $100 to encourage widespread participation, and prohibited the spending of campaign funds from out-of-state sources in a federal election. Despite broad popular support for some kind of reform, and the embarrassment generated by the Case incident, by June 1956 the "Honest Elections" bill, proposed by Senate Democratic Leader Lyndon B. Johnson (D-TX) and Senate Republican Leader William F. Knowland (R-CA), was dead in the water. Dogpaddling under the weight of dual objections from labor leaders, fearful about limits on their PACs, and concerns raised by conservative Republicans anxious to curb what they saw as the growing power of unions to coerce their members out of contributions, the bill received only lukewarm congressional support. Unions were particularly opposed to the plan, since they felt that multiple campaign committees would be restricted, and that they could not otherwise compete with business organizations in the raising of funds. Union leader Walter P. Reuther proposed an alternative that limited to $5 all individual contributions to candidates, with another $5 for political parties, and a maximum limit of $20 per individual in a presidential election year. Senator Curtis and Senator Barry Goldwater (R-AZ) offered an amendment that would prevent unions from making political contributions from money collected as dues, the earliest version of "paycheck protection." With opposition from both sides, the "Honest Elections" bill failed to win congressional approval to the muted lamentations of the congressional proponents and the reform coalition.[31]

The failure of the reform effort in 1956 was not due to a lack of public support for the plan, but instead, to a fear by the political players that the new regulations would alter their competitive balance. In addition, media executives, whose corporations profited handsomely from new techniques being used in the political marketplace, opposed proposals for free or reduced political advertising costs, and strongly advocated for an end to the equal time provisions. Congress rejected plans to require free airtime for major candidates when the officials of the three major television and radio networks equated those proposals with free market conceptions of private property that privileged the individual over the communal interest. These arguments signaled a growing movement to redefine the rights of public ownership of the airwaves quite different from those that had undergirded the 1934 Federal Communication Act. The media attack on the "equal time" provision of Section 315 of the Federal Communication Act began in earnest when Ernest Lee Jahncke, vice president of the American Broadcasting Company, testified that despite the "areas of responsibility assigned to broadcasters under their basic obligation to serve the public interest," none specifically defined that as relating to political broadcasting.[32]

While the media conglomerates opposed the fairness doctrine, more significantly, they wanted the decision on the amount and nature of political programming that they would broadcast left to their own business judgment. Regarding proposals that the networks and broadcast stations be required to provide free airtime, Jahncke concluded, "economically, this is just not feasible." The free publicly owned airwaves by 1956 had evolved into national businesses, and congressional reformers soon discarded the option of reducing campaign costs by providing free airtime to candidates. What resulted was a bill that teased at only the edges of reform, one that generated concomitant opposition from unions, the PACs, and those politicians who felt that they would experience electoral disadvantage by its reformist ideals. These attitudes died hard, and by the end of the 1960s, reform of the campaign finance system from inside the system —a system then building its own institutional inertia with a huge cadre of campaign professionals—appeared a daunting, thankless task. Despite those obstacles, energized by the Civil Rights movement and nurtured in the civic activism of the Warren court, legal reform appeared to be the only viable option for challenging systemic electoral corruption and reinvigorating the democratic ideals of American elections.[33]

THE SUPREME COURT RESPONDS—*United States v. Classic* to *Red Lion*

From the 1941 decision in *United States v. Classic* to the 1969 decision in *Red Lion Broadcasting Co., Inc. v. FCC,* the Supreme Court took increasing interest in deciding legal-political questions that had formerly been considered beyond their institutional competency and demanded an ordering of a democratic philosophy that would support and substantiate their rulings. That period coincided with a rising worldwide challenge to democratic institutions and ideas, and a growing domestic movement demanding civil rights for African Americans. Those dual forces shaped the nature of the debate over democratic ideas and forced the judiciary to adopt constitutional protections for what they considered instrumental devices to protect democratic institutions. First Amendment free speech protections came to be seen, by democratic theorists and by civil rights activists alike, as not simply necessary tools, but the most essential means to ensure the steady evolution of those democratic ideals threatened by fascism, Nazism, communism, and racism.[34]

During that period the Supreme Court decided a wide variety of cases indirectly related to campaign finance that altered democratic conceptions of the electoral system. Election law questions became the "important testing ground for constitutional theory" because they often involved conflicts between principles central to theories of our government. The Court's choices between principles in a particular election law case often had an unusually direct relationship to its underlying assumptions about the nature of democracy. As the Court decided these cases, it focused less on civic conceptions of the common good that it had formerly used to sustain the right of Congress to regulate elections, and relied more on emerging conceptions of individual rights, especially First Amendment protections, as the best way to promote deliberative democratic ideas. The influence of the Civil Rights movement had invigorated the concept of individual rights by demonstrating the irrationality and undemocratic nature of group discrimination, and the Court began in earnest to apply that concept to cases affecting the electoral system.[35]

At the same time, the Court's preappointment experience underwent a change. During the period before 1965, the Supreme Court membership possessed an institutional political acumen largely arising from the direct political experiences of its members. As the composition of the Court began to change after 1955, with the appointing of former law clerks and judges who lacked practical, electoral political experiences similar to those of their predecessors, the values of the Court began to prefer a doctrinal, theoretical implementation of First Amendment rights. That shift of the Supreme Court composition away from members with practical political experience toward a judicial temperament that evoked a theoretical defense of First Amendment rights dramatically diminished communitarian equality as a value in election and campaign finance cases. That preference helps explain why the Supreme Court in the 1976 case of *Buckley v. Valeo* could ignore a century of campaign finance precedent favoring equality as an instrumental democratic value, yet maintain that their decision was a victory for free speech rights.

The 1941 *Classic* decision, which granted Congress the right to regulate primary elections, arose during a time when democratic institutions and democracy itself faced worldwide challenges. Nazi Germany rolled across

Europe, leaving many formerly democratic countries prostrate in its evil wake. The Atlantic Charter commanded as one of its principal objections the restoration of democracy to all European nations, as well as an end to racial and ethnic discrimination. The United States, smarting from its inherent internal hypocrisies, faced challenges at home, as the presence of Jim Crow discrimination in the United States undercut American claims of moral superiority. For African Americans denied the opportunity to participate in the American bounty, their nation's call on them to participate in its wartime military obligation crystallized the inherent injustice of denying them the right to vote. The military battles of World War II were of immense concern, but so too was the ideological resurrection of democracy, which became a national political project.[36]

Even before *Classic,* antecedent legal challenges to the all-white primary in 1927 led to the Supreme Court decision in *Nixon v. Herndon* that overturned the all-white primary and ruled that denying to African Americans the right to vote in a primary election was a violation of the equal protection clause of the Fourteenth Amendment. By 1932, the recalcitrant Texas legislature had innovated its way around *Nixon v. Herndon* by creating private political parties, each of which could "prescribe the qualifications of its own members and shall in its own way determine who shall be qualified to vote or otherwise participate in such political party." The power to regulate party membership, the Court found, came not from inherent political rights of parties but from the state statute. Having found no rational basis for state action regarding the discrimination by the Democratic Party in Texas, which excluded from membership all African-American voters, and finding no rational basis for the exclusion, the Supreme Court struck it down as invidious discrimination in violation of the Fourteenth Amendment. The Court determined that the right to vote was an individual right, because it believed that group discrimination could best be addressed by characterizing rights violations as individual claims. Justice McReynolds, joined by Van Devanter, Sutherland, and Butler, dissented, arguing that the right to regulate and conduct elections was a state prerogative, as was the regulation of party membership. Parties, being voluntary organizations, could define their own membership. This power was essential, the dissenters argued, to "secure order, prevent fraud . . . and in part from obligation to prescribe appropriate methods for selecting candidates whose names shall appear upon official ballots used at regular elections." Since the new act did not specifically exclude African Americans, the dissenters were willing to leave the regulation of primary elections to state officials and party leaders, but it was clear that the Court was moving in a vastly different direction.[37]

The final setback for African-American voters before the *Classic* decision came in *Grovey v. Townsend,* a case again arising out of the Texas primary system. The petitioner, an African-American citizen of Harris County, Texas, and a member of the Democratic Party, sought an absentee ballot to vote in the party primary. Townsend, the county clerk refused him the ballot based on a 1932 Democratic Party resolution that said "all white citizens of the State of Texas who are qualified to vote under the Constitution and laws of the state shall be eligible to membership in the Democratic Party and as such entitled to participate in its deliberations." Grovey filed suit and the Supreme Court found that since Texas had laws permitting political parties to establish membership requirements, and since no violation of Grovey's rights to vote in the general election occurred, there was no violation of his right to vote in the Democratic Party primary. The primary, and party membership, remained outside of the regulation by federal authorities and of Fourteenth Amendment equal protection principles.[38]

By 1941, however, both the political landscape and the democratic implications of restricted electoral participation had changed. The rising tide of "isms" that seemed at every turn to threaten democratic principles compelled the Court to reexamine *Grovey v. Townsend* and its racially discriminatory party primary decisions. The crux of the issue in *United States v. Classic* was whether Congress could regulate federal primary elections by making applicable the federal criminal code to acts of voter and election fraud. The Louisiana Democratic Party had held its party election for the office of the Second Congressional District on September 10, 1940. The evidence demonstrated that nomination as a Democratic candidate always ensured election as the representative, there being no effective Republican opposition in the state. The criminal allegations alleged that Classic and other election officials had "altered eighty-three ballots cast for one candidate and fourteen cast for another, marking and counting them as votes for a third candidate, and then falsely certified the number of votes cast for the respective candidates to the chairman of the Second Congressional District Committee."[39]

Justice Stone, writing for the majority (Chief Justice Hughes took no part in the case having earlier argued for the plaintiff in *Classic,* while Justices Douglas, Black, and Murphy dissented), found that the primary election was, in all respects, a state enterprise. The state paid for, organized, carried out, and set the rules for the nomination process. Facing the precedent of *Newberry,* which held that Congress had no power to regulate the processes of state primary elections, the majority characterized the historical basis of the *Newberry* finding—that the founders knew of no primaries and thus could not have meant to authorize their regulation as "stultifying narrowness." "The right to vote in a congressional election is a right secured by the Constitution" and any conspiracy to deprive any voter of that right "is a conspiracy to injure or oppress the citizen . . . in the free exercise of the right to participate in choosing a representative." In *Classic,* the court found that elections were integral to democratic principles because in many states, beginning in 1900, the primary winner became the elected representative since there was limited opposition party competition. Yet at the conference deliberations, some justices expressed concern at the reach of that decision, which extended even into party nominating conventions. Although there remained a concern about the judicial role in political affairs, in *Classic* those fears were overridden by the facts of blatant vote fraud, and by the values adopted by the majority regarding the democratic value of individual voting rights.[40]

The emerging judicial consensus that the right to vote was integral to the development and preservation of American democracy connected with earlier legal strands that wove free speech liberties into that theoretical tapestry. While most of the free speech cases of the 1910s–1930s only indirectly involved the electoral system, the Court developed the doctrine privileging individual free speech rights as the strongest way to stimulate deliberative debate and ensure the protection of minority rights against oppressive majority interests. The decision in *Near v. Minnesota* implicitly recognized the growing complexities of American political life and urbanization, and the attendant concerns about corrupt public officials bent on corrupting democratic institutions and principles. "[T]he administration of government," the Court stated, "has become more complex, the opportunities for malfeasance and corruption have multiplied, crime has grown to most serious proportions, and the danger of its protection by unfaithful officials and of the impairment of the fundamental security of life and property by criminal alliances and official neglect, emphasizes the primary need for a vigilant and courageous press." The Court, considering a series of cases after *Classic,* affirmed the interconnectivity between practical political rights, such as voting rights, ballot access, and equalization of voting apportionment, and the necessity of protecting free speech rights essential to fight those battles. The free speech rights of newspapers soon expanded beyond the limited application of *Near v. Minnesota* to cover other circumstances involving individuals shut out of the political process. First Amendment rights became a substantive way for the courts to announce and then protect political rights in an otherwise inhospitable climate.[41]

During the 1950s–1960s that connectivity made the Civil Rights movement the catalyst for legal change. But the political questions doctrine obstructed the path toward change. The "political question doctrine" held that courts, as unrepresentative bodies lacking political accountability, should avoid deciding political questions, policy issues considered beyond the competence and constitutional authority of the judicial branch. Those decisions were, the doctrine went, better decided by legislatures and remained unenforceable by courts because they clearly fell outside "the conditions and purposes that circumscribe judicial action." The judicial branch refrained from acting in those political areas because institutional constraints required that judges exercise their powers in a principled, neutral manner, in a manner that "they did not systematically prefer one class of litigants to another except to the extent that the rules the judges invoked made the characteristics of the favored class relevant to the outcome." The political question doctrine supported the separation of powers doctrine, according to each branch a particular competency over certain kinds of decisions.[42]

The political question doctrine seemed to provide a response to complaints that the Court had itself developed into a dangerous political branch of government, its excesses not pruned by the sharpened tools of regular popular elections. Yet despite the widespread acceptance of the political question doctrine, when the Supreme Court saw recalcitrant state legislatures denying civil and political rights to African Americans, and an executive branch that appeared unwilling to implement the Court's vision of participatory democracy, it transformed the meaning of the political question doctrine. The difficulties faced during the 1950s–1960s by African Americans who fought to implement their political rights guaranteed them under the Constitution exposed for the Supreme Court, with a clarity that could not be ignored, that the states, Congress, and the executive branch could not be relied upon to implement or enforce the rights demanded by the Supreme Court's democratic vision of equality and justice.[43]

INTEGRATING FREE SPEECH AND COMMUNITARIAN THEORIES OF DEMOCRACY IN *BAKER V. CARR, NEW YORK TIMES V. SULLIVAN,* AND *RED LION*

An examination of three cases decided in the mid-1960s illustrates how the Court confronted political questions relating to fundamental principles of electoral equality, and used the First Amendment to construct a democratic theory that privileged the deliberative democratic values courts had used since 1876 in deciding campaign finance cases. At the same time, the Court found that its balancing tests and bifurcated review process for free speech cases caused it to "intertwine the ideological predisposition of those doing the balancing." Along with the heavy criticism the Court endured during Warren's tenure as chief justice for "making law" and "politicizing the court," this realization had by the early 1970s forced the judicial focus away from those deliberative communitarian values of a common good arrived at through open and equal deliberation, toward a process that narrowed the legitimate rationale for regulation of corruption in the campaign finance system into quid pro quo corruption.[44]

Baker v. Carr arose out of one of the most contested political controversies of the twentieth century. Chief Justice Earl Warren, who had authored the breathtaking revolution by desegregating America's apartheid school system in *Brown v. Board of Education,* considered *Baker,* not *Brown,* his most lasting achievement. The 1950 census demonstrated the stark disparities in the Memphis, Tennessee, voting districts. Memphis, with its 312,000 voters, had seven representatives in the state legislature; the surrounding twenty-four counties with an identical population, chose twenty-six representatives. Rural interests controlled the state legislature and, since 1901, had refused to reapportion or equalize the voting districts. Stymied by the Court's political question doctrine in *Colegrove v. Green,* aggrieved voters found the judicial remedy unavailable and the legislative remedy unattainable.[45]

As governor of California, Chief Justice Warren had defended its system of apportionment, which accorded each county one representative, regardless of population. By 1958, Warren, facing the political reality of the growing disparity between voters and representation, and fully aware of the recalcitrance of those in power to voluntarily reapportion their political bodies, began to rethink the political question doctrine. The Court, with Warren writing the majority decision, concluded that "it was unconstitutional to overweigh the value of some voters and underweigh the value of others." He reached this conclusion by resorting to his set of cardinal principles. He believed that our democracy was a representative form of government through which the rights and responsibilities of all people were protected; that protection, he contended, could only be effected "through representatives who are responsible to all the people, not just those with special interests to serve." Expressing this democratic ideal in *Baker v. Carr,* Warren wrote that the constitutional basis for "one-man, one-vote" could be found in the "constitutional right to vote freely for the candidate of one's choice" and that meant that "a debasement or dilution of the weight of a citizen's vote" unduly and unconstitutionally infringed on that right.

For the *Baker* majority, the organizing principles of American democracy required the eradication of corruption, "the presence of special interests, the selfishness of public servants, and the imperfect vindication of participatory rights held equally by all citizens," that made good government impossible. To a remarkable degree, *Baker v. Carr* echoed the principles announced in earlier decisions of the Supreme Court beginning with *Ex Parte Curtis,* which reconciled legislative regulation of the campaign finance system with equality of voting rights, encouraged the end of coercion against the free will of the voter, and protected congressional regulation of speech where that speech tended to drown out the opportunity for voters to hear the full range of political opinion.[46]

Free speech rights became the major cog in the Warren court's democracy project. The most famous Warren court free speech case arose on March 23, 1960, when John Murray placed a full-page advertisement in the *New York Times* on behalf of a civil rights organization called the Committee to Defend Freedom. The ad, entitled "Heed Their Rising Voices" described a series of events that had occurred in South Carolina, Georgia, Alabama, Tennessee, North Carolina, and Virginia, which violated the civil rights of African Americans. The advertisement requested that "[d]ecent-minded Americans cannot help but applaud the creative daring of the students and the quiet heroism of Dr. King" but questioned whether that passive support would be enough to stand against "an unprecedented wave of terror," and requested financial support. "The America whose good name hangs in the balance before a watchful world," the ad declared, "the America whose heritage of Liberty these Southern Upholders of the Constitution are defending, is our America as well as theirs. . . . We must heed their rising voices-yes-but we must add our own."[47]

One copy of the *Times* reached Grover Cleveland Hall, Jr., editor of the Montgomery, Alabama, *Advertiser,* who had been known for his curious mix of racial liberalism. Citing several claims in the advertisement, Hall wrote an editorial that called the advertisement "Lies, lies, lies—possibly willful ones on the part of the fund-raising novelist who wrote those lines to prey on the credulity, self-righteousness and misinformation of northern citizens." Montgomery City Commissioner L. B. Sullivan, in charge of the police alleged to have violated the rights of the protesters, demanded a full and complete retraction for what he called "grave misstatements and defamatory matter." Soon, several public officials, brought suit for libel against the *New York Times* and several other civil rights leaders responsible for placing the ad. The trial of the Sullivan case occurred over three days, November 1–3, 1960, and resulted in a jury verdict, reached after only two hours and twenty minutes of deliberation, against the *Times* and the four civil rights ministers in the amount of $500,000. The judgment against public newspapers and civil rights officials struck a lethal blow at the vitality and power of the Civil Rights movement.[48]

The case moved slowly through the appeals process toward the Supreme Court. The uncontroverted evidence was that the ad contained several misstatements of fact. In the South, a man's reputation and honor remained culturally and socially important, and the common law of libel protected even public figures from libelous utterances. For the civil rights advocates, and eventually, for the Supreme Court, the case came to represent the "emerging notion of the public marketplace of ideas" that Justice Brennan described in his opinion.[49]

Previous cases had held that libel, a specially derogated kind of speech, had only limited First Amendment protection. A unanimous court in *New York Times v. Sullivan* decided for the first time that freedom of speech and press limited the right of a public official to recover damages for comments critical of their official conduct. Justice Brennan wrote that the Court, in deciding this issue, "must consider this case against the background of a profound national commitment to the principle that debate on public issues should be uninhibited, robust and wide-open, and that it may well include vehement, caustic, and sometimes unpleasantly sharp attacks on government and public officials." Failure to permit some false statements in public debate would choke off the "breathing space" that free debate needs to survive and lead to self-censorship. Limiting free debate, the Court concluded, "dampens the vigor and limits the variety of public debate." Only when a false statement was made with the knowledge that it was false, or with a reckless disregard of whether it was false or not, would a cause of action for libel of a public official exist. The belief that free speech best protected and promoted fundamental democratic ideals of deliberation and debate created a condition during the Cold War and during the equally repressive times of the Civil Rights movement that free speech rights, essential yet frail, demanded special legal protection from the Court. The historic decision represented the high point of what some have called the "bifurcated review project," the process by which the Supreme Court has implemented Justice Stone's footnote 4 from *Carolene Products Co.*, which elevated certain freedoms to a preferred position.[50]

The problem that *Sullivan* created nearly swallowed the problem that *Sullivan* solved. The purpose of the *Sullivan* limitations on public libel actions was to promote a free and open debate. While deliberative democratic ideals were essential to the marketplace of ideas, making free speech an individual right furthering individual autonomy in a pluralistic society invited "a world in which any speaker is free to talk on any subject." Individualizing free speech rights to the effect of minimizing their communal, deliberative value seemed to make free speech easier to protect but less easy to regulate on the basis of equality of opportunity. When everyone can speak, and everything can be said, "speech has ceased to become special and has become the equivalent of noise." Rising critics of the Warren court complained that the Court, in taking on apportionment and state libel laws, was promoting a political agenda they saw as both injudicious and undemocratic. But the Warren court's emphasis on individual rights was meant to promote, not interfere with, the communal concepts of deliberation that free speech also protected and promoted.[51]

Although the acrimony and contention over the Warren court's democracy project grew in the last years of his tenure, Warren issued two more opinions in 1969 that epitomized the strength of the Court's democratic idealism, and emboldened the growing challenge to the Court's judicial temperament and institutional competence to resolve political questions. Flamboyant U.S. congressman Adam Clayton Powell, Jr. (D-NY) had represented his Harlem, New York, constituency for many years and had been reelected by a wide majority in the 1966 general election. Responding to allegations of ethical and financial improprieties, the House leadership appointed a Select House of Representatives Committee to conduct an investigation into the allegations and determine Powell's eligibility. Before he was seated, it declared that although Powell met the "age, citizenship, and residence requirement specified in the Federal Constitution, he had asserted an unwarranted privilege and immunity from the processes of the courts of New York, he had wrongfully diverted House funds for the use of others and himself, and he had made false reports concerning expenditures of foreign currency." The House, by resolution, voted to exclude him from membership and declare his seat vacant. Powell filed a challenge to the refusal of the House to seat him after his 1966 election. Under Article I, Section 5, the Constitution gave Congress the power to determine the elections and qualifications of its members. Opponents contended that this meant the power lay in the Congress and not the Court, and this contest represented the epitome of a political question over which the Court had no jurisdiction. After *Baker v. Carr,* the political question doctrine had become one of the most contentious weapons in the Court's armament.[52]

In *Powell v. McCormack* the Court reasoned that neither the textual interpretation of the Constitution nor the history of the Constitutional Convention provided any "textual commitment" to defer to Congress on the qualification of members, especially since this case involved not the constitutionally prescribed expulsion, but the less certain prerogative of Congress to deny an elected member the right to his seat. Having determined the issue was not a political question, and was thus within the purview of the Court, Warren, writing for the majority, returned to the ideals of the democracy project. "A fundamental principle of our representative democracy," Warren wrote, "is . . . that the people should choose whom they please to govern them." Congress could protect the integrity of its membership by punishing a member or in an extreme case, expelling a member with a two-thirds vote, but "an examination of the basic principles of our democratic system persuade us that the Constitution does not vest in the Congress a discretionary power to deny membership by a majority vote."[53]

The Warren court's interpretation of the power of Congress to exclude members continued the thematic construct of the Warren court democracy project by protecting voters otherwise denied equal access and influence in the political system from majorities bent on limiting their rights. Equal access to the electoral system often required the Court to limit the rights of stronger, more powerful actors. This theme carried over to the final case in which the Court melded its democratic ideals with politics, which was one of the last decisions Warren wrote. Having resigned in 1968 "at the pleasure of the President," Warren intended to stay on only until Congress confirmed President Lyndon Johnson's nominee for chief justice, sitting justice Abe Fortas. Led by opponents of the Warren court, the Fortas confirmation became a referendum on the Warren court as conservatives raged against all forms of Warren court activism. Senator J. Strom Thurmond (R-SC), a member of the Senate Judiciary Committee, questioned the timing and arrangement of Warren's retirement. "Justice Fortas is not only a friend of President Johnson," Thurmond fumed, "he is also a protégé of Earl Warren." Comparing their voting records, Thurmond claimed that Fortas had agreed with Warren on 97 out of a possible 112 decisions, a record exceeded only by Justice Brennan. Warren's delayed retirement especially hackled his detractors. "If the Senate confirms this appointment," Thurmond declared, "we will be confirming an extraconstitutional arrangement by which the Supreme Court justices can so arrange their resignations as to perpetuate their influence and ideology on the Supreme Court." Soon, the Fortas nomination became entangled in allegations of impropriety and Warren, facing embarrassment at withdrawing his nomination to avoid having his replacement appointed by Richard Nixon, instead waited out the end of his last year on the Court. While the controversy swirled, the Court granted certiorari in *Red Lion Broadcasting Co. v. FCC*.[54]

In many ways, *Red Lion Broadcasting* epitomized the highest ideals of the Warren court democracy project intended to protect equality of access in order to promote democratic deliberation. As previously discussed, *Red Lion* involved a challenge to the FCC equal time and the fairness doctrine rules, which required broadcast companies to provide full and equal, and—when the party could not afford to pay the going rate—free equal access to persons attacked in broadcasts, or to political opponents of those candidates who were endorsed by a station. Every major broadcast company challenged the rules as violations of the free speech rights of those companies, arguing that requiring a broadcaster to provide free time for controversial opposing viewpoints forced self-censorship on those broadcasters.[55]

The *Red Lion* decision, written by Justice White, and sounding very much in tune with the tenets and tenor of the democracy project, held that the fairness doctrine regulations promulgated by the FCC were valid and constitutional, because they "enhance, rather than abridge the freedoms of speech and press." The advances in technology, and the increasing use of broadcast media in political campaigns, did not change the fundamental fact that the public owned the broadcast medium, and that therefore the FCC must administer the medium in the public interest. To ensure the vigorous public debate that the public interest standard required, Congress had legitimately concluded that the characteristics of the electronic media justified "differences in First Amendment standards applied to them" and it was legitimate to take into account "the ability of new technology to produce sounds more raucous than those of the human voice." Just as the government could constitutionally limit the use of sound-amplifying equipment potentially "so noisy that it drowns out civilized private speech," it could also regulate the use of the broadcast medium. The Court recognized that, if misused, abused, or concentrated such that the radio spectrum drowned out the small voices of the minority, the power of the medium could cause great damage to the deliberative tools of the democracy project. "The right of the public to receive suitable access to social, political, esthetic, moral, and other ideas and experiences" was crucial to the Court's finding that the fairness and equal time doctrines were constitutional assertions of congressional authority. The communitarian democratic values evidenced by the Warren court in deciding election and free speech cases reflected assumptions about democracy that privileged the values of free speech, but balanced them against reasonable congressional attempts to promote egalitarian practices of equality. Earl Warren's pragmatic political experience made his tenure especially willing to bend the political question doctrine, because he believed that the Supreme Court possessed a special kind of political competency to formulate and implement a democratic vision that the states, Congress, and the executive branch seemed unwilling to embrace.[56]

PAC SCANDALS, THE KENNEDY COMMISSION, AND THE ORIGINS OF PUBLIC FINANCING—1962–1967

By 1960 the reassessment of rights and democracy by the Warren court extended deep into the political culture. The denial of voting rights to millions of African Americans symbolized both the promise and the ambiguity of American democratic ideals, even as that very denial vitalized the growing Civil Rights movement. The Cold War competition between democratic ideals and communism became part of the campaign rhetoric during the 1960 presidential election between John F. Kennedy and Richard M. Nixon. At a $100-a-plate fund-raiser in San Francisco, Nixon's running mate Henry Cabot Lodge called on the U.S. to "prove its democracy," and noted the recent vote against admitting the People's Republic of China to the United Nations as proof of a "clear-cut defeat for communism." "We will win the world struggle on a spiritual basis," Lodge claimed, "or victory will elude us." School children held mock elections, preceded by weeks of campaigning, electioneering, and speechmaking, to demonstrate the vitality of the democratic system. Kennedy's election was hailed by the Vatican as "proof of American democracy" because it strengthened the appreciation for "high democratic principles of freedom that guide American public life and assure access to the highest office to every citizen regardless of social class, race, or religion."[57]

Once again, the power of campaign finance money to reshape political debate became a question of significant interest to a select group of policy reformers concerned about the vitality of American democratic institutions. At the heart of those democratic ideals was the traditional and now revitalized conception about equality of access to the machinery of democracy. The Warren court led the executive and legislative branches toward a conception of equality that broke down institutional barriers to political access, while at the same time cementing a conception of individual liberty that accorded to each American the political rights protected by the Constitution.[58]

The professionalization of elections also raised serious challenges to democratic ideals. Policy experts called on Congress to revamp the antiquated and ignored Federal Corrupt Practices Act, which had proven ineffective in controlling the rising amount of campaign money spent in elections. The rise of political action committees and scandals involving Senators Thomas Dodd (D-CT) and Senator Case concerning the use of campaign funds for illicit personal purposes raised the concerns of reformers about the ineffectiveness of the act. Lobbyist and political action committees formed a nexus of campaign money and influence that some claimed threatened the ability of average citizens to access and influence their elected representatives. The rising cost of American campaigns, estimated at $140 million for all elections in 1952 ($1.40 per eligible voter) to $200 million in 1960 ($3.04 per eligible voter) was a problem, but not the only concern. The problem of raising large amounts of campaign finances necessary to run a modern political campaign while ensuring that no contributor gained an unfair advantage over an elected representative evolved to become the fundamental question of the campaign finance debates from 1960 to 1974.[59]

Responding to a chorus of campaign finance experts voicing concerns, President Kennedy ordered a study of the system in 1960. The critics, however, rarely focused simply on the amount of campaign spending. They understood that there were good reasons for the increase in spending, including the massive influx of eligible voters due to the abolition of the poll tax by the Twenty-Fourth Amendment, the passage of the Voting Rights Act of 1965 that brought additional millions of formerly excluded blacks and poor whites into the electorate, and the increase of voters due to the coming of age of the baby boomers. The host of new campaign technologies and expertise also came at a price, and the days of mass rallies created by personal appeals directed to the populace were long gone. Modern campaigning demanded the use of the modern media to appeal to an inert electorate only sporadically interested in politics.[60]

Reformers decried the corruption of the electoral system, which they had broadly defined to include the quid pro quo component of political access and influence, and the conception that campaign funds were used to drown out competing voices in the din of the political process. The inability of the system to ensure full discussion concerned the reformers. The lack of reliable information about the sources of contributions and the nature of expenditures was seen as a major impediment to informed voting. Big contributions from individuals, corporations, or political action committees that could not be accounted back to those contributors also created an impression that those contributors gained special and unequal access to their representatives. But that dual conception of corruption began to unravel. By 1976, when the Supreme Court in *Buckley v. Valeo* redefined corruption to privilege individual rights of free speech over communal concerns about equal access to the political marketplace, the only corruption Congress could legitimately regulate in the campaign finance arena became the highly limited and formalistic conception of "quid pro quo."

Kennedy invited Alexander Heard, a leading campaign finance expert, to head the commission. Herbert Alexander, another expert on campaign fund-raising and spending, headed the staff. The Commission on Campaign Costs produced a study and recommended to the president on May 29, 1962, that Congress make major changes to the system. The commission believed it fundamental to the preservation of American democracy that the financial burdens of presidential campaigns "be widely shared" and that some incentives be established to encourage "broad solicitation and giving." The proposed incentives, necessary to end the reliance by candidates on the large contributions of those with "special interests," included income tax credits and deductions for those who made political contributions. Furthermore, the commission recommended ending the mother of all political loopholes by requiring campaigns to establish one uniform committee for all contributions, and required reports for "corporations, labor unions, trade associations, and other groups, spending $5,000 or more for bipartisan or multi-partisan political activities in any year." Also, to reduce costs, the commission recommended a temporary suspension of Section 315 of the Federal Communication Act, the "equal time" provision, which had been suspended in 1960 for the Kennedy-Nixon debates, to be accompanied by a study and review by Congress of "broadcasting and campaigning practices that occur under ever-changing conditions." The argument, promoted by the national broadcasting industry, was that if Congress relaxed the "equal time" provisions, media outlets would voluntarily provide free time and facilities for political uses. Another proposal of the commission was to permit free use by local election boards, registration commissions, and political parties of the U.S. Postal Department for registering voters during presidential elections.[61]

The commission's recommendations were shelved in 1964 by Lyndon Johnson. But calls for campaign finance reform grew especially strong during the bribery scandal of Senator Francis Case, which played out on the front pages of American newspapers during 1964–1965, and during the scandal over political fund-raising from corporate executives with large military contracts during the Vietnam War. Although the scandals created public concern over the connections between campaign contributors and congressional influence, public support for campaign finance reform remained less than overwhelming. Part of the problem resulted from the unclear definition of corruption. Despite the notoriety of the Case scandal, the corruptive effects of campaign funding remained ambiguous. Elected officials, quick to recognize the political implications of direct bribery, soon established indirect ways to offer access and influence, ways that would not call attention to their activities and that could, if disclosed, be explained away as constituent service. Even as the campaign apparatus became professionalized and complex, professional politicians found ways to offer access to their major contributors without tying the knot of corruption around their political necks.[62]

In 1966 pressure on congressional Democrats to address the appearance of campaign impropriety prompted a renewed effort, led by Senator Russell Long (D-LA), to reform the campaign finance system. Long proposed a direct subsidy for presidential elections as an amendment to President Johnson's proposal of campaign finance reform, which would have substantially enacted the recommendations of the Kennedy Commission. Senator Long, who felt that the tax incentives proposed by the Kennedy Commission were insufficient to promote the goals of widespread public participation in campaign financing, offered an amendment, the "Presidential Election Campaign Fund Act of 1966," that provided for a tax checkoff whereby individual taxpayers could allocate $1.00 of taxes to go to a fund to help defray the costs of presidential campaigns for major political parties (those receiving fifteen million votes or more in the last presidential election). Major parties would get the public money, but minor parties could also earn access to the fund by obtaining a threshold of five million votes in the last general election. Long admitted his approach was not a "full answer to all of the problems in connection with regulating political contributions," but he viewed his proposal as legislation that "will give assurance that presidential campaigns are not necessarily obligated to any financial interests as a result of the necessity to raise funds to finance their campaigns." Long asserted that "there are sizable groups of citizens in our country who suspect that these financial contributions have influenced governmental decisions," and this amendment would "remove this shadow and prevent the possibility of anything like this in the future."[63]

The passage of the first public campaign financing provisions for federal elections was due in part to recognition that the costs of modern campaigning had exceeded the capacity of the citizenry to adequately support that campaigning. Only through the measure of an income tax checkoff, where the federal government would collect and then distribute general revenue dollars to the parties, could those costs be met. The spending limits still in place under FCPA, long considered antiquated, unenforceable, and inadequate, were repealed. The move toward public financing, coupled with the repeal of spending limits, cautioned opponents of the proposal like Senator Gore, could substantially change the voluntary system of political participation and provide a boondoggle to major parties and incumbents. Nevertheless, the bill passed Congress and President Johnson signed it into law, but only after approving a delay in implementation proposed by Gore. Johnson also created a new task force that would, one year later, facing the new financial constraints from the costs of the Vietnam War, recommend a delay in implementing the public financing provisions.[64]

The debates over the Long Act of 1966 and its repeal focused the campaign finance reform community on two seemingly intractable problems. First, any system of public financing that failed to impose sensible spending limits would not curb the rising costs of campaigns. Related to that concern, restrictions on campaign contributions or expenditures became inimical to free speech rights preserved and protected by the Constitution, as expressed in the last decade of Warren court decisions that emphasized essential connections between preserving free speech and protecting democratic ideals. Commentators who have examined that conundrum, however, have ignored the changing conception of corruption and how that limited quid pro quo conception, which discounted civic ideas of protecting the election process and voters from the coercive effects of money, became the preeminent judicial value by 1976. Critics of the Warren court's activism first exposed those changes, which originated with the submergence of political experience and acumen to a particular privileging of a formalist, apolitical ideology in assessing the qualifications of Supreme Court nominees between 1952 and 1974.[65]

RAISING THE BAR—The Diminishing Political Experience of the Supreme Court after Warren

President Eisenhower's appointment of Chief Justice Earl Warren, sworn in on October 5, 1953, marked both a beginning and an end to a period of activism in American judicial history. Sixty-two years old, Warren was known nationally as a seasoned politician, serving ten years as Governor of California and earning high marks there for his administrative and political capabilities. While few questioned Warren's ability as a politician and compromiser, many wondered aloud about his lack of judicial experience. Only the seventh justice in the Court's history with no prior judicial service, Warren faced criticism from academics and conservatives who dominated the American Bar Association, who carped that he "was not a legal scholar." Others, who knew Warren and trusted his judgment, countered that in the entire history of the Court, only two of the thirteen chief justices before Warren had spent their lives as working lawyers. Most, in fact, had run for or been elected to office before their appointment to the bench.[66]

However, the appointment of Warren also signaled the end of a different kind of era. Up to and including the appointment of Warren, the vast majority of Supreme Court justices had elective political experience—running for elections, serving in public office, being public officials. Of the fifty-four justices appointed from 1858 to 1953, thirty had been elected to state or local office before their appointment; another fourteen held some form of national elective office. Another six ran for either state or national office, but lost. After the Warren appointment, partly as a reaction to the activism of the Warren court, partly as a response to changes in the selection process and criteria for choosing judges, and partly as a result of the transformation of the prerequisites for serving in high judicial office created by perceptions about legislative deference, originalism, and judicial competence originating among top legal and political academics, the number of justices appointed that had elective political experience dropped dramatically. From 1955 to 2004, there were twenty Supreme Court appointments; only two, Justice Potter Stewart, who served from 1949 to 1958 on the Cincinnati City Council, and Sandra Day O'Connor, who served in the Arizona State Legislature from 1969 to 1974, had ever been elected to public office.

On the Supreme Court that decided *Brown v. Board of Education* in 1954 sat no justice that had ever served in a judicial capacity before their appointment. While several of the justices had acquired substantial judicial experience while serving on the Court, it is remarkable that no member of what many have called the Court's most significant twentieth-century decision had any preappointment judicial experience. To a large degree, the perception of the activism of the Warren court, which became more controversial after the 1952 election of President Eisenhower, is based on the assumption that the members were acting in a political instead of a judicial manner. Eisenhower's postelection change in philosophy on the appointment of judges was a reaction to an impression that the Supreme Court, populated with "political appointees," had violated strict-interpretative and apolitical principles of judging. In response to that reaction, Eisenhower established specific criteria for appointees to the high court. Eisenhower's criteria for judicial appointments included a character and ability that could command the "respect, pride, and confidence of the populace"; a basic philosophy of "moderate progressivism, common sense, high ideals, the absence of extreme views"; prior judicial service, in the belief that such service would "provide an inkling of the nominee's philosophy"; geographic balance; religious balance; an upper age limit of sixty-two, unless, as Ike put it, "other qualifications were unusually impressive"; and a thorough FBI check of the candidate *and* the approval of the American Bar Association (ABA). Eisenhower's insistence on prior judicial experience and ABA approval produced a dramatic shift in the composition of judicial candidates thought fit for service on the Supreme Court.[67]

Attorney General Herbert Brownell convinced Eisenhower that the ABA could act as an independent body to review potential nominees; as a result, the ABA created a rating system that ranged from "Well Qualified," to "Qualified," to "Not Qualified," for all judicial nominations. The ratings were based on criteria that included *experience,* meaning being a member of the bar for at least 10 years and having been engaged in the practice or teaching of law, public interest law, or service in the judicial system; *integrity,* being of a high moral character and enjoying a general reputation in the community for honestly, integrity, and diligence; *professional competence,* including intellectual capacity, professional and personal judgment, writing and analytical ability, knowledge of the law and breadth of professional experience, and for appellate judgeships, scholarly writing, academic talent, and the ability to write to develop a coherent body of law; *judicial temperament,* including a commitment to equal justice under law, freedom from bias, ability to decide issues according to law, courtesy and civility, open-mindedness and compassion; and *service to the law,* meaning a contribution to the effective administration of justice, including professionalism and a commitment to improving the provision of justice to all those within the jurisdiction. These criteria for evaluating the nominees, which Eisenhower implicitly accepted in 1954, remained the mainstay of the presidential Supreme Court appointment process until 2001, when the administration of George W. Bush altered the practice from a prenomination to a postnomination process.[68]

The arbiters of the ABA standards became a geographically distributed committee of fifteen members who would conduct interviews about the professional qualifications of the nominees. This process was supplemented by a team of law school professors who would examine the legal writings of the candidate, and by a team of practicing lawyers, often including former Supreme Court clerks, who would also examine the legal writings of the candidate, all intended to weigh not the ideology, but the professional competence of the candidate. This process continued after Eisenhower's administration due in part to the political reaction against the perceived activism of the Warren court during the presidential election of 1964, and during the campaign of 1968, which made the activism of the Warren court, and thus the issue of judicial appointments, a highly charged political issue.

In 1964 both Republican presidential nominee Senator Barry Goldwater (R-AZ) and Alabama Governor George C. Wallace, a candidate for the Democratic nomination, criticized the Warren court for its decisions on desegregation, school prayer, reapportionment, and criminal justice. In remarks made in Richmond, Virginia, in June 1964, Wallace said that "with the power in the United States Supreme Court to construe the Constitution in a manner to negate limitations upon the power of the federal government, we are confronted with the cold hard fact that the people are not sovereign over their government any longer and that we, in fact, are bordering on an entirely different form of government. . . . It is judicial oligarchy pure and simple . . . accomplished by revolution." The 1964 Republican Party platform called for constitutional amendments to undo the damage the Court had done in its apportionment and school prayer decisions. Goldwater made the Warren court's activism a major issue in the campaign. In a speech delivered to the American Political Science Association in Chicago, he called the Court's reapportionment decisions "raw and naked power" that damaged the principles of political legitimacy and was inconsistent with the doctrine of separation of power and limited government. His attacks, part of a broader criticism about the excessive exercise of federal government authority that fundamentally changed the federal relationship between state and national government, evoked long-standing conservative critiques that political judicial appointees were improperly making, rather than interpreting, the law. The conservative critique connected the opposition to big and activist government, and would later become a fundamental tenet of mainstream conservative thought.[69]

The election of 1968 threatened to swamp the careful construction that Warren and the Court had built in a tidal shift of American public opinion. Californians had elected conservative Ronald Reagan as their governor in 1966. During the campaign Richard Nixon, sensing a national animus against judicial activism, refurbished Goldwater's conservative criticism of the Warren court. Relying on a strategy intended to win the votes of white southerners, Nixon criticized the Court for excessive activism and made law and order his central theme, which played well to enthusiastic audiences who greeted his stump speech punch line, "Some of our courts have gone too far in weakening the peace forces as against the criminal forces," with enthusiastic applause. Nixon promised to appoint judges who would be "strict constructionists who saw their duty as interpreting and not making law . . . who would see themselves as caretakers of the Constitution and servants of the people, not super-legislators with a free hand to impose their social forces and political viewpoints on the American people." Nixon's vision for the judiciary rejected the Warren court's activism and challenged much of the Warren court's legacy, making the Court a political issue. Nixon contended that the Supreme Court should not "become a political issue," which has often been misinterpreted to mean that Nixon wanted judges who were "strict constructionists who saw their duty as interpreting law and not making law." In fact, Nixon meant more than that. Nixon called for a Supreme Court that deferred to the legislative and executive branches on exactly the kind of political questions that the Warren court had regularly answered in constructing their vision of and hope for American democracy.[70]

With Nixon's election that new view, along with the increasing role of the ABA in vetting and recommending approval of judicial nominations guided by their expressly apolitical criteria of qualifications, led to a narrowing of potential nominees nearly devoid of elective political experience. Warren, the penultimate political appointee, had adroitly navigated the complicated legal-political questions the Court faced precisely because his practical pre-Court experience taught him well the values of American democracy. His ability to form compromising coalitions on the Court came from his political competence learned over long years of experience as attorney general, California governor, and vice presidential candidate.

The composition of the Warren court was particularly suited to understanding the fundamental conflicts between the ideals of liberty and equality, because at their heart, those conflicts were political questions, thrust by changing social conditions into the legal arena through the development of legislative doctrine or the abdication of legislative responsibility to enforce individual rights. When confronted with political issues such as malapportionment of legislative districts, the "equal time" provisions of the Radio Act, Hatch Act restrictions on federal workers, or congressional regulation of the campaign finance system protecting against electoral coercion and ensuring the principles of electoral equality, the Warren court drew out of its ideological quiver not only a principled belief in First Amendment freedoms, but a straight arrow of understanding about modern political changes and efforts to prevent the corruption of the process and public interest.

By 1969 the Warren court, with its patina of political expertise, was aging. The spoils of American politics, however, along with Nixon's peculiar conception of corruption, would ensure that he would, through his four

Supreme Court appointments over the next five years, cast his own cloud over the ideals and principles of American democracy. Nixon's appointments to the Supreme Court reflected the continuing professionalization of judicial selection and the de-political nature of court nominees that had begun in the Eisenhower presidency. Selecting Warren Burger to succeed Earl Warren as chief justice laid the groundwork for a change in the Court's judicial philosophy, but also for a limiting of the available weapons the Court had when confronted with the clashing political questions inherent in American democracy in *Buckley v. Valeo*. The Burger court, populated not with former legislators, governors, or senators, but with former Supreme Court clerks, law school academics, and federal and state judges, and increasingly separated from electoral politics, spoke to those clashing political questions with the distinct legal language they best understood. It was a language that privileged formalist ideas of freedom of speech over deliberative equality, and one that presumed the "free marketplace of ideas" would adequately regulate political corruption.[71]

As the Supreme Court evolved into one composed almost exclusively of a membership from academia, or members of former state or federal courts, the theoretical preferences its members had imbued during their training and judicial experience gained jurisprudential favor. While early Warren court decisions maintained and even expanded the pragmatic democratic principles and ideas, by 1970 formalist First Amendment principles began to overshadow certain political values that for a century had explicitly formed the foundation of the campaign finance system. Even as the Supreme Court continued after 1969 to decide America's deepest political disputes, its membership became "depoliticized." This ironic trend had dramatic ramifications on how the Court would address impending campaign finance controversies. By 1976, when the Supreme Court in *Buckley v. Valeo* ignored the congressional determination that excessive money coerced voters and corrupted the electoral system, it was not because they looked the other way to avoid those values, but instead because they looked at those issues differently. As academics and judges, the Court membership preferred and expressed a different set of tools and values with which to support and defend their own democratic assumptions. Confronted with the conflict of regulating free political speech as a means of protecting the political system from corruption, it is no wonder that the Burger court in *Buckley* took little account of the political history of campaign finance regulation, since those values could only be expressed in a distinctly political language that this newly depoliticized Court could barely understand.[72]

Chapter Seven

COINING CORRUPTION

Watergate, FECA, and the Limits of Reform, 1970–1976

In the dank, dark corner of a mostly vacant parking garage, Deep Throat offered *Washington Post* reporter Bob Woodward the trenchant advice that became the mantra for the post-Watergate generation of reforms. "Follow the money," he rasped, nervously puffing a cigarette, leading Woodward and fellow reporter Carl Bernstein to the evidence that would lead to the truth behind the emerging political scandal. But that famous vignette never occurred. Deep Throat never uttered those words to Woodward. Instead, that scene was the imaginative product of screenplay author William Goldman, hired to put to paper the words Woodward promised he would never directly quote. The popular movie version of Woodward and Bernstein's Watergate history, *All the President's Men,* shaded the truth about Deep Throat's admonition and revealed a broader misconception about the excesses of the Watergate scandal. The misconception, that narrow directive to "follow the money" as the source of the truth about the political corruption of Watergate, eventually became a crabbed conception of quid pro quo corruption that undermined the persuasiveness and possibilities of comprehensive campaign finance reform in the Federal Election Campaign Act (FECA) of 1974. In addition, the focus of reformers, scholars, and eventually the Supreme Court on the political process of reforming the campaign finance system would divert attention from the ideals of deliberative democracy that had for a century formed the foundation of the system.[1]

The Watergate scandal undoubtedly catalyzed the reform coalition that had been advocating reform of the campaign finance system since the mid-1950s. Revelations of widespread collection of unreported cash contributions to finance a variety of political dirty tricks by President Richard Nixon's Committee to Re-Elect the President ("CRP") shocked most Americans. These efforts to dissuade voters from supporting specific Democratic nominees thought to pose the most severe general election challenge to Nixon represented the worst excesses of American politics. But FECA was not only constructed to deal with the excesses of Watergate, it also built upon earlier reforms, specifically the short-lived Honest Elections Act of 1966, the failed Political Broadcast Act of 1970, and the reforms enacted in the FECA of 1971, which was, until passage of the new FECA in 1974, the most comprehensive reform of the campaign finance system since the Federal Corrupt Practices Act of 1925. In many ways, those earlier reforms provided the intellectual foundation for the Watergate reforms. Yet despite the widespread notoriety of the Watergate disclosures, the reforms proposed by the Watergate Committee, which were based on broad deliberative principles that reformers had evoked throughout a century of campaign finance history, evolved in FECA as more limited conceptions of deliberative equality. Even those more limited reforms were rejected by the Supreme Court when first heard in the 1976 case of *Buckley v. Valeo*.[2]

Broad attempts to reform the campaign finance system were undercut by both the politics of reform that failed to develop a consensus on a specific set of democratic assumptions, and by a Supreme Court increasingly preferring formalist free speech values over political principles to protect the democratic process. This failure was complicated by the promethean concept of corruption that the executive, legislative, and judicial branch held, and the ways that pragmatic political experience created those different understandings. Richard Nixon, Congress, and the Supreme Court all saw corruption and its effects on democratic institutions differently. When the lens of Watergate focused their conception on the limited quid pro quo concept as the preeminent political evil, broader attempts at reform in FECA 1974 became problematic. In addition, the different interests of the House and Senate played a role in the inability to agree upon broad proposals made by the Watergate committee to reform the entire electoral system. Elections in the Senate and House were fundamentally different affairs in the 1970s, and the reform interests of those two bodies more often clashed than coincided. When Congress tried to ameliorate the differences in the conference committee handling the Watergate reforms, their interests clashed incessantly.

Finally, the evolution of the political acumen of the Supreme Court, increasingly distanced from pragmatic electoral experience, played a major role when the Court, facing the complexities of the reforms of FECA 1974, had to choose between First Amendment values and congressional interests in protecting the electoral system. Much of the criticism of the Supreme Court for its decision in *Buckley* comes from the Court's apparent lack of political expertise in splitting the contribution and spending limits of the campaign finance system so inextricably connected by Congress in 1974. Further, critics contend that by ignoring the free speech equality principles that were established in FECA 1974, the Supreme Court ignored the long history of judicial sanction of that principle. The history of the modern campaign finance system begins, not with the tragedy of Watergate, but with the evolving concept of corruption, coined over a century of political-legal conflict, that both created and constrained changing principles and practices of political deliberation.[3]

CONGRESSIONAL SCANDAL AND RICHARD NIXON'S CORRUPTION—
Checkers, "Law and Order," and the Victory of Quid Pro Quo

At the center of the story about the FECA 1971 and 1974 campaign finance reforms is the darkly conflicted public figure of Richard Nixon. His actions and the actions of his campaign committees in 1968 and 1972 catalyzed the most significant overhauling of the campaign finance system since the passage of the Federal Corrupt Practices Act of 1925. Nixon was a reluctant reformer, careful to protect his own political interests in the battles with Congress over FECA 1971. But it was not only legislative maneuvering and self-interest that shaped the FECA 1971 and 1974; they were shaped in large part by Nixon's peculiar conception of corruption practiced in his political campaigns and affected by his political philosophy on judicial appointments as he filled the four Supreme Court vacancies of his presidency, which would shape the *Buckley* decision.[4]

Clues to Nixon's conception of corruption can be found years before the exposure of the events of Watergate. In 1952, while Nixon was running as President Eisenhower's vice presidential nominee, reports of a secret Nixon slush fund challenged the viability of his continuation on the Republican ticket. On September 18, the *New York Post* announced a sensational revelation: "SECRET NIXON FUND! SECRET RICH MEN'S FUND KEEPS NIXON IN STYLE FAR BEYOND HIS SALARY." Nixon's opponents jumped on the story, and within a day, it became clear that Nixon would have to defend himself to the American people, and to Eisenhower, who true to form, remained noncommittal about Nixon's remaining on the ticket. By September 23, the situation had grown into a political maelstrom, although in retrospect, the Democrats seemed foolish for making it a major issue. Nixon decided to appear on national television to explain the nature of the fund, and to defend his actions to the American public.[5]

Nixon's "Checkers Speech" was a turning point in his career, a do or die moment of high political theater. The truth about the fund was that it had not profited Nixon personally, and he played on that theme in his televised address to the American people. "I, Senator Nixon," he began his explanation on television, "took $18,000 from a group of my supporters . . . And let me say that it was wrong. I am saying that it was wrong, just not illegal, because it isn't a question of whether it was legal or illegal, that isn't enough." But here Nixon drew the line. "The question is," he added, "was it morally wrong? I say that it was morally wrong if it was secretly given and secretly handled. . . And I say that it was morally wrong if any of the contributors got special favors for the contributions that were made." Nixon had done none of these things, and his defense concluded "and to answer those questions let me say this: not one cent of the $18,000 or any other money of that type ever went to me for my personal use. Every penny of it was used to pay for political expenses that I did not think should be charged to the taxpayers of the United States."[6]

Nixon knew that the other campaigns had used similar funds. He had not used the money in his fund for personal gain. Nixon believed that the fund was not corrupt because he did not personally gain from it, and that it had helped him pay for campaign expenses that "were primarily political business." The fund paid for reprints of his speeches he gave exposing the Truman Administration, "the Communism in it, the corruption in it." Since he was not a rich man, Nixon reasoned, the only way to perform this public service was with the funds of friends who supported him because they held the same beliefs.[7] Nixon listed for the listening audience his modest personal income and assets, including his dog "Checkers," which made him appear much more like the average American than the recipient of a rich man's fund used for corruptive purposes. The speech saved his candidacy. The Republican National Committee received more than 300,000 letters and telegrams of support, and state and local Republican committees announced thousands of telegrams that ran 350 to 1 in favor of Nixon. More importantly, it exposed and then reaffirmed Nixon's conception of political corruption. So long as the money did not personally profit him, and so long as he used it to spread his political message, the source and methods of acquisition were irrelevant.[8]

Congress also began to take a more narrow view of the concept of corruption in the 1960s. In 1967 Congress faced numerous ethical challenges, including the decision not to seat Congressman Adam Clayton Powell, Jr.; the censure of Senator Thomas Dodd; the investigation into charges that Senator Edward V. Long (D-MO) had used his position and accepted fees to aid imprisoned Teamster Union President James R. Hoffa; and the conviction of the former secretary to the Senate majority leader by a federal district court jury of income tax evasion. All these events helped to create an ethical storm. Calls for internal reform challenged Congress, and in 1967, in the midst of a bitter battle to repeal or salvage the Honest Elections Act of 1966, the Senate three times defeated proposals to require disclosure of senators' financial assets and income. Both chambers began work on separate congressional codes of ethics, and the Senate created the Select Committee on Standards and Conduct, while the House formed its own Committee on Standards of Official Conduct, to recommend codes of ethical conduct for their members. In each of these cases, the dominant theme became the corruption of individual members who profited personally from an abuse of their official position. While the overall perception of Congress had been tarnished, the remedies dealt almost exclusively with demonstrating that the individual congressman had nothing to hide because he had not profited personally from his congressional contacts and duties.[9]

Nixon's 1968 campaign provided additional clues about his conception of corruption. In addition, the 1968 campaign themes also dovetailed with his political beliefs about the role of the judiciary that influenced his nomination of Supreme Court judgeships. By juxtaposing his "law and order" theme with criticism of the activism of the Warren court, Nixon established the parameters for the role of the judiciary in the management of the social order. During his 1968 campaign, Nixon decried the "lawless society" that he saw in America, and conflated public perceptions of judicial leniency with judicial activism. Warren defended the Court against attacks, saying that "all of us must assume a share of the responsibility" for the increase in crime rates. Warren warned that the attacks could damage the judiciary, which he called the "most susceptible to attack, because it cannot enter the political arena and trade blow for blow with those who would discredit its work."[10]

In 1973, when deeply embroiled in the Watergate scandal that would destroy his presidency, Nixon spoke with White House Counsel Charles Colson about why so much attention had been focused on the events. Nixon understood political corruption through a myopic lens "They say this is the greatest corruption in history," he told Colson. "That's baloney." Nixon then defined corruption much the way he had during his earlier political career, metaphorically following the money as the Watergate investigation had. "Nobody stole anything. The whole point about this," he emphasized, "nobody has made any money. And I haven't seen one of our little boys make that point." Nixon's law and order ideology insulated him from the realities that corruption could also involve violations of the constitutional rights of others and corruption of the political system, even in the misguided belief that illegal acts were committed to protect the national interest.[11]

The law and order theme that Nixon employed during his 1968 presidential campaign challenged the propriety of the Supreme Court's entering the political arena to decide cases. He also believed that the Warren court's foray into social policy was a corruptive departure from the proper role of traditional judicial review. The depoliticization of the nomination process begun during the Eisenhower administration continued under Nixon as he nominated justices he felt would be "strict constructionists," would curtail the Court's forays into interpretative social policy, and would instead begin to curtail the activism of the Warren court. Even as Nixon sought to make his appointments reflective of his understanding of the proper role of the Supreme Court in American politics, his own view of corruption would, during the Watergate crisis, embolden his approval of the cover-up.[12]

The Burger court, authorities claim, was the counterrevolution that wasn't.[13] It did not transform constitutional doctrine by rolling back or abandoning the activist Warren court's most controversial decisions, many of which remained steadfast American law years after the replacement of a majority of the Court membership. The most salient feature of the early years of the Burger court was an "absence of any common understanding of mission held by all the Justices." While the early years of the Burger court demonstrated limited substantive doctrinal change from Warren court doctrines, Nixon's ability to appoint four new justices in the first five years of his presidential tenure, and the makeup of those appointments, continued a trend begun in 1959 of appointing justices who privileged formalist doctrinal understandings of judicial theory over political ones. This process, and the lens through which the Eisenhower, Kennedy, and Nixon appointees viewed the law, politics, and the role of judicial review all help explain why the campaign finance decisions concerning FECA 1971 and 1974 seemed to ignore congressional imperatives about political corruption on which the previous century of Supreme Court decisions in the campaign finance field had been based.[14]

FOUNDATIONS OF REFORM—The Federal Election Campaign Act of 1971

The 1974 campaign finance reforms were part of a cumulative process that began with the Presidential Election Campaign Fund Act of 1966 (or "Long Act," which established the first public funding for campaigns), its repeal in 1967, the Political Broadcast Act of 1970, vetoed by President Nixon, and the Federal Election Campaign Act of 1971 (FECA 1971). From 1966 to 1970, Congress attempted to deal with political corruption by addressing the relationship of campaign fund-raising, and the costs of the new media-driven campaigns, to political corruption. State initiatives in Florida, Massachusetts, and elsewhere, which required full disclosure of political contributions and spending, often provided both the model and impetus for federal action. The Long Act legalized income tax checkoffs to fund a public campaign finance system and demonstrated congressional support for some form of campaign finance reform. The plan provided for a voluntary taxpayer checkoff of $1 allocated to public funding of presidential campaigns. Although Congress authorized the fund, the checkoff plan went down to defeat in 1967 when disaffected Democrats and Republicans joined to end the plan they felt would strengthen the political hand of President Johnson.[15]

In 1967, led by Senator Albert H. Gore (D-TN) over five weeks of bitter and vitriolic debate, the Senate changed its position several times during key roll call votes. Gore felt that the bill, which did not limit spending, nor regulate congressional campaigns, would prove ineffective at reforming the system. Republicans, who traditionally had larger sources of private funds, were almost unanimously behind repeal of public financing. The repeal of the funding provisions of the Long Act in 1967, however, did not end the reform attempts, and the principle of public financing and the tax checkoff mechanism remained favored reform principles that would soon be resurrected. In 1970 Congress, reacting to the emergence of television advertising as the major medium in campaigns, enacted the Political Broadcast Act, which limited radio and television spending by candidates for all federal offices, and for governor and lieutenant-governor in both primary and general elections. The cost of campaigns, focused on the most expensive media costs, led to this reform attempt. The concept of limiting costs, particularly the most expensive costs of the electronic media, hearkened back to the principles established in the 1934 Federal Communication Act, which reminded legislators that the air waves were public, and played an important role in political speech and communication. Although President Nixon vetoed the act on October 12, 1970, and the Senate failed to override Nixon's veto, the concept of limiting electronic media costs would again be utilized in the reform efforts of FECA 1971.[16]

Increasingly, the inertia of reform emboldened by a new reform coalition led to the passage of the FECA 1971. President Nixon grudgingly accepted the act in 1972. The act amended the Communication Act of 1934 by ending the equal time provisions of Section 315(a) for legally qualified candidates for president and vice president in primary and general elections. It also required that broadcast licensees charge qualified candidates for public office no more than the lowest unit rate for the medium during the forty-five days before a primary, and 60 days before a general or special election. Finally, the law established limitations on spending for broadcast and nonbroadcast media for legally qualified candidates for federal office in all primary, general, and special elections. The law defined broadcast media as any media using airwaves, including community antenna television stations, and placed the spending limits on the use of media at $50,000, or 10 cents multiplied by the estimate of resident population of voting age for such office as determined by the more recent census, whichever was less. Expenditure restrictions for nonbroadcast media (defined to mean newspapers, magazines, and other periodical publications and billboard facilities) expenditure restrictions were set at the same level.[17]

FECA 1971 had three goals. First, Congress intended to "give candidates for public office greater access to the media so that they may better explain their stand on the issues, and thereby more fully and completely inform the voters." Secondly, Congress, in setting spending limitations for candidates for federal office, intended to "halt the spiraling cost of campaigning for public office." Additionally, Congress meant to permit states, where they desired, to adopt similar spending limitations in the broadcast media for candidates for state and local office to make the Federal Communication Commission a federal partner in any state reform.[18]

The repeal of Section 315 of the Federal Communication Act of 1934 became an important reform of FECA 1971. The "equal time provision" and "fairness doctrine" had been applied to require broadcast media outlets to provide time for opposing candidates if any media outlet had broadcast views or positions in opposition to those candidates. The fairness doctrine originated in the 1940 *Mayflower* decision in which the FCC ruled that stations could not advocate the political causes of the licensee without violating their licenses. In 1949 the FCC, responding to broadcasters unhappy with *Mayflower,* required stations to provide a reasonable amount of time for the presentation of public issues and reasonable opportunities for contrasting issues or contrasting views of public importance.[19] During the 1960 elections, because of complaints about the effects of the ruling, Congress temporarily suspended operation of the equal time provision with respect to presidential and vice presidential nominees specifically for that campaign year. Continuing complaints about the rising costs of broadcast media and the equal time and fairness doctrines compelled congressional action in FECA 1971.[20]

Interestingly, the complaint about the rising costs of campaigns made by incumbents during congressional hearings on the bill allied closely with the end of equal time provision arguments made by network and media executives, but for very different and conflicting reasons. Campaign reform advocates reasoned that specific limitations on the amount of spending, along with limits on the maximum charge for media time, would increase opportunities for qualified but poorly funded candidates. "The danger," the committee report asserted, "is that the cost of campaigning, chiefly swollen by the cost of television, will exclude (as candidates) the honest poor." Citing a survey that showed nearly 70 percent of U.S. Senate campaigns cost over $100,000 and that 30 percent of all House candidates spent over $60,000 to be elected, the committee found these costs excessive. "How many men of talent and interest, but not of means," the report asked, "are discouraged from seeking office?"[21]

Yet setting spending limits without limiting broadcast media costs would severely diminish the amount of political discourse many thought essential to a campaign of education. On this issue, there was a wide diversity of opinion. Senator Hugh Scott (R-PA) and Senator Charles Mathias (D-MD) opposed spending limitations, fearful that low limits would hurt challengers, and that high limitations would set the benchmark for the amount of money raised, in effect encouraging more spending. Sen. Scott also questioned the free speech implications of the spending limitations. But the committee generally agreed that Congress had a legitimate interest in stopping the rise of campaign finance spending, and reasonable spending limits tied to numbers of potential voters, yet generous enough to permit a full campaign on the issues, were both rational and constitutional.

The repeal of the equal time provision and the regulation of the cost of political broadcast advertising costs worked closely with the overall spending limitation. Network executives testified that repeal of Section 315 (which had been approved in the Political Broadcast Act but was vetoed by President Nixon in 1970) remained an important objective. The presidents of the three major television networks, long critical of the equal time provision, argued that instead of opening up the avenues of debate, Section 315 established roadblocks on the information highway because networks tended to avoid controversial or political broadcasts, fearful that opponents using the rule would insist on increasing amounts of media access that would eat into the networks' bottom line. As a compromise, CBS President Frank Stanton testified that his network "was prepared to offer next year between Labor Day and Election Day eight hours of free time on CBS

Television and Radio Networks for the major party candidates for President and Vice President to present their views." That offer, he added, was contingent on the repeal of Section 315. The promise of voluntary network access for the major candidates became the driving rationale for the repeal of the equal time provision.[22]

FECA 1971 established limits on broadcast media costs to candidates consistent with the lowest unit charge of the station for the same amount of time during the same time period, and limited the total amount candidates could spend on broadcast and nonbroadcast media. The committee acknowledged congressional authority over "the integrity of Federal elections, and its authority to regulate radio and television in the public interest," but refused to impose the lowest-unit charge rule for nonbroadcast media because the majority believed that the federal interest did not extend to permitting congressional regulation of political advertising for media sources traditionally considered private. However, Congress clearly felt that reduction of rates to candidates alone would be insufficient to stop the spiraling costs of campaigns. It was this concern that led to the reaffirmation by Congress in FECA 1971 of the concept of overall spending limits that had been part of the loophole-ridden Federal Corrupt Practices Act since 1911, but became so constitutionally problematic in *Buckley.*

While FECA 1971 limited the amount of permissible nonbroadcast media expenditures for candidates to federal office, the act also repealed the $5,000 limitation on spending and contributions found in Section 608 of the Federal Corrupt Practices Act. Congress realized that the FCPA 1925 had limited enforceability because it applied only to multistate committees. Congress opted to end the unenforceable ruse of the spending limitations established in the FCPA and instead expose all contributions and expenditures to broader, clearer, and stricter disclosure. "The Committee is of the general opinion," the report concluded, "that the voters, having full knowledge of all sources of contributions and the nature of all expenditures, and, having the privilege of demonstrating at the polls their approval or disapproval with respect to particular candidates or political parties for excessive contributions received or expenditures made, will serve as a deterrent to abuses or excesses."[23]

The disclosure requirements developed as a viable alternative as a result of congressional recognition about the limited effectiveness of the spending limits imposed in the FCPA of 1925. A supplement to the committee report filed by Senators Scott, Winston Prouty (R-VT), and John Cooper (R-KY) stated that "[t]he Federal Corrupt Practices Act of 1925 has probably been worse than having no law regulating Federal elections," arguing it was "full of loopholes" and provided neither the candidates nor the public "with any guidance or information concerning the election process." In a Freudian slip, the report called it a dangerous "shame" (sham) "because over the years it has created an illusion of regulation of the Federal elective process."[24]

Disclosure of contributions and spending, supporters contended, would act as a means to garner useful information on the amount of broadcast and nonbroadcast media spending, as well as on other traditional expenses. In the future, with that information, Congress could revisit the issue. The report stated that "how much spending is enough to ensure truly democratic elections and how much is too much are at this point in history impossible to determine. An even greater risk is inherent in making binding decisions for the future." The reporting requirements also ended the loophole of FCPA 1925 that allowed unregulated political committees that organized in the District of Columbia, a particularly beneficial provision for incumbents. It required reporting of all expenditures or contributions over $100, and Section 304 required every committee and every candidate, whether organized in a single state or not, to file reports detailing the amount donated, name, and address of each contributor, as well as each expenditure over $100. The reports would be filed on a schedule to ensure their availability and disclosure during the election cycle with two final reports filed fifteen and five days before the election. Each report would be filed with the comptroller general and with the appropriate state office. FECA 1971 gave the comptroller general the power and authority to regulate the reporting requirements, rejecting the Senate version that would have established a federal election commission. According to its sponsors, FECA 1971 restored faith in democratic ideals essential to the success of the democratic process. While the broadcast provisions and spending restrictions were important to ending the spiraling costs of elections, the essential purpose of the act exemplified by the disclosure rules remained the restoration of the integrity of the election process.[25]

In addition, Congress argued that the limitations on spending posed significant problems. Since the creation of the first spending restriction, campaign-spending demands had grown exponentially. As the campaigns avoided the requirement by establishing multiple committees, each subject to the spending limitation, the cost of campaigning made the paltry $5,000 spending limit of FCPA clearly too small. In opting for the disclosure regime, Congress intended to end the sham and require increased reporting and disclosure of all contributions and expenditures over $100 in all federal campaigns. Although FECA 1971 limited spending on broadcast media, spending on other traditional means of political communication such as direct mail, door to door canvassing, phone bank calling, yard signs, and mass meetings were excluded from any spending restrictions.

Finally, the act relaxed long-standing restrictions on corporate and union contributors. The Tillman and Taft-Hartley acts made illegal any corporate or union contribution or expenditure for any candidate, campaign committee, political party, or organization concerning any federal election. Remarkably, the provisions of FECA 1971 created a new exemption from that broad sixty-five-year prohibition by permitting communications by a corporation to its stockholders and their families, or by a labor organization to its members and their families; nonpartisan registration and get-out-the-vote campaigns by a corporation aimed at its stockholders and their families, or by a labor organization aimed at its members and their families; and *"the establishment, administration, and solicitation of contributions to a separate segregated fund to be utilized for political purposes by a corporation or labor organization."* This provision legalized the establishment of political action committees that used corporate or union money contributed for political purposes to support particular candidates. While a major goal of FCPA 1971 was limiting the spiraling cost of campaigns, the elimination of the individual contribution limits and the candidate expenditure limits and the passage of the PAC provision effectively created new opportunities for increased campaign spending.[26]

Yet Congress's concern was not merely the limitation of aggregate spending. As it passed FECA 1971, Congress enacted legislation that created tax deductions and credit for small campaign contributions in order to promote more involvement by citizen-contributors in funding campaigns. Democratic Party leaders, facing a national committee debt of $9 million on the eve of the 1972 election pushed for a tax checkoff, and Senate Democrats added this provision to the Revenue Act of 1971. House leaders, fearing a veto by President Nixon, deferred the tax checkoff provision until the 1973 tax year. The overall scheme of FECA 1971, building upon important campaign finance principles, was to pass reforms intended to combat corruption damaging to electoral deliberation. Those ideas would soon shape debate over the more famous 1974 Act.[27]

LEGAL CHALLENGES TO FECA 1971—Constitutionalizing the Regulation of Quid Pro Quo Corruption

After passage of FECA 1971, the judiciary played a significant role in shaping the campaign finance reform debate. In a troika of cases challenging the constitutionality of FECA 1971, those ideas emerged and served as a precursor to the political debate and legal challenges that would soon embroil the 1974 reform and revamping of the campaign finance system. Plaintiffs filed two cases in New York. *Pichler v. Jennings* challenged the provisions of the FECA 1971, which regulated the expenditure of moneys "on behalf of" a candidate. Pichler and other state and district members of the Conservative Party in New York sued Pat Jennings, the clerk of the House of Representatives, and the comptroller general, seeking injunctive relief against application of the FECA 1971 regulations. They alleged that the regulations effectively required that any broadcast media outlet certify first that the expenditures did not violate the candidate limit on expenditures before accepting them for publication, and that the disclosure provisions of the act "would have the effect of deterring some people from serving as officers of plaintiffs' clubs and deterring others from contributing money for use by the Conservative Party and the clubs of which they are officers." Together, they alleged these regulations violated their freedoms of expression and association, and that the state interest supporting FECA 1971 was not so compelling as to override those constitutional protections.[28]

The District Court eventually dismissed the case, citing the vague and unsupported allegations of a threat to party participation or contribution, and finding the lawsuit moot under the ripeness doctrine. In so doing, it performed a balancing test that weighed the congressional interests to safeguard the integrity of elections against those individual rights. Relying on *Burroughs and Cannon v. United States,* in which the Supreme Court sustained FCPA 1925, the District Court agreed that Congress possessed "every other power essential to preserve the departments and institutions of general government from impairment and destruction, whether threatened by force or by corruption." However, the court found that Burroughs did not foreclose the inquiry because although "Congress reached the conclusion that public disclosure of political contributions, together with the names of contributors and other details, would tend to prevent the corrupt use of money to affect elections," that undoubtedly compelling governmental interest did not automatically override an individual's interest in maintaining privacy in his associations. In *Pilcher,* the court would not render a decision because the plaintiffs had failed to plead adequately any concrete facts on which the court could determine the constitutional protection of their individual interest.[29]

The second New York case, *United States v. The National Committee for Impeachment,* involved the prepublication certification of an advertisement advocating the impeachment of President Nixon because of the broadcast media limits in FECA 1971. Congressional representatives and private citizens purchased a two-page advertisement in the *New York Times* entitled "A Resolution to Impeach Richard M. Nixon as President of the United States." The ad consisted of 5,100 lines and cost the group $17,850. It advocated the impeachment of Nixon based on the violation of his duties as president in his handling of the Vietnam War. As part of FECA 1971, media outlets were required to ensure that "political committees" not spend more than the law permitted if such committees spent money for the "purpose of influencing" federal elections. Each committee was also required to file statements and reports of contributions and expenditures. The issue in *National Committee for Impeachment* was defining what Congress intended in FECA 1971 by the term "political committee" and deciding whether the group who solicited the ad met that definition.[30]

The Circuit Court had little trouble finding that it did not. "We construe the words," held the Court, "'made for the purpose of influencing' in Section 301(e) and (f) to mean an expenditure made with the authorization or consent, express or implied, or under the control, direct or indirect, of a candidate or his agents." Consistent with the requirements of free speech in the campaign finance context, the broadcast media regulations must have limited ends that dealt with limited subject matter. To permit a broad definition of a political committee to include the kind of committee that advocated impeachment as a public policy goal, without direct candidate endorsement or engagement, would present too great a potential for abuse. The concern about subverting the campaign finance limits by prohibiting the coordination of expenditures by ostensibly separate committees did not seem to the court to be a legitimate congressional concern where the expression published was the epitome of political speech. A main concern of Congress in FECA 1971 was political campaign financing coordinated by candidates, and not the funding by independent organizations advocating national policy issues. The system of free expression, the court concluded, meant that the act applied "only to committees soliciting contributions or making expenditures the major purpose of which is the nomination or election of candidates," and thus the National Committee for Impeachment could not be prosecuted.[31]

Although this interpretation would require regulators to glean from the facts the purpose of the organization in order to determine the act's applicability, the court felt this administrative burden "would not be incompatible with the first amendment which requires that administrative standards regulating free expression be precisely drawn." The court feared that a broad interpretation, as advocated by the government, would eventually subject every group (citing examples such as the Audubon Society or the Girl Scouts) expressing any political sentiment to the act's jurisdiction and burdensome contribution, spending, reporting, and disclosure requirements. "The dampening effect on First Amendment rights," ruled the court, "that would result from such a situation would be intolerable." While not ruling directly on the constitutionality of the contribution or expenditure limitations of FECA 1971, the court limited the First Amendment boundaries of legitimate congressional regulation of political campaign speech and spending.[32]

The final case, arising from the United States District Court for District of Columbia, the same court that would eventually hear the *Buckley* case, set a high standard of constitutionality for future campaign spending regulations. Under FECA 1971, the comptroller general established the procedural requirements for compliance and required a certification process whenever any group sought to place an ad that could conceivably constitute spending "on behalf" of a specific candidate. FECA 1971 limited total nonbroadcast and broadcast media spending to a maximum of $50,000 per candidate per election cycle, and the law carried criminal penalties for anyone, including any media outlet, that violated those requirements. When the American Civil Liberties Union and the New York Civil Liberties Union (ACLU/NYCLU) submitted a proposed advertisement to the *New York Times* in early September 1972, expressing opposition to the administration-backed legislation limiting court-ordered busing for school desegregation, the *Times* acted to ensure they would not violate the law. On the advice of their lawyers, the *Times* notified the ACLU/NYCLU officials that their failure to comply with the certification requirements mandated by FECA 1971 precluded publication of their advertisement, and the ACLU filed suit challenging the regulations. In *American Civil Liberties Union v. Jennings,* the District Court found that the regulations constituted a prior restraint on publication that chilled the First Amendment rights of the groups seeking publication. While the government attempted to moot this case by arguing that ACLU/NYCLU was not a political committee under the act, the court found that the provisions and the regulations requiring prepublication candidate certification of the spending limits violated the free speech rights of those groups.[33]

The conundrum the FECA 1971 regulations imposed was emblematic of the problems inherent in the implementation of modern campaign finance reform. The FECA 1971 limits on media spending required the certification by the candidate on whose behalf the spending, either in support of his candidacy or in derogation of his opponent, was to occur, in order to ensure the spending limits had not been exceeded. If, however, the spending was independent of the candidate, the law did not apply. The regulations, anticipating an obvious loophole, required that the would-be advertiser state in writing before publication that no federal candidate had given authorization or consent for placing the advertisement, after which the media outlet must "take reasonable precautions under the particular circumstances to verify the identity and affiliation of such person and the accuracy of the written statement." This requirement subjected media outlets to substantial criminal penalties for any violation, if they failed to discover and disclose before publishing the submitted political advertisement the intention of the advertiser and any connection with any candidacy. The court concluded that this was an unconstitutional attempt at prior restraint despite the fact that Congress imposed the restrictions "in furtherance of matters of legitimate governmental concern." In balancing the congressional interest of regulating excessive campaign expenditures and the rights of free speech, the court concluded that the government failed to demonstrate the restraints were necessary and appropriate, and clearly and narrowly drawn, to achieve the legislative purpose.[34]

The court also considered plaintiffs' claim that the broad disclosure regime of FECA 1971 violated their freedom of privacy and association. Citing *United States v. National Committee for Impeachment,* the court held that since Congress was concerned with political campaign financing and the funding of movements dealing with political policy, the act did not violate freedom of association and privacy rights because the regulations clearly limited the act's applicability to committees concerned with "the nomination or election of candidates." The court concluded that the interest of regulating and reforming the alarming rise of candidate expenditures would not unduly restrict the views of groups concerned with the open discourse of views on prominent national issues. The court left unresolved the privacy and associational concerns affected by the disclosure regulations for those organizations that advocated policy views in opposition to or in favor of a candidate, where the spending was not coordinated with any particular candidate.

The three cases demonstrated a fundamental conflict between First Amendment assumptions and renewed reform efforts in the 1960s–1970s to address the political corruption of the campaign finance system. Several constitutional problems became apparent. Spending limits were going to be difficult to administer, especially if connected to support for or against particular candidates. Whether the limits were media-type selective as in FECA 1971, or whether they set overall spending/contribution limitations, the constitutionality of the regulation remained uncertain in a system that protected free expression by political groups as a fundamental principle of American democracy. Second, while it was clear that congressional regulation of campaign finance spending was a legitimate goal, when that regulation conflicted with the free expression or association rights of individuals or groups, the constitutional burden became very high. Legal doctrine appeared to sanction strong disclosure requirements because the integrity of election rationale tipped the scale toward that kind of impartial regulation intended to provide notice of contributions and expenditures as part of the educative process of elections. But prior-restraint regulation of campaign spending would be very difficult to sustain using the compelling state interest rationale of protecting electoral integrity.

By the time these issues came before the Supreme Court and many lower courts, most were composed of judges trained to prefer free speech as the value most capable of protecting democratic freedoms. The judicial preferment of the First Amendment as a preeminent value essential for the protection of democracy made it more difficult to balance other political interests, such as promoting deliberative equality, that legislatures deemed just as important. In a wide range of cases involving individual rights, courts protected individualist claims over communitarian interests. Claims of inadequate political influence became personalized to represent an individual loss of rights and liberties by contending that although the constitutionally established political system was a given, "the tools of political influence had been unfairly denied" to the claimant. Courts protected claims of individual rights over communal challenges because communal claims meant that the system itself denied equal rights for entire groups. Accepting that position would require courts to first resolve those issues by agreeing on the fundamental values of republican government.[35]

While courts in the past had decided election law cases by promoting a particular vision of democracy, the decreasing political competence of courts caused them to evaluate and decide cases using individualist principles in which they were trained and with which they were most familiar that allowed them to decide cases without engaging the bigger democratic questions. Although the courts were not afraid of slashing into the political thicket of campaign finance regulation, they often sought limited legal avenues out of that thicket, relying on individualist constitutional issues of free speech and privacy and association rights. By avoiding communitarian principles of political equality, courts avoided, as much as they had earlier embraced, their own ideas about the kind of democratic system that they preferred for America. Because of this, the judiciary created obstacles to drafting and passing constitutional campaign finance legislation that remained as daunting as the political ones. That would become evident in two short years as Congress and the judiciary reacted to the emerging scandal of Watergate, which would provide the next great impetus for reform.

UNDERSTANDING WATERGATE—The Committee to Reelect the President's Abuse of Deliberative Democracy

Improving the democratic system was the last thing on the mind of the politicos in the Nixon administration as the 1970 midterm elections approached. The all-out effort by Republican operatives to fund successful congressional candidates turned into a major disappointment. The potential presidential run of former Alabama governor George Wallace in 1972 posed a huge challenge to Nixon's southern strategy of peeling southern white voters away from their traditional allegiance to Democratic candidates. Nixon and his advisors anticipated that the 1972 election would be very close, and Nixon directed his personal attorney Herbert Kalmbach to provide over $400,000 in secret, unreported campaign funds left over from his 1968 presidential campaign to Wallace's 1970 gubernatorial opponent, then Governor Albert Brewer. Brewer won the primary without a majority, and despite Nixon's efforts, Wallace went on to win the general election. Nixon's campaign use of his secret campaign funds to support opponents of his opponents would multiply in both quantity and cupidity as the 1972 primary election season got underway.[36]

The tragedy of Watergate arose from a complex set of psychological stimuli in Richard Nixon that he demonstrated in a pattern of political malpractice subversive of democratic choice. In the campaign and in the cover-up that followed, Nixon conflated his political interest with what he imagined to be the national interest, and in that strange and perverse understanding created a calculus of corruption that had no moral equation. The crimes of Watergate have become synonymous with the concept of political corruption.[37]

The Senate Select Committee on Presidential Campaign Activities, referred to as the Watergate or "Ervin Committee," after its chairman Senator Sam J. Ervin (D-NC), investigated the 1972 election activities and revealed a pattern of widespread political manipulation intended to stifle the voice of the opponents of the Nixon administration and to subvert the political will of the people. The burglary of the Democratic national headquarters at the Watergate hotel complex in Washington, D.C., was only part of a pervasive scheme to rig the 1972 electoral process and ensure that the weakest Democratic candidate would become Nixon's opponent. Surrounded by men willing to use any means to achieve the ends of the Nixon White House, and fueled by Nixon's pathological misunderstanding of the rule of law, the crimes of Watergate revealed the depth of political corruption during the Nixon years. Instinctively, Nixon explained Watergate in a 1977 interview with David Frost by obscuring the fundamental "law and order" theme of his own career. "Well, what I, at root I had in mind," Nixon analogized, "was perhaps much better stated by Lincoln during the War between the States. Lincoln said, and I think I can remember the quote almost exactly, he said, 'Actions which otherwise would be unconstitutional could become lawful if undertaken for the purpose of preserving the Constitution and the nation.'"[38]

Many begin the story of Watergate in the early morning hours of June 17, 1972, when James McCord, Bernard L. Barker, Frank Sturgis, Eugenio Martinez, and Virgilio Gonzales entered the Democratic National Committee headquarters in the posh Watergate situated along the banks of the Potomac River. Inside the Watergate complex, Howard Hunt and G. Gordon Liddy listened attentively to walkie-talkie communications with their five burglars. Across the street in the Howard Johnson Motor Lodge (now a dormitory for George Washington University), Alfred Baldwin stood lookout to the traffic below. Truth be told, the story of Watergate began in 1970 with the development of the "Huston Plan," and with Nixon's reaction to the passage and implementation of the campaign finance reforms of FECA 1971. Developed by Tom Charles Huston in various memorandums to H. R Haldeman and John Dean, the Huston plan envisioned unlimited presidential power manifested in schemes of illegal wiretapping, illegal break-ins, and illegal mail covers (when the government records without a warrant all information on the outside of an envelope delivered by US mail) for domestic intelligence purposes. The initial plan involved the FBI, CIA, National Security Agency, and Defense Intelligence Agency in domestic spying on Nixon's political opponents, intent on locating and monitoring domestic opponents of Nixon administration policies. The rise of domestic antiwar protests and domestic bombing attacks on federal facilities encouraged the president and his advisors to consider the Huston plan as a viable option. Resistance by FBI Director J. Edgar Hoover squelched the plan, but soon Committee to Reelect the President ("CRP") hirelings formulated an alternative plan specifically designed to plug information leaks from government sources.[39]

The special investigation unit designed to plug leaks, which consequently came to be known as the "Plumbers," was created after Daniel Ellsberg leaked the *Pentagon Papers* in June 1971. Egil Krogh supervised the groups, and John Erlichman, Nixon's right-hand man, supervised Krogh. The unit added G. Gordon Liddy and Howard Hunt, a former CIA agent, as key operatives in the unit. Their initial role was to investigate and uncover personnel who stole and disclosed secret government documents. Soon the group began to participate in illegal activities, including the burglary of the office of Dr. Lewis Fielding, Daniel Ellsberg's psychiatrist, in an attempt to get evidence to discredit Ellsberg. This 1971 burglary preceded the Watergate burglary by a year, and became part of the modus operandi of the Plumbers unit that preceded Watergate.

At about the same time, the CRP geared up for its own intelligence gathering and political dirty tricks campaign. In September 1971 White House counsel John Dean met with Jeb Stuart Magruder and Jack Caulfield, an investigator, to discuss "Project Sandwedge." Project Sandwedge in effect created a private intelligence-gathering organization to serve the president's campaign. Attorney General John Mitchell, who also served as the president's campaign manager, rejected Project Sandwedge, but it resurfaced when Dean recruited G. Gordon Liddy, who had moved from the Plumbers unit, to work with the CRP. The CRP divided into two subcommittees, the political committee and the finance committee, both under the control of the White House presidential staff, and directed and run by White House personnel.[40]

What emerged from the CRP intelligence-gathering brainstorm was project "Gemstone." Cooked up by Liddy, the plan proposed the use of CRP staff and hired personnel to use mugging squads and kidnappings to deal with anti-Nixon demonstrators, hiring prostitutes to infiltrate the Democratic National Convention in Miami, and conducting electronic surveillance and break-ins at a variety of locations. Its modest budget would be $1 million. Mitchell again initially rejected the proposal and advised Liddy to come back with a more modest plan focusing on the problems of demonstrations. In February 1972 Liddy presented a scaled-down proposal of burglary and intelligence-gathering that would form the basis for the plans that became the Watergate break-in. Targets included Democratic National Chairman Larry O'Brien and Las Vegas publisher Hank Greenspun, who allegedly had explosive and damaging material on Senator Edmund Muskie in his office safe. The goal was to steal the material, then use it to damage Senator Edmund Muskie (D-ME), whom the CRP considered a potentially strong general election opponent, ensuring that Muskie would lose the Democratic nomination for president. Throughout the campaign, the political arm of CRP twisted the campaign with "sophomoric stunts" (like ordering unwanted pizzas to a Democratic rally) and "underhanded personal attacks" (manufacturing libels about the sexual preferences of candidates or forging letters on opponents' stationery), as well as more serious illegalities, such as bugging and intercepting conversations and breaking into Democratic campaign headquarters. Liddy and Attorney General John Mitchell coordinated their efforts using government agencies to further their plots, and when the plots began to unravel, they used same federal agencies to subvert the investigation of their illegality.[41]

These campaign tactics were expensive, and CRP became the steady source of the funds. Political candidates attempted to raise as much money as possible before April 7, 1972, the effective date of FECA 1971, in order to evade the disclosure requirements of the new law. Those funds would be reportable under the old Federal Corrupt Practices Act, which carried little accountability and less enforcement. The CRP initially authorized Hugh Sloan, CRP campaign treasurer, to distribute up to $250,000 to Liddy for Project Gemstone. Liddy's first request for $83,000, most of it held in cash in the CRP safe, surprised Sloan, because it was more than he had disbursed during the entire campaign.

In the early morning hours of June 17, 1972, Frank Wills, a security guard at the Watergate complex, noticed a door lock taped open by the burglars employed in the Huston Plan and called the Washington District Metropolitan Police to assist him in the arrest of the burglars. Soon those CRP campaign funds kept in Sloan's safe became instrumental in preventing the burglars from talking to investigators. Liddy eventually received $199,000 in hush-money disbursements, and the other defendants and their attorneys received payoffs for their silence and quiet acquiescence in the operation. As the Ervin Committee commenced their investigation, the General Accounting Office audited the campaign funds, disclosing that by the end of the sordid affair, the CRP had disbursed over $1,777,000 in campaign-generated cash to buy the silence of the Watergate burglars. But the full breadth of the wrongdoing remained hidden throughout the summer of 1973.

Before the FECA 1971 became effective, the CRP demanded more and more money from its supporters. The raising and diversion of substantial and secret campaign funds created new avenues of corruption for the CRP. With the former FCPA limits on individual contributions and overall spending now gone, CRP fund-raisers used every tactic to exact from supporters increasingly large contributions. The Ervin Committee investigated the "sale" of ambassadorships, whereby large contributors bid their way into the most desired foreign capitals. After his election, Nixon appointed thirteen noncareer ambassadors. Eight of them contributed a minimum of $25,000, and taken together contributed over $706,000 to the reelection campaign. Including those persons already holding ambassadorships, the total contribution from that class of public servants came to $1.8 million. In the instance of businessman Roy Carver, chairman of the board of Bandag, Inc., he hired the public relations firm Hill & Knowlton to promote his visibility with the president's campaign. Contributing was a significant way to do that, and those businessmen testified that throughout the campaign they monitored the amount of campaign contributions others had given. "[H]e, particularly in the final weeks," the public relations officer testified, "got very anxious that he be on record as having given more than someone else. I don't know if he ended up with that distinction or not: but he likes to be first in what he does, and he was determined in the final weeks to be first if he could." On November 2, 1972, Carver gave to the CRP Bandag, Inc. stock worth $275,000. Evidently Carver's largess was not enough; he got State Department interviews, but no ambassadorial appointment.[42]

In addition to these abuses, the Ervin Committee exposed the massive evasion of the 1907 Tillman Act prohibiting direct corporate contributions to federal political campaigns. While the fear about corporate-generated wealth's overwhelming ordinary candidate fund-raising, and corporate directors' spending of shareholder funds to support political candidates, remained a strong policy rationale for corporate campaign-spending restrictions, the CRP found a multitude of ways around the Tillman Act restrictions. When CRP officials solicited contributions from corporations, at least thirteen corporations, interested in obtaining access or, as they put it "staying on the good side of the administration," contributed over $749,000 to the 1972 Nixon campaign. CRP officials were indifferent to the source of the money, and did not attempt to obtain assurances that the corporate contributions complied with the Tillman Act restrictions on corporate contributions. In many cases, the corporate officers prepared a list of names of individuals from which they would assert the contributions came. Since individual corporate officers or employees could lawfully contribute unlimited amounts under FECA 1971, this deception succeeded until they were placed under oath. During the campaign, Common Cause filed a lawsuit against the CRP, alleging a violation of the Tillman Act. This sent corporate and campaign officials scrambling to create a paper trail of names of corporate executives who had "contributed" to the fund. Many of them refused to perjure themselves when they testified, and the truth about most of the corporate contributions became known. Absent the lawsuit, none of this would have come to be known short of a legal investigation, since the reporting under FECA 1971 would have accepted the list of names the corporations offered with their "bundled" contributions.[43]

In a continuous pattern of abusive, undemocratic attempts to influence the selection of the Democratic opponent, the political and fund-raising arms of CRP worked together in a large-scale effort to disrupt and deceive the internal campaigns of their Democratic opponents, deceive public opinion, and siphon votes from candidates in a steady and overt effort to deny the average voter his free and reasoned electoral choice. Campaign espionage and spying, use of paid protesters for Senator George McGovern (D-SD) at Muskie rallies, and the creation and publication of slanders against the Democratic candidates on Democratic candidate stationery all demonstrated the scope of the deception. Efforts at vote-siphoning, the direct interference by one political party or campaign in the affairs of another party or campaign for the purpose of weakening or eliminating the opposition candidate, exemplified the extent and manner of the Nixon campaign. For example, in the New Hampshire primary, CRP spent campaign funds to organize and support a write-in campaign supporting Senator Edward Kennedy (D-MA), intended to siphon votes from the front-running Muskie. Nixon campaign operatives mailed between 100,000 and 150,000 letters to New Hampshire Democrats. In the Illinois primary, CRP directed campaign funds to Senator Eugene McCarthy, hoping again to divert support from Muskie. Later in California, which had at that time a ballot law that required a party to have registered voters of one-fifteenth of one percent of total registered voters in the state in order to qualify for the ballot in a primary election, CRP gave money to a reregistration effort. CRP tried to convince members of the American Independent Party, which supported George Wallace, to change their registration before the deadline to keep Wallace from gaining their support as a primary ballot candidate. CRP spent $10,000 in that effort, all of which went unreported to the public. What effect these dirty tricks and unethical efforts directed against Democratic campaigns may have had remains unknown. But Muskie campaign officials testified that the CRP dirty tricks "took a toll in the form of diverting our resources, changing our schedule, altering our political approaches, and being thrown on the defensive."[44]

Throughout the campaign and the cover-up that followed, Nixon steadfastly maintained that he had done no wrong. Ethically straitjacketed by his conception of political corruption, he agreed with his presidential assistant John Ehrlichman that these were "technical violations of the Campaign Spending Act." As press accounts grew more ominous, Nixon questioned how the Ervin Committee could believe he had acted corruptly, since "I don't have a damn thing. . . . I don't own anything," and "if I had a billion dollars of stolen money in that (my) house or I had campaign money in that house. . . then that would be a different matter." "But I haven't, you see," Nixon complained to Press Secretary Ron Ziegler in a May 14, 1973, Oval Office meeting, "That's the whole point."[45]

COMBATING CORRUPTION THROUGH LEGAL REFORM—
The Ervin Committee Report and FECA 1974

On February 7, 1973, Senate Resolution 60, authorized because of newly discovered evidence of 1972 campaign abuses, directed the Ervin Committee to make a "complete investigation and study into the extent to which illegal, improper, or unethical activities occurred in the 1972 Presidential campaign and election," and further, to determine whether new legislation was needed "to safeguard the electoral process by which the President of the United States is chosen." The Ervin Committee documented the litany of electoral abuses that occurred during the 1972 primary and general campaign. The committee, which issued its report during the middle of the Nixon impeachment inquiry, called for a multitude of political reforms, not limited to changes in the campaign finance system, that served as a clarion call for electoral reform. However, during the negotiations between the Senate and House versions of the bills and when examined by the Supreme Court in *Buckley v. Valeo*, the broad reform recommendations promoting deliberation in the electoral system devolved into the campaign finance reforms of FECA 1974, more narrowly balanced against First Amendment rights of individual contributors and candidates. How and why that happened poses significant questions about the process and limits of legislative reform in the aftermath of Watergate.[46]

One chapter of the story, reminiscent of the anticampaign finance backlash of the late 1920s that began in the states, was the growing antipathy to federal institutional solutions to the problem of political corruption. Post-Watergate progressives "looked longingly back to the first two decades of the century and saw how political reform had changed the country," and then sought similar reforms in FECA 1974. But by 1974 conservative resistance to national solutions for reforming political behavior questioned the value and efficacy of congressional political reform.[47]

But perhaps the main failure of FECA 1974 was that at one point, it aspired to be so much more, but suffered at the hands of some in Congress who feared that broader reforms might endanger their ability to get elected. Congressional efforts at structural reform of the political system, intended to restore the faith of the people in government and the democratic system, led Congress to enact a system of campaign finance in FECA 1971 that included a belief in principles of free speech equality that had a 100-year progeny in the legislative and judicial construction of the American campaign finance system. Despite the initial focus on those reform ideals, as enacted, FECA 1974 focused much more narrowly on fixing the political process and thus tended to ignore the broad principles of equality and democratic deliberation that most previous campaign finance reforms had addressed. The values that Congress preferred when it enacted FECA 1974 help explain the decision of the Supreme Court in *Buckley v. Valeo* when it confronted the constitutional conflict between free speech doctrine and the congressional mandate to safeguard the electoral process from corruption. When it considered the constitutionality of FECA 1974, the Supreme Court also too singularly "followed the money," narrowly defining the evil as quid pro quo, privileging First Amendment rights over the deliberative ideas of campaign finance reform. Congress and campaign finance reformers confronted the conflict between free speech and deliberative democracy in 1974, but the failure to come to a common understanding about what values our electoral system should embody meant that those reforms were delivered to the Supreme Court on life support in *Buckley*. The Court pulled the plug, but the same conundrum that challenged proponents of campaign finance reform in 1976 still challenges them today.[48]

Congress expected that the Ervin Committee would recommend a broad, comprehensive, and systematic set of reforms of the entire campaign system. The Ervin Committee proposals should be examined in light of the previous decade of congressional attempts, this "rolling thunder" of campaign finance reform, which came to a crescendo in FECA 1974. A short summary of the findings of the Ervin Committee are necessary to understand the scope of both the problem and the reform proposals eventually recommended to the entire Congress to address the pattern of political abuse uncovered by the investigation.

The committee divided its report into eleven separate chapters that dealt with specific parts of the investigation, which although distinct, often intertwined with one another. They included the Watergate break-in and cover-up, campaign practices, the use of incumbency, campaign financing, the Milk Fund investigation, the 1972 presidential campaigns of

Senator Hubert H. Humphrey and Congressman Wilbur D. Mills, the Hughes-Rebozo investigation over illegal campaign funding, a chapter on the legal difficulties of Congress called the Senate Select Committee in Court, and another on the committee's use of computer technology intended to offer Congress information on the difficulties and opportunities for future congressional investigations. Each chapter concluded with specific reform recommendations to Congress as solutions to the corruption that had been uncovered. The final chapter presented the individual views of the Senators of the Select Committee.[49]

While acknowledging that their report was "not an exhaustive compendium of every campaign practice investigated by the Select Committee," the Ervin Committee focused on those abuses that raised the most serious questions of campaign propriety and ethics. The report emphasized several themes. The committee regarded the power of incumbency and the consequent abuse of position, power, and prerogative by the Nixon administration as a significant abuse. The second area was the "misuse of large amounts of money," particularly cash secretively solicited and sequestered, that paid for the myriad of unethical campaign practices. This, the committee reasoned, demonstrated the need for "strict regulation of its use in political campaigns." The third theme discussed was the search for and use of intelligence on opposing candidates. The intelligence involved illegal wire-tapping, illegal use of income tax information, and the illegal and unethical use of public agencies to do the work of the CRP. Finally, the committee strongly objected to the means and manner in which CRP attempted to "mislead and deceive the press," which eventually made it impossible for the public to know the whole truth about the issues of campaign contributions and expenditures that had formed the basis for the disclosure provisions in the major campaign finance acts from FCPA 1925 to FECA 1971.[50]

Not willing to limit their proposals to campaign financing, the committee made three recommendations intended broadly to reform political ethics. It recommended that Congress should prohibit anyone involved in any campaign directly or indirectly from spying on or obstructing the campaign of any other candidate. Second, Congress should prohibit the disbursal of campaign funds for the purpose of promoting or financing the violation of federal election laws. Third, Congress should enact new legislation that prohibits the theft, unauthorized copying, or taking by false pretenses of any campaign material, documents, or papers belonging to any candidate for federal office.[51] This modest code of ethical behavior was backed up by the meat of the campaign finance recommendations that formed the basis of FECA 1974, but which in many respects, became a ghost of reform once the bill had churned its way through Congress.

The Ervin Committee offered eleven campaign finance recommendations. They included establishing an independent, nonpartisan Federal Elections Commission that would replace the present tripartite administration of the clerk of the House, secretary of the Senate, and GAO Office of

Federal Elections and would have certain enforcement power; enactment of a statute prohibiting cash contributions and expenditures in excess of $100 in connection with any campaign for nomination or election to federal office; enactment of a statute intended to end the long-standing FCPA loophole by requiring each candidate for the office of president or vice president to designate one political committee as his central campaign committee, with one or more banks as his campaign depositories. The committee also recommended enactment of a statutory limitation on overall campaign expenditures of presidential candidates, imposing a limit on expenditures of twelve cents times the voting age population during a general election, and a statutory limitation of $3,000 on political contributions by any individual to the campaign of each presidential candidate during the prenomination period and a separate $3,000 limitation during the postnomination period. Contributions to a vice presidential candidate of a party would be considered, for the purposes of the limitation, as contribution to that party's presidential candidate. As a way to expand the involvement of small citizen contributors, the committee recommended the creation of a tax credit in a substantial amount on individual and joint federal income tax returns for any contribution made in a calendar year to a political party or any candidate seeking election to any public office, federal, state, or local.

In one area where the final bill seemed to support deliberative principles more than the committee's recommendations, the committee opposed the adoption of any form of public financing in which tax moneys are collected and allocated to political candidates by the federal government. It recommended enactment of a statute prohibiting the solicitation or receipt of campaign contributions from foreign nationals, and stipulated that no government official whose appointment required confirmation by the Senate or who was on the payroll of the executive office of the president be permitted to participate in the solicitation or receipt of campaign contributions during his or her period of service and for a period of one year thereafter. Finally, the committee recommended that stringent limitations be imposed on the right of organizations to contribute to presidential campaigns, and that any violation of the major provisions of the campaign financing law, such as participating in a corporate or union contribution or a contribution in excess of the statutory limit, or making a foreign contribution, be a felony.[52]

Importantly, individual members of the committee made several recommendations to reform the electoral process that added substantially to the overall reform package. Senator Howard Baker (R-TN), the ranking minority member on the committee, examined the proposed reforms in light of FECA 1971. Baker personally felt FECA 1971 was a major reform, an exception to the generally held belief that FECA 1974 was the first "significant attempt by Congress to regulate political campaigns since the Corrupt Practices Act of 1925, and even that was more loophole than law." Elections, he said, had taken on the appearance of a "political free-for-all in which the distinction between illegal, unethical, and immoral conduct is generally obscured," resulting in "a devastating erosion of public trust and confidence in the process by which public officials are elected." Because he understood the political system based on his own experiences, Baker supported reform of the campaign finance system but advocated broader reforms aimed at the ethical lapses in the election process itself. Baker opposed public financing of elections because, he maintained, voter participation by campaign contributions was a civic-political act that was essential to the voluntary nature of the American process. Baker supported an overall expenditure limitation, a requirement for full public disclosure of all contributions and expenditures before elections, and a single campaign committee and depository for all contributions. These, Baker argued, along with a strict prohibition of contributions from all organizations, would solve the problem of excessive money in elections.[53]

Although he opposed full public financing, Baker proposed that Congress fund a tax incentive for small contributions that would alleviate concerns about drying up the financial spigot by the new limit on contribution size. He also advocated automatic voter registration of all adults at age 18. In order to shorten campaigns and help control their expenses, he proposed creating a primary system of regional primaries held on four or five dates at three-week intervals. Additionally, Baker proposed a 24-hour voting period to eliminate the harmful effects of the national media projecting the outcome of elections based on early returns, and he called for the abolition of the Electoral College system. Finally, Baker demanded greater party control of elections, and a requirement that the presidential and vice presidential campaigns become the sole responsibility of the national party structure, necessary to avoid the problems created by control of the campaign by an unaccountable organization like the Committee to Reelect the President. Congress meant these reform proposals, which demonstrated a broader understanding of the problem exposed in Watergate, to increase voter participation, deliberation on positions and issues, and equal access for both candidates and voters.[54]

Committee chairman Senator Sam J. Ervin (D-NC), the moral poet of the committee, described Watergate as a "conglomerate of various illegal and unethical activities in which various officers and employees of the Nixon reelection committees" attempted to "destroy, insofar as the Presidential election of 1972 was concerned, the integrity of the process by which the President of the United States is nominated and elected." They accomplished this, he continued, by exacting "enormous contributions—usually in cash—from corporate executives," all in violation of the Tillman Act ban on corporate contributions. They then used these funds to slander and libel opposing candidates, manufacture stories intended to shape public opinion and squelch deliberate debate on the political issues of the day, all out of "a lust for political power" that caused good men to resort to evil means to promote what they conceived to be a good end. The law alone, Ervin cautioned, even as his committee delivered their massive report to the Senate for legislative action, "will not suffice to prevent future Watergates." The law merely deters some human beings from offending; "it does not make men good. This task can be performed only by ethics or religion or morality."[55]

Senator Lowell Weicker, Jr. (R-CT), the most critical Republican member of the Ervin Committee, provided a lengthy summary of what he understood to be the evils of Watergate, which he described as nothing less than an attack on the laws, institutions, and principles of American constitutional democracy. Weicker's report read like a primer on constitutional civics. For Weicker, the Watergate abuses, which he methodically detailed in the summary, were fundamental challenges to the constitutional system. The excesses of the CRP that the committee uncovered undermined legitimate values inherent in the doctrines of executive power and the separation of power, and in the protective value of the Bill of Rights. The break-ins, bugging, electronic surveillance, and domestic spying created a chilling effect on the free speech and deliberative capacity of political participants. The Nixon reelection machine violated a litany of constitutional rules and democratic doctrine, Weicker asserted, but the political process that had been most abused by the Watergate crimes occurred when the CRP "emasculated important party functions" by taking the election process and operation away from the Republican Party and putting it into the hands of a few men without any ethical compass and "unresponsive to the checks and balances of party politics." The problem with illegally unreported and spent campaign funds was that they distorted the political process by undemocratically coercing voters. While normally a legitimate function of party politics, the process of voter education, in the hands of the CRP, became an undemocratic effort at immoral suasion. Weicker decried CRP's illegal and unethical use of funds because the true task of politics and political campaigning was to influence the voters based on tangible facts, reasoned positions, and articulated differences between the candidates. The idea that one candidate would use his own campaign funds to influence the votes for or against an opponent in an opposition primary, simply to ensure the weakest general election candidate, ranked as the worst kind of political subversion. "It was," Weicker concluded, "nothing short of a massive operation to deprive the American voter of information about Democratic candidates for President—it was an attack on voters and their opportunity to cast a fully informed vote."[56]

Because Weicker saw those abuses as a direct attack on deliberative democracy, he proposed a code of candidate responsibility with a grievance procedure enforced through a Federal Election Commission. He also proposed that all campaigns be run not by the nominee, but by the party of the nominee, assuming this would provide more accountability. Additionally, he suggested that all nominations for federal elective office be by direct primary, with unaffiliated voters free to participate in the party primary of their choosing. These institutional changes would help avoid the problems endemic to the Nixon campaign by making the campaigns themselves more responsive and responsible to democratic control. Weicker was clearly troubled by what had happened, but he too realized that institutional reform of the political system, and particularly the campaign finance system that bred and fed the potential for corruption, may not be enough. "It is no source of pride to me as an American," he lamented, "that the coinage of responsibility has been in inverse measure to rank and power. I was taught early on, first by my dad and then by the U.S. Army, that rank has its privileges because rank has its responsibilities."[57]

THE DEMOCRATIC PARADOX OF THE PROPOSED REFORMS
AND THE FINAL FORM OF FECA 1974

Although FECA 1974 is widely regarded as the most significant reform of the campaign finance system since the FCPA 1925, Congress reshaped the original Ervin Committee recommendations after often contentious floor debate and the conference committee reconciliation of the Senate and House versions. What the conference committee left for the inevitable court challenge was a reform package that largely ignored, except in terms of the effect of campaign money on elections, the effects of systemic corruption on deliberative democratic institutions and principles that the original package of reform proposals had addressed. Instead of the broad and ubiquitous reform of the election system proposed by the committee and its leading members intended to reaffirm deliberative principles, FECA 1974 became a more narrow process-focused reform of the campaign finance system.[58]

A brief comparison of the Senate and House versions of FECA 1974, and the conference committee results, demonstrate the limits of the Watergate-inspired reforms to revamp the political system. At its heart, FECA 1974 was quite limited in scope and was handicapped by a failure to consider the connections between corruption and the deliberative democratic functions that Senators Baker, Ervin, and Weicker had explicitly made in their Ervin Committee summaries. In addition, the severability clause in FECA 1971 found at Section 313, which remained in FECA 1974, created a problem during the judicial review of the law. The clause provided that though a court may find one part of the law unconstitutional, that would not invalidate the entire law. This ironically encouraged the Supreme Court to approve what many critics considered to be the most unintended result of *Buckley v. Valeo*—the limitation of contributions but not expenditures —a condition of reform none of the supporters of FECA 1974 intended or would have supported when the bill passed.

The original draft of FECA 1974 (S. 3044) expanded FECA 1971 in several significant ways. First, it imposed specific contribution limits on political committees of $5,000 per candidate annually, and for individuals of $1,000 per candidate annually, with a total individual limitation of $25,000 each year for all candidates. Every candidate was required to create one campaign committee responsible for collecting and reporting all receipts and expenditures in excess of $100 (none of which could be in cash). Candidates for president and vice president were limited to total expenditures for nomination to $10 million, and $20 million for the general election. Senate candidates were limited to a maximum of $150,000 or twelve cents times the voting age population of the state, and candidates for the House to $100,000 or eight cents times the voting age population in their respective districts, whichever was greater.[59]

Parties were limited to spending on behalf of presidential and vice presidential candidates to two cents times the national voting age population, and in the case of senators and representatives, to the greater of two cents times the voting age population of the state or district if the state had but one district, or $20,000. Candidates could spend from their personal funds, or the funds of their immediate families, to support the election for any federal office the aggregate of $50,000 for president and vice president, $35,000 for senator or representative if the state had only one representative, or $25,000 for the office of representative in multidistrict states. Violations of the candidate contribution or spending limits carried fines of up to $25,000 or one year imprisonment. Labor unions and corporations, long prohibited from contributing any funds to federal campaigns, were given the authority to act like any other political committee provided they established and administered a segregated fund to collect and spend money to influence the nomination or election of candidates.

Additionally, S. 3044, in an attempt by Congress to end the too vigorous regulatory control exercised by the comptroller general (as authorized by FECA 1971), established the Federal Election Commission (FEC). Congress granted to the FEC the regulatory power to collect and disseminate all campaign finance reports, to make regulations and issue advisory opinions to enforce and administer FECA 1974, to investigate all alleged violations of campaign laws, and to recommend prosecution of any such violations. All political committees would be required to register with the Federal Election Commission, and meet specific reporting requirements that would include the names of all contributors giving in excess of $100.[60]

Finally, in a separate provision entitled the "Presidential Primary Matching Payment Account," Congress enacted, along with amendments to the Revenue Act of 1971, tax deductions and credits for small campaign contributions and a tax checkoff to fund the Presidential Election Campaign Fund reminiscent of the Long Act of 1966. These provisions, which would take effect in 1973, were a compromise toward partial public financing of presidential and vice presidential campaigns, and the tax deduction and credit provisions were encouragement for small voluntary contributions to offset the potential loss of revenue from the contribution limitations enacted in FECA 1974.[61]

The Subcommittee on Privileges and Elections, chaired by Senator Claiborne Pell (D-RI), met in September 1973 to consider the reforms. More than forty witnesses testified in support of public financing of elections. Senator Cranston (D-CA), speaking on behalf of a third of the Senate membership, submitted a set of eight principles intended to form the basis for any public financing legislation the court would consider. Those principles included (1) an extension of the checkoff system to provide sufficient funds for effective campaigns not reliant on large donors; (2) full funding for major parties, and up to full funding for minor, new, and independent party candidates based on their demonstrable success in the last election; (3) an extension of funding to primaries for candidates once they had demonstrated broad public support, which could include petition support; (4) establishment of an overall spending limit for primary and general election campaigns; (5) permitting candidates to raise limited private funds from very small contributors; (6) providing a role for political parties as a pooling mechanism for contributions to candidates in general elections; (7) a requirement of central financial reporting and recordkeeping; and (8) administration of all campaign finance reporting and regulations by an independent elections commission with enforcement powers.[62]

All of these provisions were intended to remedy the most corrosive causes of the Watergate scandal. They would, argued supporters, "check the excessive influence of great wealth" in such a way as to eliminate reliance on large private contributions and "still ensure adequate presentation to the electorate of opposing viewpoints of competing candidates." Public financing would allow a candidate to have the public funds to run a "fully informative and effective campaign" once he had become "an unquestionably serious candidate, by virtue of his being a major party nominee." Supporting truly deliberative campaigns of education remained an essential element of reform, but only if the campaign performed that civic function primarily with large campaign donations reflective of widespread grassroots support.[63]

Lawmakers believed that political parties were essential to the reform process. Providing a statutory role for parties in pooling small contributions, and making them available to their nominees, would reestablish the role of parties disregarded by the Nixon campaign of 1972. Parties, thought the reformers, would be easier to regulate, and parties ought to play a role in "building strong coalitions of voters and in keeping candidates responsible to the electorate through the party organization."[64] Specifically, to address the potential of small faction parties that could undermine the stability provided by a strong two-party system, minor party candidates would only receive funds if they could demonstrate electoral support from the prior election. The supporters of public financing hoped that this would diminish the possibility of a "proliferation of splinter parties or independent candidates" that would undermine stability and could polarize voters based on a single volatile issue.[65]

The expenditure limits in S. 3044 arose not from the system of public financing, which became the most contentious provision of the act, but from the pragmatic understanding that without such individual limits, the system of public financing with aggregate spending limits was unworkable. Independent expenditure limits on behalf of a candidate, and political contribution limits for individuals and political action committees, necessarily coordinated with the overall spending limitation to establish reasonable boundaries for political spending, and to ensure effective policing of those limits. While recognizing the free speech problems posed by this approach, the Senate Watergate committee, relying on the numerous Supreme Court precedents it considered decisive, believed that "[i]f Congress may, consistent with the First Amendment, limit contributions to preserve the integrity of the electoral process, then it also can constitutionally limit independent expenditures in order to make the contribution limits effective." These spending limitations, along with permitting unlimited communication by a person or group if the communication did not advocate specific candidates, seemed to pose no First Amendment problems.[66]

Senators Pell and Robert P. Griffin (R-MI), who opposed parts of the bill, described in their opposition to the legislation terms that explained their conception of the corruptive evil that should be remedied. Pell granted the FECA 1974 reforms historic significance, calling them in accord with "Jeffersonian principles which place abiding confidence in the wisdom of the individual and in the individual's fundamental role in the development of an enlightened democracy." For Senator Pell, the corruption rampant in the campaign finance system was epitomized by the Watergate-like connection between the misuse of power and the influence of large political contributions. The most important part of the legislation removed the temptation of any candidate from seeking or accepting a compromising gift, and returned to individual voters casting individual ballots based on a campaign of education, the rightful responsibility in the choosing of candidates. Senator Griffin, an opponent of public financing, said that "[t]he only thing more dangerous to democracy than corrupt politicians may be politicians hellbent on reform." Griffin supported the provisions of the bill limiting expenditures and contributions, and the creation of an independent Federal Election Commission, but he feared that public financing would not reform the system and would instead increase levels of campaign spending. He also lamented that real reforms, such as those recommended by Senators Baker and Weicker to shorten the duration of campaigns and regulate their operation, were excluded from the bill. In the end, Griffin reluctantly voted to send the bill to the full Senate. The Senate passed S. 372, which included the broad range of campaign finance and election reforms that closely mimicked the Ervin Committee recommendations.[67]

The bill, however, stalled in the House of Representatives largely through the efforts of Administration Committee chairman Wayne Hays (D-OH), and John Dent (D-PA), chairman of the Subcommittee on Elections. By 1974, catalyzed by the outrageous Watergate examples, public support for campaign finance reform moved forward in both houses, and the Senate passed S. 3044 on April 11, 1974. Though the House delay continued, by August 8, 1974, a bill moved to the floor that contained many of the Senate bill provisions on contribution and spending limitations, but rejected public financing of congressional campaigns, approved a weak enforcement agency, and rejected public financing of presidential nominating conventions. The conference committee would engage in bitter disagreement as it reconciled the two competing versions of campaign finance and broader reform.[68]

The conference committee made several changes to the bill, some of which altered the deliberative principles expressed by reform proponents in the Ervin Committee report and in the Senate Subcommittee markup of S. 3044. Those changes focused the final FECA 1974 reforms on addressing the limited concept of quid pro quo corruption. That narrow focus meant that many of the broad, institutional reforms of the political process proposed to address the integrity of the electoral system did not become part of the law, and thus would not be considered as part of the overall reform enacted by Congress when the Supreme Court considered its constitutionality two years later.

The original Senate bill contained three provisions dealing with larger concerns about the integrity of the campaign system. It prohibited the embezzlement or conversion of political contributions, provided for new rules meant to curb voter fraud (including casting an unauthorized ballot, miscounting votes, tampering with a voting machine, or committing any act with the intent of causing an inaccurate count of votes in any election), and regulated the release of public information about votes cast in a presidential election before midnight EST on the day of the election. The Conference Committee struck those three provisions from the bill. The Senate bill required the national committee of a political party to approve every expenditure of more than $1,000 made by the candidate of such party for president or vice president. As it was clearly intended to remedy the expenditure of cash funds for illegal purposes and to permit party control over campaigns, the Conference Committee likewise omitted this provision.

The Senate bill also included a provision that excess contributions received by a candidate for the purposes of supporting that candidate for office "may be used by such candidate or individual to defray ordinary and necessary expenses incurred in connection with his duties as a holder of federal office, or may be made as a charitable contribution." The House bill contained no such provision, but the Conference Committee elected to adopt the Senate bill, thus permitting the use of excessive campaign contributions for the use of the officeholder in the performance of his duties. Also, the Senate bill prohibited any senator or representative from making any mass mailing of a newsletter or mailing with a simplified form of address under the frank during the immediately preceding sixty-day preelection period. The Conference Committee removed this provision from the final bill. Finally, the Senate bill required financial disclosure and reporting of taxes, sources of income, any gifts received, and the value of honoraria, and the annual reporting of all such items of income or value for all federal elected officials. The Conference Committee omitted the provisions of the disclosure requirement.[69]

To be sure, in its final form FECA 1974 modified FECA 1971 in several significant respects. In its final form, FECA 1974, which was approved on October 10, 1974, provided for expenditure limits on presidential candidates of $20 million in elections and $10 million in nomination races. No presidential candidate could spend more than twice the Senate limit in any state. Senatorial candidates were limited to the greater of eight cents times the voting-age population or $100,000 in primaries, and to twelve cents times the voting-age population in general elections. House candidates bore a similar limit of $70,000 in each primary and general election, unless the House candidate came from a single-district state, in which case that race fell under the Senate limitations. Fund-raising expenses permitted an additional 20 percent of the respective limits. National party committees retained a role in campaign fund-raising. Each national party committee could raise and spend an additional 2 cents times the voting age population for national candidates, and up to 2 cents to support Senate and House candidates, with an upper limit for the latter of $20,000 and $10,000 respectively.[70]

FECA 1974 also limited contributions to campaigns. Individuals could contribute $1,000 for each nomination and $1,000 for each general election campaign per candidate for any federal office. No individual could give more than $25,000 annually to all candidates and in all elections combined. A candidate's contribution to his own campaign could not exceed $50,000 for president, $35,000 for senator, and $25,000 for representative. The act further limited contributions by political committees, now defined to include corporate and union organizations that raised and held funds in segregated, exclusively political accounts, to $5,000 for each federal office candidate in each nomination and election contest. Any indirect or earmarked contributions counted against those limits. Donations by foreign nationals were specifically prohibited. No contributions or expenditures made in cash could exceed $100.

The act reinforced long-standing campaign finance principles regarding public disclosure that had their origins in FCPA 1925 and FECA 1971. These disclosure principles were further strengthened by the requirements for specific campaign treasurer reporting deadlines, repealing the requirement of keeping the occupation and principal place of business of contributors (felt to be abusive, obstructive, and not helpful in aiding public disclosure), and making each campaign committee maintain a single depository bank through which all transactions would flow for easier public tracking. Further, to end the persistent FCPA 1925 loophole that had permitted multiple campaign committees to slip the knot of full disclosure, FECA 1974 required that each campaign have only one committee responsible for all accounting and all reporting, to be centrally recorded and available for public inspection.[71]

The most controversial provision of the act involved public financing and independent enforcement. The act initiated public financing for presidential nominating conventions and for nominating and general elections. Major party candidates could receive up to $20 million in public funds. Major party presidential candidates could receive matching funds in nominating contests for each individual contribution up to $250, by first qualifying by raising $5,000 in such total contributions in each of twenty different states. Matching grants were limited to $5 million or one-half of the total nominating expenditure limits. Minor parties were eligible for proportional participation in public financing, with their grants calculated as a percentage of major party subsidies equal to the percentage that their vote in the preceding general election was of the average major party vote. New parties yet unable to establish such a ratio could qualify for postelection public reimbursement based on their proportional vote in the present election. Congress retained the $1 checkoff formula from FECA 1971 and provided that all grants be indexed to the consumer price index. Finally, FECA 1974 created the Federal Election Commission and gave it power to supervise and enforce the full disclosure provisions of the law, but the secretary of the Senate and clerk of the House remained the depositories for the disclosure filings. While the commission could make rules, each house could consider the rules and could veto them by majority vote within thirty days.[72]

Clearly, many critics today regard these provisions as the most innovative of the bill. But in light of the root causes and consequences of the Watergate scandal that animated its consideration, the removal of the many other broader reform provisions from the final bill meant that Congress had limited the scope of the reforms to a carefully circumscribed regulation of corruption that directly led to the granting of political access or favors. Critics of the *Buckley* decision underestimate how the Conference Committee itself began to limit the compelling interest of Congress to regulate broad electoral corruption when it eliminated the most deliberative reforms of the political system that the Ervin Committee had proposed. Just as in *Buckley* the Court illustrated its views on the kind of democratic values it sought to create when deciding election law cases, so the legislature provided a window into its democratic values when it avoided enacting broader reforms proposed by the Senate. Given that Watergate created the best political opportunity at campaign finance reform in fifty years, the final form of FECA 1974 demonstrated the institutional difficulty of achieving electoral reform at the hands of those most likely to be affected by it.[73]

THE SUPREME COURT SPEAKS—Coining Corruption in *Buckley v. Valeo*

The legislative history of FECA 1974 demonstrated the difficulties inherent in reforming the campaign finance system in the post-Watergate-clouded climate of moral revulsion and political ambiguity about the effect of the scandal on American democracy. Key to both the revulsion and moral ambiguity was the conflicted understanding about the nature of the corruption that Watergate exposed and that the reforms of FECA 1974 intended to address. Lawmakers of both parties, concerned that reform may overreach and damage their own fund-raising capabilities, coined a limited definition of corruption that "followed the money" and that prevented a full reformation of the campaign finance system based on the principles of 100 years of campaign finance legislation and judicial decisions.

When the Supreme Court considered the challenge to FECA 1974 in *Buckley v. Valeo*, it employed a similarly limited corruption rationale to weigh the balance of congressional interests against the general free speech doctrine the judiciary had created outside the specific campaign finance arena. The Supreme Court used the more limited rationale not because, like Congress, it feared regulatory overreaching and desired to protect its own interest, but because its members, since the appointment process changes beginning during the Eisenhower administration, and since the departure of Chief Justice Warren, privileged a free speech value system that promoted individualist over communitarian interests, and that encouraged the adoption of an explicitly apolitical language of corruption. This language bespoke of a narrow understanding of the connections between free speech and campaign finance that largely ignored the deliberative democratic function of American political campaigns.[74]

FECA 1974 included a provision proposed by New York Conservative Party senator James Buckley that required an expedited judicial review of the law. That review would occur in a milieu of definitional confusion and limitation. When the Watergate investigators began to follow the money, so too did the political reform community. Corruption took on the garb of "crude pecuniary bribery," not simply because that was the most available definition, but because the political climate of the 1960s and the facts of Watergate exposed political abuses so closely related to that understanding. FECA 1974 failed to address, except in the attenuated regulation of money, the Ervin Committee's exposure of the abuses of the political system, the dirty tricks, the manipulation by one candidate of another party's voters, and the public lies, deceit, and misrepresentation used to dissuade and persuade voters away from objective and rational deliberation that had formed the most egregious Watergate abuses. Instead, in FECA 1974, Congress focused on the direct misuse of campaign funds to garner political power and disburse political favors in reforming the political process. This meant that Congress minimized historically broader understandings about the effect of corruption on deliberative democracy that had long formed the heart and sinew of the regulatory scheme of the campaign finance system. Little wonder then that when the Supreme Court examined FECA 1974 in *Buckley*, it would likewise fail to consider the broader public interest in promoting democratic values and in sustaining "a strong and compelling collective interest" in representative democracy.[75]

The challenge to FECA 1974 came on January 2, 1975, before the United States District Court of the District of Columbia in *Buckley v. Valeo*.

The plaintiffs included Senator James L. Buckley, Eugene J. McCarthy, Representative William A. Steiger, Stewart R. Mott, Committee for a Constitutional Presidency McCarthy '76, the Conservative Party of New York, the Mississippi Republican Party, the Libertarian Party, the New York Civil Liberties Union, the Conservative Victory Fund, and Human Events, Inc. Defendants included Hon. Francis R. Valeo, secretary of the U.S. Senate; Hon. W. Pat Jennings, clerk of the U.S. House of Representatives; Hon. Elmer B. Staats, comptroller general; Hon. Edward H. Levi, attorney general of the United States; and the Federal Election Commission, created by FECA 1974 but not yet appointed or confirmed. Collectively, they brought action against the enforcement officials seeking declaratory and injunctive relief against certain provisions of FECA 1971 and FECA 1974, as well as the public financing provisions of Subtitle H of the Internal Revenue Code. The plaintiffs challenged several of the provisions because they violated their First Amendment rights to free speech and association. That decision was quickly appealed to the United States Supreme Court.[76]

Buckley remains one of the most analyzed and criticized Supreme Court cases in modern history. Critics focus on two main elements in the court decision. First, they are highly critical of the Supreme Court's finding that money was the equivalent of speech, deserving of First Amendment protection and thus subject to strict scrutiny overcome only by a compelling state interest. Second, although the Court found that there was a legitimate state interest in protecting the integrity of elections, it held that with regard to corruption, FECA 1974 went beyond what was needed to guard against quid pro quo corruption that the Court felt that statute intended to regulate. When confronted with the potential state interest of preserving voter equality beyond the one-man, one-vote formulation found in the apportionment cases, the *Buckley* Court dismissed that claim.[77]

Focused on the speech implications of restricting contributions and expenditures in political campaigns in an attempt to limit the rising costs of campaigns or prevent corruption or the appearance of corruption, the court found that expenditure limits unconstitutionally impaired the free speech rights of both candidates and voters. The Supreme Court starkly rebuked the third possible interest, that of "equalizing the relative ability of all citizens to affect the outcome of elections," stating that "the concept that government may restrict the speech of some element of our society in order to enhance the relative voice of others is wholly foreign to the First Amendment, which was designed to secure the widest possible dissemination of information from diverse and antagonistic sources and to ensure unfettered interchange of ideas for the bringing about of political and social changes desired by the people."[78]

The Court distinguished the equality rationale it had employed in the apportionment cases, arguing that "the principles that underlie invalidation of governmentally imposed restrictions on the franchise do not justify governmentally imposed restrictions on political expression." Furthermore, the Court distinguished the equality language in *Red Lion*

Broadcasting Company v. FCC by arguing that "the broadcast media pose unique and special problems not present in the traditional free speech case" since the individual right to broadcast is not the same as the individual right to speak, write, or publish. The Court further recharacterized *Red Lion* by arguing, against that decision's own logic and against the clear purposes of both FECA 1971 and 1974, that the effect of the fairness doctrine was merely one of "enhancing the volume and quality of coverage." It was neither the volume or quality of, but the accessibility to, the publicly owned airwaves that in *Red Lion* compelled the Warren court to insist that the congressional mechanisms of media access—fairness and equal time—were vital to maintaining free political speech for those least able to afford the cost of the electronic marketplace.[79]

On those points, however, the Supreme Court failed to consider the long and distinct legislative and judicial history of the regulation of the American campaign finance system. The construction of a "quid pro quo" definition of corruption that permitted Congress to regulate campaign finances limited the potential for other legitimate interests to balance public access to deliberative ideas and discussion. Focused on quid pro quo corruption akin to bribery, the Supreme Court ignored the historically broader definition of corruption that had long been considered a legitimate object of the state regulation of elections.[80]

The conference notes from the Buckley case provide some clues as to how the Court examined the legal conflict between restricting campaign contributions and expenditures and protecting political speech. Leading off the discussion, Chief Justice Burger said that he "seriously doubted" the constitutionality of the contribution and expenditure limits. Justice Brennan sustained the contribution limits, but reserved judgment on the expenditure limits. Justice Stewart was "predisposed to say that the statute is constitutional at first, but the more I get into this the more doubtful I become." He found the expenditure limitations "wholly unconstitutional under the First Amendment." Justice White believed that contributions were an act "regulable" by Congress because the "dangers to fuel corruption require regulation." He would have approved the expenditure limits "because otherwise, despite the contribution limits, you can get and spend all the money you want." Justice Marshall would have sustained the expenditure limits, and the contribution limits, but worried about the constitutionality of the $10 and $100 publicity limits. Justice Rehnquist disagreed with Brennan, stating that "this act does not further First Amendment values—this law abridges, rather than furthers, First Amendment values." He believed that campaign contributions to a candidate constituted action and not speech, and would vote to uphold them. Justice Powell called the law "a revolutionary change in the system under which we have lived for two hundred years." The entire act, he said, "perpetrates the grossest infringement upon First Amendment rights" by advantaging incumbents and disadvantaging challengers. "Instead of a system neutral on its face, where all scramble for all money they can get, this law rigs the structure for incumbents." He continued, "Moreover, exemptions for media, corporations, and labor unions only guarantee a greater concentration of power to keep the 'ins' in office, or at least determine who shall be the representatives." He would have voted to find both the contribution and expenditure limits unconstitutional. Finally, Justice Blackmun called for a balancing of interests—"the effect," he said, "is to equalize the interested with the disinterested person." He found a serious First Amendment infringement "that is simply indefensible in the expenditure provisions." Only Justice Blackmun expressed the belief that Congress had a larger interest in mind when it passed FECA 1974, but even then, he had no problem finding the expenditure provision inimical to First Amendment rights over the regulation of the amount of political speech.[81]

In the drafting of the *Buckley* opinion the Court effectively assigned a committee of justices. Chief Justice Burger proposed that Justice Stewart and Justice Powell would form what he called a "drafting team" to prepare the opinion. Burger would draft the "statement of facts, issues, and contentions," Powell would draft the disclosure provisions, Brennan would draft the public funding section, Stewart the contribution and expenditure limitations section, and Rehnquist the FEC composition issue. Burger had assigned each justice to write in an area where five of more justices appeared be in agreement. The complicated opinion, which ran to over 138 pages with concurring and dissenting opinions adding an additional 83 pages, failed to produce an overall coherence. The drafting process, created in part due to the expedited review process, and exacerbated by the long, involved, and politically difficult provisions of FECA 1974, "obscured some fundamental disagreements about the nature of the equality rationale for campaign finance regulation."[82]

Yet it was not simply the drafting process that prevented that clarity. It was, to a great degree, the lack of overall agreement by the Court as to what kind of democratic interests Congress in FECA 1974 had intended to promote, and that the Court itself would agree to protect. In large part, this lack of clarity arose because of the failure to clearly define the kinds of corruptive forces that the campaign finance reform meant to attack. Faced with an uncertain and attenuated reform proposal from Congress that itself did not propose systemic reforms of the democratic process, the Court, lacking the political acumen derived from practical electoral experiences, employed its own formalistic free speech value system to interpret the law.[83] The Court divvied up the campaign finance provisions in a way Congress never intended, permitting contribution but not spending limits, and then inserted new language about express advocacy in footnote 52 that would lead to ironic and unintended consequences as political actors struggled with the explicitly disjunctive system that the Court created. The problem that Congress and the Supreme Court created in *Buckley* continued to handcuff the next generation of reformers seeking to create a truly deliberative electoral system that provided equal political opportunities for all Americans.

CONCLUSION

From *Buckley* to BCRA and Beyond

The Supreme Court decision in *Buckley v. Valeo* failed to end the debate over the problems of campaign financing and the meaning of political corruption. For many observers, the Court's limited "quid pro quo" definition nagged at their pragmatic sense of how modern politics worked. Congress modified FECA 1974 twice in five years after the *Buckley* decision. In 1976 Congress amended FECA 1974 by limiting individual contributions to national parties to $20,000 annually and individual contributions to PACs, which saw explosive growth after the approval FECA and Buckley accorded them, to $5,000 annually. In 1979, reacting to complaints that the party contribution restrictions hampered party efforts to mobilize voters, Congress approved amendments permitting state and local parties to fund "get-out-the-vote" drives and other grassroots activities. Parties proceeded to funnel hundreds of millions of unregulated or "soft" campaign dollars into those efforts. The passage of the Bipartisan Campaign Reform Act of 2002 (BCRA), commonly known as the McCain-Feingold bill, and the Supreme Court decision testing its constitutionality in *FEC v. McConnell* a year later failed to resolve the conflict. These congressional efforts only addressed the edges of reform, having accepted the free speech limits on campaign spending that the *Buckley* decision had installed. The most recent campaign finance decision of the Supreme Court in *Randall v. Sorrell*, decided on June 26, 2006, added yet another layer of law, but little resolution to the debate. Vermont's attempt to regulate contributions and spending fell victim, as had all efforts since Buckley, to the resiliency of the Supreme Court's *Buckley* conception preventing the regulation of campaign spending, which it believed was an unconstitutional regulation of political speech unrelated to the interest of controlling quid pro quo corruption.[1]

Since the *Buckley* decision the Court developed and applied a three-part examination when considering campaign finance regulations. The first part, *Buckley's* most resilient principle, was the distinction between regulations of contributions and of expenditures. Contribution limits were more likely to be upheld than expenditure limits because the Court found the legislative interest in combating quid pro quo corruption directly relevant to contributions to candidates. The Court reaffirmed this dichotomy in *Nixon v. Shrink Missouri Government PAC,* where it found that a 1994 Missouri statute limiting campaign contributions to candidates for state office was constitutional. Relying heavily on *Buckley,* the Court found the Missouri limit of $1,075 per candidate per year was a reasonable state contribution regulation. The prevention of corruption and the appearance of corruption remained a "constitutionally sufficient justification" for the state regulation of contributions because "to the extent that large contributors are given a political quid pro quo from current and potential office holders, the integrity of our system of representative government is undermined." The power of the quid pro quo rationale remains the most significant and controversial legacy of *Buckley*.[2]

The second part, which sustained corporate limits on candidate elections but found that the state's interest in controlling real and apparent corruption was not generally applicable to ballot measure elections, arose from *First National Bank v. Belotti.* First National Bank was a corporate bank that challenged a Massachusetts state law that prohibited business corporations from making contributions or expenditures "for the purpose of . . . influencing or affecting the vote on any question submitted to the voters, other than one materially affecting any of the property, business or assets of the corporation." First National Bank proposed to spend money to publicize its view on a proposed constitutional amendment to be submitted to the Massachusetts voters that would have assessed a graduated income tax on voters. Free speech was again at the heart of the state corporate restriction. "The question in this case," the Court said, "is whether the corporate identity of the speaker deprives this proposed speech of what otherwise would be its clear entitlement to protection." The Court, in finding the law unconstitutional, found the rationale for the law (to sustain the interest of individual citizens, and protect the rights of shareholders whose views differ from those expressed by corporate management) too unrelated to its actual effect to pass constitutional free speech muster.[3]

While the corruption rationale had sustained prior anticorporate campaign finance restrictions since the Tillman Act, and while the *Buckley* court had affirmed that "preserving the integrity of the electoral process, preventing corruption, and sustaining the active, alert responsibility of the individual citizen in a democracy for the wise conduct of government" were interests of the highest importance, the Court nevertheless found the anticorruption interests in the Massachusetts law preventing corporate speech on a referendum issue constitutionally insufficient. Again, the

Court focused on quid pro quo corruption. Finding no foreseeable way in which corporate campaign speech could corrupt the vote by exerting undue influence over the referendum and thereby destroying the "confidence of the people in the democratic process and the integrity of government," the Court held the law was an unconstitutional restriction on the political free speech rights of Massachusetts businesses.[4]

The majority believed that the limited amounts spent and the eventual defeat of the referendum were proof of the lack of undue influence by the corporation. In dissent, Justice White argued that the natural advantages of the corporate form to amass wealth and to "dominate" the debate on an issue provided a legislative rationale to regulate or restrict corporate speech. But again, relying on the *Buckley* precedent that the state may not control "the volume of expression of wealthier, more powerful corporate members of the press in order to enhance the relative voices of smaller and less influential members," the Court rejected the limitations.[5]

Buckley also distinguished between legitimate restrictions placed on corporate and union political contributions and those placed on other groups. Two somewhat confusing and highly criticized cases demonstrate the current constitutional rigor of that distinction. The first case involved Massachusetts Citizens for Life (MCFL), a nonprofit, nonstock corporation that promoted pro-life positions to its membership. FECA 1974 prohibited any corporation from using treasury funds to make any expenditure "in connection with" any federal election, requiring any corporate expenditure made for such purpose to be financed with voluntary contributions in a separate, segregated PAC fund. In September 1978, MCFL published a newsletter distributed to its members identifying pro-life candidates, but specifically disclaiming any endorsement of any particular candidate. At issue was whether MCFL had violated the FECA 1974 corporate expenditure restrictions (whose antecedent were the Tillman Act restrictions in FCPA 1925) by publishing and distributing the brochure.

MCFL forced the Court to confront its own phantom from *Buckley,* the "express advocacy" language specified in footnote 52 of the decision. In interpreting the meaning of the operative language that brought certain contributions within the FECA 1974 restrictions, the Court had to determine what the legislative language "any expenditure . . . relative to a clearly identified candidate" actually meant. In the hastily drafted footnote 52, the *Buckley* court concluded that for expenditures to be "relative to" a candidate, the communication must contain "express words of advocacy of election or defeat, such as 'vote for,' 'elect,' 'support,' 'cast your ballot for,' 'Smith for Congress,' 'vote against,' 'defeat,' 'reject.'" Examining the MCFL brochure, the Court fairly determined that the brochure urged voters to vote for pro-life candidates, and thus fell within the prohibitions of FECA 1974.[6]

However, in considering the constitutionality of the prohibition as it applied to nonstock, nonprofit corporations, the Court found that the speech restrictions on MCFL were significant. While MCFL could establish a separate, segregated fund with which to fund express advocacy publications, the Court found that the administrative burden of complying with the Federal Election Commission's accounting and reporting requirements was substantial in relation to the state interest in regulating corporate political expenditures. Even as the Court affirmed the long tradition of permitting corporate campaign finance regulation because of the "corrosive influence of concentrated corporate wealth" that disturbed the free marketplace of ideas, it held that MCFL, which made no direct contributions to candidates and gained its contributions from members who expressly supported its purposes and advocacy, was a different kind of corporation. In effect, the Court found that the FECA 1974 restriction on independent expenditures was unconstitutional because "voluntary political associations do not suddenly present the specter of corruption merely by assuming the corporate form."

The three features that the Court found distinguishing from other corporate forms were (1) MCFL was formed for the express purpose of promoting political ideas, and could not engage in business activities, (2) it had no shareholders or other persons affiliated so as to have a claim on its assets or earnings, and (3) it was not established as a business or labor organization, and it was its policy not to take contributions from such entities. "This prevents," the Court said, "such corporations from serving as conduits for the type of direct spending that creates a threat to the political marketplace." While the Court sustained the regulation of corporate and labor union contributions based on the rationale that aggregate wealth accumulated and spent by those organizations could corrupt the marketplace of ideas, it found that MCFL did not pose the kind of threat to electoral integrity that those entities did because nonstock, nonprofit corporations did not have the same corruptive effect on political spending that business corporations and unions possessed.[7]

In the second case, *Austin v. Michigan State Chamber of Commerce,* the Court reaffirmed the strong presumptions against direct corporate political spending. The Michigan statute prohibited the spending of corporate treasury funds for independent expenditures in support of or in opposition to any candidate for election to state office. The Michigan State Chamber of Commerce, a nonprofit corporation with 8,000 members, three-quarters of whom were for-profit corporations, proposed to spend treasury funds generated by annual membership dues for political activities, promoting their pro-business agenda. In a 6–3 opinion by Justice Marshall, the Court sustained the Michigan regulation, finding that the Michigan law aimed at a legitimate, though different kind of corruption in the political arena: "the corrosive and distorting effects of immense aggregations of wealth that are accumulated with the help of the corporate form and that have little or no correlation to the public's support for the corporation's political ideas."[8]

Denying that *Austin* had somehow overruled the equality of political speech rationale rejected by the majority in *Buckley,* the Court held that the special state-conferred benefits of the corporate form that "facilitates the amassing of large treasuries warrant the limits on independent expenditures" because that wealth could "unfairly influence elections when it is deployed in the form of independent expenditures, just as it can when it assumes the guise of political contributions." The fact that the Chamber of Commerce, and its members, had a business connection to the political ideas they espoused therefore meant that a presumptive economic incentive for a quid pro quo corruptive connection made the Michigan regulation legitimate. The long-standing rationale for regulating business corporations remains the most resilient constitutional basis for limiting political contributions and spending in the campaign finance system.[9]

Created in *Buckley,* this three-part dichotomy has changed little since 1976. In 1992–1996, when the campaign controversies over the rise of the expenditure of "soft money" by the major political parties exploded, Congress reacted similarly to how it had in the aftermath of Watergate, proposing a major revamping of the political system, but settling for a more limited reform that touched only the edges of the system. While many commentators have called BCRA and the 2003 Supreme Court decision in *FEC v. McConnell* "the most far-reaching and controversial attempt to restructure the national political process in a generation," this is less because of its reach than because of the generation that has passed since the Court decided *Buckley.* For all the attention given the recent Supreme Court decision in *McConnell,* the main controversy stubbornly remains about how we define corruption to permit the legislative regulation of corruptive political influences that limit political free speech in the marketplace of ideas.[10]

The story of reform from 1976 to the Bipartisan Campaign Finance Reform Act of 2002 (BCRA) and the challenge to BCRA in *McConnell* are reminiscent of the reformist reaction to the political abuses of the deliberative function of the political process made evident during the Watergate scandal. But this most recent redux of reform came about during a period that saw an increasing professionalization of politics, the rise of special interest groups that, through their fund-raising functions, grew increasingly divorced from their own memberships, and the unabated increases in the individual and civic costs of modern campaigning. Coupled with a belief by both parties that electoral success or defeat not only involved individual candidates, but also raised the stakes that elections could shape the future of certain cultural and constitutional rights, the success of political campaigns became increasingly dependent on the ability of the candidate to raise enormous sums of campaign money. The process of raising immense amounts of money through PACs and parties, and more recently through 527 organizations, more than any other modern development, came to symbolize how separated candidates had become from their individual constituencies.

The rise of PACs, authorized by FECA 1974 as a device of permissible campaign fund-raising for corporations and unions, did not take off until the 1980s. FECA 1974 established spending limits that many argued were unreasonably low, given the rising costs of media advertising. Unadjusted for inflation, the rising costs of campaigns and the failure of FECA 1974 to provide for any free public airtime required that politicians find other outlets for campaign funds. Reminiscent of how the Anti-Assessment Act caused Gilded Age politicians to solicit campaign funds from corporations, FECA 1974 created a shortage of reliable campaign funds that parties and candidates efficiently replaced by appealing to PACs to take up the slack. PACs, organized by corporations and labor unions that could not otherwise legally contribute to federal candidates, recognized this mutual dependency as an opportunity to obtain access to their elected representatives.[11]

The corruptive effects of the kind of access that contributors wanted, however, were often hard to define, much less regulate. The quaint concept of quid pro quo, where the candidate supported legislation or the economic position of a contributor *because* of the contribution, almost disappeared. Quid pro quo corruption as understood by the *Buckley* court, except for the ham-handed attempt by Nixon's reelection committee to sell ambassadorships and promote milk legislation, had gone underground, covert and difficult, if not impossible, to connect to campaign contributions. That is not to say that quid pro quo arrangements did not happen, simply that politicians and their contributors, through evolving the labyrinthine congressional process of bill-drafting, committee hearings, debate, earmarks, and conference committees, could easily hide the most direct forms of access corruption bought with campaign contributions.

In 1994, when the Republicans for the first time in forty years took over the House of Representatives, President William J. Clinton's reelection committee, led by strategist Dick Morris and a plethora of election law attorneys, devised a scheme to evade the contribution limits of the federal campaign finance laws. President Clinton viewed the scheme to raise enormous amounts of money unregulated by the campaign finance system that would be delivered to the Democratic Party as essential to competing with the Republicans, who generally held an advantage in hard money fund-raising. Though not illegal, the unseemly use of the White House, the "Motel 1600" aspect of the fund-raising, the use of foreign money in the election, and the transformation of the political parties from invigorated voter mobilization machines into fund-raising conduits caused renewed concerns about the effectiveness of existing campaign finance law to promote deliberative democratic goals.[12]

The congressional investigations that ensued disclosed that the campaign finance system had once again failed in its objectives to force full disclosure, to regulate and control campaign fund-raising and spending, and to protect the equal deliberation goals of the American electoral process. The reports of the Senate and House disclosed over $3.2 million in illegal campaign contributions collected by the Democratic National Committee, half of which was raised by former DNC vice chairman John Huang from mostly foreign sources. Republicans also were forced to return over $150,000 of foreign campaign contributions illegally raised during the 1996 campaign. Near the end of the investigation, Clinton told reporters that "I don't think you can find any evidence of the fact that I had changed government policy because of a contribution." In the mind of every politician, the *Buckley* safe harbor of quid pro quo lived on.[13]

The public disapproval motivated the newest generation of campaign finance reformers to act. What resulted from the hearings was the Bipartisan Campaign Finance Reform Act of 2002. But BCRA 2002 addressed only the most prominent concerns uncovered by the congressional investigations, and was a limited version of what its earlier versions in BCRA 1995 and 1997 had aspired to be. Both of those earlier proposals, like FECA 1974, were far-reaching proposals for reform of the political process that included provisions such as substantial free or discounted television time and mailing privileges, conditioned on the acceptance of spending limits. By the time BCRA passed in 2002, supporters in Congress had scaled it back, emphasizing regulating soft money and the addressing the problem of sham issue advertisements. The rise of sham issue ads, masquerading under the safe harbor of *Buckley* footnote 52 but avoiding the "express advocacy" language, and in every other respect advocating the election or defeat of a candidate, created an immediate and overriding demand in Congress that reform, albeit not broad limitations on the political system originally intended, be undertaken.[14]

BCRA made three main changes to the campaign finance scheme of FECA. BCRA increased the amount of some individual contribution limits (doubled from $1,000 to $2,000 per election), increased the individual contribution to national parties from $20,000 to $25,000 per year (from $5,000 to $10,000 for state parties), and raised the individual aggregate annual contribution limit from $25,000 to $95,000 per year (with sub-limits of $37,500 to all candidates, and $57,500 to all parties). It also indexed many of the contribution limits to the cost of living. Second, BCRA defined and regulated a new category of "electioneering communication" (limited to broadcast advertising) intended to plug the "issue advocacy" loophole, and provided for a bright-line limit on spending by certain independent groups sixty days before a primary and thirty days before a general election. Finally, BCRA severely restricted the ability of federal, state, and local parties to receive soft money, or money unregulated by the contribution and source limits of federal law. Critics of these reforms argued that they did more harm than good because their unintended effects would outweigh the limited reform value of the legislation. While proponents called it only a first step in a longer effort at more substantive reforms, they lauded the act, which they argued would work to transform the system by ending a reliance on large contributors, thus making more accountable those elected officials formerly reliant on and corrupted by large campaign contributions.[15]

The BCRA drafters had learned part of their history well. Aided by professional election law experts dominating the legal field since *Buckley*, the drafters wanted to develop a legislative history and trial record directly connected to the modest legislative goals of the act. Foremost, they meant to plainly set forth the legislative intention of Congress, something that the *Buckley* record had failed to do. They wanted the trial record to fully reflect the facts behind the reform motivations of BCRA, to show how the measures in BCRA were aimed to serve the legislative objectives of prohibiting soft money corporate and union contributions that evaded the campaign contributions limits the Court had sustained in *Buckley*. Finally, they wanted to demonstrate how the reform measures of BCRA related to the broader values of ending the campaign finance abuses, which they contended damaged the healthy functioning of American democracy. By doing this, supporters felt they could convince the Court that the legislative interests in regulating campaign finances had a long, historical, and constitutionally recognized basis, that the reforms prevented the evasion of those regulations necessary to make the system work, and that the free speech restrictions were valid because they weighed against the legitimate congressional rationale of protecting the integrity of the electoral process.[16]

BCRA's proponents documented how the evasion of the campaign finance laws through the sham issue ads, and the emergence of soft money contributions solicited by and made to parties specifically to evade the law, resulted in eviscerating even the long accepted principles and values of regulating and restricting corporate and union contributions. This evasion of the law demanded that the Court consider the principles of BCRA in light of such activity. While the bright-line thirty- and sixty-day restrictions on independent expenditures were an infringement on the speech rights of those groups, they had shown by their evasion that such a restriction was necessary to keep the campaign finance structure whole. The lessons learned from the contribution/expenditure separation in *Buckley* were not lost on the BCRA proponents. The pragmatic *McConnell* decision, drafted not surprisingly by Justice O'Connor, the justice most experienced in electoral politics, reflects the historical rebirth in election law of a pragmatic view of the necessity and attendant evils of political money, and the appropriate deference to Congress to carefully address the issue.[17]

Finally, the BCRA proponents meant to broaden the concept of corruption so as to include the values expressed by Justice Souter in *Shrink Missouri* when he acknowledged a "concern not confined to bribery of public officials but extending to the broader threat from politicians too compliant with the wishes of large contributors." But on this point, the debate over corruption continued throughout the *McConnell* opinion to represent a crabbed conception of corruption that wavered between real and apparent corruption, requiring proof of corruption akin to bribery. On that key issue, the corruption rationale and arguments remain stubbornly tied to *Buckley,* and the advocates of comprehensive campaign finance reform will continue to face the misunderstanding and misreading of that ahistorical speech impediment.[18]

One cannot blame BCRA proponents for lack of trying. The legislative and trial record provided ample evidence of the rationale for BCRA, but more importantly, it provided thousands of pages of testimony by sitting and former members of Congress about the corruptive effects of the campaign finance system. Time and time again, witnesses such as Senators John McCain, Alan Simpson (R-WY), Russ Feingold (D-WI), Olympia Snow (R-WA), former senators David Boren (R-OK) and Dale Bumpers (D-AR), and others testified to the corrupting effects of the campaign finance system. They testified that while they had not been bribed, they had personally experienced and felt the pressure from campaign contributors seeking undue access and favors. Opponents would later contend that the decision was "short on serious analysis and long on anecdotal evidence" of corruption, but for the trial and appellate lawyers working to sustain BCRA, and for the Supreme Court who confronted the voluminous record, the anecdotal testimony of those politicians affected by the system became circumstantial evidence in a case where there was never a smoking gun. The Court understood the reality of pragmatic campaign fund-raising and its connection to the desire to gain and use political access bought with contributions, something that the supporters of *Buckley* and opponents of BCRA had ignored for twenty-five years.

The *McConnell* dissents of Justices Scalia, Thomas, and Kennedy are particularly instructive about the continuing political-legal battle over the definition of corruption. All three justices discounted the value and evidentiary significance of the trial record testimony about the corruptive effects of soft money. Scalia derided the "danger to the political system from amassed wealth," calling the most direct form from undisclosed favors and payoffs to elected officials "no more discoverable" as a result of BRCA. While any quid pro quo agreement for votes would violate criminal law, Scalia discounted the argument that increased access provided by candidates to their largest campaign contributors was corruptive, contending instead that that very arrangement was "the nature of politics."[19]

Campaign finance disclosure provisions, he argued, were enough to check the "evil corporate (and private affluent) influences" of in-the-pocket politicians. Even more discredited was the governmental interest of eradicating the "appearance of corruption," the fall-back position from *Buckley* on which BCRA supporters, unable to find direct evidence of corruption, heavily relied. Scalia cited the floor debate and testimony that called attack ads the "crack cocaine," "drive-by shootings," and "air pollution" of political speech—but then Scalia misinterpreted the concern of those in Congress, recharacterizing the debate into one about the amount and not the quality of speech. To be sure, many congressional supporters of BCRA were themselves tongue-tied to explain their concerns, often conflating the dangers of the increasing costs and amount of attack ads with their effect on the nature of political deliberation. But Scalia's dissent discounted the very real fear that the increasing attack ads created an impediment to real deliberation on the issues, costing too much money and thereby increasing the time spent by candidates raising money and limiting the time they spent reading, studying, and passing legislation. This, proponents argued, created a widespread public perception that average people have little or no voice in the political system, which damaged the integrity of the system Congress was obliged to protect.

Justice Clarence Thomas attacked the anti-circumvention rationale, the legislative strategy that the drafters of BCRA built into the legislation and the trial record, which permitted them to argue successfully that the bright-line cutoffs on primary and general election issue ads, and on the soft money provisions for parties, were justified to end the appearance of corruption. Thomas suggested, even while decrying the excessive breadth of BCRA, that a more broadly drawn antibribery statute would be sufficient to address "attempts . . . to influence government action." But Thomas argued this because he believed that the root problem remained quid pro quo corruption. He therefore found that soft money contribution limits on parties were so attenuated to the corruption of any candidate that the free speech restrictions on parties should override the congressional interest in preventing real or apparent corruption.[20]

Especially telling was Thomas's assertion that the cited evidence of party soft money contributions by "lobbyists, CEOs and wealthy individuals" for the express purpose of securing influence over federal officials, in his opinion consisted of "nothing more than vague allegations of wrongdoing." Since Thomas ignored the corruptive connections between soft money contributions and the implementation or delay of policy initiatives, he referred to the evidence as "personal conjecture" and dismissed it as insufficient to sustain the First Amendment restrictions on party and corporate speech.[21]

Concern about the mainstream media exemptions (BCRA explicitly did not limit their corporate speech during the thirty- or sixty-day preelection periods) animated Justice Anthony Kennedy's dissent in *McConnell*. In part, his criticism was justified because the majority opinion improperly justified all of the BCRA limits to the accepted anticorporate campaign finance rationale previously accepted by the Supreme Court. But Kennedy, like Scalia and Thomas, found one, and only one, interest sufficient to justify the BCRA burdens on free speech and association: "eliminating, or preventing, actual corruption or the appearance of corruption stemming from contributions to candidates," the *Buckley* mantra that would not die. Kennedy contended that the majority's definition of corruption, which he believed was improperly expanded in *Austin v. Michigan,* concludes that access proved that influence was undue. Kennedy believed that under the majority ruling, quid pro quo corruption had become access to influence, which Kennedy found too amorphous and unprovable a standard to justify significant First Amendment restrictions on political speech. He found that "though the majority cites common sense as the foundation for its definition of corruption, in the context of the real world only a single definition of corruption has been found to identify political corruption successfully and to distinguish good political responsiveness from bad—that is quid pro quo."[22]

Especially with party soft money, Kennedy claimed, there was a lack of clarity about defining corruption damaging to First Amendment interests. The very aim of a political party was to influence its candidates' stances on issues and, once elected, on votes. Given this view, it was not surprising that Kennedy found the majority's definition of corruption dangerous and unworkable. *Buckley's* "quid pro quo" definition of corruption, derived from the myths about the Watergate abuses, had become so baked into the political rhetoric of campaign finance reform that the principles of deliberative debate and equality of voice were for Kennedy and the other dissenters but distant echoes of the earliest and most fundamental campaign finance reforms.

To be sure, *McConnell's* majority opinion offered little defense to that indictment. The renewed deference that the majority showed to congressional determinations about the corruptive effects of soft money, unregulated issue ads, and independent expenditures appeared in the decision as little more than a generous and uncritical acceptance of the circumstantial evidence in the record. In that regard, BCRA's proponents did their job well. By presenting a voluminous record of testimony from sitting and former members of Congress about the corruptive effects of the current campaign finance system, they overcame *Buckley's* lack of an adequate record and the Supreme Court's consequent narrow reliance on a "quid pro quo" definition of corruption.

But search the record for a definition of corruption that addresses the concerns of the dissenters, or of those BCRA opponents who contend that the regulation of political speech demands more than naked assertions and anecdotal evidence, and you will come up empty-handed. When the majority in *McConnell* stated that "the idea that large contributions to a national party can corrupt or, at the very least, create an appearance of corruption of federal candidates and officeholders is neither novel or implausible," the Court relied on the position that "common sense and the ample record confirm Congress's belief that they do." That reliance hardly inspired confidence that the Court has a firm understanding of what kind of corruption BCRA was meant to address. The fact that candidates will feel "grateful for such donations" from corporate, union, and wealthy individual donors and that "donors will seek to exploit that gratitude" may very well be true, but that fails to explain why that gratitude and exploitation, which was not illegal, demanded the creation of a campaign finance system designed to regulate and limit that activity. The apparent purchase of access by large donors who contribute in the same election to both parties and opposing candidates in a single election, while ideologically inconsistent, does not help define corruption much beyond the Madisonian understanding of self-interest expressed in *Federalist 10*. While the majority seemed to expand the *Buckley* definition of direct or apparent quid pro quo corruption, its singular focus on the candidate and on access to the candidate belied that understanding. Except as to the deference accorded the congressional assumptions, which were at their heart mostly evidentiary presumptions, *McConnell* failed to advance the definition of corruption much beyond that in *Buckley*.[23]

The debate over BCRA in Congress, among the experts, and in the Supreme Court once again demonstrated that at the heart of the confusion and conflict over the making of the campaign finance system is the failure to consider a definition of corruption consistent with reform goals for the political system, one that reflects broader values about deliberative democracy. While the Supreme Court in *McConnell* sustained nearly every provision of the BCRA reforms, it was not so much the judicial decision as it was the drafting, legislative, and trial techniques the proponents employed in presenting the litigation, and the politically pragmatic and deferential values the Court used in deciding the case, as well as the continuing debate over the kind of corruption that legitimates free speech restrictions, that make the lessons of *McConnell* in the context of the history of the campaign finance system so relevant.

The manner in which *Buckley* continues to prevent a full understanding and examination of the historical nature of corruption redounded in the most recent Supreme Court decision examining Vermont's attempt to regulate campaign contributions. In 2002 the Vermont legislature enacted one of the most stringent campaign finance regulations in the country. It limited both the amounts that candidates for state office could spend on their own campaigns, and the amounts that individuals, organizations, and political parties could contribute to those campaigns. For example, a single individual could contribute a maximum of $400 for statewide offices, $300 for state senator, and $200 for state representative. None of the contribution limits were indexed for inflation. Political committees and parties were subject to the limits.[24]

Several individuals who had run for state office in Vermont sued in Federal District Court to overturn the law on First Amendment grounds, contending that the expenditure limits violated the rule of *Buckley*. The District Court, following the *Buckley* precedent, found the expenditure limits unconstitutional but generally upheld the limits on contributions. The Vermont legislature sought to distinguish *Buckley's* application from the limits by advancing several other reasons for the limits on spending, namely that such limits help to protect candidates from spending inordinate amounts of time soliciting large contributions instead of devoting that time to legislative activities and fund-raising among ordinary voters. By adopting the expenditure limits of the Vermont Act, the legislature intended to regulate the corruptive effects of the demands of inordinate fund-raising on the electoral system and on the deliberative functions of elections. As in most pre-FECA efforts to reform the campaign finance system, the Vermont legislature broadly defined corruption as a threat to the deliberative equality of elections, especially where candidates spent excessive time on campaign fund-raising efforts from big contributors.

Randall v. Sorrell became the Supreme Court's first opportunity since *Buckley* to reconsider the contribution-expenditure dichotomy and the nature of corruption that would justify regulation of political spending and speech. The majority rejected that opportunity, striking down the Vermont law and finding that "Vermont's primary justification for imposing its expenditure limits" did not differ significantly "from Congress' rationale for the *Buckley* limits: preventing corruption and its appearance." Yet the opinion continued the judicial myopia that has afflicted the generation of judicial decision-making since 1976. Fearful that the Vermont limits were so low as to "harm the electoral process by preventing challengers from mounting effective campaigns against incumbent officeholders, thereby reducing democratic accountability," the Court dismissed the Vermont legislature's rationale as "outside the tolerable First Amendment limits." The Court worried that the severe limits on contributions would "reduce the voice of political parties in Vermont to a whisper." As a whole, the Court found that nothing in the record indicated that "corruption (or its appearance) in Vermont is significantly more serious a matter than elsewhere," and therefore, the law was not narrowly tailored enough to withstand the constitutional challenge.[25]

Justice Samuel Alito, following the stare decisis of *Buckley,* voted to sustain the expenditure restrictions. Justice Kennedy mimicked his dissent in *McConnell* concurring in the majority judgment but objecting to the "universe of campaign finance regulation" that the Court in part created and in part permitted by its decisions. "That new order," Justice Kennedy wrote, "may cause more problems than it solves" because "our own experience gives us little basis to make these judgments, and certainly no traditional or well-established body of laws exist to offer guidance" on the proper level of scrutiny that ought to be applied to campaign contributions and expenditures. Justices Thomas and Scalia again dissented, as they did in *McConnell,* arguing that the contribution limits permitted in *Buckley* be overturned because they provided "insufficient protection to political speech." For all of these justices, and for the majority, the blind acceptance of the *Buckley* corruption rationale made it difficult for them to recognize the interests of protecting deliberative equality in the political process on which the Vermont legislature based their reform efforts.

The decision in *Randall v. Sorrell* surprised no one because the history of the campaign finance system has not reached back beyond *Buckley* to examine the traditional body of campaign finance law that Justice Kennedy longs for but the Court ignores.[26]

Both critics and defenders of *Buckley* have, much like the Hollywood screenwriter in *All the President's Men,* created their own mythic assumptions about what FECA 1974 did and about what the Supreme Court's rebuttal in *Buckley* meant. Prominent opponents of FECA 1974 contend that "the most compelling and only legitimate argument advanced by our adversaries was that the limitation or size of contributions would reduce corruption." Their central concern was about quid pro quo corruption, where contributors gained access to candidates who decided issues in their interests, or proposed or supported legislation, or exchanged some form of governmental benefit in direct return for those campaign contributions. While important, that concept of corruption ignored both the broad congressional purposes expressed in FECA 1971 and in the first drafts of FECA 1974, and the most trenchant reform goals of campaign finance legislation. The effect of such a limited concept of corruption bolstered the *Buckley* opinion because it dismissed any other substantive governmental interest, such as increasing electoral equality or avoiding voter coercion, in regulating election processes or campaign finances.[27]

Other critics argue that the campaign finance legislation passed in the 1970s was based on faulty assumptions concerning the excessive use of money in elections and the related concept of corruption. The cost of elections does not come close to the amount of money Americans spend on popular CDs, cigarette advertising, or potato chips. Critics contend that if adjusted for market changes and costs, the gross amount of campaign spending remains historically low. In fact, they reason, the abysmal civic education most Americans demonstrate cries out for more, not less, political spending. Reform legislation such as FECA 1971 and 1974, they counter, instead of reforming the system tends to promote antidemocratic aspects of elections by limiting the amount of speech and debate. They deny assumptions that campaign finance laws promote political equality, prevent corruption, and reduce the time spent by legislators on fund-raising. They dispute that small contributions make electoral politics more democratic, and instead argue that they eventually fail to provide money adequate to run a modern campaign. Furthermore, limiting large donations has the effect of "reducing the flow of information to voters and aiding more radical candidacies at the expense of centrist candidates."[28]

More importantly, they disagree with the fundamental assumption that money buys elections and influence for contributors, which they say underlay the corruption rationale Congress used in FECA 1971 and 1974. The connection between money and electoral success is not a direct one, and while most candidates who spend more win, this is merely evidence of preexisting political support. The problem is not that candidates spend too much and therefore ensure their electoral success, but that challengers spend too little to "reach the mass of voters." Finally, many assert that the concept of corruption central to the earliest campaign finance laws is simply wrong. Money does not "corrupt" the legislature or individual legislators, because corruption, defined as the "responsiveness to the wishes of moneyed constituents" is not really corruption at all. In our political system, legislators should and will be responsive to contributors and constituents, and without some "causal link between contributions and legislative behavior" this concept of corruption remains illegitimate. Since no empirical studies exist that smoke out this kind of corruption, the notion must rest on the older conceptions of a common good, which, by virtue of vast campaign contributions, is blotted out of the political process. Critics of campaign finance reform are dismissive of this notion because, while it is clear that legislators respond to their campaign backers in often disproportionate stridency, no one can know that the common good is not thereby further advanced by that very response. The concept of the common good is not empirical, and more a value judgment determined by competing political claims. Proponents who "claim to know what good public policy is" and therefore to know "when legislators are violating their trust," and then seek to justify speech limits on their opponents' political advocacy, strike campaign finance reform critic Bradley Smith as the most dangerous kinds of reformers.[29]

Opponents of the *Buckley* decision can barely restrain their response to those arguments. At their core, the basic dispute between the opponents and supports of the *Buckley* decision involve three fundamental disagreements. Did the Supreme Court in *Buckley* too narrowly define corruption as quid pro quo, thereby ignoring the deleterious effects of money in elections on the democratic ideals implicit in the American political process and system? Two, is money, as used in modern political campaigns, a corrupting influence on the process, candidates, or voters? And three, do notions of political equality permit state regulation of political contributions or spending without violating the First Amendment? While there are subparts to each of these arguments, at the heart of the vast and raucous debate, these three issues continue to fundamentally divide opposing views on the question.

Campaign finance proponents contend that those assumptions are themselves faulty, unsubstantiated, and even overtly deceptive. The idea of corruption, they argue, means and has historically meant, "the personal enrichment of a legislator in exchange for a vote" that in the campaign finance context involves both the explicitly negotiated deal where the candidate promises a favor in return for a campaign contribution, but also, "a subversion of the political process." It includes the real or imagined "coercive influence of large financial contributions on candidates' positions and on their actions if elected to office." The influence of money on officeholders, which reform opponents contend is mostly anecdotal, unmeasured, and a natural part of politics, is, for proponents, the fundamental blind spot in the argument. Although the political influence of campaign contributions remains mostly unmeasured by political scientists hamstrung by the refusal of legislators to admit the direct connections between campaign contributions and legislative initiatives, reliance on anecdotal and circumstantial evidence that money buys access and results and exacerbates the need for increasing contributions is entirely legitimate.[30]

The expectation that empirical data tell the full story is wrong because most legislative action occurs outside of the formal voting process, away from the stark tradeoff of an up-or-down vote on a discrete issue that a moneyed interest may support or oppose. For *Buckley* opponents, the corruption that permeates the political process is no less real despite the obvious problems of measurement. This process corruption extends beyond the kind of empirical data presently available to support the claims of the influence of large donations in political campaigns. Similar to the Supreme Court in *Buckley*, reform opponents disregard the threat of corruption because it is not easily measured and because using any means to sway, influence, and gain access to individual legislatures is the warp and woof of the American political process.

Yet the historical concern about corruption of the deliberative process, found in the regulatory examples of *Ex Parte Curtis*, the Tillman Act, the Federal Corrupt Practices Acts of 1911 and 1925, the Hatch Acts, War Labor Disputes and Taft-Hartley Act, the Lobbying Act, and FECA 1971 and 1974, remain the most important rationale for the regulation of the campaign finance system. The congressional interest in protecting the "integrity of the electoral process" has always involved fighting corruption that diminished equal deliberative opportunities for public debate. The *Buckley* court, while noting that the Court of Appeals had sustained FECA 1974 and cited "a clear and compelling interest in preserving the integrity of the election process," nonetheless redefined that state interest based on a formalist set of assumptions when it decided the case. The Supreme Court's limited "quid pro quo" definition of corruption resulted in an unduly and ahistorical state interest in protecting democratic institutions that ignored long-held beliefs about the role of money in a proper and healthy deliberative process.[31]

That campaign finance reform remains a contested issue, and that the failure to arrive at a generally accepted understanding of what kind of corruption campaign finance reform is intended to address, should caution policymakers about advancing further reforms. The emergence of 527 organizations, independent nonprofit political action groups such as MoveOn.org and America Coming Together, now raising and spending unregulated campaign funds in the 2004 election, has increased the shrill call for more immediate changes to the current system. George Soros, the billionaire philanthropist, pledged to spend $10 million of his own money to defeat President George Bush. House Majority Leader Tom DeLay (R-TX) offered big donors a chance to spend time with him at private dinners and yacht cruises at the September 2004 Republican National Convention, in exchange for contributions to his "Celebrations for Children, Inc.," his nonprofit charity formed under the federal tax laws. Both presidential candidates opted out of the public finance system for the 2004 primary elections, which provides $75 million in public funds for each major candidate but prohibits the expenditure of more, because they could raise more than those limits. In 2002 reformers acknowledged that the BCRA changes were but a first step, and they are aggressively moving to tighten, change, and strengthen the campaign finance system. At the same time, the predictions that BCRA would somehow limit overall contributions had proven wrong, with estimates that over $2.9 billion would be spent on the 2006 midterm elections. Calls to abolish the Federal Election Commission and replace it with a nonpartisan commission with stronger enforcement powers await formal committee deliberation in Congress.[32]

Perhaps it is time to take a break. At the heart of any reform is a clear-headed conception of the evil to be remedied. The legislative history of BCRA and the *McConnell* and *Randall* decisions demonstrate that neither Congress nor the Supreme Court has a clear understanding of the nature, much less the definition, of corruption that campaign finance reform should address. Given the fundamental requirement that the congressional interest in regulating the corruption of the political process by limiting First Amendment rights must be clear, consistent, and substantial, coming to a consensus on the nature and definition of corruption would seem a reasonable and essential first step.

The history of the making of the campaign finance system offers a firm foundation for answering those questions, but the resolution of those legal-political issues cannot simply be tied to the past. What made sense for the reformers of the spoils system in 1876 may have little relevance to the modern professionalized political system. Yet the values of the proponents of the Tillman Act may be just as important today, where issues of corporate citizenship and the role of national and international corporations in the political system remain contested and controversial issues. While we may laud the political acumen of the lawyers who prepared the BCRA legislation and the trial record for succeeding where others have failed, the hardest work of reform comes first in addressing and answering the substantive and fundamental questions about what political values we want to promote in our system. It is no longer sufficient to know corruption when we see it. Engaging in debate and establishing a consensus on those values will make the reform of the system, if such reform be needed, an effective and valuable improvement to our mutual democracy.

Understanding the *Buckley* controversy requires an examination of the legal-political history of campaign finance reform as a century-long effort to correct American problems of deliberative democracy. That requires an examination of how each new generation of reformers coined their own definition of corruption, and spent their political capital in an effort to remedy the ills of democracy they saw sickening the body politic. These legislative efforts faced review by earlier generations of courts whose members brought their own tools of interpretation, promoting distinct views about the kind of democratic values to promote. In *Buckley*, the Burger court favored a different set of values that repaired the institutions of democracy in distinctly legalistic ways. The key then to understanding the Supreme Court's rationale for the *Buckley* decision, and the Court's role in shaping the campaign finance system, requires both a focused snapshot and an expansive panorama, so that the broader trends and understandings of corruption and reform are exposed in the light of contextual legal, historical, and political debate.

From the Anti-Assessment Act in 1876 to the decision in *Ex Parte Curtis*, from the Tillman Act of 1907 to the Progressive Era passage of the Federal Corrupt Practices Acts, from the Supreme Court decisions in *Burroughs*, *Brewers Association, Newberry*, and *Classic*, through the New Deal regulation of the media, public utilities, labor unions, lobbyists, and political action committees, legislatures and courts defined and then regulated the kinds of corruption that affected the candidates because it was seen as detrimental to the free democratic will of the voter and to the deliberative principles of American democracy. For a century, these legislative efforts and judicial decisions stoutly stood for the proposition that Congress could regulate the solicitation, assessment, and expenditure of campaign finance money from a variety of sources to eliminate the coercive and corruptive effects of campaign money. Since 1882 the right of the voter to cast his vote fairly and freely in the interest of the common good animated the Supreme Court to permit reasonable restrictions on campaign funding and political speech. While the courts often accorded significantly higher protections for political free speech, they also viewed corruption of the electoral process a significant problem that ate first at the free will of the voter and then corroded the deliberative function of the body politic.

By 1976 the formalist conception of corruption adopted by the Supreme Court exposed its glaring lack of political acumen that had been building since the changes in the appointment process that began during the Eisenhower administration. Predisposed through a course of legal training and experience to view challenges to the free speech project formalistically, the Burger court came to privilege values that permitted it to separate the corruptive effects of campaign contributions from expenditures. In part, the Burger court's lack of elective political experience, as distinguished from the Supreme Court memberships' political experience during the period of 1876–1954, caused the Court to focus their view singularly on quid pro quo corruption. Trained to think about free speech like lawyers and judges, in the *Buckley* decision, when confronted with the realities of political fundraising, the nuances of corruption, and the values of legislative regulation to promote electoral equality and liberty, the Burger court relied on a formalist rationale with which it was familiar and comfortable.[33]

But Congress, too, shares some of the blame for that myopic vision. In passing FECA 1974, it cast aside the most comprehensive recommendations for reforming the electoral system that were intended to revitalize the democracy project by recognizing that the real threat from campaign finance corruption was on the deliberative free will of the voter rather than on the corrupt politician. Congress gave the *Buckley* court a limited law that followed the money to a narrow view of quid pro quo corruption that itself had no overriding vision of deliberative democracy. The *Buckley* court, in turn, ignored the long train of campaign finance precedent, which regarded the regulation of the electoral system to prevent the coercion of the voters' free will away from a reasoned, deliberative choice based on the common good, as a legitimate congressional interest.

The point of this history is not to answer all those questions. The point, instead, is to ask them—to examine and understand the significance and limits of the law to implement political reform, and to address the needs of a modern political society within the modern political processes. It is to recall a lost history in which the values of deliberative democracy, free speech equality, and communal political interests are principles over which Americans can debate and decide, before proceeding to make reforms.

The history of the making of the campaign finance system demonstrates how the law shapes politics, and how politics shapes the law, but more significantly, how in the well-intentioned rush to reform, Americans have created a system that often failed to accomplish its goals, led to unintended negative consequences, and failed to promote a coherent value system of democratic ideals. Arriving first at a consensus on those values would promote the goals of rational policy making and effective legislation. But more than that, it would, through the process of deliberation, force us to engage our differences openly, fairly, and with the requisite comity essential for good citizenship and good lawmaking. In these times of contested elections and bitter partisan fighting, we should remind ourselves that deliberative democracy is as much about listening to a good argument with an openness to change your opinion as it is about sealing the deal. Once we to do that, the making of the campaign finance system will become a catalyst to reaffirm and invigorate, for a citizenship desperately in need of civic revival, the principles and best practices of deliberative democracy.[34]

Notes

INTRODUCTION—IGNORING HISTORY AND THE CONUNDRUM OF REFORM

1. Congressional Record, 106-2, Senate, 12585–90 (2002); Helen Dewar, "Campaign Bill Debate Turns Personal; McCain Challenged to Back Up Charge that 'Soft Money' Corrupts Colleagues," The *Washington Post*, 15 October 1999, A4.

2. Ibid.

3. Public Law 107-155, 116 Stat. 81 (2002); Herbert E. Alexander, "The Political Process after the Bipartisan Campaign Reform Act of 2002," *Election Law Journal* 2 (Spring 2003): 47–54.

4. Anthony Corrado, Thomas E. Mann, Daniel Ortiz, and Trevor Potter, *The New Campaign Finance Sourcebook* (Washington, D.C.: The Brookings Institution Press, 2003).

5. Elizabeth Drew, *The Corruption of American Politics* (New York: The Overlook Press, 1999), 61–85.

6. *McConnell v. Federal Election Commission*, 540 U.S. 93 (2003).

1—THE BEGINNINGS OF THE CAMPAIGN FINANCE SYSTEM

1. *The Utica Saturday Globe*, 15 January 1910; Newton Martin Curtis, *From Bull Run to Chancellorsville* (New York: G.P. Putnam's Sons, 1906), 274–89.

2. 19 Stat. 169, Chap. 287, Section 6 (1876).

3. Ari Hoogenboom, *Outlawing the Spoils: A History of the Civil Service Reform Movement* (Urbana: University of Illinois Press, 1961), 195–97; Dean McSweeney, "Parties, Corruption and Campaign Finance in America," in Robert G. Williams, ed., *Party Finance and Political Corruption* (Durham: St Martin's Press, 2000), 37–60; Robert D. Marcus, *Grand Old Party: Political Structure in the Gilded Age, 1880–1896* (New York: Oxford University Press, 1971), 59–100; Paul Van Riper, *History of the United States Civil Service* (Westport, CT: Greenwood Press, 1958), 85, 110–11.

4. "A Centennial Guide," *The New York Times*, 7 May 1876, 1; "Mr. Evart's Oration," *The New York Times*, 5 July 1876, 3.

5. Morton Keller, *Affairs of State* (Cambridge: Belknap Press, 1977), 239.

6. Richard Franklin Bensel, *The Political Economy of American Industrialization, 1877–1900* (Cambridge: Cambridge University Press, 2000), 17.

7. Glenn C. Altschuler and Stuart M. Blumin, *Rude Republic* (Princeton: Princeton University Press, 2000), 171–79; Joel Silbey, *The American Political Nation, 1838–1893* (Stanford: Stanford University Press, 1991), 201; Keller, *Affairs of State*, 243; Mark Walgren Summers, *The Era of Good Stealings* (Oxford: Oxford University Press, 1993), 93–94.

8. Keller, 243; "Reform Cheap for Cash," *The New York Times*, 9 June 1876, 4; 22 U.S. Stat 403 (1883); 20 U.S. Stat 403 (1883); Congressional Record, 46-3, Senate Report. *The Regulation and Improvement of the Civil Service* (Washington, D.C: Government Printing Office, 1881).

9. Fred Perry Powers, "The Reform of the Federal Service," *Political Science Quarterly* 3 (June 1888): 247–81, 252; 14 Stat. 497, Chapter 172 (1868); *The New York Times*, 6 January 1882, 8.

10. Matthew Josephson, *The Politicos, 1865–1896* (New York: Harcourt Brace & Co., 1938), 320–23; Mark Walgren Summers, *The Gilded Age* (Princeton: Princeton University Press, 1997), 186.

11. *The Princeton Review* 42 (January 1870): 2; Rev. R. L. Dorman, "Some New York Custom House Investigations," *New Englander* 136 (October 1877): 785, 790.

12. Ibid., 793; "Desperate Radicals," *The Washington Post*, 25 September 1878, 1; "Politics in Brooklyn," *The New York Times*, 3 July 1877, 8; "The Corruption Fund," *The New York Times*, 15 April 1876, 3.

13. William G. Sumner, "The Theory and Practice of Elections," *Princeton Review* 1 (January–June 1880): 265, 266, 271–72.

14. Ibid., 280.

15. Altschuler, *Rude Republic*, 215–27; Dorman B. Eaton, "The Public Service and the Public," *Atlantic Monthly*, 41 (February 1878): 242, 248–49.

16. "The President's Message," *The New York Times*, 6 December 1876, 1; "Mr. Tilden's Centennial Message," *The New York Times*, 1 July 1876, 4; "The Disconsolate Democracy," *The New York Times*, 15 December 1876, 4; "The Reform Movement," *The New York Times*, 9 April 1876, 6; Robert Marino and David Schultz, *A Short History of the United States Civil Service* (Lanham, Maryland: University Press of America, 1991); David Schultz and Robert Marino, *The Politics of Civil Service Reform* (New York: Petersburg Press, 1998); Frederick C. Mosher, *Democracy and the Public Service* (New York: Oxford University Press, 1968); Patricia W. Ingraham and David H. Rosenbloom, eds., *The Promise and Paradox of Civil Service Reform* (Pittsburgh: University of Pittsburgh Press, 1992); Frank Mann Stewart, *The National Civil Service Reform League: History, Activism, and Problems* (Austin: University of Texas Press, 1929); Ari Hoogenboom, "The Pendleton Act and the Civil Service," *American Historical Review* 64 (Jan. 1959): 301–18; George F. Howe, "The New York Customhouse Controversy 1877–1879," *Mississippi Valley Historical Review* 18 (Dec. 1931): 350–63; Ari Hoogenboom, "Thomas A. Jenckes and Civil Service Reform," *Mississippi Valley Historical Review* 47 (March 1961): 636–58; Patricia Wallace Ingraham, *The Foundation of Merit: Public Service in American Democracy* (Baltimore: The Johns Hopkins University Press, 1995), 1–55.

17. Ibid., *Foundation of Merit*, 139–40; Summers, *Good Stealings*, 287–300.

18. "Senator Blaine's Speech," *The New York Times*, 12 December 1876, 1; "The Suffrage," *The New York Times*, 2 January 1876, 1; "The Right of Suffrage," *The New York Times*, 15 September 1876, 1.

19. Hoogenboom, *Outlawing*, 2–3.

20. Marino and Schultz, *Short History*, 58–59; 22 U.S. Stat 403 (1883); U.S. Congress, 46-3, Senate, *The Regulation and Improvement of the Civil Service* (Washington: Government Printing Office, 1881); E. L. Godkin, "The Democrats and Civil Service Reform," *The Nation* 31 (December 2, 1880), 388.

21. "House of Representatives," *The New York Times*, 22 March 1876, 2; Clifton K. Yearly, *The Money Machines* (Albany: SUNY Press, 1972), 109–10.

22. Keller, *Affairs of State*, 238–40, 249–68.

23. Congressional Record, 44-1, House, 2281-2282, 2808 (1876).

24. Ibid.

25. Hoogenboom, *Spoils*, 199; James K. Pollock, Jr., *Party Campaign Funds* (New York: Alfred A. Knopf, 1926), 7; "Political Assessments," *The New York Times*, 18 September 1880, 4.

26. Roy Morris, *Fraud of the Century: Rutherford B. Hayes, Samuel Tilden and the Stolen Election of 1876* (New York: Simon & Schuster, 2003); Paul Haworth, *The Hayes-Tilden Disputed Presidential Election of 1876* (New York: AMS Press, 1970); Summers, *Gilded Age*, 188; "Political Assessments," *The New York Times*, 18 September 1880, 4; "A Plea for Political Assessments," 16 May 1882, 4.

27. Record of the Supreme Court, *U.S. v. Curtis*, 58. The Conference Committee had struck the criminal penalties from the Whitehouse amendment, leaving the maximum penalty a $500 fine. Record of the Supreme Court, *Ex Parte Curtis*, Petition for Writ of Habeas Corpus, 1–4.

28. 106 U.S. at 373–75.

29. Record of the Supreme Court, *Ex Parte Curtis*, Brief of Petitioner, 9.

30. 106 U.S. at 376–78.

31. "The Conviction of General Curtis," *The New York Times*, 26 May 1882, 4; "Gen. Curtis' Conviction, The Political Assessment Law Sustained," *The New York Times*, 19 December 1882, 3; *The New York Times*, 20 December 1882, 4.

32. Hoogenboom, *Spoils*, 227, 275. He estimates that only 10 percent of employees actually paid assessments in 1880, and small responses to voluntary assessment solicitations occurred in many state and local parties. Yearly reports that in 1878, the Republican National Congressional Committee sent out over 100,000 demands, with a measly 11.5 percent response rate. Yearly, *Money Machines*, 108. General Curtis's trial record indicates that the New York Committee he chaired sent out increasingly threatening dun letters to recalcitrant employees because the response rate was so low. Record of Supreme Court, *Ex Parte Curtis*, Trial Record, 15–59.

33. Van Riper, *History of Civil Service*, 105; U.S. Congress, 46-3, Senate Report. *The Regulation and Improvement of the Civil Service* (1881).

34. Fred Perry Powers, "The Reform of the Federal Service," *Political Science Quarterly* 3 (June 1888): 263.

35. Hoogenboom, *Outlawing Spoils*, 234; Congressional Record, 47-2, Senate, 12 December 1882, 204.

36. Congressional Record, 47-2, Senate, 12 December 1882, 207; Ari Hoogenboom, "The Pendleton Act and the Civil Service," *The American Historical Review* 64 (January 1959): 303.

37. Congressional Record, 47-2, Senate, 14 December 1882, 279–80.

38. Congressional Record, 47-2, Senate, 16 December 1883, 355–60.

39. Congressional Record, 47-2, Senate, 16 December 1882, 364.

40. Dorman B. Eaton, "The Public Service and the Public," *The Atlantic Monthly* 41 (February 1878): 248–50; William G. Sumner, "Presidential Elections and Civil-Service Reform," *Princeton Review* 1 (January–June 1881): 143.

41. Congressional Record, 47-2, Senate, 22 December 1882, 526.

42. Ibid., 621.

43. Ibid., 623–25.

44. Ibid., 641.

45. Ibid., 629, 639.

46. Summers, *Gilded Age*, 193; Geoffrey Blodgett, "The Mugwump Reputation, 1870 to the Present," *Journal of American History* 66 (March 1980): 867–87.

47. Louis W. Koenig, *Bryan: A Political Biography of William Jennings Bryan* (New York: G. P. Putman & Sons, 1991), 231; David K. Ryden, "The United States Supreme Court as an Obstacle to Political Reform," in Christopher Banks and John C Green, eds., *Superintending Democracy: The Courts and the Political Process* (Akron: University of Ohio Press, 2001), 163–86; John R. Schmidhauser, *Constitutional Law in the Political Process* (Chicago: Rand McNally & Co., 1963), 321–36; Michael E. McGregor, *The Decline of Popular Politics: The American North 1865–1928* (New York: Oxford University Press, 1986), 108–9; Alexander Keyssar, *The Right to Vote* (New York: Basic Books, 2000), 118–27; Jesse Macy, *Party Organization and Machinery* (London: T. Fisher Unwin, 1905): 227; David Paul Nord, *Newspapers and New Politics: Midwestern Municipal Reform 1890–1900* (Michigan: Research Press, 1981).

48. David M. Rabban, *Free Speech in Its Forgotten Years* (Cambridge: Cambridge University Press, 1997), 132–73.

2—FUNDING THE NATIONAL INTEREST

1. Frederick Jackson Turner, *The Frontier in American History* (Tucson: University of Arizona Press, 1997), x; ibid., quoting Wilbur R. Jacobs, Foreword, xii.

2. Turner, *Frontier,* 22, 37, 52.

3. Ibid., 12.

4. James C. Bryce, *American Commonwealth,* Volume II (New York: Macmillan and Company, 1893), 639–40.

5. Paul Kens, *Justice Stephen Field* (Lawrence: University of Kansas Press, 1997), 236–65, 11–43.

6. *Remarks of Mr. Justice Field to the New York State Bar Association,* found at 134 U.S. 729 (1890), 744–45 (italics added).

7. Ibid., *Remarks of Justice Field,* 745.

8. Kens, *Field,* 138–39.

9. Turner, *Frontier,* 2–3; Robert McCloskey, *American Conservatism in the Age of Enterprise* (Harvard University Press: Cambridge, 1961), 1–9; Charles W. McCurdy, "The 'Liberty of Contract' Regime in American Law," in *The State and Freedom of Contract,* ed. Harry N. Scheiber (Stanford: Stanford University Press, 1998), 161.

10. Alfred D. Chandler, Jr., *The Visible Hand* (Cambridge: Harvard University Press, 1977), 122–45; Olivier Zunz, *Making America Corporate: 1870–1920* (Chicago: University Press of Chicago, 1990), 15–36; Alan Trachtenberg, *The Incorporation of America* (New York: Hill and Wang, 1982), 6–13; William C. Robbins, *Colony and Empire: The Capitalist Transformation of the American West* (Lawrence: University of Kansas Press, 1994); Sarah H. Gordon, *Passage to Union* (Chicago: Ivan R. Dee, 1997); David Howard Bain, *Empire Express* (New York: Viking, 1999); Samuel P. Hays, *The Response to Industrialization: 1855–1914* (Chicago: University of Chicago Press, 1957).

11. Chandler, *Visible Hand,* 127–28.

12. Ibid., 141–42; Clare Cushman, ed. *The Supreme Court Justices: Illustrated Biographies, 1789–1995,* 2nd edition (Washington, D.C.: Congressional Quarterly, Inc., 1995).

13. Bruce R. Trimble, *Chief Justice Waite: Defender of the Public Interest* (Princeton: Princeton University Press, 1938), 151.

14. J. R. Pole, *The Pursuit of Equity in American History* (Berkeley: University of California Press, 1993), 254–55, 261; *The National Anti-Slavery Standard,* 20 March 1869, quoted in William Gillette, *The Right to Vote: Politics and the Passage of the Fifteenth Amendment* (Baltimore: Johns Hopkins University Press, 1965), 87; Alexander Keyssar, *The Right to Vote* (New York: Basic Books, 2000), 166.

15. 110 U.S. 651 (1884), 655–58.

16. 110 U.S. at 662.

17. 110 U.S. at 665.

18. Ibid.

19. *Santa Clara County v. So. Pacific RR,* 118 U.S. 394 (1886), 394; Charles W. McCurdy, "The Knight Sugar Decision of 1895 and the Modernization of American Corporation Law, 1869–1903," *Business History Review* 3 (Autumn 1979): 308–9.

20. Kens, *Field,* 117–30; Charles W. McCurdy, "Justice Field and the Jurisprudence of Government-Business Relations: Some Parameters of Laissez-Faire Constitutionalism, 1863–1897," *The Journal of American History* 61 (March 1975): 989; 118 U.S. 394 (1886); Herbert Hovenkamp, *Enterprise and American Law, 1836–1937* (Cambridge: Harvard University Press, 1991); Morton J. Horowitz, *The Transformation of American Law, 1870–1960: The Crisis of Legal Orthodoxy* (New York: Oxford University Press, 1992); Owen Fiss, *Troubled Beginnings of the Modern State, 1888–1921* (New York: Macmillan Press, 1993); Howard Gillman, *The Constitution Besieged: The Rise and Demise of Lochner Era Police Power Jurisprudence* (Durham: Duke University Press, 1993); Charles A. Beard, *The Supreme Court and the Constitution* (New Jersey: Prentice Hall, 1962); Charles W. McCurdy, "Knight Sugar Decision," 304–42; Barry Cushman, "Lost Fidelities," *William and Mary Law Review* 41 (December 1999): 95–145.

21. Allan Nevins, *Grover Cleveland* (New York: Dodd, Mead & Company, 1970), xi; Joanne Reitano, *The Tariff Question in the Gilded Age: The Great Debate of 1888* (College Park: Pennsylvania State University, 1994), 8–9.

22. Nevins, *Cleveland*, 368, quoting *Messages and Papers of the Presidents*, Volume VIII, 507.

23. Reitano, *Tariff Question*, 7–9.

24. "Speeches by Leading Businessmen at the Dinner of the New England Tariff Reform League, January 18, 1894" (Woodbridge, CT: Research Publications, 1988).

25. Ibid., 19.

26. Congressional Record, 50-1 (1888) 3057, 6536; Reitano, *Tariff Question*, 18.

27. Congressional Record, 50-1, 17 April 1888, 3058.

28. Ibid.

29. Reitano, *Tariff Question*, 28.

30. "Transformation of Party," *Nation* 47, 5 July 1888, 4–5; "Proposed Sugar Bounty," *Nation* 47, 12 July 1888, 24–25; "Signs of National Progress," *Nation* 47, 23 July 1888, 65–66; "Letter to the Editor," *Nation* 47, 23 August 1888, 149–50.

31. "The Education Value of the Present Campaign," *Nation* 47, 30 August 1888, 162–63; "Tariff Reform as a Moral Issue," *Nation* 47, 13 September 1888, 204–5.

32. Reitano, *Tariff Question*, 32–35.

33. E. W. Taussig, *The Tariff History of the United States* (New York: Putnam & Sons, 1923); Sidney Ratner, *The Tariff in American History* (New York: Nostrand and Co., 1972); Edward Stanwood, *American Tariff Controversies in the Nineteenth Century* (Cambridge: Houghton Mifflin & Co., 1904); E. E. Schattschneider, *Politics, Pressures and the Tariff* (New York: Prentice Hall, Inc., 1935); Reitano, *Tariff Question*, 47–55.

34. Congressional Record, 50-1, 1 May 1888, 3595.

35. Geoffrey Blodgett, *The Gentle Reformers: Massachusetts Democrats in the Cleveland Era* (Cambridge: Harvard University Press, 1966), 37–39.

36. Elizabeth Sanders, *Roots of Reform: Farmers, Workers and the American State, 1877–1917* (Chicago: University of Chicago Press, 1999), 119; Michael Les Benedict, "Law and the Constitution in the Gilded Age," in Charles W. Calhoun, ed., *The Gilded Age* (Wilmington: Scholarly Resource, 1996), 289–308; Charles W. McCurdy, "American Law and the Marketing Structure of the Large Corporations, 1875–1890," *Journal of Economic History* 38 (September 1978): 631–49.

37. James K. Pollock, *Party Campaign Funds* (New York: Alfred A. Knopf, 1926), 62–70.

38. Nevins, *Cleveland*, 414–15.

39. Ibid., 418; Summers, *The Gilded Age*, 212–13.

40. Nevins, *Cleveland*, 419; American Iron and Steel Association, *Bulletin*, 21 December 1887, 351.

41. Nevins, *Cleveland*, 419–20; *New York Herald*, 17 June 1888; Herbert Croly, *Marcus Alonzo Hanna* (New York: The Macmillan Company, 1965), 149.

42. *Cleveland Papers*, University of Virginia, Letters from Brice to Lamont, 18 August and 2 September 1888; *Nation*, 22 November 1888; *New York Mail and Express*, 22 November 1888; *Nation*, 29 November 1888.

43. <http://www.sddt.com/features/conventions/elections/1888.html> (6 January 2004). New York's thirty-four and Indiana's fifteen electoral votes would have given Cleveland a substantial electoral and popular victory; *New York Herald*, 15 November 1888.

44. *Cleveland Papers*, University of Virginia, Letter from White, 21 November 1888.

45. Nevins, *Cleveland*, 436–42.

46. John D. Hicks, *The Populist Revolt* (Minneapolis: University of Minnesota Press, 1931), 267; Normal Pollack, *The Just Polity: Populism, Law, and Human Welfare* (Urbana: University of Illinois Press, 1987), 270.

47. Cass Sunstein, *The Partial Constitution* (Cambridge: Harvard University Press, 1993), 41.

48. Hicks, *Populist Revolt*, xiii, 17–19; *Farmers Alliance*, 28 February 1891, 22 October 1891 (Lincoln: Nebraska State Historical Society).

49. James H. Davis, *A Political Revelation* (Dallas: The Adimonte Publishing Co., 1894), 242–44.

50. W. Scott Morgan, *History of the Wheel and Alliance and the Impending Revolution* (Fort Scott, Kansas: J. H. Rice & Sons, 1889), 15–16; *Platte County Argus*, 4 June 1896 (Lincoln: Nebraska Historical Society); Hicks, *Populist Revolt*, 41.

51. James B. Weaver, *A Call to Action* (Des Moines: Iowa Printing Co., 1892), 185, 210–41; Hicks, *Populist Revolt*, 125.

52. Pollock, *Just Polity*, 3, 133.

53. Ibid., 137.

54. Hicks, *Populist Revolt*, 269; Pollock, *Just Polity*, 199; C. Vann Woodward, *Tom Watson: Agrarian Rebel* (New York: Oxford University Press, 1963), 217.

55. Summers, *Gilded Age*, 215; Nevins, *Cleveland*, 500–501.

56. <http://www.sadt/com/features/conventions/elections/1892.html> (6 January 2004). Cleveland won 5,535,426 popular votes, Harrison had 5,182,690, and Populist James Weaver 1,029,846; Nevins, *Cleveland*, 508.

57. Kurt Hohenstein, "William Jennings Bryan and the Income Tax," *Journal of Law and Politics* 16 (Winter 2000): 163–92; Nevins, *Cleveland*, 678.

58. See W. H. Harvey, *Coin's Financial School* (Cambridge: Belknap Press of Harvard University, 1963); Nevins, 680–81.

59. Nevins, *Cleveland*, 691; Louis W. Koenig, *Bryan* (New York: G.P. Putnam & Sons, 1971), 126–47; Paolo E. Coletta, *William Jennings Bryan* (Lincoln: University of Nebraska Press, 1964), 112–20, 66–91.

60. <http://www.townhall.com/documents/crossofgold.html> (6 January 2004); Alan F. Westin, "The Supreme Court, The Populist Movement, and The Campaign of 1896," 15 *Journal of Politics* (1953): 3–41.

61. Edward M. Epstein, *The Corporation in American Politics* (Englewood Cliffs, New Jersey: Prentice-Hall, Inc., 1969), 23–25; Robert A. Dahl, *Democracy and Its Critics* (New Haven: Yale University Press, 1989), 98.

62. Croly, *Hanna*, 108, 209, 211.

63. Coletta, *William Jennings Bryan*, 188; Croly, *Hanna*, 218.

64. Coletta, *William Jennings Bryan*, 220.

65. Ibid., 193–200; Matthew Josephson, *The Politicos* (New York: Harcourt Brace & Co., 1938), 695–99.

66. Coletta, 193.

67. Alan Trachtenberg, *The Incorporation of America* (New York: Hill and Wang, 1982), 170–77; Samuel Hays, *The Response to Industrialism: 1885–1914* (Chicago: University of Chicago Press, 1957), 140–52; David Vogel, *Kindred Strangers* (Princeton: Princeton University Press, 1996), 43, 47, 142–43.

3—THE PROGRESSIVE PROMISE DERAILED

1. Edmund Morris, *Theodore Rex* (New York: Random House, 2001), 360–64; Adam Winkler, "Other People's Money: Corporations, Agency Costs, and Campaign Finance Law," *Georgetown Law Journal* 92 (June 2004): 886–87.

2. "Cleveland Loss to Harrison," *Nation* 47, 8 November 1888, 365; "The Really Serious Matter," *Nation* 47, 7 November 1888, 403.

3. Kurt Hohenstein, "William Jennings Bryan and the Income Tax: Economic Statism and the Judicial Usurpation in the Election of 1896," *Journal of Law and Politics* 16 (Winter 2000): 163–92; Herbert Croly, *The Promise of American Life* (New York: Capricorn Press, 1909), 200, 149–51.

4. Walter Lippman, *Drift and Mastery* (Madison: The University of Wisconsin Press, 1985), 154; *Public Opinion* (New York: Harcourt Brace and Company, 1922); *The Phantom Public* (New York: Harcourt, Brace and Company, 1925).

5. Lippman, *Public Opinion,* 275, 292; Ronald Steel, *Walter Lippman and the American Century* (New York: Random House, 1980), 22.

6. Robert B. Westbrook, *John Dewey and American Democracy* (Ithaca: Cornell University Press, 1991), 307.

7. Washington Gladden, "Safeguards of the Suffrage," *The Century* 37 (February 1889), 622, 627, 621.

8. Jeremiah W. Jenks, "Money in Practical Politics," *The Century* 44 (October 1892), 942–47. But see Alexander Keyssar, *The Right to Vote* (New York: Basis Books, 2002), 158.

9. "Responsibility for Political Corruption," *The Century* 44 (July 1892), 473.

10. *The Federalist* 51 (Vermont: Everyman Publisher, 1996), 265–69, 265.

11. Weibe, *The Search for Order, 1877–1920* (New York: Hill and Wang, 1966), 8; *English Corrupt Practices Act,* Chapter 47; James K. Pollock, Jr., *Party Campaign Funds* (New York: Alfred A. Knopf, 1926), 7–8.

12. Ibid., *Party Campaign Funds,* 152; "Corrupt Practices Legislation in 1891," *The Century* 43 (November 1891), 151–53.

13. "The First Presidential Election under Ballot Reform," *The Century* 43 (April 1892), 952.

14. *Ex Parte Yarbrough,* 110 U.S. 651 (1884), 666.

15. Pollock, *Party Campaign Funds,* 8–9.

16. Winker, *Other People's Money,* 7–8, 26.

17. Robert Mutch, *Campaigns, Congress and the Courts: The Making of Federal Campaign Finance Law* (New York: Praeger, 1988), xvii.

18. Michael McGerr, *A Fierce Discontent: The Rise and Fall of the Progressive Movement, 1870–1920* (New York: Free Press, 2003), 155; Adam Winkler, "The Corporation in Election Law," *Loyola LA Law Review* 32 (June 1999): 1244.

19. Winkler, *"The Corporation in Election Law,"* 1246; Cass Sunstein, *The Partial Constitution* (Cambridge: Harvard University Press, 1993), 40–67; Mutch, *Campaigns,* 2–3.

20. James D. Richardson, ed., *A Compilation of Messages and Papers of the Presidents,* Volume 11 (New York: Bureau of National Literature and Art, 1908), 1905; Mutch, *Campaigns,* 176.

21. Congressional Record 59-1, 7 December 1905, 229; Congressional Record 59-1, S. 4563, 19 February 1906, 2642; Congressional Record 59-2, Senate Report 4563, 15 January 1907, 6397–98; "Roosevelt Says Nation Must Curb Plutocracy," *The New York Times,* 5 October 1906, 4.

22. Congressional Record 59-2, House, 21 January 1907, 1453.

23. Ibid.

24. David M. Rabban, *Free Speech in Its Forgotten Years* (Cambridge: Cambridge University Press, 1997); David M. Rabban, "The IWW Free Speech Fights and Popular Concepts of Free Expression Between World War I," *Va. Law Review* 1055 (August 1994): 80; Mark A. Graber, *Transforming Free Speech* (Berkeley: University of California Press, 1991), 36–40, 75–104.

25. Congressional Record 59-2, Senate, 29 January 1907, 1866.

26. 239 Fed 163 at 168–69.

27. 239 Fed 163 at 169; Nichole Bremman Casarez, "Corruption, Corrosion and Corporate Political Speech," *Nebraska Law Review* 70 (1991); Adam P. Hall, "Regulating Corporate 'Speech' in Public Elections," *Case W. Res L. Rev.* 39 (1988–1989); Larry Ribstein, "Corporate Political Speech," *Wash State L. Rev.* 49 (Winter 1992); Michael J. Garrison, "Corporate Political Speech, and First Amendment Doctrine," *Am. Bus. L. J.* 27 (Summer 1989); Charles E. M. Kold, "Campaign Finance Reform: A Business Perspective," *Cath. U. L. Review* 50 (Fall 2000).

28. Mutch, *Campaigns*, 8–9.

29. Congressional Record 61-2, House, 18 May 1908, 6520; 22 May 1908, 6470–72.

30. Congressional Record 61-2, House, 22 May 1908, 6472.

31. Congressional Record 61-2, Senate Report 689 (1908), 2.

32. Sikes, *Corrupt Practices*, 192–207; Mutch, *Campaigns*, 10–16; Daniel R. Ortiz, "The First Amendment and the Limits of Campaign Finance Reform," in Anthony Corrado, ed., *Campaign Finance Reform: A Sourcebook* (Washington, D.C.: Brookings Institution Press, 1997); Robert E. Mutch, "The First Federal Campaign Finance Bills," *Journal of Policy History* 14 (2002), 30–48; David M. Bixby, "The Roosevelt Court, Democratic Ideology, and Minority Rights: Another Look at *United States v. Classic,*" *Yale Law Journal* 90 (March 1981): 741–97.

33. Congressional Record 61-2, House, 18 April 1910, 4927.

34. Ibid., 4930–31.

35. Ibid.

36. Ibid. (italics added.)

37. Ibid.

38. Ibid., 4934.

39. Congressional Record 61-2, 25 June 1910, 9084–85, 8753.

40. Mutch, *Campaigns*, 12–13; Congressional Record 62-1, House, 13 April 1911, 254.

41. Congressional Record 62-1, House, 13 April 1911, 263; J. Morgan Koussar, *The Shaping of Southern Politics: Suffrage Restriction and the Establishment of the One-Party South, 1880–1910* (New Haven: Yale University Press, 1974), 224–57.

42. Congressional Record 62-1, House, 14 April 1911, 267–69.

43. Congressional Record 77-4, House Joint Resolution 290, House Hearings (1923); U.S. Constitution, Article IV, Section [1]; Congressional Record 62-1, Senate, 20 June 1911, 2312–13.

44. Congressional Record 62-1, Senate, 20 June 1911, 2313.

45. Edward Sait, *American Parties and Elections* (New York: D. Appleton-Century, 1942), 192–200, 222; James Bryce, *American Commonwealth,* Volume II (New York: MacMillan and Company, 1893), 77–79; David J. Rothman, *Politics and Power: The United States Senate, 1869–1901* (Cambridge: Harvard University Press, 1966), 11–42; Nancy L. Rosenbaum, "Political Parties as Membership Groups," *Columbia Law Review* 100 (April 2000): 813–42; Cornelius Cotter, "Institutional Development of Parties and the Thesis of Party Decline," *Political Science Quarterly* 95 (Spring 1980): 1–27; Frank J. Sorauf, "Extra-Legal Political Parties in Wisconsin," *The American Political Science Review* 48 (September 1954): 692–704; Robert E. Cushman, "Voting Organic Laws," *Political Science Quarterly* 28 (June 1913): 207–9; John L. Reynolds, "Outlawing 'Treachery': Split Tickets and Ballot Laws in New York and New Jersey, 1880–1910," *Journal of American History* 72 (March 1986): 835–58; Richard Briffault, "The Political Parties and Campaign Finance Reform," *Columbia Law Review* 100 (April 2000): 620–66; Kirk J. Nahia, "Political Parties and the Campaign Finance Laws: Dilemmas, Concerns & Opportunities," *Fordham Law Review* 56 (October 1987): 53–110.

46. Congressional Record 62-1, Senate, 17 July 1911, 3017, 3006.

47. Congressional Record 62-1, Public Law 32, HR 2958, 19 April 1911.

48. Congressional Record 62-1, House, 17 August 1911, 4091.

49. Ibid., 4099.

50. Ibid.

51. Ibid., 4102.

52. 256 U.S. 232 (1921).

53. Congressional Record 66-2, Senate Hearings, S. Res. 357 (1920); Congressional Record 66-3, *Senate Report 823,* 24 February 1921; Congressional Record 68-2, *Senate Resolution 248,* Unpublished Hearings (1924); Congressional Record 68-2, Senate Report 1100, 3 February 1925; Congressional Record 69-1, Senate Resolution 195, Special Committee (1926).

54. Congressional Record 66-3, *Senate Report 823,* 24 February 1921, 1, 4.

55. Ibid., 12.

56. Congressional Record 68-2, *Senate Report 1100,* 3 February 1925, 2, 12.

57. Congressional Record 69-1, *Senate Resolution 195,* 9 June 1926, 1; Congressional Record 69-2, *Senate Report 1197* (1927).

58. Harding would win the 1920 election, running on the Republican ticket with vice presidential nominee Calvin Coolidge, then Massachusetts governor. Ohio governor James M. Cox, a Progressive governor, chose Franklin D. Roosevelt as his running mate. Harding won the popular vote 16,143,407 to 9,130,328, and the electoral vote 404 to 127. Third party Socialist candidate Eugene V. Debs, running from prison, polled 919,799 popular votes. <http://www.americanpresident.org> (7 January 2004).

59. Congressional Record 66-2, Senate Hearings, *Senate Resolution 357* (1920), 51–52.

60. U.S. Constitution, Amendment XVII (1913).

61. Ralph Rossum, *Federalism, the Supreme Court, and the Seventeenth Amendment: The Irony of Constitutional Democracy* (Lexington: Lexington Books, 2001), 2, quoting John Adams to Roger Sherman, 203.

62. Congressional Record 66-2, Senate Hearings, Subcommittee on Privileges and Elections, *Sen. Resolution 357* (1920), 236.

63. Ibid., 238–39.

64. Ibid., 256, 261.

65. Ibid., 2230, 2386.

66. Elizabeth Varon, *We Mean to Be Counted* (Chapel Hill: University of North Carolina Press, 1998); Elizabeth Clemens, *The People's Lobby* (Chicago: University of Chicago Press, 1997), 89–99; Rebecca Edwards, *Angels in the Machinery* (New York: Oxford University Press, 1997), 95–110; Theda Skocpol, "How America Became Civic," in Theda Skocpol and Morris D. Fionna, eds., *Civic Organization in American Democracy* (Washington, D.C.: Brookings Institution Press, 1999), 27–71.

67. Congressional Record 66-2, Senate Resolution 357, *Kenyon Hearings* (1920), 673–75.

68. Ibid., 1282 (italics added by author for emphasis), 2038.

69. Ibid., 2038.

70. Ibid., 525; Jean H. Baker, ed., *Votes for Women* (Oxford: Oxford University Press, 2002), 13; Michael McGerr, "Political Style and Women's Power, 1830–1930," *The Journal of American History* 17 (December 1990): 882; Elaine Tyler May, "Expanding the Past: Recent Scholarship on Women in Politics and Work," *Reviews in American History* 10 (December 1982): 217, 221; Keyssar, *Right to Vote,* 202–11.

71. 243 U.S. 476 (1917).

72. Michigan Public Acts, No. 109 (1913).

73. 243 U.S. 476. (1917), at 478. The laws implemented parts of the 1870 Force Bill into the 1910 revision of the federal criminal code. 16 Stat 144, Section 19-27, 31 May 1870; 16 Stat. 254, Section 5-6, 14 July 1870.

74. 243 U.S. at 480.

75. *Blair v. United States,* 250 U.S. 273 (1919), 277, 283.

76. Records of the Supreme Court of the United States, No. 27,916, Bill of Exceptions, Indictment, 957–68 (1921); Mutch, *Campaigns,* 16; Records of Supreme Court, Testimony, 117–23.

77. U.S. Constitution, Article IV, Section 1; *The Federalist* 47, 49, 50.

78. 256 U.S. 232, 256–57.

79. 250 U.S. at 267, White, C.J., dissenting.

80. Ibid. at 286.

81. Michigan Public Laws, Act 109 (1913).

82. Records of the Supreme Court, *Truman Newberry v. United States,* No. 27,916, Ruling on Demur, 15.

83. Congressional Record 67-4, House, Committee on Elections, Hearings, HJ Res. 290, 413, 424, 435, HR 12186, 11, 18, 27 January 1923; Congressional Record 68-2, Senate, *Sen. Res. 248,* Committee on Campaign Expenditures (1925); ibid., 26 May 1924, 9506–7; Congressional Record 68-2, House, 3 June 1924, 10328–29; Public Law, Chapter 368, Title III, Section 301–19, "Federal Corrupt Practices Act," 28 February 1925; also found at 2 U.S.C Section 241–48.

84. Congress held the power under Article I, Section 5 to "be the judge of the election, returns, and qualifications of its own members." *U.S. Constitution,* Article I, Section 5. Whether that provision included the power to exclude an elected candidate because he had violated campaign finance spending limits was not challenged. The Supreme Court finally considered the power of Congress to exclude one of its own members from admittance to Congress and ruled that absent a violation of the qualifications found in the Constitution, Congress could not exclude a properly elected member from his or her seat. It could, however, under its own rules, remove a member for violations after an election; *Powell v. McCormack,* 395 U.S. 486 (1969).

85. Congressional Record 69-1, Special Committee Investigation on Expenditures in Senate Primary and General Elections, *Senate Resolution 195* (1926); 551.

86. Congressional Record 69-1, Senate, Special Committee (1924), 1824; Congressional Record 70-1, Senate, *Senate Report 92,* 17 January 1926; Carroll Hill Wooddy, *The Case of Frank L. Smith* (Chicago: University of Cincinnati Press, 1931), 241.

87. Wooddy, *Case of Frank Smith,* 245.

88. Ibid., 277.

89. Wooddy, *Case of Frank Smith,* 277; Congressional Record 70-1, Senate, 19 January 1928, 1905.

90. *Springfield Republican,* 21 January 1927, 1.

4—MANAGING THE MARKETPLACE OF IDEAS

1. Kevin Baker, "FDR's Fireside Chats," in Robert A. Wilson and Stanley Marcus, eds., *American Greats* (New York: Public Affairs Press, 1999).

2. Louise M. Benjamin, *Freedom of the Air and the Public Interest: First Amendment Rights in Broadcasting to 1935* (Carbondale: Southern Illinois University Press, 2001), 2; Gary Dean Best, *The Politics of American Individualism: Herbert Hoover in Transition, 1918–1921* (Westport, Connecticut: Greenwood Press, 1975), 94–99, 64, 101; Ellis W. Hawley, ed., *Herbert Hoover as Secretary of Commerce* (Iowa City: University of Iowa Press, 1981), 48–49; Robert F. Himmelberg, in *Herbert Hoover and the Crisis of American Capitalism* (Cambridge: Schenckman Publishing Company, 1973), 64.

3. Fred D. Ragan, "Justice Oliver Wendell Holmes, Jr., Zechariah Chafee, Jr., and the Clear and Present Danger Test: The First Year, 1919," *The Journal of American History* 58 (June 1971): 24–45; David S. Bogen, "The Free Speech Metamorphosis of Mr. Justice Holmes," *Hofstra Law Review* 11 (Fall 1982): 97–178; 249 U.S. 47 (1919).

4. 250 U.S. 616 (1919); Richard Polenberg, *Fighting Faiths: The Abrams Case, the Supreme Court, and Free Speech* (New York: Viking Press, 1987); Zachariah Chafee, "Freedom of Speech in Wartime," *Harvard Law Review* 32 (1919).

5. 250 U.S. 616, 630 (1919).

6. 268 U.S. 652 (1925).

7. *Whitney v. California,* 274 U.S. 357 (1927), 375–77.

8. Lawrence M. Friedman, *American Law in the 20th Century* (New Haven: Yale University Press, 2002), 139–47.

9. Fred D. Ragan, "Justice Oliver Wendell Holmes, Jr., Zechariah Chafee, Jr., and the Clear and Present Danger Test for Free Speech: The First Year, 1919," *The Journal of American History* 58 (June 1971): 24–45.

10. David M. Rabban, *Free Speech in Its Forgotten Years* (Cambridge: Cambridge University Press, 1997), 13, 58–59, 63.

11. Ibid., 110–11, 126.

12. Ibid., 131.

13. Michael Kent Curtis, *Free Speech: "The People's Darling Privilege"* (Durham: Duke University Press, 2000); *Ex Parte Curtis*, 106 U.S. 371 (1882); *United States v. United States Brewers' Association*, 239 F. 163 (W. D. Pa. 1916); *Burroughs and Cannon v. United States*, 290 U.S. 534 (1934).

14. *Louthan v. Commonwealth*, 79 Va. 196 (1884); *State v. Pierce*, 163 Wis. 615 (1916).

15. *Adams v. Lansdon*, 110 P. 280 (1910); Rabban, *Free Speech Forgotten*, 152–53.

16. Lawrence Friedman, *A History of American Law* (New York: Simon and Schuster, 1973), 295–340; William E. Nelson, *The Legalist Reformation* (Chapel Hill: University of North Carolina Press, 2001), 27–41; Harry Kalven, *A Worthy Tradition* (New York: Harper Collins, 1989), 3–4; Owen M. Fiss, "Free Speech and Social Structure," *Iowa Law Review* 71 (July 1986): 1405.

17. 268 U.S. 652 (1925); John Braeman, *Before the Civil Rights Revolution: The Old Court and Individual Rights* (New York: Greenwood Press, 1988), 32.

18. C. Edwin Baker, "Campaign Expenditures and Free Speech," *Harvard Civil Rights-Civil Liberties Law Review* 33 (Winter 1998): 1–46; G. Edward White, "The First Amendment Comes of Age: The Emergence of Free Speech in Twentieth Century America," *Michigan Law Review* 95 (November 1996): 299–392.

19. Rabban, *Free Speech Forgotten*, 3; G. Edward White, *First Amendment Comes of Age*, 304–5.

20. 274 U.S. 357 (1927); Melvin I. Urofsky, *Louis D. Brandeis and the Progressive Tradition* (Boston: Little, Brown and Company, 1981), 112, 119.

21. Samuel J. Konefsky, *The Legacy of Holmes and Brandeis: A Study in the Influence of Ideas* (New York: Da Capo Press, 1974), 140.

22. David Cole, "Agon at Agora: Creative Misreadings in the First Amendment Tradition," *Yale Law Journal* 95 (April 1986): 883.

23. Louis Brandeis, *The Curse of Bigness* (New York: The Viking Press, 1934); Philippa Strum, ed., *Brandeis on Democracy* (Lawrence: University Press of Kansas, 1995), 186–94; Cole, "Agon," 888; Cass R. Sunstein, *The Partial Constitution* (Cambridge: Harvard University Press, 1993); Owen F. Fiss, *The Irony of Free Speech* (Cambridge: Harvard University Press, 1996); Ronald Dworkin, *Freedom's Law: The Moral Reading of the American Constitution* (Cambridge: Harvard University Press, 1996).

24. 274 U.S. at 372; 268 U.S. 652 (1925); 274 U.S. at 377–79.

25. 274 U.S. at 375–76 (footnote omitted).

26. Robert Post, "Meiklejohn's Mistake: Individual Autonomy and the Reform of Public Discourse," *Colorado Law Review* 64 (Fall 1993): 1109.

27. Robert W. McChesney, *Telecommunications, Mass Media and Democracy* (New York: Oxford University Press, 1993), 12–37; Daniel R. Ortiz, "From Rights to Arrangements," *Loyola of Los Angeles Law Review* 32 (June 1999): 1217–18.

28. *Lamont v. Postmaster General*, 381 U.S. 301 (1965); *Nixon v. Herndon*, 273 U.S. 536 (1927); *United States v. Classic*, 313 U.S. 299 (1941) overruling *Newberry v. United States*; *Burroughs and Cannon v. United States*, 290 U.S. 534 (1933); *Grovey v. Townsend*, 295 U.S. 45 (1935). But see *Smith v. Allwright*, 321 U.S. 649 (1944); Benjamin, *Freedom of the Airwaves*, 70–77; Mark Graber, *Transforming Free Speech: The Ambiguous Legacy of Civil Libertarianism* (Berkeley: University of California Press, 1991), 93–94, quoting John Dewey.

29. Graber, *Transforming*, 178; 395 U.S. 367 (1969).

30. Federal Communication Commission, Report and Order and Notice of Proposed Rulemaking 03–127, 2 June 2003, 30–31.

31. Ibid., 32; *Schroders International Media and Entertainment Report* (New York: Schroders & Company, 2000), 256.

32. Ibid., 32–34; Alfred D. Chandler and James W. Cortada, eds., *A Nation Transformed*

by Information: How Information Has Shaped the U.S. from Colonial Times to the Present (New York: Oxford University Press, 2000); Doris A. Graber, *Mass Media and American Politics* (Washington, D.C.: Congressional Quarterly Press, Inc., 1984); Lawrence K. Grossman, *The Electronic Republic: Reshaping Democracy in the Information Age* (New York: Viking Press, 1995); Edwin Diamond and Stephen Bates, *The Spot: The Rise of Political Advertising on Television* (Cambridge: MIT Press, 1984).

33. *The Radio Act of 1912,* 62-2, Public Law 264, 13 August 1912; *Hoover v. Intercity Radio Co., Inc.,* 286 F. 1003 (D.C.CCA), 5 February 1923; *United States v. Zenith Radio Corporation,* 12 F.2d 614 (N.D. Ill.), 16 April 1926; Congressional Record 69-2, H. Doc. 483, "President Coolidge's Message to Congress on Radio," 7 December 1926.

34. *The Radio Act of 1927,* Sections 10, 11; Jonathan Weinberg, "Broadcasting and Speech," *California Law Review* 81 (October 1993): 1103.

35. *The Radio Act of 1927,* Section 18 (italics added).

36. Glen O. Robinson, "The Federal Communications Act: An Essay on Origins and Regulatory Purpose," in Max D. Paglin, ed., *A Legislative History of the Communications Act of 1934* (New York: Oxford University Press, 1989), 14–17; 94 U.S. 113 (1877); Congressional Record, 67-2 (1926), 12355; Congressional Record, 68-1 (1927), 3027.

37. J. Roger Wollenberg, "The FCC as Arbiter of 'The Public Interest, Convenience, and Necessity,'" 61–78, in Paglin; Benjamin, *Freedom of the Air,* 4–7.

38. Congressional Record, 72-2, *Hearings before the Interstate Committee of the U.S. Senate,* Part 2, 22–23 December 1932, 9; *Sorenson v. Wood,* 123 Neb. 348 (1932); Wollenberg, "FCC as Arbiter," 64.

39. Wollenberg, "FCC as Arbiter," 66.

40. Benjamin, *Freedom of the Air,* 8–31; Michele Hilmes, *Radio Voices: American Broadcasting, 1922–1952* (Minneapolis: University of Minnesota Press, 1997), 6–23; Lucas A. Powe, Jr., *American Broadcasting and the First Amendment* (Berkeley: University of California Press, 1987), 49–67; *Reading Broadcasting Co. v. FRC,* 48 F.2d 458 (CAD.C., 1932).

41. *Telecommunications Act of 1996,* P.L. No. 104, 110 Stat. 56 (1996); Report and Order and Notice of Proposed Rulemaking, FCC 03-127 (2 July 2003), 44.

42. *Loveday v. FCC,* 707 F. 2d 1443 (U.S. Court of Appeals D.C. Circuit, 1983), 1452.

43. 37 F.2d 993 (CAD.C., 1930), 993–94.

44. 47 F.2d 670 (CAD.C. 1931), 671–72.

45. Benjamin, *Freedom of the Air,* 47–48; 62 F.2d 850 (CAD.C. 1932).

46. 62 F.2d at 852.

47. 62 F.2d at 852–53.

48. Benjamin, *Freedom of the Air,* 77–78; David A. Moss and Michael R. Fein, "Radio Regulation Revisited: Coase, the FCC, and the Public Interest," *Journal of Policy History* 15 (Fall 2003): 389–416; Alexander Meikeljohn, *Political Freedom: The Constitutional Powers of the People* (New York: Harper and Brothers, 1948); G. E. White, *First Amendment Comes of Age,* 321–26.

49. Hilmes, *Radio Voices,* 10.

50. Commerce Department, *Study of Communications by an Interdepartment Committee* (Washington, D.C.: Government Printing Office, 1943), 24; Congressional Record, 73-2, Senate Hearings, S. 2910 (9, 10, 13, 14, and 16 March 1934).

51. Ibid., Congressional Hearing, at 310–11; Congressional Record, 73-2, House Hearings, HR 8301 (10 April 1934); *Federal Communication Act of 1934,* Public Law 416, 73-2 (19 June 1934).

52. *Federal Communication Act of 1934,* Section 315; Douglas B. Craig, *Fireside Politics: Radio and Political Culture in the United States, 1920–1940* (Baltimore: Johns Hopkins University Press, 2000), 113–205.

53. Charles E. Lindblom, *Politics and Markets* (New York: Basic Books, Inc., 1977), 119–31, 161–89.

54. Congressional Record, 73-2, House Hearing, HR 8301 (16 May 1934), 625.

55. Ibid., 629.

56. 319 U.S. 190 (1934).

57. Ibid., at 197, 213, 218.

58. David A. Moss and Michael R. Fein, 389–416; Editorializing by Broadcast Licensees, 25 R.R. 1901 (1949); Special Subcommittee on Investigations of the House Committee on Interstate and Foreign Commerce, *Legislative History of the Fairness Doctrine* (Washington, D.C.: 1968), 7.

59. *Mayflower Broadcasting Corporation,* 8 FCC 333 (1941), 340.

60. 25 R.R. 1901, at 1911 (1949).

61. Congressional Record, 86-2, S. 2424, HR 7985, 16160, 16375, 16588 (1959); *Legislative History of the Fairness Doctrine,* 21. The FCC had issued a Fairness Primer, 29 Fed. Reg. 10415 (1964), that defined and elaborated on its procedures for handling fairness complaints.

62. *Legislative History of the Fairness Doctrine,* 28; Donald P. Mullally, "The Fairness Doctrine: Benefits and Costs," *Public Opinion Quarterly* 33 (Winter 1969–1970): 577–82, 581; Charles H. Tillinghast, *American Broadcast Regulations and the First Amendment* (Ames: Iowa State University, 2000), 111–20; Steven J. Simmons, *The Fairness Doctrine and the Media* (Berkeley: University of California Press, 1978), 189–250; Powe, Jr., *American Broadcasting,* 108–20; Thomas W. Hazlett and David W. Sosa, "Was the Fairness Doctrine a 'Chilling Effect'? Evidence from the Post-De-Regulation Radio Market," *Journal of Legal Studies* 26 (January 1997): 279–300.

63. 400 F.2d 1002 (U.S.CA, 7th Circuit, 1968); 381 F.2d 908 (1967), 910–11.

64. 395 U.S. 367 (1969); Records of the Supreme Court, Brief of Appellant Red Lion, 101a–2a (1969), quoting comments of Bedford Broadcasting on the proposed rules of the FCC from the 1966 decision on the fairness doctrine.

65. Records of the U.S. Supreme Court, *Red Lion Broadcasting Co., Inc., v. United States,* Brief of Appellant Red Lion, 20.

66. Records of the U.S. Supreme Court, *Red Lion Broadcasting v. FEC,* Amicus Brief of Churches of Christ, et al., 6–7, quoting the *33rd Annual Report,* Federal Communication Commission, Fiscal Year 1967 (Washington, D.C.: U.S. Government Printing Office, 1968), 9; *Television Network Programming,* FCC 650277, 4 P & F Radio Reg.2d 1589, 1591; House Report No. 281, 88th Congress, 1st Session (8 May 1963).

67. Ibid., 12–13; Records of the Supreme Court, 15, 20.

68. Amy Gutmann and Dennis Thompson, *Democracy and Disagreement* (Cambridge: The Belknap Press of Harvard University Press, 1996); Robert A. Dahl, *A Preface to Democratic Theory* (Chicago: University of Chicago Press, 1956); R. Randall Rainey and William Rehg, "The Marketplace of Ideas, the Public Interest, and the Federal Regulation of the Electronic Media: Implications of Habermas' Theory of Democracy," *Southern California Law Review* 69 (September 1996): 1923–87; Neil Kinkopf, "Deliberative Democracy and Campaign Finance Reform," *Duke Law Review* 65 (Summer 2002): 151–54; Bradley Smith, *Unfree Speech: The Folly of Campaign Finance Reform* (Princeton: Princeton University Press, 2001); James A. Gardner, "Shut Up and Vote: A Critique of Deliberative Democracy and the Life of Talk," *Tennessee Law Review* 63 (Winter 1996): 421–51.

69. 395 U.S. 367 (1969), 377, 382, 387, citing the sound truck case of *Kovacs v. Cooper,* 336 U.S. 77 (1949), 390.

70. Ibid.

71. Ibid., 393–94, 401, footnote 28.

72. Mutch, *Campaigns,* 1–47; David M. Bixby, "The Roosevelt Court, Democratic Ideology, and Minority Rights: Another Look at *United States v. Classic,*" *Yale Law Review* 90 (March 1981): 741–97.

73. Syracuse Peace Council: Memorandum and Order, 2 FCC Record 5043 (1987); this decision was sustained by the District of Columbia Circuit Court in *Syracuse Peace*

Council v. FCC, 867 F.2d 654 (D.C. Cir. 1989); "CBS's Bob Mcconnell and the Story Behind the Veto," *Broadcasting,* 6 July 1987, 33; "Reagan Vetoes Fairness Doctrine Bill," *Broadcasting,* 29 June 1987, 27; Charles D. Ferris and Terrence J. Leahy, "Red Lions, Tigers and Bears: Broadcast Content Regulation and the First Amendment," *Catholic University Law Review* 38 (Winter 1989): 299–327; Jonathan Weinberg, "Broadcasting and Speech," *California Law Review* 81 (October 1993): 1103–1206; Donald P. Mullally, "The Fairness Doctrine: Benefits and Costs," *Public Opinion Quarterly* 33 (Winter 1969–1970): 577–82; Charles W. Logan, Jr., "Getting Beyond Scarcity: A New Paradigm for Assessing the Constitutionality of Broadcast Regulation," *California Law Review* 85 (December 1997): 1687–1747; Roy David Spiceland, Jr., "The Fairness Doctrine, the Chilling Effect and Television Editorials," The University of Tennessee: Knoxville, Doctoral Dissertation (December 1992).

74. Ronald M. Levin, "Fighting the Appearance of Corruption," *Washington University Journal of Law and Policy* 6 (2001): 171–79. The Supreme Court in *Buckley v. Valeo,* 421 U.S. 1 (1976) explicitly rejected the argument that there existed a governmental interest of preventing real or apparent corruption that was sufficient to justify government attempts at "equalizing" the ability of groups and individuals to influence the results of candidate elections with campaign expenditure limits. But compare *Austin v. Michigan Chamber of Commerce,* 494 U.S. 650 (1990), where the Supreme Court sustained a Michigan state restriction that prohibited corporate independent expenditures for assisting candidates for elective office due to the special benefits that states accord corporations, and the "potential for distortion" that aggregate corporate wealth has to distort the political marketplace.

5—CAMPAIGN FINANCE "REFORM" IN THE NEW DEAL

1. "Within the Law," *Time,* 11 August 1944, 19.
2. Alan Brinkley, *The End of Reform* (New York: Vintage Books, 1995), 160–61; Adolf Berle, "Corporations and the Modern State," in Thurmond Arnold, et al., *The Future of Democratic Capitalism* (New York: Holt and Company, 1941), 52–53.
3. David Plotke, *Building a Democratic Political Order* (New York: Cambridge University Press, 1996), 333–47.
4. Richard L. Gordon, "The Public Utility Holding Company Act: The Easy Step in Electric Utility Regulatory Reform," <http://www.cato.org/pubs/regulation/reg15n-1gordon.html> (6/16/2003).
5. Congressional Record, 70-1, HR 5423, 19 February 1935.
6. Arthur M. Schlesinger, *The Politics of Upheaval* (Boston: Houghton Mifflin, 1960), 303–4.
7. 49 Stat. 838, PL 102-486 (26 August 1935); Congressional Record, 70-1, House, *Hearings of the Committee on Interstate and Foreign Commerce,* HR 5423 (22 February 1935), 589.
8. Ibid., *Hearings of the Committee on Interstate and Foreign Commerce,* 343; Arthur Schlesinger, *The Politics of Upheaval* (New York: Houghton Mifflin, 1960), 306–7.
9. 49 Stat 838, Section 12(h)(1), (2).
10. 301 U.S. 1 (1937); Barry Cushman, *Rethinking the New Deal Court* (New York: Oxford University Press, 1998).
11. *Public Papers and Addresses of the President: Franklin D. Roosevelt, 1933–1944* (1946).
12. Schlesinger, *Politics of Upheaval,* 311.
13. Congressional Record, 74-1, House, 10640, 2 July 1935; Congressional Record, 74-1, Senate, 14691, 26 August 1935.
14. Schlesinger, *Politics of Upheaval,* 315–16.
15. Schlesinger, *Politics of Upheaval,* 310; "Utility Lobby War Spreads in Senate to All Other Bills," *The New York Times,* 11 July 1935, 1.

16. "Senators Seize Files, Find Lobby Spent $301,865," *The Washington Post*, 13 July 1935, 1.

17. "Utilities Aid Admits Files Were Burned," *The Washington Post*, 20 July 1935, 1.

18. Congressional Record, 74-1, Senate, S2796, 14691, 26 August 1935; *The Public Utility Holding Company Act of 1935*, 15 U.S.CS Sections 79, et seq.; *North American Co. v. Securities & Exchange Commission*, 327 U.S. 686 (1946).

19. 15 U.S.CS Section 791(h); 15 U.S.CS Section 791(i).

20. Richard S. Kirkendall, "The New Deal as Watershed: The Recent Literature," *The Journal of American History* 54 (March 1968): 839; William E. Leuchtenburg, *Franklin Roosevelt and the New Deal, 1932–1940* (New York: Harper and Row, 1963); David M. Kennedy, *Freedom From Fear: The American People in Depression and War*, 1929–45 (Oxford: Oxford University Press, 1999).

21. Dorothy Ganfield Fowler, "Precursors of the Hatch Act," *The Mississippi Valley Historical Review* 47 (September 1960): 247–62.

22. "175 in WPA Staff of 200 Join $3 Jackson Dinner," *The New York Times*, 6 January 1936, 4; "Jackson Dinner Is Called 'Fraud' on Democracy," *The Washington Post*, 8 January 1936, 3.

23. "Tax on Jobholders Laid to Democrats," *The New York Times*, 6 February 1936, 2.

24. "Vandenburg Calls for Inquiry on WPA," *The New York Times*, 6 March 1936, 15; "Protest Campaign Levy," *The New York Times*, 10 March 1936, 11 (Illinois); "New Charges Spur Inquiries by WPA," *The New York Times*, 22 May 1936, 4 (detailing 700 cases including New York and Indiana); "Republican Claim of Politics in Missouri Relief Adds Fuel to a Warm Campaign," *The New York Times*, 31 May 1936, E10; "Democratic Tickets Sent WPA Workers," *The New York Times*, 21 June 1936, 28 (California); "WPA Assailed by Candidates in Oklahoma," *The Washington Post*, 27 July 1936, X2; "Vote WPA Inquiry in Pennsylvania," *The New York Times*, 29 September 1936, 22; "Coercion Is Laid to Democrats in Tugwell Model Ohio Village," *The Washington Post*, 10 October 1936, X1; "Republicans Seek Jersey WPA Data," *The New York Times*, 15 October 1936, 21.

25. "Farley Disclaims 'Ticket' Letters," *The New York Times*, 18 June 1936, 1; "Farley Censured by Civil Service," *The New York Times*, 18 June 1936, 2.

26. "G.O.P. Charges Fund Inquiry 'Intimidation,'" *The Washington Post*, 19 October 1936, X1; "Coercion Report Held Groundless," *The New York Times*, 21 June 1936, F9.

27. Charles Michelson, *The Ghost Talks* (New York: G. P. Putnam Sons, 1944); Michael J. Webber, *New Deal Fat Cats* (New York: Fordham University Press, 2000), 70–79.

28. "Liberty League Pays Shouse Top Salary," *The New York Times*, 17 March 1936, 7. The present-day value of the salary is calculated on the helpful website <www.eh.net.hmit> (24 June 2004); "Inquiry Is Ordered on Steel 'Coercion,'" *The New York Times*, 1 September 1936, 4; "Industrialists Fighting Roosevelt by Tax Warning on Pay Envelopes," *The New York Times*, 24 October 1936, 1.

29. "Coercing Voters Penalized in Bill," *The New York Times*, 7 March 1936, 6.

30. "$3,500,000 Held Democrats 'Fund,'" *The New York Times*, 2 August 1936, 3; "$13,000,000, Record Spent in Campaign," *The New York Times*, 30 November 1936, 1; Congressional Record, 74-3, Senate Resolution 225 (24 February 1936).

31. "$500,000 Fund Ready to Unite Steel Workers," *The Washington Post*, 30 June 1936, X2.

32. Nelson Lichtenstein, *State of the Union: A Century of American Labor* (Princeton: Princeton University Press, 2002), 39–40, 43; *The Washington Post*, 30 June 1936, X2; "Labor Looms as a Mighty Political Force—But a Divided One," *The Washington Post*, 24 May 1936, B2; "Makings of Class War Seen in Pennsylvania," *The New York Times*, 4 October 1936, E3; "Steel and the Unions Join the Issue," *The New York Times*, 5 July 1936, E6.

33. Louise Overacker, "Campaign Funds in the Presidential Election of 1936," *The American Political Science Review* 31 (June 1937): 489; Louise Overacker, "Labor's Political Contribution," *Political Science Quarterly* 54 (March 1939): 5; Joseph Tanehaus, "Organized Labor's Political Spending: The Law and Its Consequences," *The Journal of Politics* 16 (August 1954): 441; Webber, *Fat Cats,* 7–16.

34. William E. Leuchtenburg, *The FDR Years* (New York: Columbia University Press, 1995), 146–50; William E. Leuchtenburg, *The Supreme Court Reborn* (Oxford: Oxford University Press, 1995), 213–58.

35. Frank R. Kent, "The Great Game of Politics," *The Wall Street Journal,* 12 May 1936, 2; Duncan Aikman, "The Campaign Thunder Begins," *The New York Times,* 26 April 1936, SM1; Joel Siedman, "Organized Labor in Political Campaigns," *Public Opinion Quarterly* 3 (October 1939): 646–54, 651–54.

36. Dorothy Ganfield Fowler, "Precursors of the Hatch Act," *The Mississippi Valley Historical Review* 47 (September 1960): 247–62.

37. Congressional Record, 76-1, Hearings, Senate Committee on Campaign Expenditures (1939); Congressional Record, 76-1, Senate, 22 June 1939, 7708; 53 U.S. Statutes at Large 1147, Section 1 (3 August 1939), Section 2.

38. Ibid., Section 5, 6.

39. Ibid., Section 9 (a).

40. Congressional Record, 76-1, Senate, 27 June 1939, 7708, 7937.

41. Congressional Record, 76-1, House, 20 July 1939, 9595; A. James Reichley, *The Life of the Parties* (Lanham: Rowman & Littlefield Publishers, Inc., 1992), 201–26; Edward McChesney Sait, *American Parties and Elections* (New York: D. Appleton-Century Company, 1942), 227–90.

42. Congressional Record, 76-1, House, 20 July 1939, 9598; Congressional Record, 76-1, Senate, 2 August 1939, 10745–47; "Roosevelt Urges Congress to Study Extension of Ban on Politics to States," *The Washington Post,* 3 August 1939, 1.

43. 54 Statutes at Large 767 (19 July 1940).

44. "Hatch Act Extension Faces Senate Fight Today," *The Washington Post,* 4 March 1940, 1.

45. "President Enters Hatch Act Fight," *The New York Times,* 5 March 1940, 4.

46. "Hatch Act Upheld by Senate, 44–41," *The New York Times,* 7 March 1940, 1.

47. Ibid.; "Barkley Offers to Resign in Fight Over Hatch Bill," *The New York Times,* 9 March 1940.

48. Congressional Record, 76-2, Report, Senate Campaign Expenditures Committee (1940).

49. Congressional Record, 76-3, Senate, S.3046, 14 March 1940, 2853; "$5,000 Gift Limit Tied to Move to Hatch Bill in Move to Kill It," *The New York Times,* 15 March 1940, 1; Congressional Record, 76-3, Senate, 18 March 1940, 2987.

50. "Party Fund Limit Set in Hatch Bill," *The New York Times,* 28 March 1940, 1.

51. "Hatch Bill Taken from Table, 14–11; Sumners Is Bitter," *The New York Times,* 8 May 1940, 1; "By Reversing Secret Ballot Committee Revives Hatch Bill," *The Washington Post,* 8 May 1940, 1.

52. *Messages of the President: Franklin D. Roosevelt, 1933–1945,* 29 December 1940.

53. David S. Muzzey, "All Is Not Lost in the Fight for Democracy," *The New York Times,* 22 January 1939, 95.

54. "World Crisis Seen for Democracy," *The New York Times,* 7 February 1939, 14; "Washington Held Democracy's Ideal," *The New York Times,* 2 February 1939, 17; "Chicago Law Group Fights All 'Isms,'" *The New York Times,* 27 February 1939, 2.

55. Congressional Record, 76-1, House, 20 July 1939, 960; Congressional Record, 76-1, House, 20 July 1939, 9604.

56. Congressional Record, 76-1, House, 20 July 1939, 9609; Congressional Record, 76-1, House, 20 July 1939, 9616.

57. "Prayer for Party Not Against Law," *The New York Times,* 7 April 1940, 17; "Talk Politics, But Privately, Mitchell Warns," *The Washington Post,* 27 July 1940, 3; "Hatch Act to Need 200 to Enforce It," *The Washington Post,* 8 August 1940, 5; "Senate Opens Inquiry into Campaign Outlays," *The New York Times,* 24 April 1940, 65; Senate Special Committee Investigating Campaign Expenditures, *Unpublished Hearings,* 1940; Louise Overacker, "Campaign Finance in the Presidential Election of 1940," *The American Political Science Review* 35 (August 1941): 701–27.

58. 330 U.S. 70 (1947); 330 U.S. 127 (1947); Ferrel Heady, "American Government and Politics: The Hatch Act Decisions," *The American Political Science Review* 41 (August 1947): 687–99.

59. Harry A. Millis and Emily Clark Brown, *From the Wagner Act to Taft-Hartley: A Study of National Labor Policy and Labor Relations* (Chicago: University of Chicago Press, 1950), 3–29.

60. Nelson Lichtenstein, *Walter Reuther: The Most Dangerous Man in Detroit* (New York: Basic Books, 1995), 50.

61. Steven Fraser, *Labor Will Rule: Sidney Hillman and the Rise of American Labor* (New York: The Free Press, 1991), 330–48; Nelson Lichtenstein, *State of the Union: A Century of American Labor* (Princeton: Princeton University Press, 2002), 20–53; J. David Greenstone, *Labor in American Politics* (New York: Alfred A. Knopf, 1969), 45–48.

62. 57 Stat. 163–68 (25 June 1943).

63. Ibid., Section 3, Section 6, Section 10.

64. Ibid., Section 9 (italics added to denote changes in the statute).

65. "The Gallup Poll," *The Washington Post,* 16 June 1943, 17.

66. Joseph Tannehaus, "Organized Labor's Political Spending: The Law and Its Consequences," *The Journal of Politics* 16 (August 1954): 441–71.

67. Congressional Record, 78-1, House, 3 June 1943, 5341; Congressional Record, 78-1, House, 3 June 1943, 5328.

68. Congressional Record, 76-3, House, 14 March 1940, 2852.

69. Ibid., 78-1, House, 3 June 1943, 5341.

70. Ibid., Senate, 12 June 1943, 5755, 5781.

71. Ibid., House, 11 June 1943, 5734.

72. Ibid., House Subcommittee of the Committee on Labor, Hearing (1943), 2–3.

73. Ibid., 32, 45.

74. Ibid., 45.

75. Ibid., 49; "Labor Legislation," *The Washington Post,* 23 January 1943, X8.

76. Congressional Record, 78-1, Senate, 25 June 1943, 6487.

77. Congressional Record, 78-1, House, 25 June 1943, 6548; Senate, 6489.

78. 61 Stat. 136 (1947), commonly known as the "Taft-Hartley Act"; Brooks Jackson, *Honest Graft: Big Money and the American Political Process* (New York: Alfred A. Knopf, 1988); Charles Lewis and The Center for Public Integrity, *The Buying of Congress* (New York: Avon Books, 1998); Susan B. Trento, *The Power House: Robert Keith Gray and the Selling of Access and Influence in Washington* (New York: St. Martin's Press, 1992); Thomas Byrne Edsall, *Power and Money: Writing About Politics, 1971–1987* (New York: W.W. Norton & Co., 1988).

79. Fraser, *Labor Will Rule,* 502; Joseph Gaier, *The First Round: The Story of the CIO Political Action Committee* (New York: Duell, Sloan and Pearce, 1944), 60–61.

80. Ibid., 62, quoting the Statement on Political Action adopted by each of three regional conferences of the CIO, held in Philadelphia (17 July), Chicago (23 July), and Birmingham (21 August); Senate Report 101, 78-3, 79-1, Special Committee to Investigate Presidential, Vice Presidential, and Senatorial Campaign Expenditures in 1944, S. Res. 263 (1945), 21; Louise Overacker, "Presidential Campaign Funds, 1944," *The American Political Science Review* 39 (October 1945): 899–925.

81. "Spangler Attacks CIO Political Funds," *The New York Times*, 31 May 1944, 1; "CIO Sets Up Group on Election Funds," *The New York Times*, 18 June 1944, 29.

82. "Hillman Defends Work of CIO-PAC, Denies Aim to Rule," *The New York Times*, 29 August 1944, 1; "CIO to Use Funds in Coming Elections," *The New York Times*, 20 July 1944; Senate Report 101, 83–84.

83. Ibid., Senate Report, 81–83; 313 U.S. 299 (1941), overruling *U.S. v. Newberry*, 256 U.S. 323 (1921); Public Law 544, 78th Congress, HR 2973, 23 December 1944; Joseph Rosenfarb, "Labor's Role in the Election," *Public Opinion Quarterly* 8 (Autumn 1944): 376–90.

84. Ibid., Senate Report, 84.

85. Congressional Record, 78-2, House, *Committee to Investigate Campaign Expenditures, Part I–II*, August–December 1944; Congressional Record 78-2, House Report, *Special Committee to Investigate Campaign Expenditures for the House of Representatives*, 1944, 2 January 1945, 7, 11–12.

86. Ibid., Special Committee, 12; Greenstone, *Labor in American Politics* (New York: Alfred A. Knopf, 1969); Terry Catchpole, *How to Cope with COPE: The Political Operations of Organized Labor* (New York: Arlington House, 1968).

87. Millis and Brown, 655–65; The Labor Management Relations Act is found at 61 Stat. 136 (23 June 1947); Congressional Record, 80-1, House, Committee on Education and Labor, Hearings, H.R. 8, H.R. 725, H.R. 880, H R. 1095, H. R. 1096 (March 1947); Congressional Record, 80-1, Senate, Hearings Before the Committee on Labor and Public Welfare, S. 55 and S. J. Res., 22 (February 1947).

88. Lichtenstein, *State of the Union*, 171–73; Frances Fox Piven and Richard A. Cloward, *The Breaking of the American Social Compact* (New York: The New Press, 1997), 17–39.

89. 335 U.S. 106 (1948), 121.

90. 352 U.S. 567 (1957).

91. Elizabeth S. Clemens, *The People's Lobby* (Chicago: University of Chicago Press, 1997); Theodore J. Eismeier and Philip H. Pollock III, "Strategy and Choice in Congressional Elections: The Role of Political Action Committees," *American Journal of Political Science* 30 (February 1986): 197–213; Nolan McCarthy and Lawrence S. Rothenberg, "Commitment and the Campaign Contribution Contract," *American Journal of Political Science* 40 (August 1996): 872–904; Harry Holloway, "Interest Groups in the Post-Partisan Era: The Political Machine of the AFL-CIO," *Political Science Quarterly* 94 (Spring 1979): 117–33; Andrew Stark, "Corporate Electoral Activity, Constitutional Discourse, and Conceptions of the Individual," *The American Political Science Review* 86 (September 1992): 626–37; Daniel Nelson, "The CIO at Bay: Labor Militancy and Politics in Akron, 1936–1938," *The Journal of American History* 71 (December 1984): 565–86; Robert J. Norrell, "Labor at the Ballot Box: Alabama Politics from the New Deal to the Dixiecrat Movement," *The Journal of Southern History* 57 (May 1991): 201–34; Harry M. Scoble, "Organized Labor in Electoral Politics: Some Questions for the Discipline," *The Western Political Quarterly* 16 (September 1963): 666–85.

6—PROFESSIONALIZING POLITICS AND THE "DE-POLITICAL" COURT

1. Stephen E. Ambrose, *Eisenhower: The President* (Simon & Schuster: New York, 1984), 190; Ed Cray, *Chief Justice: A Biography of Earl Warren* (Simon & Schuster: New York, 1997), 10; Earl Warren, *Memoirs* (Doubleday: New York, 1977), 5.

2. Julian Zelizer, *On Capitol Hill* (Cambridge: Cambridge University Press, 2004); Sidney M. Milkis, *Political Parties and Constitutional Government: Reconstructing American Democracy* (Baltimore: Johns Hopkins University Press, 1999); Sidney Milkis, *The Presidents and the Parties: The Transformation of the American Party System since the New Deal* (New York: Oxford University Press, 1993).

3. Julian Zelizer, "Seeds of Cynicism: The Struggle over Campaign Finance, 1956–1974," *The Journal of Policy History* 14 (2002): 73–111.

4. Congressional Record, 78-1, S. Res. 1, 1942; Anthony J. Badger, *The New Deal: The Depression Years, 1933–1940* (New York: Hill and Wang, 1989); Alan Brinkley, *The End of Reform* (New York: Random House, 1995); David Plotke, *Building a Democratic Political Order* (Cambridge: Cambridge University Press, 1996); John A. Perkins, "American Government and Politics: Congressional Self-Improvement," *The American Political Science Review* 38 (June 1944): 499–511.

5. George B. Galloway, "The Operation of the Legislative Reorganization Act of 1946," *The American Political Science Review* 45 (March 1951): 41; Congressional Record, 79-2, S. Rep. No. 1400, 1946; Congressional Record, 79-2, Statement by Representative Monroney on the Legislative Reorganization Act of 1946 (1946), 27–33; Estes Kefauver, "Congressional Reorganization," An Address to the Southern Political Science Association at Knoxville, Tennessee, 8 November 1946, reprinted in *The Journal of Politics* 9 (February 1947): 96; Kefauver, 97–98; Congressional Record, 79-2, "The Legislative Reorganization Act of 1946," S.2177, 2 August 1946, 10625; 60 Stat 753, PL 60 (1946).

6. George E. Outland, "Congress Still Needs Reorganization," *The Western Political Quarterly* 1 (June 1948): 155; *Strengthening the Congress* (Washington, D.C.: National Planning Association, 1945); Francis N. Thorpe, *American Charters, Constitutions and Organic Laws* (Washington, D.C.: Government Printing Office, 1909), Volume V, 3129; *Statutes of California*, Constitution, Article IV, Section 35 (1947); Edgar Lane, *Lobbying and the Law* (Berkeley: University of California Press, 1954), 37–39.

7. Belle Zeller, "American Government and Politics: The Federal Regulation of Lobbying Act," *The American Political Science Review* 42 (April 1948): 239–71, 242.

8. Hope Eastman, *Lobbying: A Constitutionally Protected Right* (Washington, D.C.: American Enterprise Institute, 1977); Outland, 155; Congressional Record, 79-2, Senate Bill 2177, 10740, 2 August 1946; *Federal Regulation of Lobbying Act of 1946*, PL 79-601, 60 Stat. 839–42 (codified at 2 U.S.C. Sections 261–70 [1994]).

9. James K. Pollock, Jr., "The Regulation of Lobbying," *The American Political Science Review* 21 (May 1927): 335–41; *The Foreign Agents Registration Act*, 52 Stat. 327 (8 June 1938); 60 Stat. Section 303, 307; Section 308.

10. Congressional Record 79-2, Senate Report 1011 (1946), 26–27; Congressional Record 79-2, Senate Report 1400 (1946), 5.

11. Congressional Record, 79-2, 2201, 13 March 1946.

12. W. Brooke Graves, *Administration of the Lobby Registration Provisions of the Legislative Reorganization Act of 1946: An Analysis of Experience during the Eightieth Congress* (Washington, D.C.: Government Printing Office, 1950).

13. *United States v. Rumely*, 345 U.S. 41 (1952), 57.

14. *United States v. Harriss*, 347 U.S. 612 (1954), 613.

15. 347 U.S. 612, 619.

16. Ibid., 625.

17. Ibid., 626.

18. Scott Ainsworth, "Regulating Lobbyists and Interest Group Influence," *Journal of Politics* 55 (February 1993): 41–56; Steven A. Browne, "The Constitutionality of Lobby Reform: Implicating Associational Privacy and the Right to Petition the Government," *William and Mary Bill of Rights Journal* 4 (Winter 1995): 717–50; Juliet Eilperin, "Ex-Lawmakers' Edge Is Access," *The Washington Post*, 12 September 2003, A1.

19. Congressional Record, 83-2, House, *Report of Special Committee to Investigate Campaign Contributions*, 2 November 1954.

20. Congressional Record, 84-1, Senate Report 629, *Federal Elections Act of 1955* (22 June 1955).

21. Ibid., 9; Ibid., *Minority Views*, 37–41.

22. Darrell M. West, *Air Wars: Television Advertising in Election Campaigns, 1952–2000* (Washington, D.C.: CQ Press, 2001), 3; G. D. Wiebe, "Merchandising Commodities and Citizenship on Television," *Public Opinion Quarterly* 15 (Winter 1951–1952): 679–91, 691; Dennis W. Johnson, *No Place for Amateurs: How Political*

Consultants Are Reshaping American Democracy (New York: Routledge, 2001); Larry Sabato, *The Rise of Political Consultants* (New York: Basic Books, Inc., 1981); Robert J. Dinkin, *Campaigning in America* (New York: Greenwood Press, 1989); Robert Agranoff, *The New Style in Election Campaigns* (Boston: Holbrook Press, Inc., 1976); David J. Swanson and Paolo Mancini, eds., *Politics, Media and Modern Democracy* (Westport, CT: Praeger, 1966); Edie N. Goldenberg and Michael W. Traugott, "Mass Media in U.S. Congressional Elections," *Legislative Studies Quarterly* 12 (August 1987): 317–39; Stanley Kelley, Jr., "P. R. Man: Political Mastermind," *The New York Times Magazine,* 2 September 1956, 6.

23. Zelizer, *Seeds,* 74; Congressional Record, 84-2, Senate Subcommittee on Privileges and Elections, *Hearings, Part I* (1956), 11; Alexander Heard, *The Costs of Democracy* (Chapel Hill: University of North Carolina Press, 1960).

24. "Senate on Trial," *The Washington Post,* 6 February 1956, 16; "Paper Official Tells Details of $2500 'Gift,'" *The Washington Post and Times Herald,* 8 February 1956, 47; George Gallup, "Public Seen Ready to Contribute $75 Million to Political Parties," *The Washington Post and Times Herald,* 11 January 1956, 1; Roscoe Drummond, "Campaign Funds; Senate Timidity Noted," *The Washington Post and Times Herald,* 17 February 1956, 29.

25. Congressional Record 85-1, Subcommittee on Privileges and Elections, *Senate Committee Report* (1957), 1.

26. Congressional Record, 84-1, Select Campaign Finance Committee Hearings (1956), 3–4, 11.

27. Ibid., 14.

28. Ibid., 61–64.

29. Congressional Record, 84-2, Senate Subcommittee on Privileges and Elections, Senate Report, *1956 General Election Campaigns* (1957), 3–4.

30. Ibid., 5

31. Robert C. Albright, "'Honest Elections' Bill Faces Dim Prospect," *The Washington Post and Times Herald,* 24 June 1956, A2; "UAW Urges Reform Plan for Elections," *The Washington Post and Times Herald,* 14 July 1956, 2.

32. Congressional Record, 84-1, Select Campaign Finance Committee Hearings (1956), 149.

33. Ibid., 153.

34. 313 U.S. 288 (1941); 395 U.S. 367 (1969); David M. Bixby, "The Roosevelt Court, Democratic Ideology, and Minority Rights: Another Look at *United States v. Classic,*" *The Yale Law Review* 90 (March 1981): 741–97; Mary Dudziak, *Cold War Civil Rights* (Princeton: Princeton University Press, 2000); S. Sidney Ulmer, "Supreme Court Behavior and Civil Rights," *Western Political Quarterly* 13 (June 1960): 288–311; Jerold S. Auerbach, *Unequal Justice* (Oxford: Oxford University Press, 1976); John Hart Ely, *On Constitutional Ground* (Princeton: Princeton University Press, 1996).

35. Bixby, *Roosevelt Court,* 786–87.

36. Alexander Keyssar, *The Right to Vote* (New York: Basic Books, 2000), 245.

37. 273 U.S. 536 (1927); *Nixon v. Condon,* 286 U.S. 73 (1932), quoting Texas Statutes, Chapter 67, Article 3107 (1927); 286 U.S. at 104.

38. 295 U.S. 45, 47 (1935).

39. Ibid., 308.

40. Ibid., 308, 320; Bixby, *Roosevelt Court,* 797, footnote 355.

41. *Near v. Minnesota,* 283 U.S. 697, 719–20 (1931).

42. *Colgrove v. Green,* 328 U.S. 549, 555; Alexander M. Bickel, *The Least Dangerous Branch: The Supreme Court at the Bar of Politics* (New Haven: Yale University Press, 1962), 183–97; Fritz W. Scharpf, "Judicial Review and the Political Question: A Functional Analysis," *Yale Law Journal* 75 (1966): 517; Herbert Wechsler, "Toward Neutral Principles of Constitutional Law," *Harvard Law Review* 73 (1959): 1, passim; Mark Tushnet, "The Transformation and Disappearance of the Political Question Doctrine," *North Carolina Law Review* 80 (May 2002).

43. Richard Kluger, *Simple Justice* (New York: Random House, 1975); Mark Tushnet, *The NAACP Strategy Against Segregated Education, 1925–1950* (Chapel Hill: University of North Carolina Press, 1987); Morton J. Horowitz, *The Warren Court and the Pursuit of Justice* (New York: Hill and Wang, 1998); Lucas A. Powe, Jr., *The Warren court and American Politics* (Cambridge: Belknap Press, 2000); Ed Cray, *Chief Justice: A Biography of Earl Warren* (New York: Simon & Schuster, 1997).

44. John Hart Ely, *On Constitutional Ground* (Princeton: Princeton University Press, 1996), 183; G. Edward White, "Free Speech and the Bifurcated Review Project: The 'Preferred Position' Cases" in Sandra F. Vanburkleo, Kermit L. Hall, and Robert J. Kaczorowski, eds., *Constitutionalism and American Culture: Writing the New Constitutional History* (Lawrence: University of Kansas Press, 2002), 99–122.

45. White, *Earl Warren*, 238; Cray, 379; *Baker v. Carr*, 369 U.S. 186 (1962); 328 U.S. 549 (1946).

46. White, *Earl Warren*, 236–39; Earl Warren, *Memoirs* (New York: Doubleday, 1977), 308–10, quoting from *Reynolds v. Sims*, 377 U.S. 533 (1964); Richard C. Cortner, *The Apportionment Cases* (New York: W. W. Norton & Co., 1970); J. Morgan Kousser, *Colorblind Injustice: Minority Voting Rights and the Undoing of the Second Reconstruction* (Chapel Hill: University of North Carolina Press, 1999); Richard K. Scher, Jon L. Mills, and John J. Hotaling, *Voting Rights and Democracy: The Law and Politics of Districting* (Chicago: Nelson-Hall Publishers, 1997); Keyssar, 266–76.

47. Anthony Lewis, *Make No Law: The Sullivan Case and the First Amendment* (New York: Vintage Books, 1991); "Heed Their Rising Voices," *The New York Times*, 29 March 1960, L25.

48. Lewis, *Make No Law*, 11, 31–33.

49. Hall, *Constitutionalism and American Culture*, 273.

50. *United States v. Carolene Products Co.*, 304 U.S. 144 (1938), 153; *Beauharnais v. Illinois*, 343 U.S. 250 (1952); 376 U.S. 254 (1964), 270, 278–79; G. Edward White, *Free Speech and Bifurcated Review*, 100–1.

51. White, ibid., 117; Cray, *Chief Justice*, 410–11; *The Gallup Poll Cumulative Index, 1937–1997* (Delaware: Scholarly Resources, Inc., 1999), 1963 results; Robert E. Semple, Jr., "Nixon Decries 'Lawless Society' and Urges Limited Wiretapping," *The New York Times*, 9 May 1968, 1; "Justices, Not Candidates," *The New York Times*, 3 September 1968, 42.

52. *Powell v. McCormack*, 395 U.S. 486 (1969); Congressional Record, 87-2, Senate Report, *Senate Election, Expulsion, and Censure Cases* (1962).

53. "Comment: Legislative Exclusion: Julian Bond and Adam Clayton Powell," *University of Chicago Law Review* 35 (Fall 1967): 157; *Bond v. Floyd*, 385 U.S. 116 (1966); 395 U.S. at 548.

54. Cray, *Chief Justice*, 500.

55. 395 U.S. 367 (1969); Records of the Supreme Court, Red Lion Broadcasting Co., Inc. v. Federal Communication Commission, *Amicus Briefs*.

56. 395 U.S. 378, 389.

57. "Lodge Asks U.S. to Prove Democracy," *The Washington Post*, 11 October 1962, A2; "Students Learn Democracy of the Voting Machine," *The New York Times*, 18 April 1962, 39; Arnaldo Cortesi, "Vatican Calls Kennedy Election Proof of American Democracy," *The New York Times*, 10 November 1960, 1.

58. Powe, Jr., *Warren Court*, 252–55.

59. Zelizer, *Seeds*, 80–81; Brooks Jackson, *Honest Graft: Big Money and the American Political Process* (New York: Alfred A. Knopf, 1988); David W. Adamany and George E. Agree, *Political Money: A Strategy for Campaign Financing in America* (Baltimore: Johns Hopkins University Press, 1975); Heard, *The Costs of Democracy*, 7–8; Herbert E. Alexander, *Studies in Money in Politics*, Volume I–III (Princeton: Citizens' Research Foundation, 1991).

60. Adamany, 23.

61. Congressional Record, 87-2, Senate, Committee on Rules and Administration, *Legislative Recommendations of the President's Commission on Campaign Costs*, 29

May 1962, 2; Congressional Record, 87-2, Senate Report 871, Federal Elections Act of 1961, S. 2426, 5 September 1961.

62. Amitai Etzioni, *Capital Corruption: The New Attack on American Democracy* (New Brunswick: Transaction Books, 1988); Elizabeth Drew, *Politics and Money: The New Road to Corruption* (New York: MacMillan Publishing Company, 1983); Elizabeth Drew, *The Corruption of American Politics: What Went Wrong and Why* (New York: Overlook Press, 1999); Philip M. Stern, *The Best Congress Money Can Buy* (New York: Pantheon Books, 1988); Larry Sabato and Glenn R. Simpson, *Dirty Little Secrets: The Persistence of Corruption in American Politics* (New York: Random House, 1996); Larry J. Sabato, *PAC Power: Inside the World of Political Action Committees* (New York: W. W. Norton & Co., 1984); Charles Lewis and The Center for Public Integrity, *The Buying of Congress: How Special Interests Have Stolen Your Right to Life, Liberty, and the Pursuit of Happiness* (New York: Avon Books, 1998); Michael J. Malbin, *Parties, Interest Groups and Campaign Finance Laws* (Washington, D.C.: American Enterprise Institute for Public Policy Research, 1980).

63. Congressional Record, 89-2, Committee on House Administration, House Resolution 15317, *Analysis of Proposed Revision of Federal Election Laws,* 1966; Congressional Record, 89-2, Senate, S. Res. 1530, Presidential Election Campaign Fund of 1966 (1966); ibid., Senator Russell Long, *Statement of the Conference Report,* 10 November 1966.

64. *1966 Congressional Quarterly Almanac* (Washington, D.C.: Congressional Quarterly, Inc., 1967), 484–500; Zelizer, *Seeds,* 85–87. In 1967 Congress repealed the short-lived provisions of the Presidential Election Campaign Fund of 1966; PL 90-27, HR 6950, 16 June 1967; Congressional Record, 90-1, Senate Report 515, Election Reform Act of 1967, 16 August 1967; Congressional Record, 90-2, House Report 1593, Election Reform Act of 1968, 27 June 1968.

65. Charles Redenius, *The American Ideal of Equality: From Jefferson's Declaration to the Burger Court* (New York: Kennikat Press, 1981), 124–38.

66. Cray, *Chief Justice,* 260–61, 272; White, *Earl Warren,* 153–55.

67. Henry J. Abraham, *Justices and Presidents: A Political History of Appointments to the Supreme Court,* 3rd edition (New York: Oxford University Press, 1992), 254.

68. *ABA Standards on Judicial Selection* (Chicago: American Bar Association, 2001); Letter from Albert Gonzales, Counsel to President George W. Bush, to Martha W. Barrett, President, ABA, 21 March 2001, <http://www.whitehouse.gov/news/releases/2001/03/2001_0322-5.html> (18 November 2003).

69. Roberta Cooper Ramo and N. Lee Cooper, "The American Bar Association's Integral Role in the Federal Judicial Selection Process: Excerpted Testimony of Roberta Cooper Ramo and N. Lee Cooper Before the Judiciary Committee of the United States Senate, May 21, 1996," *St. John's Journal of Legal Commentary* 12 (Fall 1996): 106; Governor George C. Wallace, Various Speeches (1964) (transcripts available in Reel 1 of Papers of George C. Wallace, State Archives, Montgomery, Alabama); Donald Bruce Johnson, ed., *National Party Platforms: 1840–1976,* Volume II (Urbana: University of Illinois Press, 1978), 132; Barry M. Goldwater, *The Speeches, Remarks and Press Conferences, and Related Papers of Senator Barry M. Goldwater,* Personal Papers of Barry Goldwater (Arizona Historical Foundation), 1964 Presidential Campaign Box; Alan F. Westin, "When the Public Judges the Court," *The New York Times,* 31 May 1959, SM16; Fred Rodell, "The 'Warren Court' Stands Its Ground," *The New York Times,* 27 September 1964, SM23; Fred Rodell, "It Is the Warren Court," *The New York Times,* 13 March 1966; Alexander M. Bickel, "Is the Warren Court Too Political?" *The New York Times,* 25 September 1966, 244; Lewis M. Steel, "Nine Men in Black Who Think White," *The New York Times,* 13 October 1968, SM56; John Micklewait and Adrian Wooldridge, *The Right Nation: Conservative Power in America* (New York: The Penguin Press, 2004), 40–43.

70. Stephen F. Ambrose, *Nixon: The Triumph of a Politician, 1962–1972* (New York: Simon and Schuster, 1989), 154; Donald Grier Stephenson, Jr., *Campaigns and the*

Courts: The U.S. Supreme Court in Presidential Elections (New York: Columbia University Press, 1999), 181; *Nixon/Wallace 1968 TV Election Spots* (Chicago: International Historic Films, 1985); Cray, *Chief Justice*, 497.

71. Bernard Schwartz, *The Ascent of Pragmatism: The Burger Court in Action* (Massachusetts: Addison-Wesley Publishing Company, Inc., 1990), 19–39.

72. John Hart Ely, *Democracy and Distrust: A Theory of Judicial Interpretation* (Cambridge: Harvard University Press, 1980).

7—COINING CORRUPTION

1. Carl Bernstein and Bob Woodward, *All the President's Men* (New York: Simon and Schuster, 1974), 74; Public Law 93-443, 88 Stat. 1263 (1974).

2. FECA 1971 is found at Public Law 92-225, 88 Stat. 1263 (1972); 421 U.S. 1 (1976).

3. Julian Zelizer, *On Capitol Hill* (Cambridge: Cambridge University Press, 2004).

4. Nixon appointed Chief Justice Warren Burger to succeed Earl Warren in 1969; he appointed Harry Blackmun to succeed Abe Fortas in 1970; he appointed Lewis Powell to succeed Hugo L. Black and William Rehnquist to succeed John Harlan in 1972. Charles M. Lamb and Stephen C. Halpern, *The Burger Court: Political and Judicial Profiles* (Urbana: University of Illinois Press, 1991), 21.

5. Stephen E. Ambrose, *Nixon: The Education of a Politician, 1913–1962* (New York: Simon & Schuster, 1987), 276, 284–85.

6. *Nixon Checkers Speech*, <http://www.pbs.org/wgbh/amex/presidents/nf/resource/nixon/primdocs/checkers.html> (17 February 2004).

7. Ibid.

8. Ambrose, *Nixon*, 290.

9. *1967 Congressional Quarterly Almanac* (Washington, D.C.: Congressional Quarterly, Inc. 1968), 579.

10. Robert B. Semple, Jr., "Nixon Decries 'Lawless Society' and Urges Limited Wiretapping," *The New York Times*, 9 May 1968, 1; "Nixon Links Court to Rise in Crime," *The New York Times*, 31 May 1968, 18; Fred P. Graham, "Warren Says All Share Crime Onus," *The New York Times*, 2 August 1968, 1.

11. *Watergate Plus 30: Shadow of History* (PBS Video: Carlton Productions, 2003).

12. E. W. Kenworthy, "Burger Nomination Is Lauded by Conservative Member of the Senate Judiciary Panel," *The New York Times*, 22 May 1969, 37; Louis M. Kohlmeier, "The Burger Court," *The New York Times*, 23 May 1969, 18; Fred P. Graham, "Burger Makes Some Changes," *The New York Times*, 14 December 1969, E9; James M. McNaughton, "Early Vote Asked; President Asserts His Nominees Epitomize Conservative View," *The New York Times*, 22 October 1971, 1; "The Changing of the Court," *The New York Times*, 24 October 1971, E14.

13. Vincent Blasi, ed., *The Burger Court: The Counter-Revolution That Wasn't* (New Haven: Yale University Press, 1983).

14. Bernard Schwartz, *The Burger Court: Counter-Revolution or Confirmation?* (New York: Oxford University Press, 1998), 6; Bernard Schwartz, *The Ascent of Pragmatism: The Burger Court in Action* (Boston, Massachusetts: Addison-Wesley Publishing Co., Inc., 1990).

15. Elston E. Roady, "Florida's New Campaign Expense Law and the 1952 Democratic Gubernatorial Primaries," *American Political Science Review* 48 (June 1954): 465–76; Elson E. Roady, "Ten Years of Florida's 'Who Gave It—Who Got It' Law," *Law and Contemporary Problems* 17 (Summer 1962): 434–54.

16. *1967 Congressional Quarterly Almanac* (Washington, D.C.: Congressional Quarterly Inc., 1968), 284; Congressional Record, 91-1, S. 2876, *The Campaign Broadcast Reform Act of 1970*, 10 September 1969; Robert L. Peabody, Jeffrey M. Berry, William G. Frasure, and Jerry Goldman, *To Enact a Law* (New York: Praeger Publishers, 1972).

17. U.S. Code Congressional and Administrative News, 92-2, Senate Report 92–95, Volume 2 (1972), 1773–74; Zelizer, *On Capitol Hill*, 4–13.

18. Federal Election Campaign Act 1971, Title I, Section 102(a) (1972).

19. F. Leslie Smith, Milar Meeske, and John W. Wright, III, *Electronic Media and Government* (New York: Allyn & Bacon, 1994), 311–20.

20. Congressional Record, 92-2, Senate Joint Resolution 207, Public Law 92-677 (1972).

21. U.S. Code Congressional and Administrative News, 92-2, Volume 2, Senate Report 92-96 (1972), 1775–76.

22. Ibid., 1776–77.

23. Ibid., 1826.

24. Ibid.

25. Ibid., 1832, 1857.

26. Ibid., 1880–81, 1876.

27. The Revenue Act of 1971, Public Law 91-178, 92-2, Title VII (tax deductions and credits), and Title VIII (the Presidential Election Campaign Fund Act of 1971); David Adamany and George Agree, "Election Campaign Financing: The 1974 Reforms," *Political Science Quarterly* 90 (Summer 1975): 204.

28. 347 F. Supp 1061 (United States District Court, SDNY, 1972), 1067. Those provisions appear at Section 104(b) of Title I of the act, expressed in Section 4.4 of the regulations, which reads "A use of communications media is deemed to be on behalf of the candidacy of any such candidate if the use (1) involves his participation by voice or image or advocates his candidacy; or (2) identifies the candidate, directly or by implication, or advocates his candidacy."

29. 290 U.S. 534 (1934); 347 F. Supp. at 1068–69.

30. 469 F. 2d 1135 (U.S.CA, 2nd Circuit, 1972), 1139, quoting Section 301 of FECA 1971.

31. Ibid., at 1141.

32. Ibid., at 1142; Thomas Emerson, *The System of Free Expression* (New York: Vintage, 1970), 640.

33. 11 C.F.R. Sections 4.4, 4.5, 5.5; 366 F. Supp. 1041 (U.S.D.C., District of Columbia, 1973).

34. 11 C.F.R. Section 4.5 (1972); 366 F. Supp. at 1051.

35. James A. Gardner, "Liberty, Community, and the Constitutional Structure of Political Influence: A Reconsideration of the Right to Vote," *University of Pennsylvania Law Review* 145 (April 1997): 893–985, 942.

36. Les Evans and Allen Myers, *Watergate and the Myth of American Democracy* (New York: Pathfinder Press, 1974), 38.

37. Tom Wicker, *One of Us* (New York: Random House, 1991); Stanley I. Kutler, *The Wars of Watergate* (New York: W. W. Norton Co., 1990); Richard Ben-Veniste and George Frampton, Jr., *Stonewall* (New York: Simon & Schuster, 1977); Carl Bernstein and Bob Woodward, *All the President's Men* (New York: Simon & Schuster, 1974); Stanley I. Kutler, *Abuse of Power* (New York: Simon & Schuster, 1997); Sam J. Ervin, Jr., *The Whole Truth* (New York: Random House, 1980); Philip B. Kurland, *Watergate and the Constitution* (Chicago: University of Chicago Press, 1978); L. H. LaRue, *Political Discourse: A Case Study of the Watergate Affair* (Atlanta: University of Georgia Press, 1988).

38. Wicker, *One of Us*, 679.

39. Ibid., 3

40. Ibid., 19–20.

41. Ibid., 22; Kutler, *The Wars of Watergate*, 198–209.

42. Congressional Record, 93-2, Senate, Report 93-981, *Senate Select Committee on Campaign Finance Abuses ("Watergate Committee")*, 493, 495.

43. Congressional Record, *Watergate Committee*, 446–529.

44. Ibid., 202–6.

45. Kutler, *Abuse of Power*, 122, 494.

46. Ibid., vi; Congressional Record, *Watergate Committee* (1974).

47. Robert N. Roberts and Marion T. Doss, Jr., *From Watergate to Whitewater: The Public Integrity War* (Westport, Connecticut: Praeger Press, 1997), 118; John Mickelthwait and Adrian Wooldridge, *The Right Nation: Conservative Power in America* (New York: Penguin Press, 2004), 63–93.

48. A. James Reichley, "Getting at the Roots of Watergate," in David C. Saffell, ed., *Watergate: Its Effects on the American Political System* (Cambridge: Winthrop Publishers, Inc., 1974), 3–10; Charles Peters, "Why the White House Didn't Get the Watergate Story," ibid., 25–33.

49. Congressional Record, *Watergate Committee*, ix–xii.

50. Ibid., 107–8.

51. Ibid., 211–12.

52. Ibid., 564–77.

53. Ibid., 1108–09.

54. Ibid., 1112–14.

55. Ibid., 1098, 1101.

56. Ibid., 1213, 1221.

57. Ibid., 1227–29.

58. Daniel D. Polsby, "*Buckley v. Valeo*: The Special Nature of Political Speech," *Supreme Court Review* 17 (1976), 1–43; Ralph K. Winter, "The History and Theory of *Buckley v. Valeo*," *Journal of Law and Policy* 6 (1997–1998): 93–109; Joel M. Gora, "*Buckley v. Valeo*: A Landmark of Political Freedom," *Akron Law Review* 33 (1999): 7–38; Debra Burke, "Twenty Years After the Federal Election Campaign Act Amendments of 1974: Look Who's Running Now," *Dickinson Law Review* 99 (Winter 1995): 357–91; Russell V. Burris, "The Narrow Application of Buckley v. Valeo: Is Campaign Finance Reform Possible in the Eighth Circuit?" *Missouri Law Review* 64 (Spring 1999): 437–58; Spencer A. Overton, "Mistaken Identity: Unveiling the Property Characteristics of Political Money," *Vanderbilt Law Review* 53 (May 2000): 1235–1310; David Schultz, "Revisiting Buckley v. Valeo: Eviscerating the Line Between Candidate Contributions and Independent Expenditures," *Journal of Law and Politics* 14 (Winter 1988): 33–107.

59. Public Law 93-443, 88 Stat. 1263, S. 3044, Section 101 (1974).

60. Ibid., Section 101 (f)(2), (h); Sections 103, 202.

61. Congressional Record, 92-3, The Revenue Act of 1971, Public Law 92-178 (1972), Title VII (tax deductions and credits) and Title VIII (the Presidential Election Campaign Fund Act of 1971); Adamany and Agree, *Political Money*, 204.

62. U.S. Code Congressional and Administrative News, 93-2, Volume 3, *Legislative History of Public Law 93-443* (1974), 5589.

63. Ibid., 3391–5592.

64. Ibid., 5594.

65. Ibid., 5594.

66. Ibid., 5605.

67. Ibid., 3617; Congressional Record, 93-1, S. 372 (30 July 1973). The official title of the bill was The Federal Election Campaign Act of 1973 (FECA 1974), and it was considered by both the Commerce and the Rules and Administration Committee due to its overlapping subject matter.

68. Federal Election Campaign Amendments of 1974, PL 93-443, 88 Stat. 1263, 10 October 1974. The law became effective on 1 January 1975; Adamany and Agree, *Political Money*, 207–9.

69. Congressional Record 93-1, *FECA 1974*, 5664–66, 5692–93 (1974).

70. U.S. Code Congressional and Administrative News, 93-2, Federal Election Campaign Act Amendments of 1974, Volume 1, 19074, 1436–38 (1974).

71. Ibid., 1451–58.

72. Ibid., 1457–68.

73. Sidney Milkis, *The President and the Parties* (Oxford: Oxford University Press, 1993), 300; A. James Reichley, *The Life of the Parties* (Lanham: Rowman & Littlefield Publishers, Inc., 1992), 304–6; Lewis L. Gould, *Grand Old Party* (New York: Random House, 2003); Jules Whitcover, *Party of the People* (New York: Random House, 2003).

74. Sunstein, *The Partial Constitution* (Cambridge: Harvard University Press, 1997), 253–56.

75. Sorauf, "Politics, Experience and the First Amendment," *The American Political Science Review* 48 (September 1954): 1350; Philip B. Kurland, *Watergate and the Constitution* (Chicago: University of Chicago Press, 1978), 180–88.

76. *Buckley v. Valeo*, 387 F. Supp. 135 (U.S.D.C., D.C.), 24 January 1975.

77. The 2003 decision in *McConnell v. FEC* examined the history of the campaign finance law, and considered but did not overrule *Buckley*. In that most recent case, the debate continued about the definition of corruption as it related to the interest of Congress to regulate money in elections. See particularly, the opinions of Justice Sandra Day O'Connor and the dissent of Justice Anthony Kennedy.

78. 424 U.S. 1, at 48, quoting *New York Times v. Sullivan*, 376 U.S. at 266.

79. 424 U.S. at 649; 395 U.S. 367 (1969).

80. Del Dickson, ed., *The Supreme Court in Conference: 1940–1985* (Oxford: Oxford University Press, 2001), 866–72.

81. Ibid.

82. Ibid., 249.

83. Christopher P. Banks and John C. Green, eds., *Superintending Democracy: The Courts and the Political Process* (Akron: University of Akron Press, 2001); David K. Ryden, ed., *The U.S. Supreme Court and the Electoral Process* (Washington, D.C.: Georgetown University Press, 2000); Richard Pacelle, *The Role of the Supreme Court in American Politics: The Least Dangerous Branch?* (New York: Westview Press, 2001); John E. Schmidhauser, *Constitutional Law in the Political Process* (Chicago: Rand McNally & Company, 1963).

CONCLUSION—FROM *BUCKLEY* TO BCRA AND BEYOND

1. Public Law 94-283, 90 Stat. 1339 (1976); *FEC v. McConnell*, 539 U.S. 911 (2003); *Randall v. Sorrell*, No. 04-1528 (26 June 2006).

2. Daniel H. Lowenstein, "BCRA and *McConnell* in Perspective," *Election Law Journal* 3 (Spring 2004): 277–83; 528 U.S. 377 (2000), 388; Richard L. Hasen, "Shrink Missouri, Campaign Finance, and the 'Thing That Wouldn't Leave,'" *Constitutional Commentary* 17 (Winter 2000): 483–509; *Nixon v. Shrink Missouri*, 528 U.S. 377 (2000).

3. 435 U.S. 765 (1977), 778.

4. Ibid., 789.

5. Ibid., 792; *Citizens Against Rent Control v. Berkeley* 454 U.S. 290 (1981); *Buckley v. American Constitutional Law Foundation, Inc.*, 525 U.S. 182 (1999); David S. Broder, *Democracy Derailed: Initiative Campaigns and the Power of Money* (New York: Harcourt Inc., 2000).

6. *Buckley v. Valeo*, 424 U.S. 1 (1976), 44. The express language footnote would, in the 1992 and 1996 election, allow the opening of the floodgates for "sham issue ads," ads that avoided the express advocacy language, but clearly advocated for a party or candidate position. Avoiding the language of footnote 52 permitted the collection and expenditure of vast sums of "soft money," money unregulated by FECA 1974.

7. *FEC v. Massachusetts Citizens for Life, Inc.*, 479 U.S. 238 (1986), 251.

8. 494 U.S. 652 (1990), 659–60.

9. Ibid., 665; *California Medical Association v. FEC*, 453 U.S. 182 (1981), sustaining the FECA provision against unincorporated associations contributing more than $5,000 to multicandidate political committees; *FEC v. National Right to Work Committee*, 459 U.S. 197 (1982), permitting solicitation of campaign funds by a nonstock corporation from persons who may be members, even though they had no prior membership

arrangement with the corporation; *FEC v. Beaumont,* 123 U.S. 2200 (1003), ruling that the provisions of FECA 1974 prohibiting direct contributions to candidates for federal elections applied to nonprofit advocacy corporations; Charles D. Watts, Jr., "Corporate Legal Theory Under the First Amendment: Belotti and Austin," *University of Miami Law Review* 47 (November 1991): 317–78.

10. Daniel R. Ortiz, "The Unbearable Lightness of Being *McConnell,*" *Election Law Journal* 3 (Spring 2004): 299.

11. Elizabeth Drew, *The Corruption of American Politics* (New York: Overlook Press, 1999), 65.

12. Kathryn Dunn Tenpas, "The Clinton Reelection Machine: Placing the Party Machine in Peril," *Presidential Studies Quarterly* 29 (Fall 1998): 761–68; Bruce D. Brown, "Alien Donors: The Participation of Non-Citizens in the U.S. Campaign Finance System," *Yale Law and Policy Review* 15 (Summer 1997): 503–52; Ed Henry, "Hill Democrats Tied to DNC Scandal," *Roll Call,* 27 February 1997; Susan Schmidt, "Clinton Aide Suggested Tracking Donors in White House Database; Documents Outline Idea to 'Recreate the General Campaign Structure,'" *The Washington Post,* 11 March 1997, A6; Sharon LaFraniere, "The Undoing of White House Damage Control; As More Documents Emerge, Clinton's Involvement in Fund-Raising Becomes Clear," *The Washington Post,* 6 April 1997, A1.

13. Congressional Record, 105-1, Senate, Committee on Governmental Affairs, *Investigation of Illegal or Improper Activities in Connection with the 1996 Campaign, Parts I–X* (1997); Congressional Record, 106-1, House, Committee on Government Reform, *Campaign Finance Investigation* (1999); William Safire, "Bribes from the Tribes," *The New York Times,* 31 December 1997, A15.

14. Russ Feingold, Statement to Introduce the Bipartisan Reform Act of 1997 (21 January 1997) <http://feingold.senate.gov/speeches.99.05/2002916925.html> (17 July 2004); 1993 *Congressional Quarterly Almanac,* "The Struggle for Campaign Finance Reform," (Washington, D.C.: Congressional Quarterly Inc., 1994), 37–49; Melvin I. Urofsky, *Money and Free Speech: Campaign Finance Reform and the Courts* (Lawrence: University Press of Kansas, 2005), 89–134.

15. *Bipartisan Campaign Finance Reform Act of 2002,* Public Law 107-155, 116 Stat. 81 (2002); Herbert Alexander, "The Political Process after the Bipartisan Campaign Reform Act of 2002," *Election Law Journal* 2 (Fall 2003): 47–54.

16. The Campaign Legal Center, "Lessons Learned from McConnell v. FEC: An Analysis by Key Participants in this Historic Supreme Court Case," <www.campaign legalcenter.org> (17 July 2004).

17. Ibid., Comments by Thomas Mann, 67; Linda Greenhouse, "The Year Rehnquist May Have Lost His Court," *The New York Times,* 3 July 2004, A1; Charles Lane, "Courting O'Connor: Why the Chief Justice Isn't the Chief Justice," *The Washington Times Magazine,* 4 July 2004, 10.

18. 528 U.S. 377, 389.

19. 540 U.S. at 14 (2003).

20. Ibid., Dissent of Justice Thomas at 5, footnote 2.

21. Ibid., at 8.

22. Ibid., Dissent of Justice Kennedy, 7, 13.

23. 540 U.S. at 35 (2003); Bradley A. Smith, "*McConnell v. Federal Election Commission:* Ideology Trumps Reality, Pragmatism," *Election Law Journal* 3 (Spring 2004): 345–53; Ellen L. Weintraub, "Perspectives on Corruption," *Election Law Journal* 3 (Spring 2004): 355–60; Richard L. Hasen, "Buckley Is Dead; Long Live Buckley: The New Campaign Finance Incoherence of *McConnell v. Federal Election Commission,*" *University of Pennsylvania Law Review* 152 (Jan. 2004).

24. Vt. Stat. Ann., Title 17, §2801 et seq. (2002).

25. *Randall v. Sorrell,* 17–18, 27.

26. Ibid., Thomas dissent, 7–8.

27. Ralph Winter, "The History and Theory of *Buckley v. Valeo*," *Journal of Law and Policy* 6 (1997–1998): 99.

28. Ibid., 48.

29. Ibid., 50, 63; Bradley Smith, "Money Talks: Speech, Corruption, Equality and Campaign Finance," *Georgetown Law Journal* 86 (October 1987): 45–99.

30. E. Joshua Rosenkranz, "Faulty Assumptions in 'Faulty Assumptions': A Response to Professor Smith's Critique of Campaign Finance Reform," *Connecticut Law Review* 30 (Spring 1998): 875; 867–96; 421 U.S. 1, 25 (1975); *FEC v. National Right to Work Committee*, 459 U.S. 197, 208 (1982) quoting *First National Bank v. Bellotti*, 435 U.S. 765, 788, fn. 26 (1978).

31. Frank J. Sorauf, "Politics, Experience, and the First Amendment: The Case of American Campaign Finance," *Columbia Law Review* 94 (May 1994): 1349; 421 U.S. 1, 630 (citing the Court of Appeals decision found at 519 F.2d at 841).

32. Glen Justice, "Advocacy Groups Allowed to Raise Unlimited Funds," *The New York Times*, 19 February 2004, A1; Ben Johnson, "'Charitable' Foundation: ATMs for the Left," *Frontpagemag.com*, 2 March 2004 <http://frontpagemag.com/Articles/Read Article.asp?ID=12423> (18 July 2004).

33. Richard L. Pacelle, Jr., *The Role of the Supreme Court in American Politics* (Colorado: Westview Press, 2002); David K. Ryden, ed., *The U.S. Supreme Court and the Electoral Process* (Washington, D.C.: Georgetown University Press, 2002); Ronald Kahn, *The Supreme Court and Constitutional Theory, 1953–1993* (Lawrence: University of Kansas Press, 1994); Martin Shapiro, *Law and Politics in the Supreme Court* (London: The Free Press, 1964).

34. Robert D. Putnam, *Bowling Alone* (New York: Simon & Schuster, 2000), 340–41; Barry M. Casper, *Lost in Washington* (Amherst: University of Massachusetts Press, 2000), 300–16.

Works Cited

PRIVATE PAPERS

Cleveland Papers, University of Virginia, Letters from Brice to Lamont, 18 August and 2 September 1888.

Compilation of the Messages and Papers of the Presidents, 1789–1897. Edited by James D. Richardson. Volumes 2–4. Washington, D.C.: GPO, 1907.

Goldwater, Barry M. *The Speeches, Remarks and Press Conferences, and Related Papers of Senator Barry M. Goldwater.* Personal Papers of Barry Goldwater. Arizona Historical Foundation (1964).

Richardson, James D., ed. *A Compilation of Messages and Papers of the Presidents, Volume 11.* New York: Bureau of National Literature and Art, 1908.

Wallace, Governor George C. *Papers of George C. Wallace.* State Archives, Montgomery, Alabama (1964).

SPEECHES

Field, Justice Stephen. *Remarks to the New York State Bar Association.* 134 U.S. 729 (1890).

Nixon, Richard M. *Checkers Speech.* <http://www.pbs.org/wgbh/amex/presidents/nf/re source/nixon/primdocs/checkers.html> (1952).

Speeches by Leading Businessmen at the Dinner of the New England Tariff Reform League, January 18, 1894. Woodbridge, CT: Research Publications, 1988.

NEWSPAPERS AND PERIODICALS

American Iron and Steel Association Bulletin. 1887.
Atlantic Monthly. 1878.
Broadcasting. 1987.
Century. 1889–1892.
Farmers Alliance. 1891.
Nation. 1880.
New Englander. 1877.
New York Herald. 1888.
New York Mail and Express. 1888.
New York Times. 1876–2006.
New York Times Magazine. 1956.
Platte County Argus. 1896.
Princeton Review. 1870.
Roll Call. 1997.
Springfield Republican. 1927.
Time. 1944.

Utica Saturday Globe. 1910.
Wall Street Journal. 1936.
Washington Post. 1935–2006.
Washington Post and Times Herald. 1956.
Washington Times Magazine. 2004.

GOVERNMENT DOCUMENTS

CONSTITUTIONAL PROVISIONS AND FEDERAL AND STATE STATUTES

U.S. Constitution.
———. Article IV, Section [1]
———. Amendment XVII (1913).
Amendments to Federal Election Campaign Act of 1974. 90 Stat. 1339 (1976).
Anti-Assessment Act of 1876. 5 U.S.CA Section 1180 (1876).
Bipartisan Campaign Finance Reform Act of 2002. 116 Stat. 81 (2002).
Bipartisan Campaign Reform Act. 116 Stat. 81 (2002).
Campaign Broadcast Reform Act of 1970. S. 2876 (1969).
Civil Service Reform Act. 20 Stat 403 (1883).
Election Reform Act of 1967. 90-1, S. 1880 (1967).
Election Reform Act of 1968. 90-2, H.R. 11233 (1968).
Federal Communication Act of 1934. 48 Stat. 1083 (1934).
Federal Corrupt Practices Act. 40 Stat. 1070 (1925).
Federal Election Campaign Act of 1971. 86 Stat. 3 (1972).
Federal Election Campaign Act of 1974. 92 Stat. 225 (1974).
Federal Elections Act of 1955. (1955).
Federal Elections Act of 1961. S. 2426 (1961).
Federal Regulation of Lobbying Act. 60 Stat. 839 (1946).
Force Bill. 16 Stat 144 (1870).
Foreign Agents Registration Act. 52 Stat. 327 (1938).
Hatch Act. 53 Stat. 1147 (1939).
Hatch Act II. 54 Stat. 767 (1940).
Labor Management Relations Act. 61 Stat. 136 (1947).
Legislative Reorganization Act of 1946. 60 Stat. 753 (1946).
Michigan Public Acts. No. 109 (1913).
National Labor Relations Act. 9 Stat. 838 (1935).
Presidential Election Campaign Fund of 1966. S. Res. 1530 (1966).
Public Utility Holding Company Act of 1935. 53 Stat. 1150 (1935).
Radio Act of 1912. Public Law 264 (1912)
Radio Act of 1927. Public Law 632 (1927).
Revenue Act of 1971. Public Law 178 (1971).
Statutes of California. Constitution, Article IV, Section 35 (1947).
Telecommunications Act of 1996. 110 Stat. 56 (1996).
Vermont Act 64. Vt. Stat. Ann., Title 17, §2801 et seq. (2002).
War Labor Disputes Act. 57 Stat. 163–68 (1943).

CONGRESSIONAL AND ADMINISTRATIVE DOCUMENTS

Commerce Department. *Study of Communications by an Interdepartment Committee.* Washington, D.C.: Government Printing Office, 1943.
Congressional Record. Washington, D.C., 1876–2005.
Federal Communication Commission. *Report and Order and Notice of Proposed Rulemaking 03-127* (2003).
———. *33rd Annual Report.* Washington, D.C.: U.S. Government Printing Office, 1968.

U.S. Code Congressional and Administrative News. Senate Report 92–95, Volume 2 (1972).
———. *Legislative History of Public Law*. Volume 3, 93–443 (1974).
U.S. Congress. House.
———. Committee on Education and Labor (1947).
———. Committee on Elections (1923).
———. Committee on Government Reform. Campaign Finance Investigation (1999).
———. Committee on House Administration. Analysis of Proposed Revision of Federal Election Laws (1966).
———. Committee on Interstate and Foreign Commerce (1935).
———. Committee to Investigate Campaign Expenditures, Part I–II (1944).
———. Report of Special Committee to Investigate Campaign Contributions (1954).
———. Report of Special Committee to Investigate Campaign Expenditures for the House of Representatives, 1944 (1945).
———. Special Subcommittee on Investigations of the House Committee on Interstate and Foreign Commerce. Legislative History of the Fairness Doctrine (1968).
———. Statement by Representative Monroney on the Legislative Reorganization Act of 1946 (1946).
———. Subcommittee of the Committee on Labor (1943).
U.S. Congress. Senate.
———. Committee on Campaign Expenditures (1925).
———. Committee on Governmental Affairs, Investigation of Illegal or Improper Activities in Connection with the 1996 Campaign. Parts I–X (1997).
———. Committee on Labor and Public Welfare (1947).
———. Committee on Rules and Administration. Legislative Recommendations of the President's Commission on Campaign Costs (1962).
———. Regulation and Improvement of the Civil Service (1881).
———. Senate Committee on Campaign Expenditures (1939).
———. Senate Report (1926).
———. Senate Report on Election, Expulsion and Censure Cases. 87-2 (1967).
———. Senate Select Campaign Finance Committee Hearings (1956).
———. Senate Special Committee Investigating Campaign Expenditures, Unpublished Hearings, 1940.
———. Senate Subcommittee on Privileges and Elections. Part I, 11 (1956).
———. Senate Subcommittee on Privileges and Elections, Report on 1956 General Election Campaigns (1957).
———. Special Committee (1924).
———. Special Committee Investigation on Expenditures in Senate Primary and General Elections (1926).
———. Special Committee to Investigate Presidential, Vice Presidential, and Senatorial Campaign Expenditures in 1944 (1945).
———. Subcommittee on Privileges and Elections (1920).
———. Subcommittee on Privileges and Elections. Senate Committee Report (1957).
———. Watergate Committee (1974).

JUDICIAL DOCUMENTS

CASES

Abrams v. United States, 250 U.S. 616 (1919).
ACLU v. Jennings, 366 F. Supp. 1041 (1973).
Adams v. Lansdon, 110 P. 280 (1910).
Austin v. Michigan Chamber of Commerce, 494 U.S. 650 (1990).
Baker v. Carr, 369 U.S. 186 (1962).

Beauharnais v. Illinois, 343 U.S. 250 (1952).
Blair v. United States, 250 U.S. 273 (1919).
Bond v. Floyd, 385 U.S. 116 (1966).
Buckley v. American Constitutional Law Foundation, Inc., 525 U.S. 182 (1999).
Buckley v. Valeo, 421 U.S. 1 (1976).
Burroughs v. United States, 290 U.S. 534 (1934).
California Medical Association v. FEC, 453 U.S. 182 (1981).
Citizens Against Rent Control v. Berkeley, 454 U.S. 290 (1981).
Colegrove v. Green, 328 U.S. 549 (1946).
Everson v. Board of Education of Ewing Township, 330 U.S. 70 (1947).
Ex Parte Curtis, 106 U.S. 371 (1882).
Ex Parte Yarbrough, 110 U.S. 651 (1884).
FEC v. Beaumont, 539 U.S. 146 (2003).
FEC v. Massachusetts Citizens for Life, Inc., 479 U.S. 238 (1986).
FEC v. McConnell, 539 U.S. 911 (2003).
FEC v. National Right to Work Committee, 459 U.S. 197 (1982).
First National Bank v. Bellotti, 435 U.S. 765 (1978).
Gitlow v. New York, 268 U.S. 652 (1925).
Great Lakes Broadcasting v. Federal Radio Commission, 37 F.2d 993 (1930).
Grovey v. Townsend, 295 U.S. 45 (1935).
Hoover v. Intercity Radio Co., Inc., 286 F. 1003 (1923).
KFKB Broadcasting Ass'n v. FRC, 47 F.2d 670 (1931).
Kovacs v. Cooper, 336 U.S. 77 (1949).
Lamont v. Postmaster General, 381 U.S. 301 (1965).
Louthan v. Commonwealth, 79 Va. 196 (1884).
Loveday v. FCC, 707 F.2d 1443 (1983).
Mayflower Broadcasting Corporation, 8 FCC 333 (1941).
McConnell v. Federal Election Commission, 540 U.S. 93 (2003).
National Broadcasting Co. v. United States, 319 U.S. 190 (1934).
National Committee on Impeachment v. United States, 469 F. 2d 1135 (1972).
Near v. Minnesota, 283 U.S. 697 (1931).
New York Times v. Sullivan, 376 U.S. 254 (1964).
Newberry v. United States, 256 U.S. 232 (1921).
Nixon v. Condon, 286 U.S. 73 (1932).
Nixon v. Herndon, 273 U.S. 536 (1927).
Nixon v. Shrink Missouri, 528 U.S. 377 (2000).
NLRB v. Jones & Laughlin Steel Corp., 301 U.S. 1 (1937).
North American Co. v. Securities & Exchange Commission, 327 U.S. 686 (1946).
Pichler v. Jennings, 347 F. Supp 1061 (1972).
Powell v. McCormack, 395 U.S. 486 (1969).
Randall v. Sorrell, U.S. Supreme Court. No. 04-1528 (June 26, 2006).
Reading Broadcasting Co. v. FRC, 48 F.2d 458 (1932).
Red Lion Broadcasting Co. Inc., v. Federal Communication Commission, 400 F.2d 1002, 395
      U.S. 367 (1969).
Reynolds v. Sims, 377 U.S. 533 (1964).
Santa Clara County v. So. Pacific RR, 118 U.S. 394 (1886).
Schenck, 249 U.S. 47 (1919).
Smith v. Allwright, 321 U.S. 649 (1944).
Sorenson v. Wood, 123 Neb. 348 (1932).
State of Oklahoma v. U.S. Civil Service Com'n, 330 U.S. 127 (1947).
State v. Pierce, 163 Wis. 615 (1916).
Syracuse Peace Council v. FCC, 867 F.2d 654 (1989).
Trinity Methodist Church v. Federal Radio Commission, 62 F.2d 850 (1932).
United States v. Auto Workers, 352 U.S. 567 (1957).
United States v. Carolene Products Co., 304 U.S. 144 (1938).

United States v. Classic, 313 U.S. 299 (1941).
United States v. Congress of Industrial Organizations, 335 U.S. 106 (1948).
United States v. Gradwell, 243 U.S. 476 (1917).
United States v. Harriss, 347 U.S. 612 (1954).
United States v. Rumely, 345 U.S. 41 (1952).
United States v. United States Brewers' Association, 239 F. 163 (W.D. Pa. 1916).
United States v. Zenith Radio Corporation, 12 F.2d 614 (1926).
Whitney v. California, 274 U.S. 357 (1927).

BRIEFS AND PLEADINGS

Buckley v. Valeo. Record of the United States Supreme Court. Washington, D.C.: National Archives and Records Administration (1975).
Red Lion Broadcasting v. FCC. Record of the United States Supreme Court. Washington, D.C.: National Archives and Records Administration (1969).
Truman Newberry v. United States. Record of the United States Supreme Court. Washington, D.C.: National Archives and Records Administration (1921).
United States v. Curtis. Record of the United States Supreme Court. Washington, D.C.: National Archives and Records Administration (1876).

BOOKS AND ARTICLES

ABA Standards on Judicial Selection. Chicago: American Bar Association, 2001.
Abraham, Henry J. *Justices and Presidents: A Political History of Appointments to the Supreme Court, 3rd edition*. New York: Oxford University Press, 1992.
Adamany, David W., and George E. Agree. "Election Campaign Financing: The 1974 Reforms." *Political Science Quarterly* 90 (Summer 1975): 201–20.
———. *Political Money: A Strategy for Campaign Financing in America*. Baltimore: Johns Hopkins University Press, 1975.
Agranoff, Robert. *The New Style in Election Campaigns*. Boston: Holbrook Press, Inc., 1976.
Ainsworth, Scott. "Regulating Lobbyists and Interest Group Influence." *The Journal of Politics* 55 (February 1993): 41–56.
Alexander, Herbert E. "The Political Process after the Bipartisan Campaign Reform Act of 2002." *Election Law Journal* 2 (Spring 2003): 47–54.
———. *Studies in Money in Politics*, Volume I–III. Princeton: Citizens' Research Foundation, 1991.
Altschuler, Glenn C., and Stuart M. Blumin. *Rude Republic*. Princeton: Princeton University Press, 2000.
Ambrose, Stephen E. *Eisenhower: The President*. Simon & Schuster: New York, 1984.
———. *Nixon: The Education of a Politician, 1913–1962*. New York: Simon & Schuster, 1987.
———. *Nixon: The Triumph of a Politician, 1962–1972*. New York: Simon and Schuster, 1989.
Auerbach, Jerold S. *Unequal Justice*. Oxford: Oxford University Press, 1976.
Badger, Anthony J. *The New Deal: The Depression Years, 1933–1940*. New York: Hill and Wang, 1989.
Bain, David Howard. *Empire Express*. New York: Viking, 1999.
Baker, C. Edwin. "Campaign Expenditures and Free Speech." *Harvard Civil Rights—Civil Liberties Law Review* 33 (Winter 1998): 1–46.
Baker, Jean H. ed. *Votes for Women*. Oxford: Oxford University Press, 2002.
Baker, Kevin. "FDR's Fireside Chats." In Robert Wilson and Stanley Marcus, eds., *American Greats*. New York: Public Affairs Press, 1999: 76–78.
Banks, Christopher P., and John C. Green, eds. *Superintending Democracy: The Courts and the Political Process*. Akron: University of Akron Press, 2001.

Beard, Charles A. *The Supreme Court and the Constitution*. New Jersey: Prentice Hall, 1962.

Benedict, Michael Les. "Law and the Constitution in the Gilded Age." In Charles W. Calhoun, ed., *The Gilded Age*. Wilmington: Scholarly Resource, 1996: 289–308.

Benjamin, Louise M. *Freedom of the Air and the Public Interest: First Amendment Rights in Broadcasting to 1935*. Carbondale: Southern Illinois University Press, 2001.

Bensel, Richard Franklin. *The Political Economy of American Industrialization, 1877–1900*. Cambridge: Cambridge University Press, 2000.

Ben-Veniste, Richard, and George Frampton, Jr. *Stonewall*. New York: Simon & Schuster, 1977.

Berle, Adolf. "Corporations and the Modern State." In Thurmond Arnold, ed., *The Future of Democratic Capitalism*. New York: Holt and Company, 1941.

Bernstein, Carl, and Bob Woodward. *All the President's Men*. New York: Simon and Schuster, 1974.

Best, Gary Dean. *The Politics of American Individualism: Herbert Hoover in Transition, 1918–1921*. Westport, Connecticut: Greenwood Press, 1975.

Bickel, Alexander M. *The Least Dangerous Branch: The Supreme Court at the Bar of Politics*. New Haven: Yale University Press, 1962.

Bixby, David M. "The Roosevelt Court, Democratic Ideology, and Minority Rights: Another Look at *United States v. Classic*." *The Yale Law Journal* 90 (March 1981): 741–97.

Blasi, Vincent, ed. *The Burger Court: The Counter-Revolution That Wasn't*. New Haven: Yale University Press, 1983.

Blodgett, Geoffrey. *The Gentle Reformers: Massachusetts Democrats in the Cleveland Era*. Cambridge: Harvard University Press, 1966.

———. "The Mugwump Reputation, 1870 to the Present." *Journal of American History* 66 (March 1980): 867–87.

Bogen, David S. "The Free Speech Metamorphosis of Mr. Justice Holmes." *Hofstra Law Review* 11 (Fall 1982): 97–178.

Braeman, John. *Before the Civil Rights Revolution: The Old Court and Individual Rights*. New York: Greenwood Press, 1988.

Brandeis, Louis. *The Curse of Bigness*. New York: The Viking Press, 1934.

Briffault, Richard. "The Political Parties and Campaign Finance Reform." *Columbia Law Review* 100 (April 2000): 620–66.

Brinkley, Alan. *The End of Reform*. New York: Random House, 1995.

Broder, David S. *Democracy Derailed: Initiative Campaigns and the Power of Money*. New York: Harcourt Inc., 2000.

Brown, Bruce D. "Alien Donors: The Participation of Non-Citizens in the U.S. Campaign Finance System." *Yale Law and Policy Review* 15 (Summer 1997): 503–52.

Browne, Steven A. "The Constitutionality of Lobby Reform: Implicating Associational Privacy and the Right to Petition the Government." *William and Mary Bill of Rights Journal* 4 (Winter 1995): 717–50.

Bryce, James. *American Commonwealth, Volume II*. New York: MacMillan and Company, 1893.

Burke, Debra. "Twenty Years after the Federal Election Campaign Act Amendments of 1974: Look Who's Running Now." *Dickinson Law Review* 99 (Winter 1995): 357–91.

Burris, Russell V. "The Narrow Application of *Buckley v. Valeo*: Is Campaign Finance Reform Possible in the Eighth Circuit?" *Missouri Law Review* 64 (Spring 1999): 437–58.

Casarez, Nichole Bremman. "Corruption, Corrosion and Corporate Political Speech." *Nebraska Law Review* 70 (1991): 45–78.

Casper, Barry M. *Lost in Washington*. Amherst: University of Massachusetts Press, 2000.

Catchpole, Terry. *How to Cope with COPE: The Political Operations of Organized Labor*. New York: Arlington House, 1968.

Chafee, Zechariah, Jr. "Freedom of Speech in Wartime." *Harvard Law Review* 32 (1919): 937–60.

Chandler, Alfred D., and James W. Cortada, eds. *A Nation Transformed by Information: How Information Has Shaped the U.S. from Colonial Times to the Present.* New York: Oxford University Press, 2000.

———. *The Visible Hand.* Cambridge: Harvard University Press, 1977.

Clemens, Elizabeth. *The People's Lobby.* Chicago: University of Chicago Press, 1997.

Cole, David. "Agon at Agora: Creative Misreadings in the First Amendment Tradition." *Yale Law Journal* 95 (April 1986): 857–903.

Coletta, Paolo E. *William Jennings Bryan.* Lincoln: University of Nebraska Press, 1964.

"Comment: Legislative Exclusion: Julian Bond and Adam Clayton Powell." *University of Chicago Law Review* 35 (Fall 1967): 157–77.

Congressional Quarterly Almanac. Washington, D.C.: Congressional Quarterly, Inc., 1966–1997.

Corrado, Anthony, Thomas E. Mann, Daniel Ortiz, and Trevor Potter. *The New Campaign Finance Sourcebook.* Washington, D.C.: The Brookings Institution Press, 2003.

Cortner, Richard C. *The Apportionment Cases.* New York: W. W. Norton & Co., 1970.

Cotter, Cornelius. "Institutional Development of Parties and the Thesis of Party Decline." *Political Science Quarterly* 95 (Spring 1980): 1–27.

Craig, Douglas B. *Fireside Politics: Radio and Political Culture in the United States, 1920–1940.* Baltimore: The Johns Hopkins University Press, 2000.

Cray, Ed. *Chief Justice: A Biography of Earl Warren.* Simon & Schuster: New York, 1997.

Croly, Herbert. *Marcus Alonzo Hanna.* New York: The Macmillan Company, 1965.

———. *The Promise of American Life.* New York: Capricorn Press, 1909.

Curtis, Michael Kent. *Free Speech: "The People's Darling Privilege."* Durham: Duke University Press, 2000.

Curtis, Newton Martin. *From Bull Run to Chancellorsville.* New York: G. P. Putnam's Sons, 1906.

Cushman, Barry. "Lost Fidelities." *William and Mary Law Review* 41 (December 1999): 95–145.

———. *Rethinking the New Deal Court.* New York: Oxford University Press, 1998.

Cushman, Clare, ed. *The Supreme Court Justices: Illustrated Biographies, 1789–1995.* Washington, D.C.: Congressional Quarterly, Inc., 1995.

Cushman, Robert E. "Voting Organic Laws." *Political Science Quarterly* 28 (June 1913): 207–9.

Dahl, Robert A. *Democracy and Its Critics.* New Haven: Yale University Press, 1989.

———. *A Preface to Democratic Theory.* Chicago: University of Chicago Press, 1956.

Davis, James H. *A Political Revelation.* Dallas: The Adimonte Publishing Co., 1894.

Diamond, Edwin, and Stephen Bates. *The Spot: The Rise of Political Advertising on Television.* Cambridge: The MIT Press, 1984.

Dickson, Del, ed. *The Supreme Court in Conference, 1940–1985.* Oxford: Oxford University Press, 2001.

Dinkin, Robert J. *Campaigning in America.* New York: Greenwood Press, 1989.

Drew, Elizabeth. *The Corruption of American Politics.* New York: The Overlook Press, 1999.

———. *Politics and Money: The New Road to Corruption.* New York: MacMillan Publishing Company, 1983.

Dudziak, Mary. *Cold War Civil Rights.* Princeton: Princeton University Press, 2000.

Dworkin, Ronald. *Freedom's Law: The Moral Reading of the American Constitution.* Cambridge: Harvard University Press, 1996.

Eastman, Hope. *Lobbying: A Constitutionally Protected Right.* Washington, D.C.: American Enterprise Institute, 1977.

Eaton, Dorman B. "The Public Service and the Public." *Atlantic Monthly* 41 (February 1878): 242–49.

Editorializing by Broadcast Licensees. 25 R.R. 1901 (1949).

Edsall, Thomas Byrne. *Power and Money: Writing About Politics, 1971–1987.* New York: W. W. Norton & Co., 1988.

Edwards, Rebecca. *Angels in the Machinery.* New York: Oxford University Press, 1997.

Eismeier, Theodore J., and Philip H. Pollock III. "Strategy and Choice in Congressional Elections: The Role of Political Action Committees." *American Journal of Political Science* 30 (February 1986): 197–213.

Ely, John Hart. *Democracy and Distrust: A Theory of Judicial Interpretation*. Cambridge: Harvard University Press, 1980.

———. *On Constitutional Ground*. Princeton: Princeton University Press, 1996.

Emerson, Thomas. *The System of Free Expression*. New York: Vintage, 1970.

Epstein, Edward M. *The Corporation in American Politics*. New Jersey: Prentice-Hall, Inc., 1969.

Ervin, Sam J., Jr. *The Whole Truth*. New York: Random House, 1980.

Etzioni, Amitai. *Capital Corruption: The New Attack on American Democracy*. New Brunswick: Transaction Books, 1988.

Evans, Les, and Allen Myers. *Watergate and the Myth of American Democracy*. New York: Pathfinder Press, 1974.

The Federalist. Vermont: Everyman Publisher, 1996.

Ferris, Charles D., and Terrence J. Leahy, "Red Lions, Tigers and Bears: Broadcast Content Regulation and the First Amendment." *Catholic University Law Review* 38 (Winter 1989): 299–327.

Fiss, Owen F. "Free Speech and Social Structure." *Iowa Law Review* 71 (July 1986): 1405–25.

———. *The Irony of Free Speech*. Cambridge: Harvard University Press, 1996.

———. *Troubled Beginnings of the Modern State, 1888–1921*. New York: Macmillan Press, 1993.

Fowler, Dorothy Ganfield. "Precursors of the Hatch Act." *The Mississippi Valley Historical Review* 47 (September 1960): 247–62.

Fraser, Steven. *Labor Will Rule: Sidney Hillman and the Rise of American Labor*. New York: The Free Press, 1991.

Friedman, Lawrence M. *American Law in the 20th Century*. New Haven: Yale University Press, 2002.

———. *A History of American Law*. New York: Simon and Schuster, 1973.

Gaier, Joseph. *The First Round: The Story of the CIO Political Action Committee*. New York: Duell, Sloan and Pearce, 1944.

Galloway, George B. "The Operation of the Legislative Reorganization Act of 1946," *The American Political Science Review* 45 (March 1951): 41–68.

The Gallup Poll Cumulative Index, 1937–1997. Delaware: Scholarly Resources, Inc., 1999.

Gardner, James A. "Liberty, Community, and the Constitutional Structure of Political Influence: A Reconsideration of the Right to Vote." *University of Pennsylvania Law Review* 145 (April 1997): 893–985.

———. "Shut Up and Vote: A Critique of Deliberative Democracy and the Life of Talk." *Tennessee Law Review* 63 (Winter 1996): 421–51.

Garrison, Michael J. "Corporate Political Speech, and First Amendment Doctrine." *Am. Bus. L. J.* 27 (Summer 1989): 163–214.

Gillette, Gillette. *The Right to Vote: Politics and the Passage of the Fifteenth Amendment*. Baltimore: Johns Hopkins University Press, 1965.

Gillman, Howard. *The Constitution Besieged: The Rise and Demise of Lochner Era Police Power Jurisprudence*. Durham: Duke University Press, 1993.

Goldenberg, Edie N., and Michael W. Traugott, "Mass Media in U. S. Congressional Elections." *Legislative Studies Quarterly* 12 (August 1987): 317–39.

Gora, Joel M. "*Buckley v. Valeo*: A Landmark of Political Freedom." *Akron Law Review* 33 (1999): 7–38.

Gordon, Richard L. "The Pubic Utility Holding Company Act: The Easy Step in Electric Utility Regulatory Reform." <http://www.cato.org/pubs/regulation/reg15n-1gor don.html> (2003).

Gordon, Sarah H. *Passage to Union*. Chicago: Ivan R. Dee, 1997.

Gould, Lewis L. *Grand Old Party*. New York: Random House, 2003.

Graber, Doris A. *Mass Media and American Politics*. Washington, D.C.: Congressional Quarterly Press, Inc., 1984.

Graber, Mark A. *Transforming Free Speech*. Berkeley: University of California Press, 1991.

Graves, W. Brooke. *Administration of the Lobby Registration Provisions of the Legislative Reorganization Act of 1946: An Analysis of Experience during the Eightieth Congress*. Washington, D.C.: GPO, 1950.

Greenstone, J. David. *Labor in American Politics*. New York: Alfred A. Knopf, 1969.

Grossman, Lawrence K. *The Electronic Republic: Reshaping Democracy in the Information Age*. New York: Viking Press, 1995.

Gutmann, Amy, and Dennis Thompson. *Democracy and Disagreement*. Cambridge: Belknap Press of Harvard University Press, 1996.

Hall, Adam P. "Regulating Corporate 'Speech' in Public Elections." *Case W. Res L. Rev.* 39 (1988–1989): 1313–42.

Harvey, W. H. *Coin's Financial School*. Cambridge: Belknap Press of Harvard University Press, 1963.

Hasen, Richard L. "Buckley Is Dead; Long Live Buckley: The New Campaign Finance Incoherence of *McConnell v. Federal Election Commission*." *University of Pennsylvania Law Review* 152 (January 2004): 31–72.

———. "Shrink Missouri, Campaign Finance, and the 'Thing That Wouldn't Leave.'" *Constitutional Commentary* 17 (Winter 2000): 483–509.

Hawley, Ellis W., ed. *Herbert Hoover as Secretary of Commerce*. Iowa City: University of Iowa Press, 1981.

Haworth, Paul. *The Hayes-Tilden Disputed Presidential Election of 1876*. New York: AMS Press, 1970.

Hays, Samuel P. *The Response to Industrialization: 1855–1914*. Chicago: University of Chicago Press, 1957.

Hazlett, Thomas W., and David W. Sosa. "Was the Fairness Doctrine a 'Chilling Effect?' Evidence from the Post-De-Regulation Radio Market." *Journal of Legal Studies* 26 (January 1997): 279–400.

Heady, Ferrel. "American Government and Politics: The Hatch Act Decisions." *The American Political Science Review* 41 (August 1947): 687–99.

Heard, Alexander. *The Costs of Democracy*. Chapel Hill: University of North Carolina Press, 1960.

Hicks, John D. *The Populist Revolt*. Minneapolis: University of Minnesota Press, 1931.

Hilmes, Michele. *Radio Voices: American Broadcasting, 1922–1952*. Minneapolis: University of Minnesota Press, 1997.

Himmelberg, Robert F. *Herbert Hoover and the Crisis of American Capitalism*. Cambridge: Schenckman Publishing Company, 1973.

Hohenstein, Kurt. "William Jennings Bryan and the Income Tax." *Journal of Law and Politics* 16 (Winter 2000): 162–92.

Holloway, Harry. "Interest Groups in the Post-Partisan Era: The Political Machine of the AFL-CIO." *Political Science Quarterly* 94 (Spring 1979): 117–33.

Hoogenboom, Ari. *Outlawing the Spoils: A History of the Civil Service Reform Movement*. Urbana: University of Illinois Press, 1961.

———. "The Pendleton Act and the Civil Service." *American Historical Review* 64 (January 1959): 301–18.

———. "Thomas A. Jenckes and Civil Service Reform." *Mississippi Valley Historical Review* 47 (March 1961): 636–58.

Horowitz, Morton J. *The Transformation of American Law, 1870–1960: The Crisis of Legal Orthodoxy*. New York: Oxford University Press, 1992.

———. *The Warren Court and the Pursuit of Justice*. New York: Hill and Wang, 1998.

Hovenkamp, Herbert. *Enterprise and American Law, 1836–1937*. Cambridge: Harvard University Press, 1991.

Howe, George F. "The New York Customhouse Controversy 1877–1879." *Mississippi Valley Historical Review* 18 (Dec 1931): 350–63.

Ingraham, Patricia W., and David H. Rosenbloom, eds. *The Foundation of Merit: Public Service in American Democracy*. Baltimore: Johns Hopkins University Press, 1995.

———. *The Promise and Paradox of Civil Service Reform*. Pittsburgh: University of Pittsburgh Press, 1992.

Jackson, Brooks. *Honest Graft: Big Money and the American Political Process*. New York: Alfred A. Knopf, 1988.

Jenks, Jeremiah W. "Money in Practical Politics." *The Century* 44 (October 1892): 942–47.

Johnson, Dennis W. *No Place for Amateurs: How Political Consultants Are Reshaping American Democracy*. New York: Routledge, 2001.

Johnson, Donald Bruce, ed. *National Party Platforms: 1840–1976*, Volume II. Urbana: University of Illinois Press, 1978.

Josephson, Matthew. *The Politicos, 1865–1896*. New York: Harcourt Brace & Co., 1938.

Kahn, Ronald. *The Supreme Court and Constitutional Theory, 1953–1993*. Lawrence: University of Kansas Press, 1994.

Kalven, Harry. *A Worthy Tradition*. New York: HarperCollins, 1989.

Kefauver, Estes. "Congressional Reorganization." An Address to the Southern Political Science Association. *The Journal of Politics* 9 (February 1947): 96–107.

Keller, Morton. *Affairs of State*. Cambridge: Belknap Press of Harvard University Press, 1977.

Kennedy, David M. *Freedom from Fear: The American People in Depression and War, 1929–1945*. Oxford: Oxford University Press, 1999.

Kens, Paul. *Justice Stephen Field*. Lawrence: University Press of Kansas, 1997.

Keyssar, Alexander. *The Right to Vote*. New York: Basic Books, 2000.

Kinkopf, Neil. "Deliberative Democracy and Campaign Finance Reform." *Duke Law and Contemporary Problems* 65 (Summer 2002): 151–54.

Kirkendall, Richard S. "The New Deal as Watershed: The Recent Literature." *The Journal of American History* 54 (March 1968): 839–52.

Kluger, Richard. *Simple Justice*. New York: Random House, 1975.

Koenig, Louis W. *Bryan: A Political Biography of William Jennings Bryan*. New York: G. P. Putman & Sons, 1991.

Kold, Charles E. M. "Campaign Finance Reform: A Business Perspective." *Cath. U. L. Review* 50 (Fall 2000): 87–109.

Konefsky, Samuel J. *The Legacy of Holmes and Brandeis: A Study in the Influence of Ideas*. New York: Da Capo Press, 1974.

Koussar, J. Morgan. *Colorblind Injustice: Minority Voting Rights and the Undoing of the Second Reconstruction*. Chapel Hill: University of North Carolina Press, 1999.

———. *The Shaping of Southern Politics: Suffrage Restriction and the Establishment of the One–Party South, 1880–1910*. New Haven: Yale University Press, 1974.

Kurland, Philip B. *Watergate and the Constitution*. Chicago: University of Chicago Press, 1978.

Kutler, Stanley I. *Abuse of Power*. New York: Simon & Schuster, 1997.

———. *The Wars of Watergate*. New York: W. W. Norton Co., 1990.

Lamb, Charles M., and Stephen C. Halpern. *The Burger Court: Political and Judicial Profiles*. Urbana: University of Illinois Press, 1991.

Lane, Edgar. *Lobbying and the Law*. Berkeley: University of California Press, 1954.

LaRue, L. H. *Political Discourse: A Case Study of the Watergate Affair*. Atlanta: University of Georgia Press, 1988.

Leuchtenburg, William E. *The FDR Years*. New York: Columbia University Press, 1995.

———. *Franklin Roosevelt and the New Deal, 1932–1940*. New York: Harper and Row, 1963.

———. *The Supreme Court Reborn*. Oxford: Oxford University Press, 1995.

Levin, Ronald M. "Fighting the Appearance of Corruption." *Washington University Journal of Law and Policy* 6 (2001): 171–79.

Lewis, Anthony. *Make No Law: The Sullivan Case and the First Amendment.* New York: Vintage Books, 1991.

Lewis, Charles, and The Center for Public Integrity. *The Buying of Congress: How Special Interests Have Stolen Your Right to Life, Liberty, and the Pursuit of Happiness.* New York: Avon Books, 1998.

Lichtenstein, Nelson. *State of the Union: A Century of American Labor.* Princeton: Princeton University Press, 2002.

———. *Walter Reuther: The Most Dangerous Man in Detroit.* New York: Basic Books, 1995.

Lindblom, Charles E. *Politics and Markets.* New York: Basic Books, Inc., 1977.

Lippman, Walter. *Drift and Mastery.* Madison: University of Wisconsin Press, 1985.

———. *The Phantom Public.* New York: Harcourt, Brace and Company, 1925.

———. *Public Opinion.* New York: Harcourt Brace and Company, 1922.

Logan, Charles W., Jr. "Getting Beyond Scarcity: A New Paradigm for Assessing the Constitutionality of Broadcast Regulation." *California Law Review* 85 (December 1997): 1687–1747.

Lowenstein, Daniel H. "BCRA and *McConnell* in Perspective." *Election Law Journal* 3 (Spring 2004): 277–83.

Macy, Jesse. *Party Organization and Machinery.* London: T. Fisher Unwin, 1905.

Malbin, Michael J. *Parties, Interest Groups and Campaign Finance Laws.* Washington, D.C.: American Enterprise Institute for Public Policy Research, 1980.

Marcus, Robert D. *Grand Old Party: Political Structure in the Gilded Age, 1880–1896.* New York: Oxford University Press, 1971.

Marino, Robert, and David Schultz. *A Short History of the United States Civil Service.* New York: University Press, 1991.

May, Elaine Tyler. "Expanding the Past: Recent Scholarship on Women in Politics and Work." *Reviews in American History* 10 (December 1982): 216–33.

McCarthy, Nolan, and Lawrence S. Rothenberg. "Commitment and the Campaign Contribution Contract." *American Journal of Political Science* 40 (August 1996): 872–904.

McChesney, Robert W. *Telecommunications, Mass Media and Democracy.* New York: Oxford University Press, 1993.

McCloskey, Robert. *American Conservatism in the Age of Enterprise.* Harvard University Press: Cambridge, 1961.

McCurdy, Charles W. "American Law and the Marketing Structure of the Large Corporations, 1875–1890." *Journal of Economic History* 38 (September 1978): 631–49.

———. "Justice Field and the Jurisprudence of Government-Business Relations: Some Parameters of Laissez-Faire Constitutionalism, 1863–1897." *The Journal of American History* 61 (March 1975): 970–1005.

———. "The Knight Sugar Decision of 1895 and the Modernization of American Corporation Law, 1869–1903." *Business History Review* 3 (Autumn 1979): 304–42.

———. "The 'Liberty of Contract' Regime in American Law." In Harry N. Scheiber, ed., *The State and Freedom of Contract.* Stanford: Stanford University Press, 1998: 161–89.

McGerr, Michael. *A Fierce Discontent: The Rise and Fall of the Progressive Movement, 1870–1920.* New York: Free Press, 2003.

———. "Political Style and Women's Power, 1830–1930." *The Journal of American History* 77 (December 1990): 864–85.

McGregor, Michael E. *The Decline of Popular Politics: The American North, 1865–1928.* New York: Oxford University Press, 1986.

McSweeney, Dean. "Parties, Corruption and Campaign Finance in America." In Robert Williams, ed., *Party Finance and Political Corruption.* Durham: St. Martin's Press, 2000: 37–60.

Meikeljohn, Alexander. *Political Freedom: The Constitutional Powers of the People*. New York: Harper and Brothers, 1948.

Michelson, Charles. *The Ghost Talks*. New York: G. P. Putnam Sons, 1944.

Micklewait, John, and Adrian Wooldridge. *The Right Nation: Conservative Power in America*. New York: Penguin Press, 2004.

Milkis, Sidney M. *Political Parties and Constitutional Government: Reconstructing American Democracy*. Baltimore: Johns Hopkins University Press, 1999.

———. *The Presidents and the Parties: The Transformation of the American Party System Since the New Deal*. New York: Oxford University Press, 1993.

Millis, Harry A., and Emily Clark Brown. *From the Wagner Act to Taft-Hartley: A Study of National Labor Policy and Labor Relations*. Chicago: University of Chicago Press, 1950.

Morgan, W. Scott. *History of the Wheel and Alliance and the Impending Revolution*. Kansas: J.H. Rice & Sons, 1889.

Morris, Edmund. *Theodore Rex*. New York: Random House, 2001.

Morris, Roy. *Fraud of the Century: Rutherford B. Hayes, Samuel Tilden and the Stolen Election of 1876*. New York: Simon & Schuster, 2003.

Mosher, Frederick C. *Democracy and the Public Service*. New York: Oxford University Press, 1968.

Moss, David A., and Michael R. Fein. "Radio Regulation Revisited: Coase, the FCC, and the Public Interest." *Journal of Policy History* 15 (Fall 2003): 389–416.

Mullally, Donald P. "The Fairness Doctrine: Benefits and Costs." *Public Opinion Quarterly* 33 (Winter 1969–1970): 577–82.

Mutch, Robert. *Campaigns, Congress and the Courts: The Making of Federal Campaign Finance Law*. New York: Praeger, 1988.

———. "The First Federal Campaign Finance Bills." *Journal of Policy History* 14 (2002): 30–48.

Nahia, Kirk J. "Political Parties and the Campaign Finance Laws: Dilemmas, Concerns & Opportunities." *Fordham Law Review* 56 (October 1987): 53–110.

Nelson, Daniel. "The CIO at Bay: Labor Militancy and Politics in Akron, 1936–1938." *The Journal of American History* 71 (December 1984): 565–86.

Nelson, William E. *The Legalist Reformation*. Chapel Hill: University of North Carolina Press, 2001.

Nevins, Allan. *Grover Cleveland: A Study in Courage*. New York: Dodd, Mead & Co., 1932.

Nixon/Wallace 1968 TV Election Spots. Chicago: International Historic Films, 1985.

Nord, David Paul. *Newspapers and New Politics: Midwestern Municipal Reform 1890–1900*. Michigan: Research Press, 1981.

Norrell, Robert J. "Labor at the Ballot Box: Alabama Politics from the New Deal to the Dixiecrat Movement." *The Journal of Southern History* 57 (May 1991): 201–34.

Ortiz, Daniel R. "Election Law as Its Own Field of Study: From Rights to Arrangements." *Loyola of Los Angeles Law Review* 32 (June 1999): 1217–26.

———. "The First Amendment at Work: Constitutional Restrictions on Campaign Finance Reform." In Anthony Corrado, ed., *Campaign Finance Reform: A Sourcebook*. Washington, D.C.: Brookings Institution Press, 2005: 61–92.

———. "The Unbearable Lightness of Being *McConnell*." *Election Law Journal* 3 (Spring 2004): 299–304.

Outland, George E. "Congress Still Needs Reorganization." *The Western Political Quarterly* 1 (June 1948): 154–64.

Overacker, Louise. "Campaign Finance in the Presidential Election of 1940." *The American Political Science Review* 35 (August 1941): 701–27.

———. "Campaign Funds in the Presidential Election of 1936." *The American Political Science Review* 31 (June 1937): 473–98.

———. "Labor's Political Contribution." *Political Science Quarterly* 54 (March 1939): 56–68.

———. "Presidential Campaign Funds, 1944." *The American Political Science Review* 39 (October 1945): 899–925.

Overton, Spencer A. "Mistaken Identity: Unveiling the Property Characteristics of Political Money." *Vanderbilt Law Review* 53 (May 2000): 1235–310.

Pacelle, Richard. *The Role of the Supreme Court in American Politics: The Least Dangerous Branch?* New York: Westview Press, 2001.

Peabody, Robert L., Jeffrey M. Berry, William G. Frasure, and Jerry Goldman. *To Enact a Law.* New York: Praeger Publishers, 1972.

Perkins, John A. "American Government and Politics: Congressional Self-Improvement." *American Political Science Review* 38 (Jun. 1944): 488–511.

Piven, Frances Fox, and Richard A. Cloward. *The Breaking of the American Social Compact.* New York: The New Press, 1997.

Plotke, David. *Building a Democratic Political Order.* New York: Cambridge University Press, 1996.

Pole, J. R. *The Pursuit of Equity in American History.* Berkeley: University of California Press, 1993.

Polenberg, Richard. *Fighting Faiths: The Abrams Case, the Supreme Court, and Free Speech.* New York: Viking Press, 1987.

Pollack, Norman. *The Just Polity: Populism, Law, and Human Welfare.* Urbana: University of Illinois Press, 1987.

Pollock, James K., Jr. *Party Campaign Funds.* New York: Alfred A. Knopf, 1926.

———. "The Regulation of Lobbying." *The American Political Science Review* 21 (May 1927): 335–41.

Polsby, Daniel D. "*Buckley v. Valeo*: The Special Nature of Political Speech." *Supreme Court Review* 17 (1976): 1–43.

Post, Robert. "Meiklejohn's Mistake: Individual Autonomy and the Reform of Public Discourse." *University of Colorado Law Review* 64 (Fall 1993): 1109–37.

Powe, Lucas A., Jr. *American Broadcasting and the First Amendment.* Berkeley: University of California Press, 1987.

———. *The Warren Court and American Politics.* Cambridge: Belknap Press of Harvard University Press, 2000.

Powers, Fred Perry. "The Reform of the Federal Service." *Political Science Quarterly* 3 (June 1888): 247–81.

Putnam, Robert D. *Bowling Alone.* New York: Simon & Schuster, 2000.

Rabban, David M. *Free Speech in Its Forgotten Years.* Cambridge: Cambridge University Press, 1997.

———. "The IWW Free Speech Fights and Popular Concepts of Free Expression before World War I." *Virginia. Law Review* 80 (August 1994): 1055–1158.

Ragan, Fred D. "Justice Oliver Wendell Holmes, Jr., Zechariah Chafee, Jr., and the Clear and Present Danger Test: The First Year, 1919." *The Journal of American History* 58 (June 1971): 24–45.

Rainey, R. Randall, and William Rehg. "The Marketplace of Ideas, the Public Interest, and the Federal Regulation of the Electronic Media: Implications of Habermas' Theory of Democracy." *Southern California Law Review* 69 (September 1996): 1923–87.

Ramo, Roberta Cooper, and N. Lee Cooper, "The American Bar Association's Integral Role in the Federal Judicial Selection Process: Excerpted Testimony of Roberta Cooper Ramo and N. Lee Cooper Before the Judiciary Committee of the United States Senate, May 21, 1996." *St. John's Journal of Legal Commentary* 12 (Fall 1996): 93–110.

Ratner, Sidney. *Tariff in American History.* New York: Nostrand and Co, 1972.

Redenius, Charles. *The American Ideal of Equality: From Jefferson's Declaration to the Burger Court.* New York: Kennikat Press, 1981.

Reichley, A. James. "Getting at the Roots of Watergate." In David C. Saffell, ed., *Watergate: Its Effects on the American Political System.* Cambridge: Winthrop Publishers, Inc., 1974.

———. *The Life of the Parties.* Lanham: Rowman & Littlefield Publishers, Inc., 1992.

Reitano, Joanne. *The Tariff Question in the Gilded Age: The Great Debate of 1888*. College Park: Pennsylvania State University Press, 1994.

Reynolds, John L. "Outlawing `Treachery': Split Tickets and Ballot Laws in New York and New Jersey, 1880–1910." *Journal of American History* 72 (March 1986): 835–58.

Ribstein, Larry. "Corporate Political Speech." *Washington and Lee L. Rev.* 49 (Winter 1992): 109–54.

Roady, Elston E. "Florida's New Campaign Expense Law and the 1952 Democratic Gubernatorial Primaries." *American Political Science Review* 48 (June 1954): 465–76.

———. "Ten Years of Florida's `Who Gave It—Who Got It' Law." *Law and Contemporary Problems* 17 (Summer 1962): 434–454.

Robbins, William C. *Colony and Empire: The Capitalist Transformation of the American West*. Lawrence: University Press of Kansas, 1994.

Roberts, Robert N., and Marion T. Doss, Jr. *From Watergate to Whitewater: The Public Integrity War*. Connecticut: Praeger Press, 1997.

Robinson, Glen O. "The Federal Communications Act: An Essay on Origins and Regulatory Purpose." In Max A. Paglin, ed., *A Legislative History of the Communications Act of 1934*. New York: Oxford University Press, 1989: 17–34.

Rosenbaum, Nancy L. "Political Parties as Membership Groups." *Columbia Law Review* 100 (April 2000): 813–42.

Rosenfarb, Joseph. "Labor's Role in the Election." *Public Opinion Quarterly* 8 (Autumn 1944): 376–90.

Rosenkranz, E. Joshua. "Faulty Assumptions in 'Faulty Assumptions': A Response to Professor Smith's Critique of Campaign Finance Reform." *Connecticut Law Review* 30 (Spring 1998): 867–96.

Rossum, Ralph. *Federalism, the Supreme Court, and the Seventeenth Amendment: The Irony of Constitutional Democracy*. Lexington: Lexington Books, 2001.

Rothman, David J. *Politics and Power: The United States Senate, 1869–1901*. Cambridge: Harvard University Press, 1966.

Ryden, David K. "The United States Supreme Court as an Obstacle to Political Reform." In Christopher Banks and John C. Green, eds., *Superintending Democracy: The Courts and the Political Process*. Akron: University of Ohio Press, 2001: 163–86.

Ryden, David K., ed. *The U.S. Supreme Court and the Electoral Process*. Washington, D.C.: Georgetown University Press, 2000.

Sabato, Larry. *Dirty Little Secrets: The Persistence of Corruption in American Politics*. New York: Random House, 1996.

———. *PAC Power: Inside the World of Political Action Committees*. New York: W. W. Norton & Co., 1984.

———. *The Rise of Political Consultants*. New York: Basic Books, Inc., 1981.

Sait, Edward McChesney. *American Parties and Elections*. New York: D. Appleton-Century Company, 1942.

Sanders, Elizabeth. *Roots of Reform: Farmers, Workers and the American State, 1877–1917*. Chicago: University of Chicago Press, 1999.

Scharpf, Fritz W. "Judicial Review and the Political Question: A Functional Analysis." *Yale L. J.* 75 (1966): 517–91.

Schattschneider, E. E. *Politics, Pressures and the Tariff*. New York: Prentice Hall, Inc., 1935.

Scher, Richard K., Jon L. Mills, and John J. Hotaling. *Voting Rights and Democracy: The Law and Politics of Districting*. Chicago: Nelson-Hall Publishers, 1997.

Schlesinger, Arthur M. *The Politics of Upheaval*. Boston: Houghton Mifflin, 1960.

Schmidhauser, John E. *Constitutional Law in the Political Process*. Chicago: Rand McNally & Company, 1963.

Schroders International Media and Entertainment Report. New York: Schroders & Company, 2000.

Schultz, David, and Robert Marino. *The Politics of Civil Service Reform*. New York: Petersburg Press, 1998.

————. "Revisiting *Buckley v. Valeo*: Eviscerating the Line Between Candidate Contributions and Independent Expenditures." *Journal of Law and Politics* 14 (Winter 1988): 33–107.

Schwartz, Bernard. *The Ascent of Pragmatism: The Burger Court in Action*. Massachusetts: Addison-Wesley Publishing Company, Inc., 1990.

————. *The Burger Court: Counter-Revolution or Confirmation?* New York: Oxford University Press, 1998.

Scoble, Harry M. "Organized Labor in Electoral Politics: Some Questions for the Discipline." *The Western Political Quarterly* 16 (September 1963): 666–85.

Shapiro, Martin. *Law and Politics in the Supreme Court*. London: The Free Press, 1964.

Siedman, Joel. "Organized Labor in Political Campaigns." *Public Opinion Quarterly* 3 (October 1939): 646–54.

Sikes, Earl Ray. *State and Federal Corrupt Practices Legislation*. New York: AMS Publishers, 1974.

Silbey, Joel. *The American Political Nation, 1838–1893*. Stanford: Stanford University Press, 1991.

Simmons, Steven J. *The Fairness Doctrine and the Media*. Berkeley: University of California Press, 1978.

Skocpol, Theda. "How America Became Civic." In Theda Skocpol and Forris D. Fionna, eds., *Civic Organization in American Democracy*. Washington, D.C.: Brookings Institution Press, 1999: 27–71.

Smith, Bradley. "*McConnell v. Federal Election Commission:* Ideology Trumps Reality, Pragmatism." *Election Law Journal* 3 (Spring 2004): 345–53.

————. "Money Talks: Speech, Corruption, Equality and Campaign Finance." *Georgetown Law Journal* 86 (October 1987): 45–99.

————. *Unfree Speech: The Folly of Campaign Finance Reform*. Princeton: Princeton University Press, 2001.

Smith, F. Leslie, Milar Meeske, and John W. Wright, III. *Electronic Media and Government*. New York: Allyn & Bacon, 1994.

Sorauf, Frank J. "Extra-Legal Political Parties in Wisconsin." *The American Political Science Review* 48 (September 1954): 692–704.

————. "Politics, Experience, and the First Amendment: The Case of American Campaign Finance." *Columbia Law Review* 94 (May 1994): 1348–68.

Spiceland, Roy David, Jr. "The Fairness Doctrine, the Chilling Effect and Television Editorials." The University of Tennessee: Knoxville, Doctoral Dissertation (December 1992).

Stanwood, Edward. *American Tariff Controversies in the Nineteenth Century*. Cambridge: Houghton Mifflin & Co., 1904.

Stark, Andrew. "Corporate Electoral Activity, Constitutional Discourse, and Conceptions of the Individual." *The American Political Science Review* 86 (September 1992): 626–37.

Steel, Ronald. *Walter Lippman and the American Century*. New York: Random House, 1980.

Stephenson, Donald Grier, Jr. *Campaigns and the Courts: The U.S. Supreme Court in Presidential Elections*. New York: Columbia University Press, 1999.

Stern, Philip M. *The Best Congress Money Can Buy*. New York: Pantheon Books, 1988.

Stewart, Frank Mann. *The National Civil Service Reform League: History, Activism, and Problems*. Austin: University of Texas Press, 1929.

Strengthening the Congress. Washington, D.C.: National Planning Association, 1945.

Strum, Philippa, ed. *Brandeis on Democracy*. Lawrence: University Press of Kansas, 1995.

Summer, William G. "The Theory and Practice of Elections." *Princeton Review* 1 (January–June 1880): 265–72.

Summers, Mark Wahlgren. *The Era of Good Stealings*. Oxford: Oxford University Press, 1993.

————. *The Gilded Age*. New Jersey: Prentice Hall, 1997.

Sunstein, Cass. *The Partial Constitution*. Cambridge: Harvard University Press, 1993.

Swanson, David J., and Paolo Mancini, eds. *Politics, Media and Modern Democracy.* Westport, CT: Praeger, 1966.

Tanehaus, Joseph. "Organized Labor's Political Spending: The Law and Its Consequences." *The Journal of Politics* 16 (August 1954): 441–71.

Taussig, E. W. *The Tariff History of the United States.* New York: Putnam & Sons, 1923.

Tenpas, Kathryn Dunn. "The Clinton Reelection Machine: Placing the Party Machine in Peril." *Presidential Studies Quarterly* 29 (Fall 1998): 761–68.

Thorpe, Francis N. *American Charters, Constitutions and Organic Laws.* Washington, D.C.: Government Printing Office, 1909.

Tillinghast, Charles H. *American Broadcast Regulations and the First Amendment.* Ames: Iowa State University Press, 2000.

Trachtenberg, Alan. *The Incorporation of America.* New York: Hill and Wang, 1982.

Trento, Susan B. *The Power House: Robert Keith Gray and the Selling of Access and Influence in Washington.* New York: St. Martin's Press, 1992.

Trimble, Bruce R. *Chief Justice Waite: Defender of the Public Interest.* Princeton: Princeton University Press, 1938.

Turner, Frederick Jackson. *The Frontier in American History.* Tucson: University of Arizona Press, 1997.

Tushnet, Mark. *The NAACP Strategy Against Segregated Education, 1925–1950.* Chapel Hill: University of North Carolina Press, 1987.

———. "Symposium: *Baker v. Carr:* The Transformation and Disappearance of the Political Question Doctrine." *North Carolina Law Review* 80 (May 2002): 1203–35.

Ulmer, S. Sidney. "Supreme Court Behavior and Civil Rights." *Western Political Quarterly* 13 (June 1960): 288–311.

Urofsky, Melvin I. *Louis D. Brandeis and the Progressive Tradition.* Boston: Little, Brown and Company, 1981.

———. *Money and Free Speech: Campaign Finance Reform and the Courts.* Lawrence: University Press of Kansas, 2005.

Van Riper, Paul. *History of the United States Civil Service.* Connecticut: Greenwood Publishers, 1958.

Varon, Elizabeth. *We Mean to Be Counted.* Chapel Hill: University of North Carolina Press, 1998.

Vogel, David. *Kindred Strangers.* Princeton: Princeton University Press, 1996.

Warren, Earl. *Memoirs.* New York: Doubleday, 1977.

Watergate Plus 30: Shadow of History. PBS Video: Carlton Productions, 2003.

Watts, Charles D., Jr. "Corporate Legal Theory Under the First Amendment: *Belotti and Austin.*" *University of Miami Law Review* 46 (November 1991): 317–78.

Weaver, James B. *A Call to Action.* Des Moines: Iowa Printing Co., 1892.

Webber, Michael J. *New Deal Fat Cats.* New York: Fordham University Press, 2000.

Wechsler, Herbert. "Toward Neutral Principles of Constitutional Law." *Harvard L. R.* 73 (1959): 1–35.

Weibe, Robert H. *The Search for Order, 1877–1920.* New York: Hill and Wang, 1966.

Weinberg, Jonathan. "Broadcasting and Speech." *California Law Review* 81 (October 1993): 1103–206.

Weintraub, Ellen L. "Perspectives on Corruption." *Election Law Journal* 13 (Spring 2004): 354–59.

West, Darrell M. *Air Wars: Television Advertising in Election Campaigns, 1952–2000.* Washington, D.C.: CQ Press, 2001.

Westbrook, Robert B. *John Dewey and American Democracy.* Ithaca: Cornell University Press, 1991.

Westin, Alan F. "The Supreme Court, The Populist Movement, and The Campaign of 1896." *Journal of Politics* 15 (1953): 3–41.

Whitcover, Jules. *Party of the People.* New York: Random House, 2003.

White, G. Edward. "The First Amendment Comes of Age: The Emergence of Free Speech in Twentieth Century America." *Michigan Law Review* 95 (November 1996): 299–392.

────. "Free Speech and the Bifurcated Review Project: The 'Preferred Position' Cases." In Sandra F. Vanburkleo, Kermit L. Hall, and Robert J. Kaczorowski, eds., *Constitutionalism and American Culture: Writing the New Constitutional History*. Lawrence: University Press of Kansas, 2002: 99–125.

Wicker, Tom. *One of Us*. New York: Random House, 1991.

Wiebe, G. D. "Merchandising Commodities and Citizenship on Television." *Public Opinion Quarterly* 15 (Winter 1951–1952): 679–91.

Winkler, Adam. "Election Law as Its Own Field of Study: The Corporation in Election Law." *Loyola of Los Angeles Law Review* 32 (June 1999): 1243–72.

────. "Other People's Money: Corporations, Agency Costs, and Campaign Finance Law." *Georgetown Law Journal* 92 (June 2004): 871–940.

Winter, Ralph K. "The History and Theory of *Buckley v. Valeo*." *Journal of Law and Policy* 6 (1997–1998): 93–109.

Wollenberg, J. Roger. "The FCC as Arbiter of 'The Public Interest, Convenience and Necessity.'" In Max D. Paglin, ed., *A Legislative History of the Communication Act of 1934*. New York: Oxford University Press, 1989: 61–78.

Wooddy, Carroll Hill. *The Case of Frank L. Smith*. Chicago: University of Chicago Press, 1931.

Woodward, C. Vann. *Tom Watson: Agrarian Rebel*. New York: Oxford University Press, 1963.

Yearly, Clifton W. *The Money Machines*. Albany: SUNY Press, 1972.

Zelizer, Julian. *On Capitol Hill*. Cambridge: Cambridge University Press, 2004.

────. "Seeds of Cynicism: The Struggle Over Campaign Finance, 1956–1974." *The Journal of Policy History* 14 (2002): 73–111.

Zeller, Belle. "American Government and Politics: The Federal Regulation of Lobbying Act." *The American Political Science Review* 42 (April 1948): 239–71.

Zunz, Olivier. *Making America Corporate: 1870–1920*. Chicago: University of Chicago Press, 1992.

Index